The
Rabbinic Parables
and Jesus
the Parable Teller

The
Rabbinic Parables and Jesus the Parable Teller

DAVID FLUSSER

TIMOTHY KEIDERLING, TRANSLATOR

HENDRICKSON ACADEMIC

an imprint of Hendrickson Publishing Group

The Rabbinic Parables and Jesus the Parable Teller

© 2024 Johanon Flusser

Translated by Timothy Keiderling

Published by Hendrickson Publishers
an imprint of Hendrickson Publishing Group
Hendrickson Publishers, LLC
P. O. Box 3473
Peabody, Massachusetts 01961-3473
www.hendricksonpublishers.com

ISBN 978-1-4964-8836-7

Originally published in German under the title:
Die rabbinischen Gleichnisse und der Gleichniserzähler Jesus
Peter Lang, 1981

Printed in the United States of America

First Printing — April 2024

Contents

FOREWORD

Ever since it first appeared in German in 1981, an English translation of David Flusser's now-classic *Die rabbinschen Gleichnisse und der Gleichniserzähler Jesus* has been sorely needed. A review of more recent works on the Gospel parables quickly reveals that Flusser's voice is as relevant now as it was when the original edition appeared. The problems that challenged the study of parables in 1981 still daunt New Testament scholarship. In his study, Flusser built on the pioneering work of Adolf Jülicher and Joachim Jeremias to reject the excessive allegorical interpretation of parables that has characterized much of Christian interpretation through the centuries. He has taken a step further, however, to demonstrate the absolute need to read the Gospel parables as part of the genre of rabbinic parables.

Flusser's literary-critical-philological approach is the necessary course to uncovering the original intent of the parables within their historical setting. Evidence of the earliest Pharisaic-rabbinic parables is reflected in the saying of Antigonus of Socho in the third century BCE: "Be not like servants who serve their master for the sake of reward; rather, be like servants who do not serve their master for the sake of reward and let the fear of Heaven be upon you" (M. Avot 1:3). It is not difficult to recognize this well-known subject of a master and his laborers as the kernel for several early rabbinic parables, as well as those of Jesus. We therefore hear that the laborers in the vineyard in Matt 20:1–16 went to work with no thought of their wages, trusting the assurance of the landlord, "Whatever is right I will give you."

Since the emergence of Jewish parables appears already during the Hellenistic period, Flusser posits that they likely resulted from the Jewish community's contact with Greek folk wisdom. Both Aesopic fables and Jewish story parables were intended to communicate a moral that lay beyond the narratives themselves. In his book, Flusser examines the structural similarities and differences between parables and other types of popular stories such as animal fables and European fairy tales. While there are points of comparison, parables possess distinctive literary features that set them apart. Indeed, the developed nature of the early parables indicates that the parable was a well-developed genre by the first century.

Flusser also compares parables with *exemplum*, another type of short story with a moral. These occur in both rabbinic literature and the Gospels. In rabbinic literature, they typically open with *ma'aseh* (מעשה): "It happened . . ." In the Gospels, *exempla* appear only in the Gospel of Luke: for example, the story of the Pharisee and the tax collector (18:9–14), the story of the rich fool (12:16–21), the legend of the rich man and poor Lazarus (16:19–31), the story of the good Samaritan (10:29–37), and the story of the prodigal son (15:11–32).

Flusser argues that insufficient literary-critical attention has been given to the historical development of rabbinic parables. He describes what he calls "classical parables," attributing them to parables that were known in the generations prior to the destruction of the temple in 70 CE. The challenge, of course, is that we have almost no rabbinic writings from this early period, and what sayings we do have are preserved only in later compilations. Nevertheless, Flusser demonstrates that the inherent resistance to structural change in parables means that these parables were preserved orally and written down only later, and therefore they can tell us something about parables and their subjects in that earlier period.

Flusser identifies a shift in the character and use of rabbinic parables from the days of Rabbi Akiba in the generation after the temple's destruction. Unlike the "classical parables," these later examples frequently served in midrashic interpretations of Scripture. On the other hand, the older parables—both those of the sages and Jesus—existed for the most part as independent stories without scriptural citations. Usually, the later parables include biblical verses; but under closer examination, it is not difficult to identify in some an earlier parable that was adapted and appended with Scripture for its use in the synagogue and in houses of study.

A few years ago, I was asked to participate in a special session on "Parables and the Historical Jesus" at the annual conference of the Society of Biblical Literature. It included scholars engaged in Gospel parables research. I was surprised to hear papers that drew parallels from stories or similitudes by classical Greek authors but largely ignored rabbinic parables.

Not only are story parables of the type associated with Jesus a distinctively Jewish genre, as Flusser notes, but they are also all found in rabbinic literature. In other words, story parables are missing from the many works of Josephus Flavius, Philo of Alexandria, Jewish apocryphal and pseudepigraphal literature, and the Dead Scrolls. While this may seem a marginal point, it informs us as to where Jesus stood on the landscape of Jewish thought in the first century CE. His world was that of Israel's sages.

Jesus' use of parables was also native. Flusser reminds us that story parables emerged from the soil of the land of Israel and not from the Jewish diaspora. Even the spiritually rich Jewish community of Babylonia did not produce a single parable. Of no less importance is the language in which parables were told. During the past hundred and fifty years, the overwhelming opinion of New Testament scholars is that Jesus told his parables in Aramaic. Yet, this assumption is controverted by the fact that we do not possess a single Jewish story parable in Aramaic. They are all in Hebrew. As with the physical setting for parables, the issue of language indicates the setting in which Jesus lived. Like others living in the trilingual environment (Greek, Aramaic, Hebrew) of Roman Judaea, Jesus would have been familiar with Greek and Aramaic. However, the distinctive language of the Jewish people in the first century was Hebrew. His use of parables demonstrates that there is no reason to assume that Jesus taught in any other language than Hebrew. Indeed, more than any other feature of Jesus' teaching, his parables embody the geographical (Israel), linguistic (Hebrew), and religious-cultural (Pharisaic-rabbinic) setting that served as the circumstance for his life and message.

For fifteen years, I studied and worked with Professor Flusser in Jerusalem. He served as my doctoral advisor at the Hebrew University, and later we collaborated on the historical biography *Jesus* (Magnes Press, 1997). My time spent with him completely changed how I read the Gospels. (I have written elsewhere of my indebtedness to Flusser for my own research in the field ancient Judaism and Christian origins.) In more recent years, his historical-philological approach has guided my efforts in historical geography of the land of Israel during the Hellenistic and Roman periods.

Professor Flusser was an original thinker whose ideas grew out of an intimate familiarity with the contours of Jewish thought in the Second Temple period and the languages in which it was expressed. Unlike many New Testament scholars today, Flusser approached the Gospel parables with an optimism that through critical treatment of the parables, we can hear the Hebraic voice of Jesus: "Let him who has ears to hear, let him hear!"

R. Steven Notley, PhD
Kinneret Institute for Galilean Archaeology, Kinneret College
Academic Director, El-Araj Excavation Project
Director, The Center for the Study of Ancient Judaism and Christian Origins
Senior Leon Charney Fellow, Yeshiva University Center for Israel Studies

PREFACE

In this book, I examine the essence of Jesus' parables and their literary nature by placing them within their natural framework of the genre of Jewish parables, as his parables undoubtedly belong to this genre. Johann Jakob Wettstein (1693–1754) established the fifth rule of New Testament hermeneutics:

> If you want to fully understand the books of the New Testament, put yourself in the person of those to whom they were first given by the apostles for reading. Put yourself in the spirit in that time and place where they were first read. As far as possible, make sure that you recognize the manners, customs, habits, opinions, contemporary ideas, proverbs, imagery, and daily expressions of those men and the way in which they try to convince others or give credence to others' justifications. Be careful where you turn to a position in which you cannot advance through any current system, whether theological or logical, or through current opinions.[1]

This rule can be fashionably reviled as rationalistic, but it is certainly not unreasonable. I think it is even more important in Christianity than in Judaism to believe in the facts, although I know that some theologians these days will not allow me to say even that! They will answer me: "Although the question of the historical Jesus may be historically possible and permissible, it is theologically, at least, if one follows the New Testament, not possible."[2] The fact that Jesus has now become a stumbling block for the faithful also seems to be new to me. I thought the Christian was, by definition, a believer in Jesus. However, I must admit that I may be mistaken in this regard. When it comes to Jesus, a Christian can't just come to me thinking that the truth is merely dialectical. Rather, truth is an important category of any religion. And Jesus is, among other things, an object of the Christian faith.

---

1. Quoted in Peter Stuhlmacher, *On Understanding the New Testament* (Göttingen, 1979), 119.
2. Walter Schmithals, *The Gospel according to Mark*, vol. 1 (Gütersloh, 1978), 70.

Therefore, it cannot be easy for a believing Christian to ignore his words as if they had never been spoken. Erasmus of Rotterdam has seen clearly here. Rhetorically, he asks:

> And we, who are initiated in so many ways and united to Christ through so many sacraments, do not see in it scorn and shame that we understand nothing of the doctrines that grant the safest happiness to all? Why do we not seek to fathom every detail with an honorable curiosity, to investigate and precisely to describe it all?[3]

One would think that this view of Erasmus is obsolete and does not fit into our witty century. Curiously, however, there are more and more "backwoods" Christians today who are interested in the "historical" Jesus. They believe that their salvation depends on their understanding of Jesus' words; only then could they live according to his teaching. The parables of Jesus are therefore an important basis for Christian moral conduct.

For many who are concerned with Jesus and his words, there is a tendency to play Jesus off against the Judaism of his time. This dualistic tendency is old and understandable. But we must vigorously interrogate this ourselves as far as it corresponds to the facts. Many find it easy to demarcate Jesus from ancient Judaism and place him as an isolated figure in the limelight. This is why this sentiment flows so easily through their pens and into the sermon: They only superficially know the Jewish sources and so tend to interpret them superficially. That is why, when dealing with Jesus' parables, Jewish parables were mostly put aside until today, or were judged disparagingly. If the dualistic superstition is unvarnished, it leads to the demonization of Judaism. In the works of Erasmus Alberus, a follower of Luther, this dualism appears in frightening nakedness. In 1534, he wrote:

> Therefore also holy people and prophets do not shy away from using images and pictures in their idle parables, indeed our dear Master Christ (who is the eternal wisdom of God) has himself taught his holy gospel by means of parables. On the other hand, the Devil also has his fables, just as the Stationier and monks lie in Bapstumb, Machomet's Alcoran and the Jew's Talmudic fables, which do nothing to serve anyone other than that they multiply the Devil's empire and lead the people away from God and truth.[4]

---

3. Erasmus of Rotterdam, *Novum Testamentum Praefationes: Selected Works*, vol. 3 (Darmstadt, 1967), 9–13.

4. Erasmus Alberus, "Dedication Preface to the Hagenauer Edition of the Book of Virtue and Wisdom (1534)," Erwin Leibfried and Joseph M. Werle, *Texte zur Theorie der Fabel* (Stuttgart: Sammlung Metzler, 1978), 12.

In recent decades, some Christians have come to realize that it is not a question of denouncing Jesus' Judaism. One begins to understand that it is hardly possible to tear the Christian faith out of its Jewish roots. Once this is understood, one notices that only through his Jewish roots can one correctly understand Jesus, and not only Jesus but also his proclamation and his person based on the Jewish material. Only then can Christianity recover. It can then banish the dangers from which it is threatened today: on the one hand, the danger of internal decay and, on the other hand, the dangerous temptation to a rabid barbarization of the Christian message amid a barbaric world. The knowledge of the needs of today's situation requires learning and re-learning, a painful renunciation of comfortable prejudices, and a pure belief in God. I know that such a path is not easy. I also see some setbacks and well-intentioned demagogic compromises. Overall, however, I am optimistic.

The concession that the parables of Jesus are also Jewish, and especially Jewish, still encounters strong internal resistance. This unusual closedness to facts is explored in this book. One defends oneself under various pretexts against the simple truth that Jesus' parables belong, without any doubt, with the Jewish rabbinic parables. And if you have no choice but to acknowledge the facts, then you usually try to live with them somehow instead of processing them. We often see the parables as a genre assigned exclusively to Jesus. But one had to take note that there are also other Jewish parables. Now, this difficulty was attempted to be overcome by diminishing the intrinsic value of the rabbinic parables and often by finding differences between Jesus' parables and other Jewish parables where, in reality, there are no real differences. If one saw the points of contact, then one nevertheless constructed a way out: One and the same statement would have a very different meaning with the rabbis and with Jesus. Refutation of the latter tendency, which at its core involves an inappropriate christological-existentialist interpretation of the parables of Jesus, is extremely difficult. Strangely enough, the difficulty of refutation lies in the fact that this research tendency is hardly based on tangible factual material. It comes from the sometimes coherent axiom that the same sentences can be interpreted differently if their speakers are not identical. On the other hand, in our case, it must be remembered that Jesus was a Jew. In terms of education, narrative style, and faith, he was not far from popular storytellers who were his contemporaries. If we now want to take the daring step of justifying and presenting the similarities between rabbinic parable tellers and Jesus the parable teller, we must first know the Jewish parables and study them impartially. Furthermore, one must keep in mind the whole proclamation of Jesus. One should approach the question of where the sublime self-conception of Jesus and his place in the economy of salvation is expressed in this proclamation, and what task Jesus devised for his parables within this proclamation. In rabbinic Judaism, parables were intended to convince the common people of a moral truth. We know that Jesus did not think otherwise. Most of Jesus' parables had the purpose of making a general moral teaching clear to ordinary people by means of a story. To accomplish this, Jesus took the usual parable form, which was known in his environment, into service.[5] It does us no harm at all today if we try to learn how to live properly from his parables. And one more thing: If Jesus' parables belong to the genre of rabbinic parables according to their form and orientation, then we need to ask ourselves whether we can understand them eschatologically in a manner different from similar rabbinic parables.

Another reason why rabbinic parables were not sufficiently considered in the interpretation of Jesus' parables is that rabbinic parables were generally lumped together: They were royal parables, or they reflected a narrow rabbinic apologetic, and so on. Hence the need to examine the history of rabbinic parables. My conclusion in this book is this: The Jesus' parables belong to the older, classical type of Jewish parables, which was maintained even after Jesus' time. It became clear to me that to understand the parables of Jesus, it is indispensable to analyze Jewish parables and Jesus' parables according to genre, motifs, subject, and style. That's why this book has a "Janus face," so to speak. It considers the problem both from a theological-moral point of view and from the point of view of a literary-aesthetic investigation. I could not and did not want to eliminate the literary side of the problem. You can only get to know Jesus as a storyteller if you learn how he told the parables; then you can also find out what he wanted to say in his parables. Finally, I want to apologize to my readers. I have not read all the scholarly studies that have been written in recent times about the parables of Jesus, and I am sure that I have left many grains of gold in the sand. But I had only the choice to write the present book or do what was necessary to

---

5. This is not as far-fetched as it may seem. An example of this is given by Johann Balthasar Schupp (1610–1661). Johann Matthesius (1504–1555) states the following: "Matthesius rightly says the allegories and parables prove and establish no article of faith, but serve to make the founded article more clearly before the eyes of the simple and illuminated than in a painting." See Leibfried and Werle, *Texte zur Theorie der Fabel*, 27.

deal with scholarly research in either an agreeable or a polemical manner. The sources I had to work through were so extensive that I wanted to devote myself intensively to them. It seems to me that my book represents a new approach, and I didn't want to be distracted by my concern. Cervantes said in the foreword to *Don Quixote*, "I am too lazy and sluggish by nature to want to look around for authors who will finally say what I know without saying it." I hope I am not so immodest and so sure of myself, but I have no choice but to ask my affectionate readers not to spare themselves the trouble of adding my book to the ever-longer chain of scientific progress.[6]

My greatest teachers in literary analysis, Gotthold Lessing and Viktor Shklovsky, have already died. The third teacher, Max Lüthi, I do not know personally, and I express my deep gratitude to him here. This book could not have been written without the help and active advice of my friend and colleague at the Hebrew University of Jerusalem, Shmuel Safrai. Sometimes I did not dare to swim on my own in the "Sea of the Talmud." But even if I swam at my own risk, I did not do so without the supervision of Safrai. The book is dedicated to Clemens Thoma from Lucerne. How can I thank him enough? He always encouraged me to write and read the book with empathetic love, improving it, and making it readable and understandable for others. It unites us both not only a deep friendship, but also the longing desire to pass on to people what is always necessary—especially today.

David Flusser
Jerusalem
May 20, 1980

---

6. The most modern work I have read in this area is *Semiology and Parables: An Exploration of the Possibilities offered by Structuralism for Exegesis*, from the Semiology and Exegesis Conference at Vanderbilt University, edited by Daniel Patte (Pittsburgh: Pickwick, 1976). You don't learn much from the volume, and what you can learn is not very exciting.

1

SETTING OUT THE PROBLEM
WITH EXAMPLES

In this book, I will explain the parables of Jesus found in the Gospels by means of the literary-critical-philological method. An attempt will here be made to possibly advance to the original form of the parable sayings of Jesus. However, critical treatment of the issue will not be exhausted. Too often it has been forgotten that Jesus' parables are not a literary device he himself created. Increasingly, the genre of rabbinic parables—to which Jesus' parables belong—has been rejected. This has obstructed the path to a proper understanding of the doctrine proclaimed in Jesus' parables.[1]

First, however, I would like to point out that there are hundreds of parables in rabbinic literature. Of course, there are those that are more successful and those that are less successful. There is also a development in the history of rabbinic parables. But all belong to a sharply profiled literary genre, which is just as independent and recognizable as the Aesopic animal fable or the European fairy tale. It is therefore inappropriate to look unilaterally for the roots of this genre in the Old Testament Scriptures, even though there are parables or similar fables there too.

Like the fairy tale, the anecdote, the riddle, and the fable (in its oldest stage), the Jewish parable is a short form that was presented orally. Its origin and its *Sitz im Leben* are therefore to be sought in such popular Jewish circles where oral teaching was important. These circles later became rabbinic Judaism, which today is usually said to have been inspired and shaped by the Pharisaic spirit. In any case, rabbinic Judaism was identical to nonsectarian Judaism. Overall, the Pharisaic teachers were a popular group, not a special class of teachers. Economically, too, they did not belong to the upper class like the Sadducees. Some of the leading Pharisees were not wealthy; they were mostly peasants or craftsmen and felt connected to the common people. Like Jesus' parables, rabbinic parables are an oral popular short form with religious content. The genre is an important expression

---

1. Here, Flusser refers to trends in scholarly discourse. —Trans.

of rabbinism, the main ideological source of ancient Judaism.[2] We would search in vain to find this genre in the Apocrypha or Pseudepigrapha. As far as we can see from the Dead Sea Scrolls, it was also alien to the Essenes.

Even more important than the intra-Jewish assignment of parables to the Pharisaic-rabbinic stream of tradition is the more general external problem that parables were common as a narrative form only in Palestinian Judaism. As far as I know, the spiritually and religiously, otherwise extraordinarily, creative Jewish diaspora of Babylonia, to which we owe the Babylonian Talmud, did not add a single parable to the collection of the Jewish parables. The linguistic nature of parables also belongs in this context: There are only Hebrew parables, no Aramaic parables. Even if a rabbi speaks Aramaic, he switches to Hebrew if he wants to tell a parable. It is true, however, that there are Aramaic sections in individual passages on similar themes. Occasionally, the parable protagonists slide back into Aramaic. The parable framework, however, always remains Hebrew. The genre of parables was thus determined linguistically and stylistically. This circumstance is also crucial to the question of whether Jesus taught the people in Hebrew or Aramaic. Why, then, should one assume that, unlike the other Jewish teachers, he was reciting his parables in Aramaic? There are hardly any other convincing arguments for Aramaic as the teaching language of Jesus!

The rabbinic parable is a special genre. One finds parables in rabbinic literature: in the Babylonian and Jerusalem Talmuds as well as in the so-called Midrashim. In literary history, the Midrashim are the works that interpret the Old Testament, usually the Pentateuch. They are also collections of ancient synagogal sermons. Thus the parables belong to Jewish antiquity. The "foothills" of this genre, however, extend into the Middle Ages. The works in which parables occur were written or collected over many centuries. Often the same parable occurs in different works, in more or less different wording. Also, a parable can occur in different variations in terms of content, and the author of the parable is not always mentioned. As we shall see, there is a literary history of rabbinic parables. In my opinion, over the second century CE, there was also a history of decay of the genre. It is understandable that the peculiarity of Jesus' parables coincides with older rabbinic parables. As far as I can see, no one has yet dealt with the literary history of rabbinic parables.

---

2. According to b. San. 38b., for example, Rabbi Meir used to break up his lecture into three parts: one-third Halakha, one-third Aggadah, and one-third parables.

The previous disregard of the rabbinic parables for understanding of the parables of Jesus is not to be understood solely by inappropriate apologetics or by an insufficient knowledge of rabbinic literature. On the contrary, there is a different problem, both in parables and in other areas of rabbinic literature. For if we really want to compare rabbinic texts with the New Testament from the ground up, we usually hear voices of caution.

It is common to argue that rabbinic parallels date back to a time later than Jesus and the New Testament. This objection is largely justified. Very few sayings in rabbinic literature can be attributed to sages who lived earlier than the last generation before the destruction of the temple (70 CE). It was only after this catastrophe that the oral tradition began to be intensively collected. But it is known that the carriers of the rabbinic oral tradition were not its actual creators. They were in a long line of tradition. In all cases, therefore, rabbinic material should be examined. If we compare it to the New Testament and Jesus' words, unspoken common sense will discover, in the vast majority of cases, how to use the rabbinic material to interpret Jesus' words. For the parallels show us that Jesus' message is rooted in the same world, the witnesses of which are mostly later rabbinic texts. It is then easy to see that the formulations, ideas, expression, and the literary forms themselves are much older than Jesus. A properly understood structuralism can help us a great deal.

The oldest rabbinic parables, as well as most of the other older rabbinic material, date from the last generation before the destruction of the temple. By this time, they were already fully developed and dealt with almost all the topics that form the content of Jesus' parables, as well as other topics. This shows that the genre existed much earlier. Due to the absence of the older material, however, the sources of the genre and its origin are shrouded in darkness. So, it is hard to agree with those who try to convince us that rabbis had to learn from Jesus how to create parables. As everyone can easily see, Jesus' parables belong to the broad field of rabbinic parables and not the other way around.

But why have the rabbinic parables not been used properly to discover the meaning of Jesus' parables? As far as I can see, there are three main reasons. The first is that rabbinic parables from different times and different types were indiscriminately conjured up as comparative material. As a result, the association of Jesus' parables to rabbinic parables could hardly be made clear. The second reason why research did not follow the right path is that it was argued that Jesus' parables were to be derived from certain individual rabbinic parables. Scholars claimed that a preserved parable in rabbinic literature was, so to speak, the father of a certain parable of Jesus. But even the idea that the rabbinic parable was primary, while the parable of Jesus was secondary, had to have been unbearable for Christian theologians. As experienced methodological experts, they could point out that such an assumption is wrong, or at least inaccurate. We will see that the literary genre of parables resembles the genre of animal fables, anecdotes, comedies, and European fairy tales in that a parable arises, so to speak, ad hoc and is constructed from certain, more or less rigid, components and motifs. Jesus' parables belong, at most, to certain types but cannot be derived from a single parable of the rabbis. The third reason why the nature of Jesus' parables has been misunderstood in recent times is that both his parables and the neglected rabbinic parables are in fact parables! Their meaning is outside their subject, and their content points to something very specific. Although this point was not completely eliminated, it became obscured by the attempt, with the help of the so-called method of form criticism and later of the method of redaction criticism, to discover the assumed original meaning of Jesus' actual parable behind any "early Christian editing."

Consequently, all interpretations of the Gospels had to be omitted as secondary. It is true that patristic and medieval allegorical interpretations of the parables were rightly rejected, but by doing this, the baby was thrown out with the bathwater. As we shall see, certain elements of the subject motifs have a strange, fixed meaning in the parables (both in rabbinic parables and in Jesus' parables) on which the narrator and the listener agreed. Other motifs gained this meaning through the situation in which the parable was spoken and by the purpose the parable served.

It will become apparent that the interpretations of the parables in the Gospels are almost always "correct." Modern research methods obscured this fact. Because scholars could not or did not want to see the parabolic features of the parables, the new meaning attached to Jesus' parables became kerygmatically nebulous. Thus, Adolf Jülicher says about the meaning of the parable of the fourfold field:

> Just as we always have death and joyful life side by side in the field, the disappointment and the rewarding gain, so also in the matter of the word of God, failure and success must go side by side, one is as sure as the other. . . . This was a wise use of generally accepted facts to ward off overstretched expectations, such as unwarranted claims for him (Jesus) and his cause; as a subject's parable, or, more vividly, in the form of a story, Jesus could recite it (II 536,538).

And Joachim Jeremias:

> It seems a lot of work, but although to be vain and unsuccessful in human eyes may seem to be a failure, Jesus is full of joy and optimism: God's hour comes and with it comes a blessing of harvest over prayer and understanding. Despite all the failure and resistance, God makes the glorious end, which he has promised, come out of the hopeless beginnings.

Later, we will see how this parable can be explained by rabbinic parallels.

The main theme in Jesus' parables and his contemporaries' rabbinic parables was the religious interpretation of human life—of man's action before God. A primary purpose of the parables was to show the listener how to do something right by describing an often-paradoxical situation, and mainly to warn him that he was perhaps doing something wrong. The old parables—and thus also most of Jesus' parables—are Socratic, so to speak. This element of ancient wisdom is, of course, expressed in the sense of Jewish monotheism's belief in an absolute commitment to the personal, almighty God who blesses the good and punishes the sinner. Furthermore, the motif of reward and punishment is not foreign to Jesus' parables. Finally, the main theme in rabbinic parables can also be changed with a certain twist: The work for the master does not necessarily mean the effort of man in his life; it can be limited, for example, to the effort of teaching. Thus, even with Jesus, the general content of the parable can be related to a specific situation. There are, however, ancient rabbinic parables that explain a biblical commandment. This type is missing from the preserved parables of Jesus.

In 120 CE, among the students of Rabbi Akiva, parables became used partly for new purposes: They began to serve as illustrations of biblical verses, to characterize persons from the Old Testament books, and to illustrate biblical stories.[3] This new kind of parable uses conventional motifs

---

3. Wilhelm Bacher, *Die Agada der Tannaiten*, vol. 1 (Strasbourg: Trübner, 1903), 109. Bacher quotes a parable of Rabbi Eliezer ben Hyrkanos, an older contemporary of Rabbi Akiva, which on the one hand belongs to a later type but which is, however, an important variant reading: "Rabbi Eleasar" (from Modiin), who belonged to the generation of students of Rabbi Akiva. See a basic book about the history of motifs in animal fables in Schwarzbaum, *The Mishle Shualim (Fox Fables) of Rabbi Berechiah ha-Nakdan: A Study in Comparative Folklore and Fable Lore* (Kiron: Institute for Jewish and Arab Folklore Research, 1979). For our book, it is particularly important what we read there on pages 14–17 ("Fables employed as an exegetical medium"). It can be seen from the rabbinic material collected there that in rabbinic literature the animal fable often serves to illustrate biblical verses and stories.

pertaining to the subject matter of the older kind. The new parable soon became predominant, although the old type did not die out until later; it is often found, for example, in the midrashic work *Tanna debe Eliyahu* and even in a relatively late work, the Midrash to the Psalms (hereafter M. Teh). It is probably no coincidence that parables closest to the spirit, subject matter, and form of Jesus' parables are found in a rather old work, the treatise Semahoth (hereafter SemH), which reflects the spirit of the old piety to which, historically speaking, Jesus once belonged.

The later type of rabbinic parable, whose theme is no longer human life and labor before God but an explanatory interpretation of the Old Testament, is not present in the parables of Jesus. It seems to me that this new type, which still works with the old material and motifs, has distanced itself from the original purpose of the genre. Such parables no longer serve to interpret a human situation. Rather, they are more of an illustration, a decorative addition to the biblical text. This new form of the parable is basically a form of generic decay. Too often, these later parables are no longer transparent. The subject of the parables is now much less natural and autonomous and much more construed. Admittedly, the old parables, as well as Jesus' parables, were not merely representations of real conditions. However, the account of their story was not, as in the later parables, in a master-servant relationship, juxtaposed with the Bible text and situation. Their linguistic and substantive autonomy was one of their most outstanding characteristics. Let us take here just one example of the later type of parables:

> "Like a servant to whom the master said, 'Wait for me in the market!' Without determining where to wait for him; the servant thinks at first: maybe he

---

Therefore, rabbis used animal fables also in a broader sense as a general moral teaching. What results from that is a fully established parallel between the history of rabbinic animal fables and the development of rabbinic parables. The restriction of the general validity of human life to these exegetical illustrations was not there from the beginning in rabbinic parables and rabbinic animal fables. This restriction is found in both related genres first in the later periods of rabbinic Judaism. Human life is the genuine object of both rabbinic animal fables and rabbinic parables, to which Jesus' parables also belong. Their change to an exegetical medium is surely observable as a more inherent, more historically connected process. One should examine whether the same changes can be found in other Halakhic or Aggadic branches of rabbinic Judaism. Such an examination would be worth it, and its results would be widely useful and meaningful. I have dealt with the above-mentioned book in "The Wisdom of the Animal Fables and Their Moral Teaching," *Davar* (October 26, 1979): 18f. This article also deals with other questions that I only touch on in this book.

waited for me at the palace or at the bathhouse or at the place of the theater. The master went up and found him, and smote him on the cheek, saying, 'I had appointed you to the gate of the palace of the ruler.' Thus, the waters also receded when they heard that God commanded them (Gen 1:9): 'The waters shall gather together under heaven in one place,' without specifying whether at noon or midnight, and they dispersed. And he said to them, 'Mountains shall ascend, valleys shall be lowered.' God smote them and said to them, 'I have told you to go to the place of Leviathan.'"[4]

It is instructive to see that in this parable of the later kind, we also find the components from which those old parables, to which Jesus' parables belong, were built: the commanding master, the servant, and the incomplete command—the incompleteness of which creates the paradoxical tension of the subject. The application to the biblical verse, however, seems almost distorted. If I am not mistaken, in the parables preserved in rabbinic literature, those belonging to this later, somewhat degenerate type predominates. Nevertheless, they are useful for understanding Jesus' parables because their subject is made up of the same elements as the older parables. These motifs are similarly intertwined, and the old paradox is preserved. It was probably the large number of these late kinds of parables that was complicit in neglecting rabbinic parables in the study of Jesus' parables and considering that rabbinic parables were inferior to his. Jülicher's judgment applies only for the later parables:

> The weakness of most rabbinic parables is that they would like to have everything similar, that they make false demands on their fabric in their invention and design, and that they demand of the imagination an unbearable burden: what they emphasize should be a foreign case, or process, and at the same time a slap in the face of the present.

Hesitantly, I will cite some old rabbinic parables here because I know it will not be easy for a Christian reader accustomed to Jesus' parables to feel the virtues of the rabbinic parables without groaning at them. He imagines that parables are only in the Gospels, but wouldn't he then allow them some good aspects?

Rabban Johanan ben Zakkai worked several decades after Jesus, and he experienced the destruction of the temple that he had foreseen. After this

---

4. Artur Weiser, *Die Knechtsgleichnisse der synoptischen Evangelien* (Munich: Kösel-Verlag, 1971), 39. The parable itself can be found in Exod. Rab. 15:22.

catastrophe, he saved the faith of Israel. He spoke by a parable to get people to repent, which must never be postponed. He began with Scripture: "Wear white garments all the time, and do not lack the oil for your head" (Eccl 9:8) and told a parable:

> Once a king invited his servants to a meal and set for them no fixed time. The wise among them adorned themselves, and sat down at the door of the king's house; And they said to themselves, "Is there anything missing from the king's house?" The foolish among them went to their work and said to themselves, "Is there a meal without preparation?" Suddenly, the king called his servants. The wise among them stood adorned before the king. But the foolish shambled before him in their filth. And the king rejoiced at the wise and was angry with the fools. He said, "These who have adorned themselves for the meal may sit down and eat and drink; but those who have not adorned themselves for the meal shall stand and watch."[5]

Another parable also follows on from a verse from Ecclesiastes: "And the Spirit returns to God who gave him" (Eccl 12:7). The parable reads,

> Give him back as he has given it to you, as he has given to you in purity, so also you return it in purity! A parable: Once a king of flesh and blood distributed royal garments to his servants. The wise among them wrapped them together and put them in a chest, and the foolish people went out with them and did their work in them. After a while, the king demanded his robes back. The wise among them returned them to him in a clean state, but the foolish among them returned them dirty. And the king rejoiced at the wise and was angry with the fools. With regard to the wise, he said, "My robes are to be brought into the treasury, and they may go home in peace." As for the foolish, he said, "My robes are to be brought to the washer, and they are to be put in prison." Likewise, the Holy One said of the body of the righteous (Isa 57:2): "He will now enter into peace, they shall rest in their resting place." And of their souls he says (1 Sam 25:29): "May the soul of my master be preserved in the cluster of life." About the body of the wicked he says (Isa 48:22): "No peace, saith the

---

5. b. Šabb. 153a. and Ignaz Ziegler, *Die Koenigsgleichnisse des Midrasch beleuchtet durch die roemische Kaiserzeit*, chapter 8, parable 20 (Breslau: S. Schottlaender, 1903). See also Bacher, *Die Agada der Tannaiten*, vol. 1, 36n1. In this context we also find the beautiful parable from Rabbi Eleazar Hakappar: Bacher, *Die Agada der Tannaiten*, vol. 2 (Strasbourg: Trübner, 1890), 516. Our parable appears also in the tractates "Semahot d'Rabbi Hiyya" 2; Michael Higger, *Treatise Semahot and Treatise Semahot of R. Hiyya and Sefer Hibbut Ha-Keber* (Jerusalem: Makor, 1970), 216 (hereafter SemH).

master, there is for the wicked." And of their soul it is said (1 Sam 25:29): "He hurls the soul of your enemies away in a slingshot."[6]

The following parable dates to the third century. Its subject does not occur in Jesus' parables. Nevertheless, it is worth getting to know.

> Rabbi Jonathan ben Eleazar said, "A king lived in a city, and the inhabitants of the city angered him. The king became angry, left the city, and stopped ten miles away. A man saw him and said to the inhabitants of the city, 'Know that the king is angry with you. He intends to send legions against the city to destroy them. Go out and reconcile with him before he distances himself from you.' There was a wise man there, and he said to them, 'You fools, as long as he was with you, you have not visited him; go out to him now before he leaves, perhaps he will receive you.' It reads: 'Seek the master now that he may be found; call him now that he is near'" (Isa 55:6).[7]

Rabbi Nathan told a parable:

> A king had built a palace and brought male and female servants there. He gave them silver and gold to trade. Then he commanded them and said, "Be careful that not one of you takes something from another and robs and steals." The king went to a province by the sea. And the servants began to snatch things from one another, to rob, and to steal. After some time, the king returned from the province by the sea, and found all that belonged to them inside, and they stood naked outside. The king took away from them all that they had robbed and stolen. This is the case with sinners in this world: they take away one's things from another, rob and steal, and when they die, they do not take anything with them, but they go naked from commandments and good deeds, as it is written: "Don't let it be challenged if one also gets rich; the glory does not go down with him" (Ps 49:17).[8]

In connection with the Jewish martyrdom after the Bar Kochba Revolt, Rabbi Meir told a parable that shows the same drastic features as some of Jesus' parables:

---

6. b. Šabb. 152b; Ziegler, *Die Koenigsgleichnisse des Midrasch beleuchtet durch die roemische Kaiserzeit*, chapter 8, parable 22.

7. Pesiq. Rab Kah., ed. S. Buber, 156b, ed. B. Mandelbaum (New York: Jewish Theological Seminary of America, 1962), 472 (Darshu). See Wilhelm Bacher, *Die Agada der Palaestinischen Amoräer*, vol. 1 (Strasbourg: Trübner, 1892), 71.

8. SemH 3, 3, ed. Higger, 221.

A king prepared a meal and invited guests to attend. He did not set any time for them to leave the meal. The wise among them rose at nine o'clock and returned to their houses. They climbed into their beds when it was still bright. Others stood up at sunset; the shops were still open and the lights were on, but they went home and climbed into their beds by the lamplight. Others got up at two and three o'clock in the night. Some shops were still open, and others were already closed, some lights were were still lit, and some were extinguished. They entered their houses and climbed into their beds in the darkness. The rest, who remained at the meal, were drunk from the wine and wounded one another and killed one another, as it is written: "I saw the Master standing at the altar, and he said, 'Strike on the knob, that the thresholds may shake: I will destroy all their heads and will kill their rest with the sword'" (Amos 9:1). And the rest of the king's servants? The great ones were smitten because of the little ones,[9] as it is written: "Therefore I have hewn them by the prophets; they have been slain by the words of my mouth" (Hos 6:5).[10]

Another parable comes from Rabbi Hanina bar Hama:

A caravan went its way. Since it had already begun to get dark, they came to a caravansary. The head of the station said to them: "Come into the station to be protected from the wild animals and predators." But the caravan leader said to him, "I don't care to enter a caravansary!" He went on, but the night came, and it got dark. So, he returned and came to the head of the caravansary. He called and asked to be let in. Then the head of the station told him, "I don't usually open the station at night, and a manager of the station doesn't tend to receive people at that hour! When I asked you, you didn't want to and now I can't open up for you." Thus, the Holy One says to Israel, "Return, renegade sons" (Jer 3:14). Further: "Seek the Master now that he is found" (Isa 55:6). But none of them are looking to return. The Holy One said, "I am going away, back to my place" (Hos 5:15). When they were delivered to the empires of the world and to the nations, they cried out, "Why, Master, do you stand far off?" The Holy One said to them, "When I asked you, you did not accept; now that you have asked me, I will not hear. Measure for measure!" It is written: "When he cried, they did not hear, so let them call now, but I will not hear" (Zech 7:13).[11]

---

9. SemH 8, 10, ed. Higger, 156; *The Tractate "Mourning" (Semahot) Regulations Relating to Death, Burial, and Mourning*, ed. Dov Zlotnick (New Haven: Yale University Press, 1966), 61.140 (Hebrew text, 21f.).

10. So it stands in Zlotnick.

11. M. Tep. to Ps 10:1, ed. Solomon Buber (Wilna, 1889), 92f.; see Bacher, *Die Agada der Palaestinischen Amoräer*, vol. 1, 15.

In the resolution of this last parable, the behavior of the head of the caravan is compared to the behavior of Israel toward God. Is this, unlike what we see in the parables of Jesus, particularistic? Does not a Jewish sage have the right to castigate his people's infidelity toward God in a parable? And what about the universalism of Jesus? The question needs to be examined in detail.[12] The answer will be favorable to Jesus both as to his being Jewish and to his humanity. As far as the parables of Jesus are concerned, they are neither universalist nor ethnically restricted. They refer to Jews, for their precondition is faith in the God of Israel. The sometimes dubious protagonists of parables are his servants.

As for the original parables of Jesus himself, we will see that only an inaccurate interpretation can find a mention of the Gentiles at the expense of Israel. And to return to the last rabbinic parable mentioned: in its form, it dates to the first half of the third century, and it speaks of God's missed offer to humanity. The parable itself can therefore be older than the time of those who passed it down. The application to Israel may also have been added at a later period. It is not certain that Israel was explicitly mentioned in Jewish parables that deal with the relationship between man and God at the time of Jesus. Although their object was the Jewish person, they were consciously applicable to all humanity.

I have given a small first selection of rabbinic parables. In this way, I want to show that they are related in their literary value and theological content to Jesus' parables. Like the rabbinic parables of the older type, Jesus' parables are not all literarily equivalent. It will be shown that his parables were restyled in the Greek stage of development by authors who did not know, or hardly knew, Palestinian Judaism. Therefore, the peculiarity of parables as such was alien to them, which is not true for the oral tradition of Jewish parables in rabbinic literature. I am not saying that there are no changes in tradition in oral literature.[13] Rabbinic parables were also changed in their written stages, although edits in the individual Gospels are much more profound. At first, however, I am concerned only with the simple evidence that Jesus' parables belong to a widespread literary genre, which is abundantly documented outside the Gospels. We find in his

---

12. See Joachim Jeremias, *Die Gleichnisse Jesu* (Göttingen: Vandenhoeck & Ruprecht, 1970).

13. The two texts of the parable of Rabbi Yochanan ben Zakkai (see note 4 above), which appear in b. Šabb. 153a and SemH, reflect two that are in a less different oral tradition of the same parable.

parables the same kind of motifs and structure as in the rabbinic parables. If so, are we then entitled to ask whether in the Gospels we may make the same statements, subjects, and elements that can also be found in other Jewish parables, and yet they enshrine a different, special meaning if there is insufficient evidence to do so?[14] Or should we not look at Jesus' parables in the context of other parables and try to clarify, with their help, what Jesus meant by his? Perhaps then Jesus' parables will sound less theological. Perhaps they will not be considered productive enough by some abstract thinkers. But for those who know and feel that these parables speak to them, they will become much more human and important. That is what Jesus himself wanted.

The distinction between the older type of rabbinic parables, which I have described as classic, and the later eisegetically and exegetically motivated rabbinic way of parable formation is important for understanding Jesus' parables. Like almost all of his parables, classical rabbinic parables are mainly oriented toward a generally valid moral doctrine. In contrast to them, later rabbinic parables were invented to illuminate a biblical situation or verse. When a verse from the Old Testament begins a classical rabbinic parable, the Bible passage is not the focal point of the parable. Rather, it is only a decorative illustration or a springboard for the parable and its teaching; the Bible passage is only loosely connected to the parable.

Is is also necessary to examine whether the biblical quotation in the classical rabbinic parables was subsequently appended to adapt the parable to the synagogal sermon, which began with a Scripture verse. It is even possible that sometimes only the editors of the collected rabbinic works provided the classical parables with biblical quotations. By classifying diverse rabbinic material according to Bible verses corresponding to their sequence, these editors wanted to give the impression that their collective works were continuous comments on biblical books.

These Bible verses, however, cannot be eliminated from all classical rabbinic parables as secondary. Often the Bible passage originally belongs to this genre. On the other hand, there is not a single parable of Jesus in

---

14. About the shift, which was made in the later Greek areas of this region, we will speak more later. It will be easily recognizable through a literary-critical examination, and it does not testify to a religiously created atmosphere but is actually rather common. By classifying diverse rabbinic material according to Bible verses corresponding to their sequence, these editors wanted to give the impression that their collective works were continuous comments on biblical books.

which an Old Testament verse is quoted literally as a springboard to the parable. As I will later conclude, neither the parable of the mustard seed (Luke 13:18f. par.) nor that of the evil vineyard workers (Luke 20:9–19 par.) are an exception to this. The former contains ornamental biblical language but no direct quotation. In the latter, listeners are expected to recognize the original wording and understand that the prophet Isaiah was comparing Israel to a vineyard.

From these distinctions between classic rabbinic parables and Jesus' parables, however, it must not be inferred from the stylistic and theological otherness of Jesus' parables that they are somehow different in genre. It is not only to be assumed that in some rabbinic parables the Bible passage was not original. On the other hand, it cannot be ruled out that Jesus began or concluded individual parables with biblical quotations, but that the evangelists or their predecessors found the Bible passage disturbing in the narrative and therefore left it out. Neither for the rabbis nor for Jesus was the Scripture quotation an integral part of the parable genre. It may be that sometime after the catastrophic destruction of the temple in 70 CE, when learning the Bible was given an ever-wider place in popular life, more and more rabbis became increasingly concerned that one or more Bible verses had to be added to the parable. In this case, biblical quotations in classical rabbinic parables would be a first step towards the later ornamental parable, in which a biblical passage or situation is illuminated by a parable.

Although as I said, while it is not impossible that Jesus sometimes began or concluded a parable with a Bible verse, this possibility remains unlikely. In the whole proclamation of Jesus, there are only a few Bible verses. Sometimes—for example, in the Sermon on the Mount—he quoted the Old Testament to develop a moral teaching from it. Elsewhere, he pointed to a Bible passage to say it was fulfilled. Jesus also often alluded to the Bible. He did so for two reasons. Either he wanted to draw the attention of the Bible scholars among his listeners to an important hidden meaning of a Scripture word by an unobtrusive "hint," or he wanted to illustrate his proclamation with biblical twists and echoes. For similar reasons, Jews and biblically literate Christians of all centuries alluded to the Bible. They were not usually concerned with high theology. Unfortunately, in some cases, the evangelists took the slightly scattered biblical illustrations in Jesus' words too seriously and too theologically. I will treat this matter below in the explanation of Jesus' saying about the purpose of parables (Luke 8:9f.; Mark 4:10–12; Matt 13:10–15).

How can we understand the fact that Jesus rarely quotes the Old Testament? Presumably, he wanted to shape his proclamation in such a way that it would at the same time appeal to both the average person and the scholar. Biblical additions might have obscured the clarity. This attitude and "strategy" correspond to the underlying humanity of Jesus. Simple, uneducated Jews were impressed. The educated also understood Jesus' learned hints and allusions. They, too, encountered and marveled at the nature of his teaching and self-revelation.

2

The Structure of Parables

One of the reasons why rabbinic parallels were neglected in the examination of Jesus' parables was the false hope that research could succeed in finding a rabbinic example for the individual parables of Jesus, a Jewish source. This path has proven to be incorrect. I have already pointed out that the investigation must not be based on a single rabbinic parable. Rather, it is necessary to grasp the nature of the genre as a whole. Luckily for us, this genre is sharply defined. There is, if we can put it like this, something creative both in the structure of Jewish parables and in the almost formulaic nature of the individual elements of which the subject is composed. I will have more to say about this later. But even with the examples of rabbinic parables quoted, we can already arrive at some conclusions. We have found in them motifs that we already know from Jesus' parables. We hear of the sensible actions of the wise and the error of the foolish, and we understand why in the end the wise are rewarded and the fools punished. Furthermore, we have also read in two rabbinic parables that the master gave his servants something to preserve. In the second case, he gave them "silver and gold to trade with." We also read that the king departed for a land beyond the sea and that in the meantime the servants acted foolishly in his absence. When the master returned, he punished them. One time, we hear that the king was not clear where the servant should wait for him, another time when the guests should leave the meal, and yet another time when they should come to the meal. Although this curious motif is lacking in Jesus' parables, the master's urgent requirement is present. In looking at rabbinic literature, we will become familiar with the hesitation to come to the banquet (Matt 22:11–13; Luke 14:16–24). We will still speak, however, about the function of omitting a condition in connection with the parable of the workers in the vineyard (Matt 20:1–16). Of the two main themes of Jesus' parables, the banquet and work, we happened to encounter only the first in our little selection; but among the rabbis, a work ethic is also one of the main themes of parables.

Already the oldest evidence for the existence of Jewish parables, which dates from about the year 175 BCE, speaks about work: "Antigonus of Socho used to say: Do not be like servants who serve the Master to receive a reward, but like servants who serve the Master not to receive a reward."[1] The word *abadim* is translated as "servants," but the rabbinic parables as well as Jesus' parables speak openly about "slaves." In this study, we will continue to follow the common way of speaking, although it makes the dependency of the slaves on their master sound humiliating without reason. But it was not the main intention of the parables to express this. In the same context of the work ethic, both Jesus and the rabbis can speak of workers. It was self-evident at the time that it did not matter whether one spoke of servants or workers in a parable. We read that in contrast to the words of Antigonus of Socho about servants and their reward an objection was raised: "Is it possible that a worker[2] shall do the work all day, and then he shall receive no wages in the evening?"[3] It is therefore inappropriate to distinguish between the function of slaves and that of workers in the parables of Jesus. In the same midrashic work I have just quoted,[4] the explanation of the saying of Antigonus of Socho speaks in one breath of man doing the will of his master and his Father. In the parable of the two sons (Matt 21:28–32), the employer is the father and the workers are the two sons. Regarding the concept of "work," the following must be said in particular: Already in the second century CE, rabbinic parables speak of tenants instead of workers. In this nuance of terminology, the influence of the starting colony is to be traced. For the sake of simplicity, we will also translate the tenants as "workers" in these cases. Both with Jesus and with the rabbinic parables, the master is spoken of as the master of the house. The second expression in Jewish parables does not mean, as we might think, the master of the house but the landlord, the "boss."[5] We shall therefore translate the expression with the word *landlord*.

---

1. 'Abot 1:3.

2. The word is missing anyway (it may be lost) in the manuscript where it speaks of "wage" as opposed to "reward."

3. *Avot d'Rabbi Natan*, ed. Solomon Schechter, version A, chapter 5 (New York: Philipp Feldheim, 1945), 26 (hereafter ARN).

4. ARN, version B, chapter 10.

5. As far as I can see, the Greek word means "master of the house" in Greek outside the New Testament (and so also in Luke 22:11); only the "master of the house," not the "boss" like in Hebrew. We can find the original Greek meaning in comparison with God in Philo, *Somn.* 1, 149, and in the beautiful parable in Epictetus, *Diatr.* 3.22:2–4. The "master of the house" in Jesus' parables is also a translation of the Hebrew expression. It appears word for word in Matt 24:42–44 and Luke

The narrators of the parables like those of Jesus want to give the impression that they use examples from daily life.

In this, they differ both from the fairy tale and from the most similar genre that there probably is to the parable: the animal fable. But the realism of the parables is only apparent. If they were merely an imitation of reality, they would be ineffective. I have learned much about the nature of the parables from the Russian formalists, chiefly from Viktor Shklovsky, though he himself has not dealt with this genre. His final book in 1970 is titled *Bowstring: On the Dissimilarity of the Similar in Art.*[6] With this twist one could, very inaccurately, define the nature and function of parables and animal fables. Shklovsky says, "We come across the concept of the example, the concept of analogy, concepts that relate to the construction of a different kind of world." This structure is carried out for the purpose of making understandable that which we call reality, for the purpose of insight and the discovery of new possibilities. What the artist chooses from his surroundings with the aim of developing a model of reality is not a mere reflection of reality. It is a reflection of a special kind: a reflection in which "the senses of the receiver are challenged by their inequality." I accept neither the theory of the literature of the formalists nor that of Shklovsky without some hesitation. If it is applied to some works, it acts one-sidedly and exaggeratedly. When Shklovsky speaks of the reflection in which the recorded features are challenged by their inequality, then, in the case of the classical parables, it means a challenge between the narrated parable and the moral failures of the listener. There is a distinction between the daily reality communicated in the example, or rather exchanged, and the moral immaturity and folly of the audience. Classical rabbinic parables and Jesus' parables always express a moral demand: Act as purposefully as the wise "in life," for it is worthwhile, and be no fool, otherwise you will fall! But the exchanged reality of the parables is consciously a different world from that of the demand itself: The narrated parable itself is only in an analogous relationship with the moral demand of the parable. If this were not so, then it would not be a parable but only an exemplary narrative from life. The parable leads the hearer to transfer and apply the story to a parallel field with the narrative from daily events and the moral imperative of the right course of action before God.

12:39. Outside rabbinic parables, *ba'al habbayit* can naturally mean the owner of the house. See m. Meṣ. 10:2–3.

6. Viktor Shklovsky, *Bowstring: On the Dissimilarity of the Similar in Art*, English trans. Shushan Avagyan (Funks Grove, IL: Dalkey Archive Press, 2011).

To produce this fruitful tension, the parables themselves, as well as animal fables and medieval exempla and their best modern descendants,[7] are never moralistic but pretend to speak only to practical reason and are consciously utilitarian. To increase the tension between the amoral story and the moral application, some parables of Jesus even bear immoral zeal. To keep the necessary distance, we never hear in the parables of the righteous and the sinners, but of the wise and the foolish. In order not to appear to be "moral gluttons," one speaks only of wise people who know how to act successfully. By this constitutive tension between the narration and the always intended moral demand, the classical rabbinic parables as well as Jesus' parables differ from the later related rabbinic literary remnants. Here, there is no moral imperative. They do not make moral demands; they just want to enhance the biblical stories and figures poetically with illustrations and strengthen the Jew in his self-confidence within the dire situation of the Jewish people.

On the other hand, as we have already seen from the examples above, classical Jewish parables are not descriptive in their intention but address the listener in order for him to improve in his actions and religious-moral attitude. Although in the parables, there is no identity between the narrative and its teaching, there is an analogy that runs parallel. Even the story told is not realistic, only pseudorealistic. If parables were imitating reality, they would be ineffective. I once spoke to a great Jewish scholar about the nature of parables. He took the view that parables sometimes seem strange and paradoxical to the reader of today only because there is too little knowledge of life in the ancient world. For example, the parable of the workers in the vineyard (Matt 20:1–16) was taken entirely from the life of that time. The landlord acted cleverly and businesslike when he paid the latecomers a dinar as a wage. The grapes were already quite ripe. If he had waited for the next day, many of them would have spoiled. Incidentally, Joachim Jeremias does not quite grasp the peculiarity of the parable when he refers to the dinar as the "subsistence minimum" and speaks of the "genuinely oriental indifference" of the workers. "The wages for an hour's work are not enough to support their families. Their children will go hungry when the father comes home with empty hands. Because he has sympathy for their poverty, let the master of the house pay them all the wages of the day."[8] So, was the

---

7. By this, I mean some of the stories of the "little treasure boxes" of Johann Peter Hebel. (See Hebel's 1811 "Treasure Chest of Rhenish Tales"—Ed.)

8. That doesn't quite agree from the standpoint of realia. A dinar as a day's wage at that time was a high sum!

Jewish scholar right when he warned against understanding parables as something other than stories that grasp real-life experiences? Immediately after the conversation, I communicated his view to a friend who is not a scholar but is concerned with practical life. "Surely the scholar is right," he replied at once. "I am concerned with the repair of transistors. If a woman is unhappy because I cannot repair her equipment on the spot, I answer her with an example from daily life: If I want to take the tuna fish out of a sandwich, I must first open the sandwich." I asked him, "And do you tend to open the pieces of bread to take out the tuna?" To which he answered, "Not at all." Apparently, his example would be much less effective and convincing if it were entirely in line with normal everyday reality. In *Theory of Prose*, Shklovsky writes, "You don't notice the path until you walk on thorns."[9] Already in 1915, he used the term "alienation" in an article of the same name.[10] We shall take a closer look at the nature of alienation in the parables. As the words of my practically gifted friend show, the alienation in examples and parables is not only a purely artistic means of making it effective but also a sign that the parables are, so to speak, Janus faced. Like the animal fables, they point to "the morality of history," which lives outside the subject; and at the same time, to appear convincing, they must pretend that they imitate everyday life. Concerning the parable of the ten virgins (Matt 25:1–13), Joachim Jeremias says "that it was originally not an allegory, but the description of a real wedding,"[11] and he succeeds in drawing similar material from antiquity and modern times. But how can one speak of a real wedding when the ten virgins behave so strangely? Perhaps it is no coincidence that the parable speaks of ten virgins, for we have ten fingers, five on each hand. Five of the virgins were foolish, and five were wise. They thus formed two groups of the same size, whose members all acted in the same way. The foolish virgins took the lamps, but they did not take oil, whereas the wise virgins took oil. All five lamps of the foolish virgins go out. The five wise virgins apparently act in a chorus. In the end, the bridegroom excluded half of the virgins from the wedding. Such strange happenings will be hard to come by at a real wedding! Each virgin is not individualized, but the event is highly stylized. The contrast between the wise and the

---

9. Viktor Shklovsky, *Theory of Prose* (Berlin: Fischer Taschenbuch, 1966). I own only the Czech translation of the book.

10. See Viktor Shklovsky, *On the Dissimilarity of the Similar* (Munich: Hansen, 1973).

11. Joachim Jeremias, *Die Gleichnisse Jesu*, 171–74.

foolish—which we also recognize from the other parables of Jesus and, as we have already seen, from rabbinic parables (which is a significant motif in the teaching of many parables)—has been artfully brought to its peak in this parable of the ten virgins. Through the two equally acting and equally treated groups of five, the polar contrast between the wise and the foolish is impressively emphasized. Thus one cannot speak of realism in the parables but only of pseudo-realism, of a stylizing selection of motifs from real life. Regarding conscious stylization and similar treatment of fixed motifs, the Jewish parable is closely related to the European folktale; although in this respect, too, there are important differences between these two genres of modern folk literature. In this area, I learned a great deal from Max Lüthi, the Swiss researcher of fairy tales. "The fairy tale works with rigid formulas. It loves clearly emphasized numbers."[12] These formulaic numbers are also found in rabbinic parables[13] and, as we have just seen, also in Jesus' parables. In the Lukan form of the parable (Luke 20:9–19), the master first sends three servants to the evil vinedressers, one after the other, and then the son. We will speak later on the artful use of numbers in the parable of the minas (Luke 19:11–27) and in the parallel in Matthew (25:14–30). Luke speaks of ten servants, but in his account, as with Matthew, only three servants are confronted by the landlord. According to Matthew (22:1–13), in the parable of the wedding feast, three groups of servants are sent to the guests in succession; in the Lukan parallel (14:16–24), the same servant is sent out three times. In Luke, we also find three individual apologies from three invitees. In the parable of the workers in the vineyard (Matt 20:1–16), Jesus is apparently speaking of three groups of workers. The importance of the number *three* is evident, then, in Jesus' parables as an expression of successive action and increase. The number *three* has the same function in European fairy tales, anecdotes and humorous tales, and some rabbinic parables. The number *three* is quite common in parables and fairy tales.[14] The same

---

12. Max Lüthi, *The European Folktale: Form and Nature* (Indiana: Indiana University Press, 1986).

13. Ziegler, *Die Koenigsgleichnisse des Midrasch beleuchtet durch die roemische Kaiserzeit*, chapter 1, parable 105; chapter 5, parable 61 (two and the son); chapter 5, parable 62 (a descending series in a beautiful parable; three kinds); chapter 6, parable 42 (three and the son); parable 76 (counted up until the fifth servant); chapter 7, parable 79; chapter 11, parable 23 (three); and parables 55 and 101 (three).

14. Lüthi, *The Fairy Tale as Art Form and Portrait of Man*, trans. Jon Erickson (repr., Bloomington: Indiana University Press, 1984), 57f. "The three stands between two singularities and amorphous majority. It is after the one, which is the

applies to the number *two*. In the parables, there are either two persons or two opposite groups. In fairy tales, it is the hero and the anti-hero. In the parables, the number *two* is used to express the polar opposition between those who do right and those who do wrong. Max Lüthi describes the structure of the fairy tale:

> The rigidity of the material is accompanied by the rigidity of the formula: conventional beginnings and closures, stereotypical recurrence of the same and similar events—similar within the individual narrative as well as similar to that described in other fairy tales—repetitions and variations, structured by the conventional as well as symbolic numbers two and three; the high degree of literary formulation in general, perfection, the measure.[15]

The same is true of the parables.

But now we want to define some basic concepts that will recur in the course of this work. We have taken them from the Russian formalists, mainly from Shklovsky. Already during our investigation, we have spoken several times of the "subject." This term is not identical to the story itself, or to the content of the "story." The "plot" is the material from which the subject is built and shaped. The subject is the theme in which the different situations or motifs are woven. What we call "motifs" is clear overall: They are the simplest epic units from which the subject is composed. We will introduce the term "main theme." These are different areas of life around which the individual parables are grouped. Of course, the main themes determine the choice of the individual motifs of the parable. For our study of Jesus' and rabbinic parables, a rather old work is an important tool: namely, Ignaz Ziegler, *The King's Parables of the Midrash in Light of the Roman Empire*.[16] This book contains a large but not complete collection of rabbinic

---

individuum, and the two, which represents both the pair and the possibility of polarity, the first representative of the actual majority. . . . The one in the person of the hero or the heroine, the two in many polarities and in the inclination toward the twofold, to two sequences, the three in the building of a group or in a series of episodes. . . . The three is not only the first but also the most impressive representative of the majority: it is optically not tangible without something further. It can also through differentiation, increase, contrast, and so on clearly be delineated. In comparison to the symmetry and equal weight of the numbers two and four, the three has something dynamic to it."

15. Lüthi, *The Fairy Tale as Art Form and Portrait of Man*, 86.

16. Ignaz Ziegler, *The King's Parables of the Midrash in Light of the Roman Empire* (Breslau, 1903).

king-parables, arranged according to the main themes, both in German translation and, in the appendix, in the original Hebrew. As the title of the book suggests, the author tries to demonstrate how the orders, customs, and conditions of the Roman Empire are reflected in rabbinic parables. It is not our task to prescribe what we can learn from them about the Roman Empire. It seems to me that the yield is quite meager, not only because of the formulaic structure of the subject and because both the motifs and the main themes are probably older than the Roman Empire, but also because, in parables, often the king does not exercise any actual royal function. Rather, he represents the function of the original landowner or host. This is easy to see from the examples of rabbinic parables given above.

There are two main themes that are often represented in rabbinic parables and that are common to them and to Jesus' parables; namely, the banquet and work ethic. There are also main themes that are missing either from Jesus or from the rabbinic parables that have been preserved. This does not prove that Jesus or the rabbis did not use them in these preserved parables. Neither all the rabbinic parables nor all the parables that Jesus spoke have been preserved. As everyone can easily learn from Ziegler's work, motifs from the agricultural world occur quite often in the rabbinic parables: growth, weeds, and the like. However, plant motifs hardly constitute a main theme in the rabbinic parables that have survived. Rather, they are mostly connected with the central motif of the landlord. As we shall see, growth is a major theme in Jesus' parables. This does not necessarily mean that Jesus invented this main theme. It may simply be that the later Jewish collectors were not mainly concerned with such. Parables whose meaning was explicitly theocentric were of interest to them. A landlord about whom one could tell parables offered a particularly suitable starting point.

How cautious we must be when deciding on the possible originality of Jesus in choosing the theme of his parables can be shown by two examples. I do not know of any rabbinic parable with the main theme of the fishnet (Matt 13:47–50). It is almost certain, however, that this main theme also existed among the rabbis. In a parable, Rabbi Akiba says, among other things: "And a net is spread over all living things" (Av 3, 16). The main theme of the children playing (Matt 11:16–19; Luke 7:31–35) is found only once in Jewish literature, in a rather obscure treatise.[17] On the other hand, there are main themes in rabbinic parables that are lacking in the preserved parables of Jesus, such as the parables spoken by the king's family

---

17. SemH 3, 5, ed. Higger, 222.

members. In the parable of the wedding feast in Matthew (22:1–13), we find the rabbinic theme of the king's son at the banquet as a "blunt motif."[18] Here, it is not further elaborated and seems secondary. On the question of the main themes of the rabbinic parables and the parables of Jesus, we should bear in mind not only that not all the parables were preserved but also that especially the old rabbinic parables known to us were sparingly delivered up to the time of Rabbi Akiba. Thus it can be assumed that the subject matter of the ancient classical parables of the Jews is much richer than we can recognize from the material we have today. A closer examination of the history of rabbinic parables will probably also show that after the destruction of the temple and the cruel subjugation of the Bar Kochba uprising, Jewish life in their country and their literary expressions became poorer and much more uniform. The actual parables are artistic. They are almost schematically constructed models that want to give the impression that they reflect real, everyday life. Without this artistry, they are ineffective. They give the impression that life itself teaches us how to behave toward God. The main themes and motifs were created and chosen for this purpose and are always adapted to the "moral" of the parables. For our investigation, it is important to know that parables are highly stylized short forms and that their motifs are actually as rigid as iron. Both the main themes and motifs give the impression that their number is limited. Because of the conventional form, it can be assumed that the hearer already knows what to expect regarding the subject and motifs and that he reacts with discomfort when the narrator suddenly says something quite unusual. A master in the creation of parables certainly proves himself not only by his epic talent in storytelling but also in the harmony between the subject and morality and in certain variations within the parable itself that are renewing or inspiring for the listeners. From a certain point of view, the parable, like similar assumptions, has an ephemeral nature that has always arisen ad hoc in a certain situation. The question of which parables were passed down to us probably depends in part on the material of the parable and in part on the authority of the creator.

The nature of the main themes and motifs in rabbinic parables remains more or less constant in the centuries-long history of the genre. This is the consequence of the parables' conventional nature. After the new kind of

---

18. See Lüthi, *The European Folktale*, 56–60: "Motifs . . . that do not stand fully without function in fairy tales but still remain without some kind of figurative direction and without a specific context, I have described as 'blunt motifs.'"

parables arose—which no longer helped the hearer to live rightly before God but were offered rather as decorative illustrations for biblical situations, figures, and passages—the main themes, motifs, and conservative nature of the parables became preserved in the new types. For example, in Genesis 1:9, we read, "Let the waters under the heavens be gathered together into one place." This passage is explained through the parable about the master who told his servant to wait for him without determining exactly where (see chapter 1, note 3). We recognize this story but with the omission of certain details. Originally, in classical parables, this omission usually had the function of referring to the responsibility of the doer in an "alienating" manner. We already saw this in the two examples of classical parables in chapter 1 (see notes 4 and 8). In the newer parable about Genesis 1:9, the moral function of the motif is lost. Another example points in this direction:

> Rabbi Judah spoke a parable: A prince had two sons; an older one and a younger one. He said to the younger one: "Go with me." And he said to the older one: "Come and go ahead of me." Thus "walked" Abraham, who had a good nature, "blamelessly before the Master." But of Noah, who had a bad nature, it is said, "Noah walked with God" (Gen 6:9).[19]

Here the theme of the two dissimilar sons, which occurs once in the Gospels (Matt 21:28–32), is applied to two biblical figures and serves to illuminate two biblical verses that speak of these two figures. In such an exegetical parable, a moral demand has no place, unlike in Jesus' parable of the dissimilar sons, which belongs to the older kind of parables. This parable also belongs to the theme of work ethic.

A later parable of Rabbi Abin also deals with the subject of work:

> A king owned a wine cellar and placed guards in it, some of whom were Nazirites (to whom the enjoyment of wine is forbidden); the others were drunkards. In the evening he came to the wine cellar to pay them their wages. To the drunkards he gave twice as much wages as to the Nazirites. The Nazirites complained, "Master King, didn't we all guard in the same way? Why do you

---

19. Ziegler, *Die Koenigsgleichnisse des Midrasch beleuchtet durch die roemische Kaiserzeit*, chapter 11, parable 21; Gen. Rab. 30, 10; Tanḥ. B 81; Yal. 1, 50. In Gen 6:9, it is written, "Noah was a righteous man, unstained in his generation." From there, Judaism stumbled onto the meaning that Noah lived in a less sinful generation and was not counted among the righteous because his perfection was only relative. Regarding the question and the parable, see Bacher, *Die Agada der Tannaiten*, vol. 2, 269.

give them a double wage, but give us only a part?" And the king said unto them, "They are drunken men, and drink wine: and yet they have guarded the wine, and unto you that drink no wine at all I give a simple reward." Thus, the superior beings, who have no evil impulse, are simply called "holy" (Dan 4:14). But about the lower beings, over whom the evil impulse has power, it is said "prove yourself holy and be holy" (Lev 11:44) that they were able to withstand their evil nature with doubled holiness![20]

This late parable is of a particular beauty. But it also seems bizarre because of the unusual manipulation of the subject. The religious background is the later rabbis' reoccurring envy toward the holy community of angels, which is in competition with holy people and whose "holy" disadvantage must therefore be emphasized. In the parable here, however, it is not about Israel but about people in general. The starting point for the parable is two verses of the Bible: In one, the word *holy* concerning the angel appears once; in the second, which speaks of Israel, twice. The parable itself is a good example of parables with the main theme of labor and wages. But I can't resist the impression that this beautiful parable is somehow wasted. How much more beautiful the parable would be if it were to end as follows: "And thus the master doubly forgives those who stumble and repent!" Thus it might be found in a classic Jewish parable of the ancients, but the parable of Rabbi Abin belongs to the later kind. This parable and the preceding example show that the new kind of parables had taken over the old motifs and theme. We will therefore be able to draw on these kinds of parables for the examination of Jesus' parables, not only because of the similar motifs and subject matter but also because the number of old rabbinic parables, which by their nature correspond to the parables of Jesus, is not very large.

Let us emphasize once again that there are two reasons for the "rigid" nature of the motifs and main themes of parables. One reason lies in the intellectual, abstract nature of the genre, which is related to other genres of oral folk poetry—such as the European fairy tale. The other reason for the schematic nature of parables is that both the subject and the individual motifs should correspond to the moral of the parable. In this matter, the parables resemble both animal fables and riddles. This necessary agreement between the subject of a parable and its application has probably also contributed to the fact that the subject matter and motifs of parables are quite fixed. As

---

20. Ziegler, *Die Koenigsgleichnisse des Midrasch beleuchtet durch die roemische Kaiserzeit*, chapter 6, parable 89; Lev. Rab. 24:8, Yal. 1, 603; Yal. 2, 505; See Bacher, *Die Agada der Palästinischen Amoraër*, vol. 3 (Strasbourg: Trübner, 1896), 424f.

we shall see, the instructions for moral conduct in parables are often quite uniform. Both causes, the inner form and the application of the parables, have thus led to the subjects of the parables and their use being highly stereotypical, to the point that they seem like they have been taken from the later type of the parables, although the illustrative portion of the parables is of a different nature than their interpretation. The stereotypical and fixed nature of parables should also be considered when examining Jesus' parables.

Like similar genres, parables, even in their conventional manner, give a gifted creator and narrator the opportunity to develop his art and talent. For example, he can vary the motifs and replace them with others that have the same or a similar function in the subject. We have already seen that it carries the same meaning whether one tells a story of "workers" or "servants." The work can be done in a field, in a garden, or in a vineyard; even for Jesus, the vineyard only once has the specific meaning of "Israel" (Mark 12:1–12 and parallels). For the same or similar purposes, subjects from different spheres of life can also be connected with different main themes. From the examples above of rabbinic parables, we can see that the parable of Rabban Yohanan ben Zakkai about wise and foolish conduct in response to an invitation to a banquet proclaims a teaching similar to that of the parable of the wise and foolish actions of the servants to whom the royal garments were entrusted. In both cases, it is about being willing to stand before God when you die. Both parables even have a common motif; namely, the filthy garments of the foolish ones. The difference is that the second parable asks us to return the soul pure at death, whereas we learn from the first parable that we should be prepared for death because we do not know the hour of its sudden arrival. That is why we are to wear, so to speak, "always white clothes." Jesus' parable about the wise and foolish actions of the ten virgins who await the arrival of the bridegroom is also about being ready for the sudden call of God (Matt 25:1–13). Here, the main theme is different, but the moral imperative is similar. The examples of the use of various main themes and motifs in various parables, which have a similar purpose, could still be multiplied, even on the basis of the already quoted material. Interesting, for example, is the variation of the motif of the appropriate festive clothing at the feast, on the one hand, in the parable of Rabbi Johanan ben Zakkai and, on the other hand, in the reference to the man without wedding attire in Matt 22:11–14. It is obvious that the same or similar moral teaching in Jesus' parables can be expressed by parables with different main themes. Thus the parables of the fishing net (Matt 13:47–52) and the weeds (Matt 13:24–30, 36–43) are actually two representations of one and the same eschatological concept. Did Jesus speak both of them on the same occasion? In any case, there are three "twin pairs" of parables in the Gospels, one after the other. Two pairs deal with the kingdom of heaven: the parables of the mustard seed and the leaven speak of the growth of the kingdom (Matt 13:31–33; Luke 13:18–21; cf. Mark 4:30–32); the second pair, the parables of the treasure and the pearl (Matt 13:44–46) speak of the "fortunate finding" of the kingdom. In the third pair, the parables of the lost sheep and the lost penny (Luke 15:1–10; cf. Matt 18:10–14), God's loving concern for the salvation of the individual person is expressed by two similar images from different areas. Jesus' teaching that one must ask God without shyness and then be heard is expressed in two parables with different themes: the parable of the pleading friend (Luke 11:5–8) and the ungodly judge (Luke 18:1–8). In both, the central concept of burden is expressed with the same Greek word (Luke 11:7; 18:5). So, Jesus mastered the art of theme variation of the Jewish parables and consciously used them.

At this point, I would like to caution us that the interpretation does not ignore the fact that variations belong to the literary genre of the parables. I know that the variations—both in terms of their themes and their motifs—sometimes, but not always, imply a shift in the tenor of the parable. But we should not exaggerate the meaning of the variations in Jesus' parables! In any case, it is not to be overlooked that sometimes the variation is due to stylistic freedom. In other, more weighty cases, one should know that the interplay between the subject, its components, and the meaning of the parable is a particularly complex matter. This artful and delicate web should not be treated with a rough hand.

One feature of the stylized nature of parables is that their content frequently exhibits a macabre and cruel exterior. Such a parable is that of the ruthless servant (Matt 18:21–35) where we see that God's mercy has its limits. In ancient times, not much thought was given to a moral obligation toward slaves. The master could allow himself to be cruel to his slaves: "But that servant, who knew the will of his master and did not stand ready or act willfully, will receive many blows. But whoever does not know him, but has done something worthy of a blow, will receive a little blow" (Luke 12:47). The background of the parable of the faithful master of the house (Matt 24:43–51; Luke 12:35–46) is therefore not all that unrealistic. It was a matter of course for many at the time: When the master delays his return, a slave begins to beat other slaves and maidservants. He gets into unhealthy eating and drinking until he is full and intoxicated. That the master would "lay hold of all his possessions" (Matt 24:47) for that servant he sees doing the right thing, or that, if he finds the servants vigilant, "he will be satisfied, and they will sit down and walk about and await them," is an exaggeration understandable from the literary character of the parables. But the idea that the master will have the disobedient slave cut into pieces is, as far as I can see, equally exaggerated. As I said, in the world of slaves and masters, one can somehow understand such cruel figures. But how is it with the parables of the banquet? Why is it sometimes grotesque and drastic, as in the rabbinic parable of Rabbi Meir where one guest even kills the other and the big ones are beaten by the small ones?[21] Such a thing hardly ever happens at a real banquet of a king. We know that a king is capable of a great deal, but is it possible that when he sees a man at his son's wedding supper who is not wearing wedding clothes, he commands his guards: "Bind him hand and foot and cast him out into the darkness" (Matt 22:11–13)? The parable of Rabbi Yohanan ben Zakkai (see chapter 1, note 4) ends in the Talmud with the words of the king: "These who have dressed themselves for the meal may sit down and eat and drink, but those who have not dressed themselves for the meal may stand and watch." In the appendix to this parable, which had certainly belonged to it at first,[22] we read:

> It may be that they went home, but the king said, "These may eat and drink, but those shall stand, watch, be beaten, and repent." Which scripture fits this? "Therefore thus saith the Master God: Behold, my servants shall eat, and ye shall hunger. Behold, my servants shall drink; ye shall thirst. Behold, my servants shall rejoice; ye shall be ashamed. Behold, my servants shall rejoice with joy of heart, ye shall cry with sorrow of heart, and wail with despair" (Isa 65:13–14).[23]

The drastic figures of the parables correspond to European fairy tales. There, too, punishment and the highest reward often stand side by side.[24]

---

21. *The Tractate "Mourning" (Semahot) Regulations Relating to Death, Burial, and Mourning*, ed. Dov Zlotnick (New Haven: Yale University Press, 1966), 61.140 (Hebrew text, 21f.).

22. This job advertisement appears in Higger. In b. Šabb. 153a, it is passed down in similar form from Rabbi Meir's son-in-law. This supplement belongs to the parable of Rabban Yohanan ben Zakkai. The word *struck* is missing in the parallel in the Talmud; it could also simply mean "suffer."

23. The Aramaic translation of that passage from the prophet says, "See my servants, the righteous, will eat, and you, evil ones, will be hungry." The text in Higger adds Mal 3:18 to this. This verse is missing in b. Šabb. 153a.

24. Lüthi, *The European Folktale*, 35.

Cruelties are common in fairy tales, especially in the form of cruel punishments. This is the consequence of the fairy tale's own stylization to the extreme. Almost everything in the fairy tale is sharply stylized. Precisely because of this the cruel punishments are not felt to be the same as in a realistic narrative. The extreme formulation is accepted as self-evident; it is a rule of the game, a tacit agreement.[25]

These words of the great researcher are not only important for the understanding of some drastic descriptions in the parables, but we also derive from them insights into the stylization of the parables that are related to fairy tales in this capacity.

In addition to the "abstract" stylization of the parables, a more or less great paradox often occurs in them. We see this in Jesus' parables. Not only is it comprehensible from the stylized nature of the parables, but it also makes them interesting. In this, they are similar to the contrasting nature of the riddle, the humorous story, the exempla, and the animal fable. But in parables, the paradox also has another function. The classical parables are a model built from real life, reflecting the action and behavior of man before God. Implicitly, they should also include the paradox of human existence. That is why themes and motifs from real life are preferred by similar parable narrators who have seen a paradoxical nature in our daily experience. This is especially true of the two main themes common to the parables of Jesus and the rabbinic parables: the work ethic and the "Knigge" for a feast.[26] Both main themes have in common an emphasis on the dependence of the servants or guests on the landlord or the host: that is, the dependence of man on God. The two main themes give the master seemingly absolute power, but there are also rules of the game that are taken from life that the guest or servant should follow in order "that it may go well." This is how it is in life: There are tense moments in the relationships between the employer and the employee. There is the question of labor and wages, of the work ethic, as well as of the diligence or laziness of the workers or slaves. The workers or the slaves can behave diligently or out of folly can be negligent in their work or do it badly. The view of the employer's rights vis-à-vis the workers in parables is extremely patriarchal in comparison with what is now thought. It probably did not completely

---

25. Lüthi, *The Fairy Tale as Art Form and Portrait of Man*, 170.

26. Here, Flusser is referring to Adolf Franz Friedrich, Freiherr von Knigge (1752–1796), who wrote a practical guide to happiness and success, written in a pleasant and easy style. —Ed.

agree with what Jesus and rabbinic parable tellers thought and felt regarding the realities and social aspects of daily life. The extreme emphasis
on the master's authority can be attributed both to the stylization of the
parables and to the function of God represented by the employer in the
parable. It was naturally easier to liken the appropriate expression for the
punishment of the sinner in a parable about the master and the slaves than
in a parable about a landlord and his workers because an owner of slaves
had the right in antiquity to punish the slaves physically. We have seen that
even in parables whose main theme is the banquet, corporeal corrections
could be made, although it was not very realistic if the landlord was a king.
It is not necessary to repeat in parables that the landlord or the host is always right, for he represents God. This circumstance precisely determines
the "reactionary" aspect of parables. But even so, the master is never the
disgusting man in classical Jewish parables or in Jesus' parables, who can
carry out whatever occurs to him based on his mood. If there were no
fixed moral laws in a parable or fairy tale according to which good is ultimately rewarded and evil punished, it would be an impossible fairy tale or
a bad parable—not only from a moral point of view, but also regarding the
subject. The fair distinction between good and evil is the backbone, so to
speak, of the two genres. In parables in which a landlord or host appears,
the mutual relationship between the master and those he commands is an
important characteristic. For the master to be just, he must follow the rules
of justice. The "rules of the game" in terms of the moral of these stories
amount to the just, though merciful, reign of God.

The rules of parables are taken from certain life situations. Since one of
the main tasks of the parables is to illustrate the alienating paradox of man's
just or sinful action on the one hand, and God's just and merciful reaction
to this action on the other, the subjects and their motifs in the parables are
often taken from those areas of human activity in which paradoxical situations often occur. These paradoxical situations are further enhanced in the
subjects through selection and stylization. It is well known that work ethics
can lead to paradoxical conditions. This paradox now manifests itself not
only in the workers' behavior but in the whole of economic life. Therefore,
the parables deal not only with work ethic in the narrower sense but also
with broader areas of the economy: for example, economic manipulation
of servants to whom capital is given, or in rabbinic parables, the pledge to
which the servants are called to be faithful. I have already mentioned a rabbinic parable that deals with pledges (see chapter 1, note 5). Now I refer to
an old parable with the same theme:

When the son of Rabban Yohanan ben Zakkai had died, Yohanan's disciple came to comfort him. Eleazar ben Arakh finally managed to comfort the master. And he stood and sat before him, and said, "Permit me a parable. This is like a person to whom a king entrusted a pledge. The man wept and lamented daily, and said, 'Woe to me! When shall I be gladly emptied of the sorrow of this pledge?' So too, Rabbi, you had a son. He read the Bible and learned the oral tradition. He then left the world without committing any wrongdoing. Therefore, you can receive the consolation since you were able to repay the pledge intact." And Rabban Johanan said unto him, "Eleazar my son, thou hast comforted me, as one should be comforted."[27]

Here, then, and in the parable above, the universally prevalent image of the soul represents a gift or pledge entrusted by God.[28] Josephus also uses this image in a kind of parable in his speech in Jotapata as an argument against suicide: "If someone destroys or badly manages assets entrusted to him by another, he is considered reprehensible and unfaithful. But if any of the good things that God has entrusted to him, does he believe that the person he has so insulted will remain hidden?"[29] In the first mentioned rabbinic parable of the pledge[30] that begins with the verse from the Preacher (Eccl 12:7), "And the spirit goes back to God who gave it," the human soul is spoken of as in other mentioned sources. In the parable of Eleazar ben Arakh, on the other hand, the interpretation of the motif is slightly

---

27. ARN, version A, chapter 14, ed. Solomon Schechter, 59; see Bacher, *Die Agada der Tannaiten*, vol. 1, 69–70.

28. Cicero, *Rep.* 6, 15, *Somnium Scipionis* 3, 5: "The soul should not leave the body early, without order" (*ne munus humanum assignatum a deo defugisse videamini*). In Greek sources, such as Jewish-Hellenistic didactic poetry from the first century CE that was transmitted in the name of the heathen poet Phokylides, we read (v. 106), "For the soul is God's loan to mortal man and is his image." See P. W. van der Horst, *The Sentences of Pseudo-Phocylides, with Introduction and Commentary* (Leiden: Brill, 1978), 180–90. There is rich material—from antiquity and modernity, Jewish and non-Jewish literature—on the popular philosophical opinion that the soul, the spirit, or life is a loan from God.

29. Josephus, *J.W.* 3.371f. The active meaning of the loan of human life also comes through the ancient practice of dream interpretation. According to the dream collection of Artemidor (Artemidorus Daldianus, *Onir.* 3.41), who lived in the second century CE, a loan in a dream symbolizes life. "A loan means the same thing as life; for we are responsible for our lives just as much as for the nature of everything as a loan for those who believe." Artemidor of Daldis, *The Dream Book*, trans. Karl Brackerz (Zurich: Artemis, 1979), 228.

30. See chapter 1, note 5.

modified: The pledge is now the son of Rabban Yohanan ben Zakkai and his pure life. Although the meaning and interpretation of the themes and motifs of classical rabbinic parables—and of Jesus' parables—are more or less determined by convention, it sometimes happens that variations occur in the interpretation of a parable. That is why it is very often helpful if we can know the situation in which the parable was told. Without this knowledge, it is sometimes impossible to discover the exact intention of the parable.

The second area of human life that contains many paradoxes is the feast. It was at that time the most striking example of an event in which established social rules of the game prevailed. The organized guests at a banquet were a more important part of life in antiquity than they are today. Since the host was the master of the rules of the game and of the guests, we can understand why in parables the banquet became an example of man's dependence on God, which is similar to the first theme of a work ethic. Man's dependence on God, which can be represented by parables of the feast, could be related to simple human life or to the end-time context. The paradox is already apparent at the guest meal, for example, when the guest is invited, since who is invited depends entirely on the host's preference. It is important to know when to appear at the feast. You must also arrive dressed appropriately. At the meal itself, there is a fixed arrangement of places according to the guest's importance. We have also mentioned a rabbinic parable about knowing when to leave the banquet.[31] Here I would like to mention one with the theme of the feast:

> Rabbi Yossi bar Hanina told a parable: "A king hosted a feast and invited the guests. The fourth hour of the day came, and they did not come. There came the fifth, the sixth hour, and they didn't come. When it was evening, the guests began to come slowly. The king said to them, 'I owe you a great debt of gratitude, for if you had not come, I would have thrown the whole meal to the dogs.' The Holy One said to the righteous, 'I owe you a great debt of gratitude. For your sake I created my world. For whom, if not for you, have I prepared all the good for the future?' It is written in this regard: 'Great is your goodness, which you have laid up for those who fear you'" (Ps 31:20).[32]

This later parable from the third century CE, because of its general application, belongs to the older type of parables—to which Jesus' parables also

---

31. See chapter 1, note 8.

32. M. Tep. to Ps 25:7, ed. S. Buber, 213; see also Ziegler, *Die Koenigsgleichnisse des Midrasch beleuchtet durch die roemische Kaiserzeit*, chapter 5, parable 42; as well as Bacher, *Die Agada der Palästinischen Amoräer*, vol. 1, 439f.

belong. The paradox is similar to the parable of the Great Supper in Luke 14:15–24. In both parables, the guests were reluctant to come; and in the end, it turns out that the prepared meal was intended for more than just the original guests.

Let us ask ourselves here how the choice of the main themes of the parables was time-bound. If the genre of parables were to flourish again today, the main theme of the feast would occur much less frequently—not because the rules of the game of reception have become less absurd today, but because today the feast plays a much smaller role in daily life than in antiquity. It is strange that parables from the life of athletes do not occur in Jesus' parables, and hardly with the rabbis, although comparisons from the actions of the athletes in ancient philosophical literature (as well as with the Alexandrian Jew Philo) are quite frequent. The topic probably did not interest Palestinian Jews enough. Given the Israeli interest in sporting events today, this may be a suitable topic, especially from team sports. In this way, we could address not only the problem of the correct execution of the coaches or the captains of the team, but also the wise or foolish behavior of the individual players.

3

AESTHETICS OF PARABLES

Like animal fables and riddles, parables are not autonomous narrations. In the parable, the riddle, and the animal fable, the focus of the action tends toward a resolution that lies outside the subject. Because of this and other affinities between the parable and the animal fable, it is important for us to factor Lessing's treatises on the fable into our consideration, as far as they are relevant for our purposes.[1] However, I must ask the reader's patience. I am now dealing with literary-critical questions and not yet with religion. Certainly, I understand those readers who read this book out of religious motivation, but the somewhat long and arduous path of literary-critical analysis is also a correct and necessary path for them to take. For only in this way can we understand the nature of Jesus' parables and experience what Jesus the parable teller wanted to say. Whoever believes in Jesus should also believe Jesus. As researching and thinking people, we value knowledge and truth. Knowledge cannot be detrimental to faith. As far as I know, truth is also a goal of faith and should not be separated from it!

The relationship between fables and rabbinic parables was known to the Jewish sages. Rabban Yohanan ben Zakkai, who has already been mentioned often, says that parables of washers and animal fables belong to the many areas in which he had expertise.[2] These parables and fables are considered here as two related genres; and as we will see, the folksy character of the parables of the washers is clear. It is also reported that Rabbi Meir, the student of Rabbi Akiva, produced three hundred animal fables.[3] In fact, the following parable of Rabbi Akiva is itself, in reality, an animal fable:

> After the insurrection of Bar Kochba was subjugated by the Roman Empire, the Jews were not allowed to deal with the doctrine of God. Then came Pap-

---

1. See also Hans G. Klemm, *Die Gleichnisauslegung Adolf Jülichers im Bannkreise der Fabeltheorie Lessings,* ZNW, vol. 60 (1969), 153–74.

2. See further b. Sukkah. 28a; b. B. Bat. 134a; see also Bacher, *Die Agada der Tannaiten*, vol. 1, 10.

3. b. Sanh. 35a; see also Bacher, *Die Agada der Tannaiten*, vol. 2, 7.

pos ben Yehuda who found Rabbi Akiva and how he had held public meetings that dealt with the Torah. He said to him: "Akiva, are you not fearful of the government?" And he said, "I will tell you a parable, to what may this matter be compared. A fox once walked along the banks of a river. Then he saw fish that were gathering from one place to another. He said to them, 'What are you running from?' They replied, 'From the nets that the people cast after us.' And he said to them 'Will you not go up to the dry land? Me and you, we want to live together, as once my and your father lived together.' But they said to him, 'Are you the one about whom it is said "He is the smartest of the animals"? You're not smart, you're stupid! If we are already fearful at the place we spend our lives, how much more at the place where we will die!' The same for us. If we are already in danger when we sit down and deal with the Torah, which is called 'your life and the length of your days' (Deut 30:20), how much more if we go and escape from it?"[4]

In rabbinic literature, water is a symbol for the Torah, so it was easy to adapt the fable to the tragic circumstances of the time. In Aesop, a similar fable is preserved:

A crab left the sea to wander the shore. A hungry fox saw him, ran, and caught him. When he was about to be eaten, the crab said, "It is right that this happens to me, because I am a sea animal and I wanted to become a dry-lander." Thus, such people deserve it who come into unfortunate circumstances because they left their own business to try things that did not fit them.[5]

Earlier, Rabbi Akiva Rabbi Joshua Ben Hananiah had discouraged the people from an uprising[6] by telling them the well-known Aesop fable of the crane and the wolf.[7]

Among the parables of Jesus that have been preserved, none of them suggest that they stem from a fable of Aesop. But Jesus, like his Jewish neighbors, knew Aesop's fables. He called Herod Antipas a fox (Luke 13:32) and said about John the Baptist, whom Antipas then executed, "What did you go out in the wilderness to see? A reed that sways in the wind? Or what

---

4. b. Ber. 61b; see Bacher, *Die Agada der Tannaiten*, vol. 1, 281f.

5. August Hausrath, "Corpus fabularum Aesopicarum," fasc. 1, *BSGRT* (1970): 118; c.f. von Halm, "Corpus fabularum Aesopicarum," *BSGRT* (1875): 186.

6. Chanoch Albeck, *Midrasch Bereschit Rabba*, ed. J. Theodor (Jerusalem: 1965) 711f, 64 (at the end); see also Bacher, *Die Agada der Tannaiten*, vol. 1, 160.

7. Von Halm, "Corpus fabularum Aesopicarum," 276 (135f.). According to Rabbi Joshua, a lion comes instead of a wolf and instead of a crane comes an Egyptian heron.

did you go out to see? A man wearing soft clothes? Behold, they that wear soft garments are in the houses of kings. But why, then, did you go out? To see a prophet?" (Matt 11:7–9; Luke 7:24–26). The wilderness, in which John the ascetic resides, is not the place for courtiers, nor for people who walk around in soft clothes in the king's house and bend and sway like a reed. One notices that the picture is taken from a well-known Aesop fable,[8] which was also familiar to the rabbis.[9] The reed survives the storm because it bends with the wind. But a strong tree that does not bow to the wind is uprooted by the storm. We shall also see that the little parable of the piping children and the weeping children (Matt 11:16–19; Luke 7:31–35), which also refers to John the Baptist, very probably depends on that fable of Aesop about the fishermen who play the pipe and the fish who do not want to dance.[10] It is probably not a coincidence that Jesus refers to Aesop's fables three times, each time directly or indirectly referring to Herod Antipas.

But now let us turn to Lessing's theory of fables. It is very instructive to see how far ahead of his time Lessing was and how close he came to the results of the Russian formalists—although he did not yet know the concept of the subject, which is not identical to the content of the narration.[11] What the formalists later referred to with the word *subject*, Lessing reluctantly called "the plot." According to linguistic usage, this generally means a plot is undertaken according to a certain purpose, and this purpose must be completely achieved if one can say the plot is over. What follows from this? That to those for whom the use of language is so sacred he does not dare to offend it in any way, he abstains from the word *plot* insofar as it should express an essential property of the fable through and through.[12] The fact that the subject does not bring the events to an end, but that the narrative is interrupted at the right point, is one of the typical characteristics of the subject in all literary genres. The end before the conclusion of further events often happens even more abruptly in popular oral creations such as anecdotes, humorous stories, exempla, fables, and parables. Everything Lessing says in the following about the fable also applies fully to the parables:

---

8. See Hausrath, "Corpus fabularum Aesopicarum," 71n5 (96); Halm, "Corpus fabularum Aesopicarum," *BSGRT* (1875), 179.

9. Herman Strack and Paul Billerbeck, *Kommentar zum Neuen Testament aus Talmud und Midrasch*, vol. 1 (Nördlingen: C.H. Beck, 1922), 596f.

10. Hausrath, "Corpus fabularum Aesopicarum," 11n5 (17f.); Halm, "Corpus fabularum Aesopicarum," 27 (13f.).

11. See the excerpt above, which follows note 14 in chapter 2.

12. Gotthold Ephraim Lessing, *Werke*, vol. 5 (Munich: Carl Hanser, 1979), 378.

The heroic and dramatic poet bring [*sic.*] the excitement of passions to their noblest end. . . . The fabulist has nothing to do with our passions, but only our knowledge. He wants to convince us of a single, living moral truth. This is his intention and this he seeks, according to the measure of truth, to obtain through the sensitive conception of an action. As soon as he has conceived it, it is equally important to him whether the action he has invented has reached its inner end or not. He often leaves his person standing in the middle of the road and does not in the least think of doing a favor to our curiosity.[13]

The same goes for parables. In the parable of the workers in the vineyard (Matt 20:1–16) and in rabbinic parallels, the landlord responded well to protesting workers. But was he able to convince the workers, or were they still dissatisfied? The parable has reached its goal, and therefore it ends!

What Lessing says in connection with the fable about the intention of the subject is also important for parable analyses. The individual case "will always be a consequence of changes which, by the intention which the fabulist associates with it, will become a whole. Are they also outside of this intention? All the better! It is a consequence of change, but the fact that there are changes that affect free moral beings is self-evident. For they are to constitute a case which is understood in a general sense, which can only be said by moral beings."[14] The moral efficacy of good parables is conditioned by the fact that the persons who appear in them, and who are representative of people upon whom the subject works, are free to choose between right and wrong action. To increase their moral freedom still further, let the Jewish narrator—and also Jesus—sometimes drive the landlords temporarily away from their land, to leave the workers or servants to their free will and their personal responsibility. Another sentence by Lessing is also worth considering for parables research: "The particular case of which the fable consists must be presented as real; it must be what we in the strictest sense call a single case."[15] This means, among other things, that the good fable is told as if it had really happened. This is true for all good fables and for most parables. For the latter, however, this is useful when their form is fully developed. Then the parable is a real narrative of a case that occurred in the past. This rule does not apply to parables that for some reason have remained stuck on the way to their completion, and whose subject could not fully develop into a narration of a single case. In classical rabbinic parables,

---

13. Lessing, *Werke*, 376f.
14. Lessing, *Werke*, 378.
15. Lessing, *Werke*, 381.

this rule was more accurately omitted. Here is a rabbinic example of the transitional stage between a comparison and a fully developed parable:

> "He who goes to the wise becomes wise" (Prov 13:20). To whom does this Scripture refer? To someone who enters the shop of a perfume dealer. Although the trader does not sell him anything and although the potential buyer does not take anything from him, in the end, he goes out with good perfumes. His clothes have taken on the perfume of the store. They are now more fragrant, and the smell does not leave him all day. Therefore it is written, "He who goes to the wise becomes wise. And whoever joins the fools: it is evil for him." (Prov 13:20) To what may this be compared? To one who enters a tanner's shop. Although he does not sell him anything and he does not take anything from him, in the end he goes out with a bad smell. His clothes are fragrant, and the smell does not leave him all day. Therefore it is written "And whoever joins the fools, he is in trouble."[16]

In my opinion, the parable would be perfect if it were told this way: A man entered the shop of a perfume merchant. Although he didn't buy anything there, he started to smell good. After a while, the smell disappeared. Then he said in his heart: If I have gotten such a good smell for one day, although I have bought nothing, how much more will I be filled when I buy fragrant perfume in the store! The interpretation is this: Man should not only associate with the wise, but he should also buy their wisdom and keep it. One could likewise dissect the second half of the rabbinic parables in a similar way. Then, we would have a nice double parable that is told about two parallel cases that supposedly happened in the past.

A merely rudimentary parable, which also did not reach completed form, is also the already quoted saying of Antigonus of Socho, which is the oldest witness of a parable in Judaism: "Be not like servants who serve the master to receive a reward, but like servants who serve the master not to receive a reward."[17] As in developed parables, this rudimentary parable also speaks of the master and his servants and of work and reward; the application to human life is present as well. Since this is neither an elaborate parable nor a description of a single case that allegedly happened but only a moral imperative, the past is not in place here. The same is true of the mixture of the teaching requirement and a parable in the New Testament pericopes of vigilance and faithfulness (Matt 24:42–51; Luke 12:35–48).

---

16. ARN, version B, chapter 2.
17. 'Abot 1:3.

The material contained in this teaching was enough for some developed parables when the subjects were completely formed. This is similar to the parable of the servant's wages (Luke 17:7–10). It is not treated as a past case, but in the form of an address to the listeners. The elements are not those of a concrete case. To build a real parable from them, one would have to completely rework the material. Also, in the teaching about the answer to prayer (Matt 7:7–11; Luke 11:9–13), motifs are contained that could occur in a parable. Luke 13:22–30 is also a parenesis. These words are also addressed to the hearers. Whether an original parable was worked out, however, remains to be seen. Also, the parable of the pleading friend in Luke 11:5–8 is apparently stylistically edited by the redactor. The deviation from the correct form of a parable, which should describe a single past case, is known by the introductory formula: "Which of you, having a friend . . ." With the same introduction ("Which of you?"), Luke 14:28–33 begins the parables of the tower and the warrior. The original form of both parables seems to have been lost by the final editors. In our context, the double parable of the lost sheep and the lost penny (Matt 18:12–14; Luke 15:1–10) is interesting. It is probably the only real exception to the rule that parables originally tell of a case that allegedly happened in the past. I suppose that originally, as in Matthew, they started with a question that was linked to the case: "What do you think?"[18] I cannot recall a similar form in a rabbinic parable when a man had a hundred sheep. The Lukan redaction works according to the well-known template, "Which one of you?" or "Which woman?" Luke's redaction of the banquet speeches is particularly drastic. We will come back to it later and see that the redactor has confused the simple rules of a meal for guests with a moral imperative within the genre of parables. In the little parable of the children playing (Matt 11:16–19; Luke 7:31–35), a certain decision regarding the original Hebrew text is hardly possible. In any case, it is a complete parable that Jesus narrated in the form of a comparison.[19]

In the days of Jesus there was a special form of parables which I would call "parable sayings." These were paratactic groups of sentences in the present form. They represent a situation typical of the subjects of the parables. From the realm of the rabbis, we have received a parable of Rabbi Akiva

---

18. Matthew (21:28) begins the parable of the unequal sons with the same words.

19. I prefer the form in Luke 7:31 over the Matthean (Matt 11:16f.). The Lukan "saying" sounds like good biblical Hebrew, better than the relative sentence in Matthew. On the other hand, Matthew is to be preferred when he speaks of "this generation" and not like Luke's embellishment, "the people of this generation."

(Avot 3:16) and of the somewhat earlier Rabbi Tarfon. As we shall see, the only "parable-saying" of Jesus that has been preserved for us (Matt 9:37; Luke 10:2) seems to depend on the parable of Rabbi Tarfon: "The harvest is rich, but the laborers are few. Ask the Master of the harvest, that he send out workers to his harvest!"[20] I suggest that parables were very popular and widespread in the time of Jesus. There are later examples of these "parable-sayings," but they seem to have slowly gone out of fashion. The not-fully-developed parable of the perfume trader and the perfume buyer, mentioned above,[21] is referred to in the original Hebrew as a "parable" (*mashal*). In the rabbinic world, this designation was not only for actual parables but also for comparisons. Apparently, it was the same with Jesus himself.

We will have more detail to add to the following comparisons of Jesus: the comparison of the new garment and the old garment (Luke 5:36–39 par.) and of the carrion and the vultures (Matt 24:28; Luke 17:37); also to the parable of the fig tree (Luke 21:29–31 par.),[22] to the Beelzebub comparisons (Luke 11:14–23 par.), to the blind as leaders of the blind (Luke 6:39; Matt 15:14), and to the saying about double service (Matt 6:24; Luke 16:13). In my opinion, the saying about the return of the demons (Matt 12:43–45; Luke 11:24–26) is also a comparison. We will deal with this saying and also the saying about the scribe who was right (in Matt 13:52), although it seems to me that this last saying does not come from Jesus.

The actual, developed parables are presented to Jesus as events that, supposedly, really happened in the past. This is true even when the action in them is simple and meagre. This is especially true of the parables of the mustard seed and leaven (Luke 13:18–21 par.), of the tares (Matt 13:24–30), and of the fish net (Matt 13:47–50).[23] For the Synoptic Problem, it is in-

---

20. Billerbeck already noted the relationship; see Strack and Billerbeck, *Kommentar zum Neuen Testament aus Talmud und Midrasch*, vol. 1, 527.

21. See note 16.

22. We will treat this parable together with the parable of the fig tree from Luke 13:6–9.

23. A fable about a fishnet with big and small fish can be found in Aesop's fables; see Halm, "Corpus fabularum Aesopicarum," 26. I present it here in Lessing's translation (*Werke*, vol. 5, 367): "A fisherman, when he pulled his net from the sea, left the big fish that were caught in there still imprisoned. The little ones, however, slipped through the net and escaped happily back into the sea." The moral is that the small thieves easily get away, but the big ones rarely stay unpunished. Lessing is correct when he says that this story is "no fable, or at least a very mediocre one." The similarity between this fable and Jesus' parable is surely no coincidence.

structive for us that the parable of the mustard seed can be found both in Luke (13:18) and in Matthew (13:31f.) and that it is correctly narrated as an event that happened in the past, while Mark uses a present-tense form (Mark 4:30–32). The same applies to the parable of the seed that grew on its own, which is found only in Mark (4:26–29). This parable is told in pure Koine Greek and no traces of a Hebrew template or source can be found. It seems to me that we are being adventurous in supposing that Mark invented this parable. But Mark probably did not work according to a written source, but rather according to oral tradition.

In addition to the parables, in the Synoptic tradition there are also narrations of past events that either really happened or were invented. We call this genre "exempla." Jülicher calls them "example stories." Such stories also occur in rabbinic literature and they are usually referred to as "stories." Jesus' exempla are found only in Luke: the story of the Pharisee and the tax collector (Luke 18:9–14), the story of the rich fool (Luke 12:16–21), and the legend of the rich man and the poor man Lazarus (Luke 16:19–31). The exemplum of the good Samaritan (Luke 10:29f.) is woven into Luke's discourse on charity, and the parable of the prodigal son (Luke 15:11f.) is also an exemplum. Although Luke does not describe this narration as a parable, it is obvious that Luke—and probably Jesus—understood the story of the prodigal son as a parable of the sinner's repentance and God's mercy. The exemplum of the prodigal son is particularly considered a parable because it contains a hero and an antihero, or two unequal sons. Interestingly, a pair of individuals somehow related to each other also appears in the exemplum of the Pharisee and the tax collector (Luke 18:9f.). The theme of the unequal son appears both in rabbinic parables and in a parable of Jesus (Matt 21:28f.).[24] Nor does the fact that one can easily identify the earthly father of the story with the heavenly father speak against the classification of the prodigal son narrative as an exemplum. In contrast to the parables in the strict sense, this identification is indeed an instructive possibility. However, the entire course of the story remains autonomous against it. The fact that an exemplum can easily be converted into a parable through one small change is shown by a Jewish example from the post-Constantine Byzantine period.[25] The beginning of this "story" is imprecisely delivered:

---

24. Exod. Rab. 27:8; b. Men. 43b; see Ziegler, *Die Koenigsgleichnisse des Midrasch beleuchtet durch die roemische Kaiserzeit*, chapter 6, notes 34 and 76, just as above chapter 2, note 19.

25. M. Tep. to Ps 25:2, ed. S Buber, 211.

Apparently, a well-known man was found dead in Constantinople.[26] The police came and arrested an innkeeper. And he said to the policemen, "Do not strike me, for I am a member of the king's household." When they heard him, they left him, but they posted guards by him until the following morning. Then they brought him into the king's palace and said to the king, "We found a member of your household last night!" The king said, "My son, I do not know you." The detainee replied, "That's correct." "If so," the king said, "why are you a member of my household?" "I beg your pardon," said the man. "I am not really a member of your household, but Master King, in you I trust, let me not be shamed [cf. Ps 25:2]. If I had not spoken like that, they would have hit me!" And the king said, "Because he trusted in me, let him go free." David said, "O Master my God, in you I trust; let me not be put to shame."

This exemplum, which probably represents a real event, became a parable in that the author put the verse from the book of Psalms in the mouth of the innkeeper and referred to this verse again in connection with the implied moral of the story. Trust in the king indicates trust in God. Similarly, in the exemplum of the prodigal son, the father's mercy on the son is understood as God's mercy to sinners. Although this is not explicitly stated in the Gospel, Jesus wanted the exemplum to be understood as such.

Let us now return to Lessing's theory of fables. Lessing describes the literary idiosyncrasy of the fable and its ultimate purpose as follows:

> I call an action a sequence of changes that together make up a whole. This unity of the whole is based on the agreement of all parts for an end purpose. The ultimate purpose of the fable—why the fable was invented—is the moral statement. Consequently, the fable has a plot when that which it tells is a consequence of changes, and each of these changes contributes somewhat to the individual recognition of the concepts which make up the "moral" of the story.[27]

What Lessing says about the plot of the fable is admirable, but what about the "moral" for which the fable was invented? Does he think that the moral sense is so clear that once he has finished reading the fable, everyone understands it without any difficulty? And is it the case that every motif of the subject contributes to "making the individual concepts that make up the moral doctrine recognizable in a perceptive manner"? In any case, the

---

26. The reading *qiston* is a correction from *qostin,* which could be an abbreviated form for "Constantinople" because only the emperor lived there.

27. Lessing, *Werke,* vol. 5, 367.

"moral" of Aesop's fables is often clumsy and inaccurate. But is this a coincidence? And can the "morals" of classic Jewish parables and Jesus' parables be clearly exaggerated? And what about the parables with the correspondence of the individual motifs of the subject with the individual concepts of their "morals"? What does Lessing mean when he opposes the notion that the fable is an allegorical poem? We will try to answer most of these kinds of questions as far as the parables are concerned, although the answer may be very difficult. In any case, it seems to me that Lessing is much more correct than many modern interpreters of Jesus' parables.

Let us now look at Lessing's summary definition of the nature of the fable: "If we bring up a general moral proposition in a particular case, give reality to that particular case, and deduce from it a story in which one recognizes the general proposition by looking at it: this story is called a 'fable.' "[28] We have already registered our concerns about the general moral proposition with regard to the fables and the parables. Although the subject of parables is stylized and often paradoxical, the main concern of the narrator of the parable is to tell a typical case from everyday reality. Only when the impression of realism is awakened can the parable take effect. What Lessing says about fables also applies to parables. They are not autonomous images; they have an end purpose that lies outside the subject. We shall still try to show that in parables the individual concepts of morality have a correspondence with their subjects. But this is not to say that, conversely, all motifs of the subject have a correspondence in the teaching of parables.

Lessing did not see clearly enough—perhaps he could not make clear distinctions from the circumstances of the time—that the fable's focus is outside the subject. In particular, however, he has not made it clear enough that the path from the fable to a "moral teaching" is a *metabasis eis allo genos*—a transition to another level. As we shall see, this applies to parables to an even greater extent. It is probably a characteristic that somehow adheres to every form of literature. Whenever an example is obtained from reality, a tension arises between the example and the reality, which is now found within the example as an alienated reflection. As far as I can see, Lessing's aesthetics and his literary theories are too committed to the Aristotelian conception of poetry as an imitation of the real and the possible. Therefore, he could not see certain moments of tension between reality and a literary example. It has become clear to me that the difference between the subject and the sphere of the moral teaching belongs not only to the

---

28. Lessing, *Werke*, vol. 5, 385.

essence of the fable but, to an even greater extent, also to the essence of the parable. When Lessing says that the "single sentence" is "led back to a single case by the fable,"[29] he is following the theory of the reduction of the general to the particular of the philosopher and student of Leibniz, Christian von Wolff.[30] But can it be said, for example, that in the case of the raven with his cheese who is deceived by the flattery of the fox, is it only a limitation of a general moral proposition to a particular case? The deceived raven is not a singular individual among many deceived by flattery. Rather, it is an example for us "now."

An example serves someone from whom—or a thing from whom—it is clearly and distinctly separated. Perhaps the animals of Aesop's fables are so popular because they strongly emphasize this separation of the example from its application. The narrated case of fables and parables are not on the same level as the moral teaching. The lower level is that of the subject, while the higher level is the moral teaching deducible from the subject. One could say it somewhat sharply: The moral principle does not really apply to the acting persons of the parable and the fable; it applies to us!

It is inaccurate and an oversimplification to think that in the fable and the parable, a certain moral proposition is primary or that these two related genera exemplify a moral proposition by a particular case. Rather, the fable and the parable are somehow incommensurable for the mind. In a good fable and a good parable, there is a correlation between the subject and the moral teaching. As we have already indicated, therefore, the moral proposition can never be articulated precisely and unanimously. And, as we also already know, the concluding teaching of Aesop's fables is usually unhelpful. It probably isn't even original. In most cases, it is quite useless there, although the heavier emphasis of the fable is outside the subject. In this, the fable is related to the exemplum—which, in contrast to the fable, is autonomous mainly because it often has a real event as its background. The exemplum, like the fable, may conclude with a moral teaching. We will examine this question when we discuss the exempla in the Gospel of Luke. In rabbinic parables and Jesus' parables, the gap between the subject and its application is even wider than in the case of the fable. When I hear a fable, I can imagine that something like this could happen to me or someone else

---

29. Lessing, *Werke*, vol. 5, 378.

30. To the same point, see also Siglinde Eichner, *Die Prosafabel Lessings in seiner Theorie und Dichtung,* Bonner Arbeiten zur Deutschen Literatur, vol. 25 (Bouvier, 1974).

in some modified way. In the fable, the content and the moral application are in transparent relation to each other. In the parable, on the other hand, the level of the subject differs in its essence from the application. If, for example, the parables that speak of work were to teach us a general, valid work ethic, then they would no longer be parables but fables. The above mentioned gap between the level of the subject and the level of moral application in the parables is that the level of the subject is daily life while the level of application is a religious truth. Precisely, the tension between everyday content and the religious sphere of the solution belongs to the essence of the parable. In this context, a paradoxical situation often arises; although the everyday level of the subject in the parable and the religious level of its sense are fundamentally different, there are cases in which the subject's interpretation of the important motifs is so obvious that the interpretation offers itself and does not have to be pronounced. More about this later! But there are also parables that are difficult to understand or even incomprehensible. Only when we know the situation in which they were told will we understand them. Sometimes an introduction to the parable can also help us understand. This applies to both the parables of Jesus and the rabbinic parables. First, a main key concept of the parable is mentioned and then it is asked: "What is this like?" Then comes the parable. Jesus said, "To whom does the kingdom of God resemble, and what do I compare it to? It looks like a mustard seed" (Luke 13:18). Often, the meaning of the parable arises only from sentences or parts of sentences that follow the actual narration of the parable. Two kinds of explanations, which cannot be sharply separated from each other, occur in such cases: It is either a moral teaching with a possible demand on the listeners or a "refined interpretation." The subsequent explanation of the parable is often introduced by Jesus and the rabbis with the word *so*.

For our purposes, these preliminary observations are important with respect to the existing or missing explanations since it is often characteristic today to diminish the importance of the interpretations and explanations of Jesus' parables in the Gospels or to assign them prematurely to a later time. In my view, too little attention is paid to the context in which the parables of the Gospels were spoken. This often blocks our way to a correct understanding of Jesus' parables.

4

Frameworks and Interpretations of Parables in the Gospels

In this chapter, we will look at the three kinds of interpretations of parables that we find in the Gospels. First, we will take every introductory formula and place it under the microscope, especially those that are offered as "solutions" to the parables. We will then turn our attention to the words at the end of the narration of a parable that form its moral proposition. Third, we will look at the contexts in which a parable appears in the Gospels. In fact, the context is often indispensable for understanding a parable. In anticipation, I can already say that there are hardly any cases in which the solutions presented would not fit in the parable—with the exception, for example, of some references to the kingdom of heaven in the Matthean introductory statements (to the parables), which are certainly secondary. With this, I realize I find myself in seemingly sharp contrast to modern research. Instructed by the rabbinic parables and enlightened by the philological-literary-critical and literary-theoretical approach, I am skeptical of all methods that attempt to dissect texts. On the other hand, I am optimistic about the reliability of the sources.

Let us begin with the parable of the four fields (Luke 8:4–8 and parallels), which has no explanatory introduction. As we will see later, there is a possibility that the sentence concluding the parable, "He who has ears to hear, let him hear" (Luke 8:8), is the moral teaching that expresses the requirement of the parable. Rabbinic parallels irrefutably show that the interpretation of the parable (for example, Luke 8:11–15) has always belonged to this parable. But even without additional material, it should be clear that this parable is barely understandable and even easy to misunderstand without interpretation. The meaning of the four types of soils can be clarified only by the following interpretation. The same applies to the seed that is scattered. But it is precisely with this parable that the strange manner of Matthew also becomes visible. Where the other Gospels speak only of the "word," he speaks (13:19) of the "message about the kingdom of heaven."

The parables of the fishing net (Matt 13:47–50) and of the wheat and the tares (Matt 13:24–30, 36–43) are also followed by a rather detailed interpretation. Like the parable of the four kinds of soil in the field, the parable of the wheat and tares is also separated from its interpretation. The parable of the fishing net, together with the parable of the weeds in the wheat, forms a double parable. Both parables and both interpretations are similar in structure. They are variations of an identical or similar teaching about the end-time division between the righteous and sinners. This double parable is a beautiful example of the fact that you can use two different main topics for one and the same purpose. Both of these parables would hardly be understandable if there were no interpretation. The two interpretations become even more similar when we consider the allegorizing verses in the interpretation of the parable of the weeds (Matt 13:37–40).[1] In the interpretation of both parables, Jesus says, "So will it be at the end of the world" (Matt 13:40–49). The Greek expression for "the end of the world" occurs only in Matthew's Gospel. In general, the vocabulary of both interpretations is typically Matthaean. However, this does not preclude the assumption that both interpretations have a core that is already connected to the two parables in their origins. The interpretations fit with the parables and make them, first of all, understandable. The situation is different with the introductory words to the two parables. They are, from a literary point of view, almost unbearably strange. Therefore, they are secondary formations: "Again, the kingdom of heaven is like a net" (Matt 13:47); "The kingdom of heaven is like a man who sowed good seeds" (Matt 13:24). We will examine similar secondary introductions in Matthew. On the other hand, the reference to the end of the world is to be regarded as original. Perhaps this expression was one of the reasons both parables were introduced with the mention of the kingdom of heaven. There is a general tendency in the Gospels to understand the kingdom of heaven as an eschatological event. But it is questionable whether Jesus, who proclaimed that the eschaton was

---

1. Matthew 13:41a (the parable of the weeds) reads, "The Son of Man shall send forth his angels." In contrast, Matt 13:49b (the parable of the fishnet): "The angels will go out." In Matt 13:37a, the Son of Man is missing if we assume, for good reasons, that the passage is interpolated. Matthew 13:41 was inserted allegorically by the same interpolator. The interpretation of the parable of the weeds was originally probably quite parallel to that of the parable of the fishnet. Therefore, Matt 13:41a can be compared to Matt 13:49b. The original interpretation of the parable of the fishnet probably began like this, "So it will be at the end of the world: The angels will go out."

being realized, understood the kingdom of heaven as purely the property of the end times. From the early days of the church, the kingdom of heaven in these two parables was often understood to mean the Christian community. In it, there are now good and bad fish and wheat and weeds. But in the end, it will be different.[2] It is true that Jesus also understood the kingdom of heaven as the community of those who gathered around him. But he hardly meant that the pious and sinners should temporarily remain together in the kingdom of heaven. It was only reinterpreted in Christianity later to be this way. Maybe Matthew was the first representative of this Christianization when he introduced the parable of the weeds with the mention of the kingdom of heaven and wrote in the interpretation that at the end of time the angels will remove from his kingdom those who commit sins and transgressions.[3] In any case, the original and simple meaning of the parable of the wheat and the weeds may have been the following: the existence of sinners can be attributed to the devil, but you have to be patient. In the final judgment, the wicked will be separated from the pious and will fall under the judgment. It is incumbent on the pious to live together with sinners in

---

2. We know what role the parable of the weeds played in the Donatist controversy. It has not been noted, however, that there was also an anti-Pauline Jewish-Christian interpretation of the parable. In the Ebionite-Jewish-Christian source of the pseudo-Clementines, Paul is referred to by the name "*echthros anthropos*" (Epistula Petri 2:3), or in Latin translation "*homo quidam inimicus*" (Recognitiones 1:70.1). See Georg Strecker, *Das Judenchristentum in den Pseudoklementinen* (Berlin: Akademie, 1958), 187. In the parable of the weeds, we read that the master sowed good seed, but someone sowed weeds. So where does the weed come from? "An enemy man (*echthros anthropos*) has done this" (Matt 13:28). The Ebionite designation of Paul as "the enemy man" thus comes from the parable of the weeds, and the parable was supposedly minted on him. He corrupted the originally pure, good church by taking in all kinds of pagans. The Ebionite interpretation forgets that later (Matt 13:39) the enemy is interpreted as the devil, but in polemics one often does not read the texts exactly!

3. In Jesus' interpretation of the parable, Matthew 13:37f. says, "He who sows the good seed is the Son of Man. The field is the world. The good seed, these are the sons of the kingdom. But the weeds are the sons of evil." If Matthew thought much about it, then according to him, it is the Son of Man—Jesus himself—who sowed the good seed, which represent the children of the kingdom. If I am not mistaken, the original meaning of the "man who sows the good seed" is God. Even if Matthew's wording cannot yet be apostrophized as an ecclesiastical interpretation of the parable, an ecclesiastical interpretation can be based on Matthew. In the sense of divine election, the kingdom is a distortion of Matthew (cf. also Matt 8:11f.; 21:43). This shows that this part of the interpretation cannot be original.

this world. The pious one should trust in the end time. In the parable of the fishing net, required endurance in the world and consolation toward the end time are not clearly expressed. But even there, in the end, sinners will be pulled out together with the pious ones. The two interpretations in the double parable of the fishing net and the weeds belong to each and they are correct. On the other hand, the mention of the kingdom of heaven at the beginning of both parables and in Matt 13:41 are the work of the evangelist.

Another group of parables sheds a particularly strong light on the proclamation of Jesus. It deals with the double parable of the mustard seed and the leaven and the double parable of the treasure and the pearl. The parable of the self-growing seed, which can be found only in Mark (Mark 4:26–29), also belongs to this group. In none of these parables is there a representative figure for God (or for the Son of Man). Their content is quite meagre. The theme of the double parable of the mustard seed and the leaven and the parable of the self-growing seed is the wonderful concept of growth and growing up. The double parable of the treasure and the pearl is about a lucky find. There is no interpretation at the end of all these parables. Without the introduction, their meaning would remain dark and ambiguous. By the treasure or the pearl, one could understand, for example, Israel or the Torah. Fortunately, however, all these parables are introduced with the mention of the kingdom of heaven. With the parable of the pearl, however, one must put up with the curious introduction: "Again, the kingdom of heaven is like a merchant who was looking for fine pearls" (Matt 13:45). It would be more correct if not the merchant but the precious pearl was compared with the kingdom of heaven. The double parable of the treasure and the pearl not only wants to point out the incomparably high value of the kingdom of heaven, but obviously also recommends that the one who has found the kingdom through Jesus and wants to be perfect should not only renounce everything else but also literally "sell everything." The three other parables of the naturally wonderful growth are vivid images of the eschaton, which, according to Jesus' view, is realized.

The double parables of the happy finding of the treasure and the pearl (Matt 13:44–46), of the mustard seed and of the leaven (Matt 13:3, 1–33; Luke 1:18–21; Mark 4:30–32), as well as the parable of the self-growing seed (Mark 4:26–29), are the only parables that certainly deal with the kingdom of heaven. Since they are an expression of Jesus' personal view of the kingdom of God, it is not surprising that one will probably look in vain for good parallels among the rabbinic parables. Again, I am well aware that what I am saying here contradicts general opinion. The trend is to look for "the mystery of the kingdom of heaven" everywhere in Jesus' sayings. However, I have not concluded from a preconceived opinion that the idea of the kingdom in the context of the New Testament parable narrations—I am not talking here about the preaching of Jesus in general—occurs in only these five parables. Before I began studying the parables of Jesus impartially, I was ready to share this general view with joy.

Let us now examine the other parables, in which the kingdom of heaven is mentioned in the introduction. We begin with the parable of the entrusted talents (Luke 19:11–27; Matt 25:14–30). The situation in which the parable was allegedly told is described by Luke (19:11) as follows: "But when they heard this, he added another parable, because he was near Jerusalem, and they thought that now the kingdom of God must immediately appear."[4]

Luke probably thought that the temporary absence of the man in the parable meant the delay in the parousia. But it will be shown that this is only a stylistic artistic expression that is often used in the rabbinic parables and in the parables of Jesus. Luke or his predecessors understood the parable in the sense that Jesus meant to express that the kingdom of heaven had not yet arrived. That is why the story about the nobleman who eventually became king was invented and inserted into the parable. This nobleman is missing in Matthew's Gospel. In Luke and Matthew, no interpretation is given. The parable itself is understandable without introduction and interpretation. Also, in the parable of the great banquet (Luke 14:15–24; Matt 22:1–14), similar to the parable of the entrusted talents in Luke, the kingdom is spoken of in the eschatological sense—not about Jesus himself: "But when one of the fellow guests heard this, he said to him: 'Blessed is he who will dine in the kingdom of God'" (Luke 14:15). In Matthew, the parable begins, "The kingdom of the heavens is like a king who prepared the wedding for his son" (Matt 22:2). Here again is a curious style we already know. So, in both Gospels, the banquet relates to the idea of the kingdom in different ways. We know that Jesus spoke of an end-times banquet. This is a common Jewish idea. On the other hand, we already expressed doubt about whether the historical Jesus thought the kingdom of heaven was purely eschatological. At the Last Supper, he connected the kingdom with

---

4. The phrase "The kingdom of heaven shall appear" is definitely Jewish; see As. Mos. 10, l (*et tunc parebit regnum illius . . .*); treatise Soferim 14:12; Mussafzu the feast days; Targum to Zech 14:9; to Isa 31:4; 52:7; to Ezek 7:7–10; to Mic 4:7; to Obad 21 (according to the text of David Kimchi).

the eschatological meal (Luke 22:15–20 par.; Luke 22:28–30), but can we be sure that the mention of the kingdom is also original there? In the case of the great banquet, it is in any case questionable whether Jesus mentioned the kingdom of heaven within the parable. In Luke, the kingdom is not mentioned by Jesus but by one of the fellow guests; and in Matthew, it is in the introduction, which could easily have been secondary. Also, with Matthew—as above with Luke—a king is mentioned in the parable. By this king is meant God himself who will punitively destroy Jerusalem. The interpretation of the kingdom of heaven in the introduction to the parable of the great banquet is therefore secondary. No interpretation is offered at the end of the parable. The parable itself is understandable without further explanation. As a conclusion of the little parable of the wedding clothes appended to Matthew (22:11–13), it is said that many are called but few are chosen. This is a beautiful moral teaching that can be applied to both the parable of the great banquet and the one of the wedding clothes. But it is more than questionable whether Jesus even mentioned the word *chosen*!

Both in the parable of the entrusted talents in Luke (19:11–27) and in the parable of the wedding banquet in Matthew (22:1–14), a king appears as an actor in the story. But this king is missing in the two parallels to the two parables. Thus the parables of the talents and the wedding banquet are the only two royal parables that occur in the Gospels. And even with them, the king was introduced only by the evangelists. So, it is likely that Jesus himself had not yet spoken of a king as a symbolic figure for God in his parables.[5] He was talking about a man, a gentleman, a nobleman, a father, a landlord, or a host, but not a king. This was also the case in the oldest rabbinic parables handed down to us. Already in the second century BCE, Antigonus of Socho's core saying (which we have already mentioned) is about servants and their master.[6] The same is true of a double parable of Samuel the Small (who died at the beginning of the second century).[7] Rabbi Tarfon, the contemporary of Samuel the Small, speaks in his parable about the workers and the landlord.[8] One can also find many examples of rabbinic parables that

---

5. In the example of warfare in Luke 14:31–33, however, there is talk of a king planning a war: but first, it is not a parable; and second, the king is not a symbol of God but an example to the disciples.

6. 'Abot 1:13.

7. b. Ta'an. 25b below; see Bacher, *Die Agada der Tannaiten*, vol. 1, 371.

8. 'Abot 2, 15–16.

were only later passed on as "king parables."[9] Earlier, they simply spoke of a gentleman, a landlord, or a host. In the late Tannaitic and Amoraic period, the king became the almost exclusive hero of rabbinic parables. The royal figure was often used only as a template. Because of the importance of the Roman Empire, this template took the upper hand. It can be observed that although the rabbinic parables speak of the king, he often continues to fulfill the function of a landlord, estate manager, or simply a father. The two cases mentioned in the Gospels in which a king appears are witnesses of the transition from the older type, which we also find with Jesus, to the newer one, which then becomes common in the rabbinic royal parables.

But let us return to the parables of Jesus and their interpretations! The parable of the ten virgins is found only in Matthew (25:1–13). There, it is introduced with the following words: "Then the kingdom of heaven will be like ten virgins." It is certain this wedding meant the end time. But we have already doubted that for Jesus himself, the kingdom of heaven was purely an eschatological concept. We also know how easy it was for Matthew to mention the kingdom of heaven in the introductions to the parables. Here, he does this after the end of the previous parable: "There will be weeping and gnashing of teeth." Then "the kingdom of heaven will be like ten virgins" (Matt 24:51–25:1). This artificial connection makes the mention of the kingdom of heaven in this introduction even more suspicious. The parable is not followed by an interpretation but by a moral teaching, which very well summarizes the requirement to which the parable is supposed to lead: "So watch now, because you do not know the day nor the hour" (Matt 25:13). The phrase already occurred earlier (Matt 24:42; cf. 13:33) in a more imprecise and "Christianized" form.[10] According to the parable of the ten virgins, the phrase is appropriate, although the parable itself would be understandable without this moral tenet. The sentence itself would probably have been older than the parable; it is an independent moral imperative.

There are two other parables in the introduction of which the kingdom of heaven is written and that occur only in Matthew. The beautiful parable of the laborers in the vineyard (Matt 20:1–16) begins with the words: "For the kingdom of heaven is like a master of the manor" —so again, the

---

9. See the parable on the workers and their master in M. Tep. to Ps 3:3, ed. S. Buber, 36–37.

10. "Watch therefore, for you do not know on what day your master will come." Here, "the hour" is missing, and it is spoken of as "your master." See also Mark 13:32 and Acts 1:7.

artificial expression. The working day is generally, even among the rabbis, a symbol of human life. Wages will be paid after the workday. The parable is eschatological only to the extent that it deals with the reward after death. The introduction with the mention of the kingdom of heaven is almost certainly the work of Matthew; the parable is understandable by itself. The sentence at the end ("So the last will be the first and the first the last," Matt 20:16) is certainly secondary. We notice how Matthew tries to point out the sentence in the parable itself. Thus the master of the vineyard commands his steward, "Call the workers and pay the wages, beginning with the last up to the first (Matt 20:8). This seems rather absurd and cannot have been part of the original parable. The landlord says to one of the first who had come to work, "I will give as much to this one, who is the last, as to you" (Matt 20:14). This was certainly part of the original parable. The inaccurate understanding of the key word *last* prompted Matthew to attach the sentence about the first and the last as a moral proposition to the parable, although the sentence does not fit the parable at all. The key point of the parable is that everyone, regardless of the time they start working, will receive the same salary. Apparently, the sentence in Luke 13:30 is in its original place. There, it concludes Jesus' saying in a natural way.[11]

In the same manner, the parable of the merciless servant is introduced in Matthew: "Therefore, the kingdom of heaven is like a king" (Matt 18:23–35). The punishment that the evil servant will receive will not be interpreted as a hint of the future kingdom of heaven. No researcher should miss how inappropriate the mention of the kingdom of heaven is here. The word *therefore* in the introduction points to the previous one (Matt 18:21f.): to Jesus' demand that one must forgive one's neighbor. This is also the teaching of the parable itself: whoever does not forgive his neighbor is punished by God. The interpretation of the parable is: "So will my heavenly father also act toward you, if you do not each forgive your brother with all your heart" (Matt 18:35). The interpretation is genuine and belongs to the parable, even if it would be quite understandable without the interpretation. The final evidence for the secondary existence of the "kingdom of heaven" in the introductions to the parables in Matthew's Gospel is the saying about the scribe who is being trained for the kingdom of heaven (Matt 13:5f.). I will

---

11. See Flusser, *Two Anti-Jewish Montages in Matthew* (Jerusalem: Immanuel, 1975), 39–43. Regarding this faulty conclusion, see Adolf Jülicher, *Die Gleichnisreden Jesu*, vol. 2 (Darmstadt, 1963), 469–71; Joachim Jeremias, *Die Gleichnisse Jesu* (Göttingen: Vandenhoeck & Ruprecht, 1970), 29–33.

still try to show that this is a Jewish saying that Jesus did not speak. Matthew could easily use this saying in connection with his interpolation about the kingdom of heaven. As a result, it was Christianized.

Exempla are instructive, autonomous stories to which one can attach a moral teaching. All the exempla in the Gospels are directed against human arrogance, complacency, and callousness. All are unique to Luke's Gospel and are understandable by themselves. Their context in Luke makes their meaning even clearer. The one exception is the exemplum about poor Lazarus (Luke 16:19f.). There is no interpretation of the story, no moral teaching, and no real connection with what comes before and what comes after. But there is a connection of a profound kind with the previous section. In 16:16, Luke speaks about the law and the prophets. At the end of the story, the dead rich man wants to send Lazarus to his five living brothers so that they will repent. "But Abraham said: 'They have Moses and the prophets; let them listen to them!' But he said 'No, Father Abraham, but if one comes to them from the dead, then they will repent.' But he said to him, 'If they do not listen to Moses and the prophets, neither will they be moved when one rises from the dead.'" That sounds almost Johannine. It is hard for me to believe that these are the real words of Jesus. My doubt is based not only on the rather clear reference to the infidelity of the Jews to Moses and the prophets, but also on the church's allusion to the resurrection of Jesus: "If they do not listen to Moses and the prophets, they will not let me move even if one rises from the dead." Who was it that composed the ending of the story of poor Lazarus? It was probably Luke. Perhaps he put the story in this place of his Gospel because he wanted to create an associative connection between the law and the prophets in 16:16 and Moses and the prophets in 16:29–31. All the other examples in Luke are in a context that makes their meaning clearer. This is true, for example, in the exemplum about the rich fool (Luke 12:16–21). First (12:13), Jesus refuses the request to be a judge or hereditary conciliator. Then he says to them, "Watch and beware of all covetousness, for abundance cannot allow one to live" (Luke 12:15). Then follows the exemplum about the rich man who makes big plans with his wealth. "But God said to him, 'You fool, tonight your life is being demanded of you. Who will then own what you have prepared?' This is the way of the one who accumulates treasures and is not rich toward God."[12] The moral teaching is thus, as with the inter-

---

12. Thus it is to be understood (cf. Rom 10:12). The usual sentimental explanation "rich toward God" does not seem to be correct. In Jülicher, *Die Gleichnisreden Jesu*, vol. 2, 614: Here, Jesus demands "an application of wealth in the service of love."

pretations of the parables, introduced with the word *so*. The exemplum is not only properly related to the previous one but also to the following section of Luke, which is about worries and collecting treasures.

The exemplum of the Pharisee and the tax collector (Luke 18:9–14) is understandable. In order to emphasize who the story is directed against, Luke introduces it with the following words: "But he also spoke the following parable to those who themselves trust that they are righteous and despise others" (18:9). The story is followed by the moral: "For he who exalts himself will be humbled, but he who humbles himself will be exalted" (Luke 8:14). That fits with the story. However, the saying itself, which also occurs in the Gospels, is older and goes back to Hillel the Elder. I will deal with it below.

The exemplum of the good Samaritan is provided with a similar introduction, also created by Luke. "But he wanted to justify himself[13] and said to Jesus, 'Who then is my neighbor?'" The questioner is described as self-righteous. Even earlier (Luke 10:25), the "expert in the law" is not described very sympathetically; he got up to try Jesus.[14] But after his first question and his answer, according to Luke, there was an agreement between him and Jesus. In my opinion, the characterization of the expert in the law as a self-righteous person and the framing of his second question "Who is my neighbor?" do not seem to be very skillful. Did the expert in the law, who had quoted the biblical passages about love for one's neighbor

---

13. The Greek phrase "to justify oneself" (with the same negative sense) appears in the New Testament only in Luke 16:15, and even there it apparently comes from Luke. The same phrase is used in the Greek translation of Ethiopic Enoch 102:10: "Behold, they who justify themselves, how was their fall, for no justice was found in them until they died." See Campbell Bonner, *The Last Chapters of Enoch in Greek* (London: Christophers, 1937), 63. See also Lamentations for another meaning.

14. It is strange that not only in Luke 10:25 but also in Matt 22:35 (but not in Mark 12:28) the questioner is a lawyer and he comes to test Jesus through his questions. This seems very unlikely to me for many reasons. This double commandment of love was not unknown in Judaism at that time; see, for example, David Flusser, "A New Sensitivity in Judaism and the Christian Message," *HTR* 61 (1968): 111–18. This state is reflected in both Mark (1:1) and Luke (10:25–28). According to both Gospels, there is a harmony between the inquiring scribe and Jesus in relation to the double commandment of love. I would think that Matt 22:34–40 is closest to the original form. Jesus began, as was customary in Judaism, by asking a rhetorical question: "What is the great chief rule in the law?" See also David Flusser, "Jesus," *Selbstzeugnissen und Bilddokumenten*, RoMo, 140 (Rowohlt: Taschenbuch, 1968), 67–70.

as himself (Luke 10:27) not understand them himself? The introduction to the exemplum of the good Samaritan seems so unnatural because it was created by Luke himself for the purpose of serving as a transition between the question of the Great Commandment and the parable itself. The question "Who is my neighbor?" takes up the previous theme.[15] The exemplum itself was originally directed against the cruel exaggeration of the priests and Levites regarding ritualistic purity regulations. The story is found only in Luke's Gospel. The previous section on the Great Commandment, which is found in all three Synoptics, is complete and does not need an appendix. Did Luke first connect the exemplum to the previous one and artificially link the two together? This transition seems to have come from Luke. Was it perhaps Jesus himself who reinterpreted the story of the Samaritan to promote mercy between people? If so, then the final question and answer can be attributed to the historical Jesus "Which of these three do you think was a neighbor[16] to the one who fell among the robbers?" And he said, "The one who has shown mercy to him." But Jesus said to him "Go, and do the same." So, this is the moral teaching that follows the exemplum. The Samaritan became the real neighbor of the wounded Jew—and not vice versa! We will mention more about this later.

The exemplum of the prodigal son (Luke 15:11–32) follows the double parable of the lost sheep and the lost penny (Luke 15:1–10). It relates to the double parable in terms of both motif and objective. God rejoices when the lost has been found (Luke 15:4 "to lose"; 15:5 "to find," "to rejoice," etc.). We find the same motifs again in the twice-recurring refrain from the father's mouth about the lost son: "Let us eat and be merry, for this son of mine was dead and came to life again; he was lost and is found. And they began to be cheerful" (Luke 15:23). These motifs also appear at the end in response to the brother: "But it is necessary to be cheerful and to rejoice. For this brother of yours was dead and has come to life; he was lost and has now been found" (Luke 15:32). For the rest, no moral teaching is attached to the exemplum. The exemplum does not need such a "lesson" explained. Luke made it follow the double parable of the lost sheep and the lost penny because he wanted to proclaim the joy of God over the lost that was found.

---

15. Jülicher is correct; see *Die Gleichnisreden Jesu*, vol. 2, 594–97.

16. This translation seems to me to be better than the usual "to have been." This is not only more correct from the Greek point of view but also from the assumed Hebrew point of view and for stylistic-logical reasons. "Been" is also weak. See Jülicher, *Die Gleichnisreden Jesu*, vol. 2, 593.

The difficult problem of the differences between the wording of the double parable of the lost sheep and the lost penny in Luke (15:1–10) and in Matthew (18:10–14; only the parable of the sheep) will be dealt with more thoroughly later. Regarding the situation in which the double parable was allegedly told, Luke says, "But the tax collectors as a whole and the sinners used to come to him and hear him. The Pharisees and the scribes grumbled about this and said, 'This one accepts sinners and eats with them'" (15:1). Luke got this introduction from other places. It is probably no coincidence that the specific Greek word for "grumbling" otherwise appears in the New Testament only in the Lukan story of the tax collector Zacchaeus: "When they saw it, they all grumbled and said, 'He has come receive the hospitality of a sinful man'" (Luke 19:7). When Luke wrote the introduction to the double parable, he recalled what he had already taken from his source earlier (5:30; cf. Matt 2:16; 9:11): "And the Pharisees and their scribes grumbled against his disciples and said: 'Why do you eat and drink with the tax collectors and sinners?'"[17] There, however, the request is in order and Jesus removes the sting from it by his apt answer. It is also worth remembering that it was customary to accuse Jesus of being a "glutton and drunkard, the friend of tax collectors and sinners" (Luke 7:34; cf. Matt 11:19). The pseudo-historical framework created by Luke for the double parable of the lost sheep and the lost coin is a beautiful example of the conscious but also unconscious tendency of the Greek editors of the Gospels to coarsely increase and expand the confrontations of Jesus with his bigoted critics and to apply the tension secondarily, even when it was not found in the original reports.

When Luke wrote the introduction, he was convinced that he had succeeded in discovering whom the double parable was directed against: namely, the Pharisees and scribes of the Jews who had self-righteously accused Jesus of taking care of tax collectors and sinners. In this sense, he edited the double parable. In Luke's Gospel, the parallel interpretations of the two parables are found in 15:7: "I say to you, there will be joy in heaven for one sinner who repents; more joy than for ninety-nine righteous people who do not need to repent." This is according to the parable of the lost sheep. This interpretation, too, is influenced by the section on the Pharisaic

---

17. Here, Luke has worked on his source. In Luke 5:30, adversaries reproach Jesus' disciples for eating with sinners and tax collectors, whereas according to Matt 9:1 (and Mark 2:16), they ask the disciples of Jesus, "Why does your Teacher eat with tax collectors and sinners?" This is more logical and correct. When Luke 15:2 says that Jesus is accused of accepting sinners and eating with them, he brings here, in a secondary place; in this point, his source is unchanged.

protest table communion with tax collectors and sinners, which inspired Luke when he composed the framework for the double parable. There, Jesus answers the grumbling Pharisees and scribes, "It is not the healthy who need the doctor, but the sick. I have not come to call the righteous, but sinners to repentance" (Luke 5:31). The parallels should not be overlooked here. In Luke 15:7, there are two expressions "do repentance" and "need repentance." In Luke 15:31, the expression "do repentance" also occurs, but also the expression "to have need to repent" can be found. This shows both Luke's ability in literary design and the underlying original interpretation.[18] The interpretation of the second parable of the lost coin (Luke 15:10) repeats the first interpretation in a shortened way: "Thus I say to you: there is joy before the angels of God over a single sinner who repents." The focus on sinners in the interpretations is caused by the secondary framework, which, as we have seen, depends on Luke (5:27–32). So, the sinners in the two interpretations were probably inserted by Luke. They are missing in the parable of the lost sheep in Matthew (18:10–14). There it is expressed more finely and vividly that God seeks and finds sinful man: three times the sheep is called lost, which is missing in Luke.

Matthew lacks the secondary, polemical framework of Luke (15:1f.). On the other hand, Jesus begins the parable with the following words: "See that you do not despise one of these little ones, for I tell you that their angels in the heavens always see the face of my Father in heaven" (Matt 18:10). Overall, the phrase sounds authentic, though I know that there are many who disagree. However, you should remember that the phrase was in front of the evangelist Luke. He modified it linguistically in the interpretations of the two parables. In the first interpretation, he speaks of the "joy in heaven" (Luke 15:7); and in the second interpretation, (Luke 15:10) of the "joy before [literally: before the face] the angels of God." Although the introductory sentence is apparently original and was spoken by Jesus, "these little ones" in Matt 18:10 and 18:14 come from the evangelist. The whole section in Matthew 18:1–20 is based on the keywords *these little ones*.[19] Did Jesus

---

18. In the two interpretations in Luke 15:7–10, the sinner is spoken of as "doing penance." In the section on table fellowship with tax collectors and sinners in Luke (5:32), Jesus says he has come to call sinners "to repentance." The words "to repentance" are missing in the parallel in Mark (2:1–7) and Matthew (9:13). I guess Jesus just said, "I have come to call sinners."

19. "These little ones" is originally found in Luke 17:1f. (cf. Mark 9:42 and Matt 18:6f.); see also Matt 10:42. For the editing of the section in Matt 18:1–35, see Erich Klostermann, *Apokrypha II, Evangelien* (Berlin: Marcus and Weber, 1929),

perhaps speak of the ones who erred here? Otherwise, there is nothing decisive to object to the originality of the introduction (Matt 18:10) and the interpretation (18:14). The exemplum of the prodigal son is followed in Luke 16:1–9 by the parable of the unjust steward. It is not literarily linked to the previous one, but it is linked to the following teaching and its practical application (Luke 16:8f.). As will be shown later, the interpretation corresponds to the parable; it forms a unity with the parable. It is more difficult to determine how to evaluate the following verses (Luke 16:10–12). In them, infidelity regarding the unrighteous Mammon is reproached, while the unjust householder is praised for having acted wisely. The tension between Luke 16:10–12 with the preceding parable and its explanation is undeniable, although these verses also contribute to the understanding of the parable. The comparison of the double service that Luke then brings (16:13) can be found in Matthew in the Sermon on the Mount (Matt 6:24). Luke made the comparison here because it also speaks of mammon, albeit with a different meaning than in the parable of the unjust householder. The appendix (Luke 16:14f.) in which, among other things, the Pharisees are condemned as greedy, self-righteous,[20] and haughty turns out to be inauthentic linguistically.[21] It is also placed at this point in Luke's Gospel because of the previous keyword *mammon*.

We have seen how Luke invents polemical situations from which he then understands the parables. This is not to say that Jesus never told a parable out of a polemical situation. An example of this is the parable of the dissimilar sons. It occurs only in Matthew (21:28–32), specifically during Jesus' last visit to Jerusalem. It stands between the question of authority (Matt 21:23–27) and the story of the wicked tenants. When the masters of the temple asked Jesus by what authority he was teaching in the temple precinct, he asked them about John the Baptist. In Matthew, the parable of the dissimilar sons is in this place because the Baptist is mentioned in its application. Jesus may have spoken the parable on another occasion. The parable fits well into the framework in Matthew. The parable was probably also

---

147; Strecker, *Das Judenchristentum in den Pseudoklementinen*, 149n2 (though not quite correct), 191n4, 232, 251, 256; Jülicher, *Die Gleichnisreden Jesu*, vol. 2, 327; Jeremias, *Die Gleichnisse Jesu*, 35f.

20. Concerning Luke's phraseology, see note 13 above.

21. The Pharisees were apparently sneering at Jesus (Luke 16:14). This word occurs in the New Testament only here and in Luke 23:35 (the rulers were sneering at the crucified master). There, the word is adopted from the Greek translation of Psalms.

known to Luke, although he does not cite it in his Gospel. One will be able to assume this because of Luke 7:29. The two verses are a pseudo-historical gloss, apparently written by Luke himself in his usual Greek.[22] Luke speaks of the fact that the tax collectors were baptized with the baptism of John, but not the Pharisees and the lawyers. This probably points not only to the section on the question of authority but also to the parable of the dissimilar sons in Matthew. The parable itself has a general moral sense, but the limiting application in Matt 21:31–32 is certainly original and probably evidenced by Luke. The parable of the wicked vintners, found in all three Synoptics, follows the parable of the dissimilar sons in Matthew, and the question of authority in Mark and Luke. The parable has no explanatory introduction. It was spoken during Jesus' last visit to Jerusalem. Jesus told it in the presence of his opponents against whom it was said.[23] It follows from the parable that Jesus wanted to confront the corrupt establishment; that is, practically, the Jerusalem hierarchy. According to the original report,[24] Jesus' attack was not without consequences. They wanted to have him arrested immediately, but the establishment did not dare because it feared the people who had well understood the goal of the parable: "So they took care and sent spies to him, who had to pose as righteous, to catch him at a word, so that they could hand him over to the authorities and the governor's authority." These spies then asked Jesus whether it was permissible to pay taxes to

---

22. The "baptism of John" occurs in Luke 7:29 in the same sense as in the Acts of the Apostles, especially Acts 19:3. Perhaps the phraseology in the Acts of the Apostles comes from the original report on the question of authority?

23. The opponents are not described in detail by Mark. In Luke (20:19), they are the "scribes and chief priests" (or in reverse order). The scribes must not have been Pharisees. It could mean, as before (Luke 20:1 par.) the scribes of the temple. Matthew (21:45) and Luke express themselves in a similar way on this question. This is significant because they stand together in a certain contrast to Mark. Matthew speaks of the chief priests and the Pharisees. The phrase "lay hands on him" in Luke is good Hebrew. The fact that the scribes and high priests were afraid of the people (not of the "crowd," as in Mark and Matthew) points to Luke's good historical foundations. The reason for their fear is correctly stated in Luke and Mark: "For they knew [lacking in Matthew] that he spoke this parable against them." According to Matt 21:46, they feared the crowds "because they thought he was a prophet." As a result, the right reason disappeared. Matthew is almost certainly dependent on his own words about the Baptist (Matt 14:5). Otherwise, he also conforms the Baptist to Jesus and Jesus to the Baptist; see *The Parables*, 39, 20.

24. Matthew (22:1–14) inserts here the parable of the great banquet. Mark 12:12b ("and they left him and went away") is an addition of the evangelist.

the emperor or not.[25] But Jesus noticed their deceit and did not let himself be caught. So, the historical situation in which Jesus told the parable of the evil vineyard workers is credible, at least according to the Gospels. This one has a special place among Jesus' parables: it is not universally valid and, in the strict sense, it is also not doctrinal. But it vividly explains Jesus' mission and its tragic end.[26] Although it has no interpretation and no moral teaching at the end, most of the parable was so easily understood by the listeners that it aroused their sympathy. But the opponents of Jesus realized that the parable was said against them. The hearers understood that the vineyard meant Israel, the master of the vineyard meant God, the evil vinedressers meant the establishment, and the messengers meant the prophets. At that time, people were already trained in the genre of parables. They could also sense that Jesus was alluding to himself as the master's "only son" and wanted to hint at his impending tragic end. Immediately afterwards, Jesus asked, "Have you not read in the scriptures[27] 'The stone that the builders rejected has become the cornerstone?'" (Ps 118:22).[28] This is neither an interpretation of the parable nor a moral teaching, but an indication that the tragic death of Jesus will turn into a victory. In what way, though, the listeners could not have guessed at that time.[29] The word from the psalm he quoted is, so to speak, a punchline outside the parable.

The little parable of the children at play (Matt 11:16–19; Luke 7:31–35) should also be understood from a context of a concrete situation in Jesus'

---

25. They are called Pharisees and Herodians. Therefore, today the whole section is usually called "the question from the Pharisees." This is hardly possible because the Pharisees paid taxes to the Roman occupation *sub reservatione mentali.* Pilate knew this too. In his eyes, this would therefore have been a strange, pharisaic indictment. On the other hand, an accusation on the side of the Sadducees, who were more foolish than the Pharisees, that Jesus was a rebel against authority was more believable to Pilate. Although Jesus had given a clear answer to his questioners, according to Luke 23:2, both the tax question and incitement to rebellion of the people were brought forward at Jesus' trial.

26. As will be seen later, the comparison of the strong (Luke 11:21f.; see also Mark 3:27 and Matt 12:29) are also closely bound to the person of Jesus. The parable of the wicked farmers applies to it with this comparison.

27. So according to Matt 21:42, which is good Hebrew. "The scriptures" is also the common name of the third part of the Old Testament, to which the Psalms belong.

28. Mark and Matthew add another psalm.

29. Neither will I measure Luke 20:18 ("Whosoever shall fall upon this stone shall be broken in pieces, but the one on whom it falls shall be broken in pieces"), though the verse is lacking in Mark and in many of Matthew's manuscripts.

life. However, it is not clear when he said it. Matthew connects it to the saying about the breakthrough of the kingdom of heaven and to the praise of the Baptist (Matt 11:7–11), but that is because John the Baptist is the common theme of the three sayings of Jesus. Luke brings the comment about the breakthrough of the kingdom elsewhere (16:16) and makes the parable follow immediately after the praise of the Baptist.[30] So the praise of the Baptist and the little parable were already connected in the original account. Perhaps, therefore, Jesus said these two sayings on the same occasion.[31] The parable begins with an explanatory introduction, which is quite consistent with similar introductions of the rabbinic parables: "To whom should I now compare this generation[32] and what are they like?"[33] "This generation" is a negative, critical term when Jesus or the rabbis use it. Through the parable, "this generation" is reproached as childish and capricious. However, as we will also see from the rabbinic parallel, the parable of the playing children could also be related to people in general. Jesus applies it to his contemporaries; namely, because of their different reactions to himself and to the Baptist (Matt 11:18–19; Luke 7:33f.). The historical application is followed by his teaching: "And wisdom is justified by her works [or: by all her children]" (Matt 11:19b; Luke 7:35). There can probably be no doubt that the historical application and his teaching at the end belong to the parable and are accordingly original.

In Matt 9:37f. and in Luke 10:2, Jesus says, "The harvest is great; the laborers are few. So, ask the master of the harvest to send workers to his harvest!" This is a special form of parable with which we will also become acquainted in the rabbinic sources. If the saying had been handed down in an unclear way, then the people could conclude that he meant there is a lot of work that urgently needs to be done. But they would hardly be able to guess what the work in the service of God is about—that is, what is to be harvested.

---

30. Luke 7:29f. is a gloss (see note 22 above), which comes from the editor.

31. This was before John was arrested; see Flusser, *Jesus in Selbstzeugnissen und Bilddokumenten*, 32–35, 41.

32. Luke 7:31: "The people of this generation." I'm sure that's secondary. The word *people* has been added.

33. Luke 7:31. Concerning the linguistic expression, cf. also Lam 2:13; Isa 40:25; 46:5. Jülicher, *Die Gleichnisreden Jesu*, vol. 2, 24, rightly quotes Isa 40:18. Almost the same introductory formula still occurs in Luke 13:18f. in the introduction to the parable of the mustard seed. There, it is secured by the edited parallel in Mark 4:30. For the originality of the formula, see also Vincent Taylor, *Gospel According to Saint Mark: The Greek Text with Introduction, Notes and Indexes* (Grand Rapids: Baker Book House, 1981), 269.

The parable is therefore only partially transparent. Fortunately, however, we know on which occasion Jesus uttered the saying; according to Matthew, it was at the sending of the disciples, and according to Luke, at the sending of the seventy. So, the parable is a gasp of surprise. Jesus is confident in his hope that many are ready to follow his message. But he sees that the crowd around him is too small to collect the rich harvest. One must therefore ask God that those who are to spread the good news should multiply. It is the context that makes the parable clear; there is no need for another explanatory sentence. Such a sentence would only be disturbing in parables of this kind.

The saying "Where there is carrion, there the vultures gather" (Matt 24:28; Luke 17:37) can only be understood with difficulty from the context. The Greek translator of the proverb translated, according to the usual way which we already know from the Greek Bible, the Hebrew נשר with the word *eagle*. But at that time, the word usually meant "vulture."[34] The vulture was the great bird of prey in the homeland of Jesus. However, no negative associations were connected to vultures. By the same Hebrew word, one could also mean the eagle, the king of birds. The eagle of the Roman legions was called נשר by the Jews. In b. San. 12a, it is said that the eagle attacked two scholars. This was an expression used to refer to the rage against the occupying power of Rome in Palestine. Since the carrion is mentioned in Matthew 24:28 and in Luke 17:37, there is no doubt that Jesus spoke of the vultures. His saying is cited in Hebrew linguistics as proof that *nesher* can mean "vulture." Jesus is paraphrasing of Job 39:30, where it is said of the vulture (*nesher*):[35] "Where the slain are, there he is." The phrase certainly became proverbial,[36] but by whom? Was it only Jesus who coined the figurative expression? If it had existed before, then it had a general sense: there are things that, so to speak, will certainly cause a specific reaction;

---

34. That Jesus speaks of a vulture is already suspected by C. H. Dodd, *The Parables of the kingdom* (London: Nisbet, 1969), 67, 1. Jülicher, *Die Gleichnisreden Jesu*, vol. 2, 134, is correct as well. See also Jeremias, *Die Gleichnisse Jesu*, 162, 6. See Jacob Levy, *Chaldäisches Wörterbuch über die Targumim*, 2 vols. (Leipzig: Baumgärtner, 1867), 454f.; Yehuda Feliks, *Animal World of the Bible* (Jerusalem: Sinai Publishing, 1962), 63–71; also, EJ 6, 338 (eagle), 16, 232f. (vultures). The *ptoma* (carcass) in Matthew is better than the *soma* (body), although the second word (since after Homer) also means "corpse."

35. In the free Greek translation of Job 39:27, both the eagle and the vulture are parallel.

36. Klostermann, *Das Matthäusevangelium*, HANT 4 (Tübingen, 1971), 194f.; cf. Rudolf Bultmann, *Die Geschichte der synoptischen Tradition* (Göttingen: Vandenhoeck & Ruprecht, 1957), 103.

they magnetically attract an event. The saying is in the same context in Matthew and in Luke, so they took it from a common source. But we must doubt that the source was compiled by an editor. Couldn't Jesus have said that already? In my opinion, Matthew (24:26–28) preserved the whole passage better than Luke. In fact, the passage about the "Day of the Son of Man" in Luke (17:22–37) is probably composed of two different eschatological series of propositions.[37] The first series (Luke 17:22–24, 37; cf. Matt 24:26–28) warns against speculation about the Day of the Son of Man; it will come like a flash. The second series (Luke 17:26–29, 31–35) also describes the suddenness of the coming of the Day of the Son of Man, yet from a different angle. Here, Jesus is not speaking of useless eschatological speculations but of the unexpected end-time catastrophe that will strike sinful humanity. So, it was in the days of Noah when the flood came, and so it was in the days of Lot when God destroyed Sodom. The generation of the flood and the inhabitants of Sodom are paradigmatic in Judaism for groups of sinners destroyed by God. Testimonies to this are Ben Sira (16:7–10), the Mishnah (m. San. 10:3), and the second letter of Peter (2:4–8).[38] In the event of future unexpected calamity, "one will be taken and the other will be left" (Luke 17:34). Matthew also brings in this second series (24:37–41) but in a shortened form.[39] Since these two series of sentences from Jesus have a common denominator, Luke, or even his predecessor, likely connected them together. It seems to me that we can see this in the connecting introduction before the image of vultures in Luke 17:37. Here, it is written, "They answered and said to him 'Where, Master?'" And then Jesus mentions the vultures by repeating the word *where*. Through this transition, the writer connects the figurative word in Luke 17:37 with Luke 17:23: "Look here! Look there!" By the unification of the second series of statements, the writer suddenly moved away from the content of the first series.

---

37. Luke has interpolated verse 17:25 from the first proclamation of suffering (Luke 9:22) into its source. Also, Luke 17:30 seems to be a secondary interpolation.

38. At Ben Sira (16:7–10), the list of God's destroyed sinners includes the evil angels, the inhabitants of Sodom, the Canaanites, and the wilderness generation. In m. San. 10:3, the list is as follows: the generation of the flood, the generation of the confusion of tongues, the inhabitants of Sodom, the desert generation, and the company of Korah. But there, Rabbi Nehemiah speaks only—like Jesus—of the family of the flood and the inhabitants of Sodom. The Second Epistle of Peter (2:4–8) speaks of evil angels, the generation of the flood, and Sodom and Gomorrah.

39. Matthew speaks only of the days of Noah, but the lists given in the preceding note speak, like Luke, of both the generation of the flood (with Ben Sira, it is evil angels) and the inhabitants of Sodom.

We now want to try to reconstruct the first series.[40] Jesus said to the disciples,

> "There will come days when you will desire to see the day of the Son of Man,[41] but you will not see it. And they will say to you: 'Look here! Look there!' Do not go out and do not run after them. For as lightning flashes in the east and shines to the west, so will be the day of the Son of Man.[42] Where the carrion is, there the vultures will gather."

Do not behave like fanatics and do not be the victim of useless expectation! If the conditions are met, then the final events will surely arrive. This has always been Jesus' opinion, which he expressed with these statements. His word picture of the vultures excellently rounds off the saying. It is in the right place, and its meaning becomes understandable through the context.

Does this also apply to the double comparison of the old and new cloths? As we can see from all three Synoptic Gospels, the section on the fasting question followed in the original report of the debate about Jesus eating with tax collectors and sinners. In Luke 5:33, the conversation about fasting is simply the continuation of the previous conversation about food. The objection is: "The disciples of John fast,[43] as well as the Pharisees, but your disciples eat and drink." (Let us pass over Jesus' words here about the bridegroom.) So, what is the aim of the double comparison of the old and new cloths? Certainly not to make a comment about the biblical fasting days, because this was common ground within Judaism. Rather, Jesus is aiming at the fast days newly introduced by the Pharisees and John the Baptist. I will try to show below why John's disciples were probably not mentioned in the original conversation. This question here is certainly about the Pharisees fasting twice a week (cf. Luke 18:12) on Monday and on Thursday (*Didache* 8:1). These fast days, however, have not prevailed even in Judaism. I don't know anyone who observes them. Jesus believed such innovations were a pointless and failed patchwork, a pouring of new wine into old wineskins. So, it turns out that we can understand the content of this double comparison only if we know something about Judaism

---

40. It is not certain whether the first sentence (Luke 17:22) is part of the utterance, or if it is part of Luke's revision.

41. In Luke 17:22, "one of the days."

42. In Matt 24:27, "the coming of the Son of Man." In Luke 17:24, "the Son of Man in his day."

43. In Luke 5:33, the words *continual* and *prayerful* are additions that are rightly lacking in the other two Gospels.

and can read this double comparison in its context in the Gospels. It has often been forgotten in research that Jesus clearly used the comparison to justify why he did not observe the fast days of the Pharisees—and perhaps also those of John's disciples. Because this is not considered, we tend to see here a principled, negative, and critical statement about the whole of Judaism that is independent of what Jesus said earlier. This blocks the way for a proper understanding of his saying about the new and old cloths. With all my advocacy for textual and contemporary historical contexts, and with all my opposition to the modern methods of consistently dismembering the texts into tiny, rather incoherent chunks, I do not want to overlook the fact that in the text, there are uneven places and jumps. In our case, too, there is a turning point in all the Synoptic Gospels between the preceding material and the comparison.[44] We will see even more clearly that the evangelists had already failed to see the connection correctly. If we take the logion about the bridegroom (Luke 5:34 par.) as an interpolation, then the comparison of the new cloth and the new wine is a convincing answer to the question of why Jesus did not keep the new Pharisaic fast days.

As with the double parable of the old and new cloths, Jesus' statement about relapse (Matt 12:43–45 par.) would not be properly understandable without the context. The saying is only clearly recognizable as a figure of speech by its place in Luke's Gospel.[45] Matthew, it seems, did not understand this figure of speech. That's why he separated it from its natural place. In his version, it should have followed 12:30. Matthew was tempted by the Markan sequence of texts to make changes in his own text. After the accusation that Jesus was driving out demons with Beelzebub, Mark concludes with the statement about sinning against the Holy Spirit. Originally, this latter saying was handed down independently (cf. Luke 12:10). As a follower of Mark, Matthew also makes the saying about the Holy Spirit follow Jesus' defensive speech. However, he then adds another logion that was also independent in the source and expands it (Matt 12:33–36; cf. Luke 6:43–45). He then brings Jesus' explanation against the addiction to miracles (Matt 12:38–42), which almost immediately follows the saying about relapse in Luke.[46] Only after that does Matthew add the saying about

---

44. See Jülicher, *Die Gleichnisreden Jesu*, vol. 2, 188f.

45. Jeremias, *Die Gleichnisse Jesu*, 196–97, correctly recognized the likeness of the word.

46. Between the proclamation of relapse and the declaration against the addiction to miracles is the short "Beatitude of the Mother of Jesus" in Luke 11:27.

relapse (12:43–45). So, he first resolved the connection of the original report, which was preserved by Luke, by allowing himself to be influenced by the sequence of sentences in Mark and then adding other sayings of Jesus. This resulted in a separation, even a distance, in his text between the saying about relapse and the defensive speech against the accusation of alliance with the devil. To reduce this discrepancy, he now reversed the order of logia found in Luke. First, he confirmed the declaration against the addiction to miracles (Matt 12:38–42; cf. Luke 11:29–32) and only then the saying about relapse (Matt 12:43–45; cf. Luke 11:24–26). He was also moved to this change by his erroneous assumption that both the saying about relapse and the explanation against the addiction to miracles were threatening words directed against "this evil generation" (Matt 12:39; Luke 11:29). That is why he added the phrase about relapse with the addition, "So it will also happen to this evil generation" (Matt 12:45b). With these throwaways, Matthew turns out to be a man who is not very sensitive to historical and literary traditions. In contrast, the original context is easy to understand in Luke's Gospel. The saying about relapse follows the words of Jesus about his exorcisms. In Luke's account, the expulsion of evil spirits is evidence of the current breakthrough of the kingdom of heaven. Jesus is the stronger one. He defeats Satan and snatches his prey from him, freeing suffering people from unclean spirits of Satan. The saying about relapse, which immediately follows, demands the person who has been freed from evil not to open his soul to evil again. Otherwise, it will return with more strength. In this case, the situation will be worse with that person than before (Luke 11:24–26). There are parable elements in this saying. The very designation of the human soul as an empty, cleaned, and decorated house to which the unclean spirit returns is reminiscent of parables. The unclean spirit says (Matt 12:44; Luke 11:24), "I will return to my house, from where I went out." It has already been subtly noticed that the unclean spirit is hiding himself, yet that he has been expelled although he speaks as if it were in his power to leave that place and then return to it.[47] He visits his former apartment and, after finding it suitable, brings with him seven—which is an abstract, symbolic number—other spirits who are worse than him. All this seems to me like a well-told story rather than a lesson in demonology. When the unclean spirit emanates from a man and moves through waterless places and seeks rest, it is an epic motif.

---

47. Johann Albrecht Bengel, *Gnomon Novi Testamenti* (Stuttgart: Steinkopf, 1891), 86.

The realia of the proverb is only the unclean spirit; the rest is a symbolic illustration. As already mentioned, the saying is in its right context in Luke's Gospel. Whether this obvious connection of the proverb about the unclean spirit with Jesus' words about the exorcisms comes from Jesus himself, or whether it was created only in the original report, is unimportant for our investigation.

For Luke, the saying about relapse (11:24–26) is thus a direct continuation of Jesus' defensive speech against the accusation of alliance with the devil (11:14–23). To defend himself against this accusation, Jesus answers the critics with two parables. He does well to reject their reproach[48] with a "rabbinic" picture about divisions or breaks[49] (Matt 12:25; Mark 3:24; Luke 11:17). The second parable Jesus uses in his defense is the saying about the strong. This is an important self-testimony from Jesus. He is the strong one! We must start from Luke (11:21–23) since Mark (3:27) did not edit the saying very well. The same is true of Matthew, who follows him (12:29). Both images are in the right place in the Gospels. They would be completely incomprehensible without the context. Jesus took the word about divisions from the rabbis. With them, it turns up in opposition to the harmful addiction to fights and quarrels. But Jesus gives this saying a new meaning: If someone were to cast out the other demons with an evil spirit, then Satan would be divided within himself (Luke 11:14 par.). Only through this reference to contemporary historical contexts does the new meaning of the traditional saying created by Jesus become understandable.

In Jesus' parable of the fig tree in Luke's Gospel, we see how important the context in which Jesus spoke it is for correctly understanding it. I will deal with it here in conclusion. The parable is a direct continuation of the previous one. For this reason, we need to examine the entire corresponding section (Luke 13:1–9). Luke begins with the fact that some people came to Jesus with the news that Pilate had "mixed the blood of the Galileans with their sacrifices." Jesus answered them:

> "Do you think that these Galileans were greater sinners than all the other Galileans because they suffered this? No, I tell you, but if you do not repent, you

---

48. According to Luke 11:15, the critics are some in the crowd who had seen the exorcism, so it was probably in the original report. Perhaps these critics were not "rabbinic" but simple Jews, for Jesus says that their sons also cast out demons (Matt 12:27; Luke 1:19). Mark speaks (3:22) of scribes and Matthew (12:24) of Pharisees.

49. See provisionally, Strack and Billerbeck, *Kommentar zum Neuen Testament aus Talmud und Midrasch*, vol. 1, 635.

will all perish in the same way. Or those eighteen, when the Tower of Siloam fell and slew them, do you think that that they were more guilty than all the other inhabitants of Jerusalem? No, I tell you, but if you do not repent, you will all perish in the same way." And he said the following parable: "One had a fig tree standing in his vineyard. He came to look for fruit on it and found none. Then he spoke to the vintner. 'Behold, it has been three years since I came and searched for fruit on this fig tree and found none. Pull it out! Why should it weaken the soil?' But he answered him: 'Master, leave it this year until I have dug around it and put fertilizer. Maybe it will bear fruit in the future. If not, you may let it be pulled out.'"

In today's world of ideological cruelty, we can better understand the urgency of the question about the Galileans who were killed and the principled importance of Jesus' answer. The Jews, who had brought this frightening news, certainly expected that he would share their justified indignation at the inhumanity of Roman power and its representative in Judea, and that he would strengthen them in their resistance to foreign rule. But this is exactly what Jesus deliberately did not do. He shared the views of those who opposed the Zealot vigilantes and, in his own special way, deepened this aversion to violence. From this point of view, he reacted to what he had just heard. First, he equated the slaughter of the Galileans by Pilate with the fall of the Tower of Siloam. By equating the violent act of the Romans with this natural disaster, he depoliticized, so to speak, the politics of this Roman misdeed. Second, he turned the political side of the terrible murder into a religious and moral concern: Do you think that you yourself are innocent and that no punishment will befall you? Now, it is necessary to pay attention to the commandment of the hour—namely, to do repentance (*teshuva*). What has befallen others can also happen to you.[50] If you do not repent, you will all likewise perish. This is neither a general theological statement nor an eschatological dictum. The great Hugo Grotius has already recognized that Jesus is talking about the impending catastrophe that will affect the whole people through the Romans and that is almost inevitable.[51] They need to

---

50. See Johann Albrecht Bengel, *Gnomon Novi Testamenti* (Stuttgart: Steinkopf, 1891), 267; Luke 13:2.

51. Hugo Grotius, *Annotationes in Novum Testamentum* (Groningen: Zuidema, 1828), to Luke 13:3: *Tota semonis haerentia, et quod de ficu sequitur, certo mihi persuadent de communi et quidem adspectabili poena Iudaeorum populo imminente hic agi: quamquam illa ipsa poenae aetemae imaginem et omen gessit.* Regarding Luke 13:5, "If you do not repent, you will all likewise perish," Grotius read "similarly" instead of "likewise": *Peribitis Simili modo, id est, inter ruinas urbis totius, cuius*

repent. The purpose of Jesus' mission was, among other things, to warn his people of future destruction. So, Jesus is a prophet of evil times similar to Jeremiah at his time. On his last visit, when Jesus approached Jerusalem and saw the city, he wept over it and said,

> "If only you, too, had at least known on this day what is for your peace. But now it has been hidden from your eyes. For days will come upon you when your enemies will dig a trench around you, surround you, and press on you from all sides. They will make you and your children like the ground inside you. They will leave no stone on another within you because you did not take advantage of the time of your opportunity." (Luke 19:42–44)[52]

In response to the news of the Galilean slaughter, Jesus warns of the coming calamity and calls for them to repent. To illustrate both, he adds the parable of the fig tree (Luke 13:6–9). Although the parable looks as if it speaks of eternal punishment, it is about this impending catastrophe that can still be prevented by repentance and renewal. If the barren fig tree will prove itself, then it will not be pulled out. It was already correctly seen by Grotius that the parable, if considered without its context, could well be understood as dealing with the end-time court of judgment. The subject of the parable and its motifs lead to this interpretation. Even today, those researchers who do not pay attention to the situation in which Jesus spoke the parable still fall for this interpretation.[53] The parable of the barren fig tree is therefore paradigmatic for the possible ambiguity of some parables, both the rabbinic kind and the parables of Jesus. Often, we cannot find the exact meaning of a parable if there is no interpretation or if we do not know the context in which the parable was spoken. In our case, the meaning of the parable is clarified by the context.

The subject of the parable of the barren fig tree belongs to the main theme of its growth—namely, in the world of plants. As we discussed earlier, some of its motifs are related to those of the parable of the tares among the

---

turris ista imaginem gerit. That the fall of the Tower of Siloam is an allegory for the destruction of Jerusalem seems unlikely to me. Jülicher has also correctly emphasized the context of Luke 13:1–9: *Die Gleichnisreden Jesu*, vol. 2, 441–44.

52. C. H. Dodd, "The Fall of Jerusalem," *JRS* (1947), here and elsewhere, states that Luke is not a *vaticinium ex eventu*. Adolf Büchler, *Studies in Sin and Atonement in the Rabbinic Literature of the First Century*, 37 (New York: Ktav, 1947), 47–54, convincingly demonstrates this.

53. E.g., Jeremias, *Die Gleichnisse Jesu*, 170f.

wheat (Matt 13:24–30). In both parables, we see that these plants are of little use. Therefore, it is being considered whether they should be pulled out now. In both parables, destruction is postponed: in the parable of the weeds, only at the harvest will someone be able to distinguish between the weeds and the wheat without damage; and in the parable of the fig tree, the gardener wants to grant the tree some time. In both cases, the motifs indicate the punishment of sinners. The differences lie in the different applications of the two parables. The parable of the weeds deals with the end-time separation between the pious and the sinners, while the parable of the fig tree deals with the deadline for repentance, which is given to sinners. In both parables, the decision is made in a conversation between the landlord and his employees (Matt 13:27–30; Luke 13:7–9). In the parable of the weeds, it is the servants who advise to pull out the plants and the master decides to wait. In the parable of the barren fig tree, on the other hand, it is the master who proposes to pull out the tree and it is the hired vintner who advises to give it more time. In both cases, the postponement of the destruction is recommended with similar words: "Let both grow together until the harvest" (Matt 13:30); "Master, leave it this year" (Luke 13:8). The interchange of roles in both parables relates to their different religious content. We are not allowed to interpret the two interlocutors in the two parables allegorically. True, in the parable of the tares, the "master" is God. But the workers cannot be transposed. We must consider that the dialogue before the decision is a "blunt motif" that could have a full meaning elsewhere. And finally, the comparison of the parable of the barren fig tree (which is not eschatological) with the parable of the weeds (which speaks of the end times) show us that the subject of the parable also fits within an end-times interpretation. Although the fig tree parable is not eschatological, it somehow has an eschatological smell.

From a Jewish-Hellenistic parallel that deals with a sermon about Jonah, we can see that the parable of the barren fig tree is not inherently eschatological but has the purpose of calling for repentance. (Although this sermon is mistakenly attributed to Philo of Alexandria, the real author is unknown. It is preserved only in Armenian.) After the inhabitants of Nineveh repented and were saved, God says to Jonah,

> "Now, if the farmers do not put their efforts on the line, but seek to make things secure, should I kill the citizens of Nineveh? After all, they are proving to be extremely obedient now! . . . I also assume that a farmer—and with this example I should convince you—who no longer hopes for the yield of a

tree, is going to tear out what he had planted. But when he sees the buds that are about to pop up, he will leave the tree unharmed for the sake of the fruit. Absolutely right! Because a tree that is useless is cut down. But if it brings fruit, they let it stand."[54]

The relationship between this parable and Jesus' parables catches our eye. In both cases, it is about impending disaster and about repentance that can avert that disaster. This Hellenistic-Jewish sermon on Jonah contains more parables. (Have you grown up based on popular Greek philosophical literature that, after all, loves parables? Much will have to be said later about the possible origin of the rabbinic parables from the parables of popular Hellenistic philosophy. We must also reckon with the possibility that, in individual cases, rabbinic parables influenced Jewish-Hellenistic authors.)

Another instructive parallel to the parable of the barren fig tree is a beautiful rabbinic parable (of the later type) from the third century:[55]

A king had a field. . . . He told the tenant, "Go and make it arable and turn it into a vineyard." The tenant went, made the field arable, and planted a vineyard. The vineyard grew up, and you could get wine from it which, however, turned sour. When the king saw that the wine was getting sour, he said to the tenant: "Go and cut down the vines! What do I have from a vineyard that brings forth vinegar?" The tenant said: "Master King, how much have you spent on the vineyard until it was able to prosper and now you want to pull it up? And that's because the wine went sour. The vineyard is still young, so it brings a sour and not a good wine. So the holy one wanted to destroy the Israelites after they had committed the deed and raised up the golden calf. And Moses said, Master of the world, have you not brought them out of Egypt, out of the place of idolatry? They are still young now, as it is written 'When Israel was young,

---

54. Cf. Folker Siegert, "Drei hellenistische–Jüdische Predigten," *WUNT* 20 (Tübingen, 1980), 471. It concerns the preaching: De Jona 52, 213–16.

55. Exodus Rab. 43:9, Ziegler, *Die Koenigsgleichnisse des Midrasch beleuchtet durch die roemische Kaiserzeit*, chapter 6, parable 81. The one responsible for passing down the tradition is Rabbi Abun in the name of Rabbi Shimeon ben Jehozadak, who was a colleague of Rabbi Johanan. About him, see Bacher, *Die Agada der Paläs-tinischen Amoräer*, vol. 1, 119–23. Our parable has escaped Bacher. Presumably, Rabbi Abun knew the parable indirectly by the name of Rabbi Johanan. In this case, the words "in the name of Rabbi Johanan" were erroneously omitted by copyists. After *Biblical Antiquities of Pseudo-Philo*, 12:8–9, Moses asks God regarding the sin of the golden calf, "Let him not tear out the vine of Israel." See Pseudo-Philo, *Les Antiquités Bibliques*, vol. 1.130 and vol. 2.115 (Paris: 1976).

I loved it; from Egypt I called my son. (Hos. 11:1)'[56] Wait a little for them and go with them, and they will do good deeds before you."

The subject and motif relationship between the rabbinic parable and the parable of the barren fig tree is obvious. In both cases, these are plants that do not bring any benefit and should therefore be pulled out. In both cases, the destruction of the plants is postponed by the advice of an employee of the landlord, who takes care of the plants, since they can still prove themselves. Both parables are about sinners and the mercy of God, who postpones his judgment against them, annihilation, in order to offer sinners the opportunity to improve in the future. For various reasons, neither parable is eschatological: the rabbinic parable is about the sin of the golden calf and Moses' intercession, and Jesus' parable is about the impending destruction by the Romans. In both parables, we learn about a similar conversation between the landlord and his worker. Another similar conversation also occurs in the parable of the weeds and the wheat, only with reversed roles. I have already mentioned that with Jesus the conversation is a "blunt motif" and that we should not and cannot identify the two interlocutors in the application of Jesus' two parables.[57] The two points of view could also have been expressed through the self-talk of the owner. The dialogue is just poor without fresher colors.[58] But didn't the "blunt motif" have a history? The conversation in the parable of the barren fig tree differs from the almost identical conversation in the rabbinic parable of the vineyard in that the conversation with Jesus is a "blunt motif" while in the rabbinic parable the two partners point to two different people: the master of the manor who wants to cut down the vineyard is God; the intercessor is Moses. According to the Jewish view, it was the Prophet's duty to defend Israel before God so that God would graciously turn to his people. In rabbinic literature, there is often talk about the figure of the heavenly intercessor. The figure of the winegrower in the parable of the fig tree hints at the traditional defender and advocate. But this realization has no significance for the understanding of the parable itself. The motif that has become "blunt" cannot be allegorized.

The parable of Jesus is a beautiful example of the fact that the narrator ends it exactly where the subject reaches its logical point:[59] whether the fig

---

56. The creator of this parable certainly also thought of Hos 10:1 where Israel is compared to a vine: "The more fruit he produced, the more altars they built."

57. See Jülicher, *Die Gleichnisreden Jesu*, vol. 2, 557f. (weeds), 442 (fig tree).

58. So Jülicher, *Die Gleichnisreden Jesu*, vol. 2, 442.

59. See Jülicher, *Die Gleichnisreden Jesu*, vol. 2, chapter 3, note 13.

tree has proven itself or not is no longer told.[60] Thus the parable dates to the time before the destruction of the temple in Jerusalem. Since we also know that one of the main purposes of Jesus' mission was to warn his people about the impending catastrophe—the destruction of the temple and the suffering associated with it—it is certain that the parable comes from Jesus. I don't know if anyone has ever doubted that.

We now turn to two parables contained only in Luke to examine their framework and interpretation. The first is the parable of the intrusive friend (Luke 11:5–8). It has been edited quite strongly, in terms of language, in the Greek stage. Luke introduces it after the Lord's Prayer, which is appropriate because the second half of the Lord's Prayer contains personal requests. The pleading friend in the parable forms a good connection. The Lukan continuation of the parable of the pleading friend is also equally successful in the admonition for trusting in prayer (Luke 11:9–13). This latter section is not only related to the parable in terms of content, but it is also composed of parables with a subject similar to this parable of the pleading friend:

> "Ask, and you will be given; seek, so you will find; knock, so it will be opened. For he who asks, receives; he who seeks, finds; to him who knocks, the door will be opened. Or where is the man among you who, when his son asks for bread, will give him a stone? Or if he asks for a fish, would give him a snake?[61] Now if you who are wicked know how to give good gifts to your children, how much more will your father in heaven give good gifts to those who ask him."

The imagery of this speech is so strong, and the relationship to the parable is so great, that it is quite possible that the connection does not come only from Luke's editorial work but that it came from Jesus. If the connection is only from Luke, then it is a sign that the evangelist correctly understood the parable. He obviously meant that the section on the answer to prayer is the moral tenet of the parable. That is why he begins it with the words that are missing from Matthew: "And I tell you" (Luke 11:9).

The Lukan parable of the unjust judge or the judge and the widow (Luke 18:1–8) is closely related to the parable of the pleading friend in terms of subject and meaning: if one urgently pleads with God, one will be heard for the very reason that—humanly speaking—God will get rid of the nuisance. To pair it with an old parable from Samuel the Little, "If a servant demands something particular from his master, the master says, 'Pay it to him, so

---

60. See Jülicher, *Die Gleichnisreden Jesu*, vol. 2, 439f.
61. So according to Matt 7:9f.

that I may not hear his voice,' "[62] the parable of the judge is understandable without any explanation. But in the case of Luke, there is nevertheless an explanatory remark at the beginning: "But he said a parable to them that one should always pray and not let go" (Luke 18:1). This is a good help for the reader. In addition, Jesus himself interprets the parable at the end: "But the master said, 'Do you hear what the unjust judge is saying? And shouldn't God give justice for his chosen ones, who call to him day and night? Shouldn't he give them kindness? I tell you, he will set them right, and speedily' " (Luke 18:6–8). This interpretation, which is correct, seems to be original but it has been greatly revised in its Greek form—and not only linguistically. The "ecclesiastical" concept of the elect, which occurs here only in Luke, was foreign to Jesus' preaching. The Greek word, which we have translated as "right," occurs only in Luke's Gospel as well as the phrase "set them right," which is found only in this parable.[63] The conclusion from Luke 18:8, "I tell you, he will soon do for them [i.e., the chosen ones] justice," is certainly the work of the editor.

"He belongs to them himself," to the elect of God who cry out to God, "to the distressed believers in Christ of the first times, who fervently plead for the day of judgment; revenge has long been a fixed concept, and it is not his intention to inculcate the duty to pray, but to promise the certain, speedy response to the prayer of longing."[64] So the editor has subsequently given the parable an eschatological punchline. Based on this new understanding, he has objectively worked on the entire interpretation. The original interpretation of the meaning is that God will hear those who fervently pray and will have mercy on them.[65] The interpretation of the parable is also accompanied by the surely secondary question: "But will the Son of Man find faith on the earth at his coming?" (Luke 18:8). I have often wondered why this is written here, but I do not know a fully satisfactory answer. The question is an invented saying of the Master, which the editor knew and suggested that "here it would be best at the right place,"[66] although it does have a background in

---

62. b. Ta'an. 25b (below); see Bacher, *Die Agada der Tannaiten*, vol. 1, 371.

63. For its meaning, see Jülicher, *Die Gleichnisreden Jesu*, 279f. Jülicher, *Die Gleichnisreden Jesu*, 284–88, considers the whole interpretation to be secondary.

64. Jülicher, *Die Gleichnisreden Jesu*, 285, rightly cites the Greek text Sir 32 (35) 14–26 as a parallel.

65. Otherwise, and certainly worth considering, Jülicher, *Die Gleichnisreden Jesu*, 286–88.

66. Jeremias, who is otherwise of a different opinion here, rightly says (155n2) from this sentence, "There is no Lukan language."

the Old Testament. The fact that the Son of Man is unlikely to find faith "on the earth" is probably an allusion to a verse from Ecclesiastes: "For there is no one who is righteous on earth, who would do good and did not lack" (Eccl 7:21). However, the real basis of Luke 18:8 is Prov 20:6, which is a difficult verse). This verse was understood by the inventor of the supposed saying of Jesus as follows: "The great man will call a man of his grace, and a man of faith—who will find him?" The "great man" was thus understood as the coming Son of Man: Will he find a man of faith when he comes? Because, as Qoheleth says, there is no one on earth who is righteous. Whoever invented this saying of Jesus was most likely already a Christian. Otherwise, he would hardly have made the connection of the Son of Man with the concept of faith. In particular, he was a Hebrew Christian. Such a reinterpretation of Eccl 7:21 is only possible because of the Hebrew original text. This saying of Jesus belongs in the framework of the expectation of the parousia, so it is eschatological. Also, if this parable is interpreted as eschatological, then Jesus' saying could be attached to it. Perhaps this development was complete even before Luke. In any case, he correctly understood the real intention of the parable and therefore continues according to the parable, which deals with the power of prayer, and moves into the example of the Pharisee and the tax collector, which deals with the answer to prayer.

The section on vigilance and faithfulness in Luke 12:35–46 also deals with the coming Son of Man in his present form. It is not objectively connected with the previous one, and we must speak here of various later editors.[67] In Luke 12:35–38, we read about lamps that should be burning, the expectation of the Master who unexpectedly arrives at the feast, as well as knocking and opening. There is certainly an influence here seen in the parable of the ten virgins (Matt 25:1–13), which is so strong that we must wonder if we can find anything original here at all. The editor has apparently reworked the material from the parable of Matthew into a parable of a servant in Luke 12:35–38 and combined it with the following two parables, both of which are about servants and have their parallel in Matthew. The common theme of the section Luke creates is vigilance. Luke knew the parable of the ten virgins, but he did not include it in his Gospel. This can be seen from another section (Luke 13:22–30), which is also secondarily composed by Luke, where Luke 13:25 is parallel to Matt 25:10–12.[68]

---

67. So, correctly, Jeremias, *Die Gleichnisse Jesu*, 50–52.

68. I examined the whole section of Luke 13:22–30 in my article, "Two Anti-Jewish Montages in Matthew," *Immanuel* 5 (1975): 39–43. Luke 13:22 is the sec-

The dependence of Luke 13:25 on Matt 25:10–12 is important because it helps us gain insight into the Lukan editorial hand. As we have already seen, Luke 12:39–46 corresponds to the two parables in Matt 24:43–51. After these two parables, Matt 25:1–13 includes the parable of the ten virgins (Luke 12:35–38). This means that in the case of Luke, the arranger reversed the order while Matthew preserved the original order. So, both parables are probably in the common source of Matthew and Luke before the parable of the ten virgins, which deals with the necessary readiness for the coming of the bridegroom. It seems to me to be certain that this motif is to be interpreted as the future coming of the Son of Man. In this case, there is a possibility that the two previous parable images were influenced by the motif of the parable of the ten virgins coming after them. The probability is even greater because it can be seen from the style that the common source of Matthew and Luke was extensively reworked in Greek here. The subject of the two parables does not itself indicate the coming of the Son of Man. The original kernel of the first parable, which admonishes to be vigilant and faithful, is: "But know this: if the master of the house had known in which night watch [Luke: "at what time"] the thief would come, he would have [Matthew: "watched and"] prevented the break-in into his house."[69] The master of the house is not the "master of the house" of the rabbinic parables and several parables of Jesus here. He is not a symbol of God here. The word in this context means the owner of the house.[70] This is strange. Perhaps the expression should be attributed to the Greek editor. Otherwise, Jesus usually speaks of watchful servants. The only important point here is that the master of the house does not stand for God but for the person addressed by Jesus. The motif of the thief in the night is an allusion to the "thieves in the night" of Jeremiah 49:9. In the New Testament epistles, this phrase became an eschatological metaphor for the coming day of the Master.[71] Also in our parable, the burglary of the thief will have meant

---

ondary geographic frame; the verses 23f. about the narrow gate are parallel to Matt 7:13f. Verse 23 comes from the parable of the ten virgins (Matt 25:10–12). Luke 13:26–30 is the second half of a saying of Jesus, the first half of which is in Matt 11 (cf. Luke 6:46). For the second half, see also Matt 7:23 and 8:11f. In this saying, Jesus turns against the cult of his personality.

69. Jeremias has exemplarily analyzed and explained the parable of the burglar at night (Matt 24:42–44; Luke 12:39f.) in *Die Gleichnisse Jesu*, 45–47.

70. See chapter 2, note 5, above.

71. See Jeremias, *Die Gleichnisse Jesu*, 47. Only in the Apocalypse of John is Christ himself compared to the thief (Rev 3:3; 16:15).

the coming catastrophe from which one can save oneself by vigilance. But already in the source of Matthew (24:44) and Luke (12:40), the parable is interpreted by the following sentence: "So be ready also, because the Son of Man is coming in the hour when you do not expect him." As the sentence stands there, it is absurd. It is clear from the parable that we are to prevent the burglary of the thief, and this cannot be true of the coming of the Son of Man! The mention of the Son of Man in Matt 24:44 and Luke 12:40 was thus incorrectly inserted by the editor of the source. The Son of Man appears in the interpretations of Jesus' parables in only three places; and in all three, this mention is secondary. We are dealing with the one case right now. The second passage is the interpretation of the parable of the tares (Matt 13:36–43), into which the allegorizing interpolator has inserted the Son of Man twice: verses 37 and 41.[72] The third passage is Luke 18:8; the spurious saying of Jesus about the Son of Man who will hardly find faith on the earth.

The reason why the Son of Man was inserted into the source of the parable of the thief is not difficult to find. We have seen that here Matthew preserved the order of his source. In it, after the two parables of readiness (Matt 24:42–51), the parable of the ten virgins follows (Matt 25:1–13). The parable of the virgins speaks of the coming of the bridegroom, who is the symbolic figure for the coming Son of Man. So, to adapt the parable of the thief to the parable of the virgins, the editor corrupted the interpretation of the parable of the thief and spoke of the Son of Man there. Matthew goes even further: he begins the picture of the thief with the words: "Then watch, because you do not know on which day your Master is coming" (Matt 24:42). This is influenced by Mark 13:35. Originally, the parable pointed to the future end-time catastrophe. Thus the interpretation of the parable used to be: "So also be ready, for the hour is coming when you do not expect it."[73] This is how Jesus spoke about the suddenness of the end-time catastrophe when he mentioned the days of Noah and Lot as a parallel (Luke 17:26–35; Matt 24:37–41).[74]

In Matthew 24:42, the image of the thief in the night is introduced by the sentence: "Then watch, because you do not know on which day the Master is coming." In the case of Luke, both this secondary introduction and the mention of watching for the master of the house, which are found in Matthew 24:43, are missing. According to Matt 24:44 and Luke 12:40,

---

72. See Jeremias, *Die Gleichnisse Jesu*, chapter 4, note l.

73. Nor is it ruled out that Luke 12:40 was not present in Luke at first but was subsequently interpolated from Matt 24:44 into the Lukan text. The verse is missing in a family of Luke's manuscripts.

74. See Jeremias, *Die Gleichnisse Jesu*, 46.

the parable concludes with: "So also be ready, for the Son of Man is coming in the hour when you do not expect it." This sentence is missing in a family of Lukan manuscripts, so it seems to have crept from Matthew into the manuscripts of the Gospel of Luke. If this happened in this way in the history of the text, then the original text of Luke received the saying of Jesus: "But know this, if the master of the house had known at what night watch [Luke: time] the thief was coming, he would have prevented the break-in into his house." This saying has certainly already been reworked in the Greek in the common source of Matthew and Luke. However, the mention of the owner of the house seems to be original. Although the master of the house usually has the meaning of "boss" in the parables, at that time, people generally spoke of the master of the house in Hebrew even if they meant the owner of the house. The absurd interpretation of the coming of the thief as the parousia of the Son of Man is therefore an exclusive invention—or interpretation—that can be attributed to Matthew. This is evident not only from the pericopes that follow in Matthew but also from the fact that Matthew spoke of the coming of the Son of Man three times before (Matt 24:47, cf. Luke 17:24; Matt 24:37, cf. Luke 17:26; Matt 24:39).

The former exegetes were not put off by the reinterpretation of Matthew but understood the saying of Jesus correctly. The great Hugo Grotius saw in Matt 24:43 a warning from Christ that we should beware of unforeseen dangers. Grotius left the eschatological point of the saying out of consideration.[75] Bengel's interpretation includes this point, and it is well worth reading. The burglary of the thief is understood as the end-time temptation, which will be the hardest, combined with hope and fear.[76] The fact that the saying is about the inbreaking crisis is ensured by the context in Matthew. The saying about the burglar is a warning and concludes the previous proclamation of the Day of the Son of Man (Matt 24:37–41, preserved better in Luke 17:29–37). So, we can only grasp the true meaning of the saying about the burglar if we read it in its original form in Luke (without Luke 12:40). It follows from the preceding pericope of Matthew that it has an imperative character. When we see this, it also makes sense to us that the saying, because of its eschatological tension, has seduced its readers (so to speak) to misunderstand it in the sense of the expectation of the parousia. That is why Matthew introduced it in this sense at the beginning and at the end, and in

---

75. Hugo Grotius, *Annotationes in Novum Testamentum*, vol. 2 (Groningen: Zuidema, 1828), 2611.

76. Bengel, *Gnomon Novi Testamenti* (Stuttgart: Steinkopf, 1891), 147.

these places, he also added the coming of the Master and the Son of Man. Luke also fell into this misunderstanding. He ripped the parable out of its original context, in which the danger of the end time was mentioned, and he put it before a saying (Luke 12:35–38), the origin of which is obscure; it is questionable whether there is any original core attributable to Jesus hidden in it. This erratic secondary structure probably has the parousia as its content, although this cannot be stated with absolute certainty. The parable that follows the saying about the burglar both in Matthew (24:45–51) and in Luke (12:42–46) is not itself about the parousia, but it belongs to the rabbinic theme of the returning master and his servant, which we have already noted. But Luke might have thought that it dealt with the parousia. Thus it can be assumed that although Luke preserved the original wording of the saying about the burglar, he, like Matthew, thought that the saying referred to the parousia. Therefore, he divided it between two sayings of Jesus, which, in his opinion, had the parousia as their subject.

The source of Matthew (24:45–51) and Luke (12:41–46), after the parable of the thief, added the parable of the servant entrusted with supervision. This parable has nothing to do with the coming of the Son of Man. The master, who placed the faithful and prudent servant above his servants, will place him above all possessions on his return when he sees that this servant is doing his duty and giving food to the rest of the servants for the time being. On the other hand, if the servant is bad and concludes from the long absence of his master that he can do whatever he wants, if he starts to beat his fellow servants, eats and drinks and gets drunk, then at the sudden and unexpected coming of the Master, he will be cruelly punished and his share will be taken from him."[77] We recognize in this parable both the subject and its motifs. The main theme is about work ethics and the relationship of the servant with his master. We have also already talked about the significance of the absence of the Master and his unexpected coming, which we also found in the rabbinic parables. There, we saw the cruel fea-

---

77. Luke says that the master will give the portion of the wicked servant "to the unbelievers" (12:46). Matthew (24:51) speaks secondarily of the "part of the hypocrites": there will be "weeping and gnashing of teeth." Here, Matthew is certainly anti-pharisaic. In his Anti-Jewish Montage in Matt 8:12, the same Matthew says, "But the sons of the kingdom shall be cast out into the darkness without; there shall be weeping and gnashing of teeth." This is what Matthew alludes to here in 24:51. On the Anti-Jewish Montage of Matthew in Matt 8:11, see Flusser, *Two Anti-Jewish Montages in Matthew*, no. 5, 78n68. See Strack and Billerbeck, *Kommentar zum Neuen Testament aus Talmud und Midrasch*, vol. 1, 969.

tures of punishment. The parable is about the responsibility of man before God, who will be rewarded for his good actions and punished for his evil. Again, as is generally the case in the rabbinic parallels and Jesus' parables, it is a question of reward and punishment after death. The good Hebrew proposition,[78] according to which the share of the wicked servant will be together with the wicked, also points in this direction. It means punishment after death. The parousia has nothing to do with the parable, because the temporary removal of the master and his sudden return is a tried and tested medium of art for those who tell parables to represent, in a surprising way, the responsibility that man imposes on himself when he acts without regard for God.

Even the small addition of the servant's wages in Luke has nothing to do with the parousia. Luke introduces that element here because he also speaks of the reward and punishment of a servant. That servant, who knew the will of his master and yet did not conform to it, will receive many blows. But those who have not known him and have done what deserves blows will receive few. To everyone to whom much has been given, much will be demanded, and to whom much has been entrusted, much more will be demanded. This is written purely in Greek, and a Hebrew source is not visible.[79] The sense of the saying is clear: just as the slave who knew his master's will and did not fulfill it experienced severe chastisement while the transgressions of the uninstructed are punished mildly, so those who knew God's commandments but did not follow them will one day face severe punishment while those who sin in ignorance are more likely to be excused.[80] The conclusion is then an explanatory interpretation: everyone to whom God has given much is judged strictly. Those who manage God's property have an even greater responsibility before God. Do the words that Luke appended to the foregoing (12:47) come from Jesus himself? Even their Greek revision gives the impression that the editor became familiar with them in the form of oral or written tradition. That is, he knew the teachings by hearsay. It seems to me that the doctrine according to which the one who knows is punished more severely for his offense than the ignorant sinner, although it does not stand in contrast to the preaching of

---

78. See Strack and Billerbeck, *Kommentar zum Neuen Testament aus Talmud und Midrasch*, vol. 1, 969.

79. Only the words "much shall be required of him" can be fully translated from Greek and well into Hebrew.

80. See Jülicher, *Die Gleichnisreden Jesu*, vol. 2, 158.

Jesus, is still somewhat atypical for Jesus.[81] The view that God takes a hair's breadth with those around him and that his judgment falls more heavily on those near than on those far away is a rabbinic doctrine.[82] Anyone who sinned knowingly will be punished by God more severely than the one who accidentally committed an offense. This teaching is illuminated by two rabbinic parables.[83] "Two people threw stones at the statue of the king. One was drunk, the other sober. The two were arrested and brought to court. The one who had acted destructively when sober was convicted, but the one who was drunk went out without punishment." In our context, the second parable is even more important:

> Two people sinned against the king. One was from the countryside and the other lived in the king's palace. The king saw that both had committed one and the same offense. He released the one who lived in the countryside, but he condemned the one who lived in his palace. The king's courtiers said to him: "After all, both have committed the same offense. But you have set the man from the country free and condemned the man from your palace." Then the king answered them: "I have released the man from the country, because he was not versed in the royal customs. However, the man from the palace is with me every day and knows what the royal customs are. The one who sinned in my environment will be condemned."

According to the two parables, the conscious sinners are punished by God, while those who act badly out of ignorance or by mistake are acquitted by God. According to Luke 12:47, the one who knows the will of the Master and yet sins is punished more severely than the one who sins out of ignorance. Another example of this view is a saying by Rabbi Yohanan. At the end of the book of Ecclesiastes (12:14), it says, "For God will bring every

---

81. In the Codex Bezae, instead of Luke 6:5, the following story is added to Luke 6:10: "On the same day he saw a man doing work on the Sabbath. And he said unto him, 'Man, if thou knowest what thou doest, be thou blessed. But if you do not know, you too are cursed and a transgressor of the law.'" Joachim Jeremias, *Unbekannte Jesusworte*, (Gütersloh: Bertelsmann: 1963), 61–64, considers the *Logion* to be genuine, but I can hardly join him. The contrast between the knowing and the unknowing offense also seems to be different in this word than in Luke 12:47f. In the apocryphal *Logion*, he who knowingly acts against the law is praised, while he who does not know what he is doing is cursed. In Luke 12:47, we read that knowledge brings more reward to a person than ignorance.

82. y. Sheq. 5 (48d); b. Yev. 121b.

83. Tan. B. 7, 9.

hidden deed to judgment." The rabbis understood the expression "hidden" as such sins that are hidden even to the sinner.[84] When Rabbi Yohanan (third century) came to this verse of Scripture while reading, he used to cry and say, "Is there any hope for the servant who sins against his master unintentionally with intentional sins?"[85] Here, as in Luke, the master and the servant are mentioned, but the view is even more pessimistic: both types of sinners are punished by God with the same severity. So we see that Luke 12:47 is easily understandable within the framework of rabbinic theology and that, although Jesus would not have rejected this saying, it is atypical for him and the words are formed in Greek. Thus we can hardly assume that the editor had a written or stylistically formed oral source for this saying. It is easier to imagine that someone told him that Jesus had said something like that. In reality, however, it was an echo of a rabbinic opinion, which may have already been handed down in the figurative language of the master and his servant.

The two parables in Matt 24:42–46 are not only found before the parable of the ten virgins (25:1–13), but they are also a continuation of an eschatological section (Matt 24:37–41). The reason for this arrangement is that, after the so-called Synoptic apocalypse[86] and before the account of the passion, Matthew wanted to append material that was either eschatological in essence or eschatological as he understood it. Mark, on the other hand,

---

84. See Schechter, *Aspects of Rabbinic Theology*, 240n3.

85. b. Hag. 5a. There are other parallel parables of Rabbi Johanan that deal with the Master and the servant.

86. See R. L. Lindsey, "A Modified Two Document Theory of the Synoptic Dependence and Interdependence," *NT* 6 (1963): 239–64; and Flusser, *Judentum und die Quellen des Christentums* (Tel Aviv: Sifriyyat Pocalim, 1979), 253–74; Flusser, "Eine Weissagung über die Befreiung Jerusalems im Neuen Testament," *ErIsr*, vol. 10 (Jerusalem, 1971), 225–36 (Hebrew); and Flusser, *Jerusalem in der Literatur des Zweiten Tempels*, Festschrift, (Jerusalem: Rubin Mass, 1975), 290–93 (Hebrew). Lindsey took the first step in the literary-critical analysis of the "Synoptic Apocalypse" in his article in the *Novum Testamentum*. Further steps were made possible by a lively exchange of ideas between the two of us. Lindsey realized that Luke (21:5–33) almost literally represents the Greek form of the Synoptic Apocalypse. The Greek editor compiled his eschatological prophecy from three sources: (1) the main source is Jesus' prophecy about the fall of the temple (Luke 21:5–7, 20–24, 28–33); (2) a prophecy about the end times and the coming of the Son of Man (Luke 21:8–11; 25–27); and (3) Jesus' words about the persecution of his disciples after the crucifixion (Luke 21:12–19), which we also find in Matt 10:17–23 in slightly edited form. See also Jeremias, *Die Gleichnisse Jesu*, 50–52.

ends the Synoptic Apocalypse with a separate appendix (Mark 13:33–37) that consists of parables, all of which deal with the vigilance of servants waiting for the arrival of the master of the house.[87] The whole thing is probably a composition by Mark from foreign phrases that were worthily created to complete the Synoptic Apocalypse. The piece, with its mixture of images, is inconsistent. The doorkeeper in Mark 13:34 is probably a modification of the one mentioned in Luke 12:35–38. This has a suitable interpretation: "But what I say to you, I say to everyone. Watch" (Mark 13:37). It also contains an explanatory introduction: "Be careful, stay awake, for you do not know when the time is coming" (Mark 13:33).[88]

The banquet speeches in Luke 14:7 also pose various riddles and are artfully embedded in the Gospel. In Luke 14:1–6, we read that Jesus once came to the house of a superior of the Pharisees to dine on the Sabbath: "and they were waiting for him."[89] He healed a man who had dropsy and then explained to the Pharisees and the experts in the law and why it was permissible to heal on the Sabbath:

> He spoke a parable to those who had been invited, as he was watching how they chose the first places for themselves, and he said to them: "If you are invited to the wedding by someone, do not take the first place. Otherwise, someone more distinguished than you might be invited by him and the one who invited you and him might come and tell you: 'Make room for him!' You would then have to take the lowest place. Rather, when you are invited, go, and settle down in the last place, so that when he who has invited you comes, he says, 'Friend, move on up!' Then you will have honor before all your fellow guests. For everyone who exalts himself will be humbled, and he who humbles himself will be exalted." But he said to the one who had invited him: "If you are organizing a lunch or a dinner, do not call your friends, nor your brothers, nor your relatives, nor rich neighbors, that they might invite you again and

---

87. See also Jeremias, *Die Gleichnisse Jesu*, 50–52.

88. This sentences from Mark (13:33) was modified from Matthew as an introduction to the parable of the thief.

89. The story of the healing of the man with dropsy (Luke 14:1–6) has two parallels in Luke: the healing of the crippled woman (Luke 6:6–1 par.) and the healing of the man with the withered hand (Luke 6:6–1 par.). In the last-mentioned parallel (Luke 6:7; Mark 3:2), it is said that someone "lurked around him" to see if he healed on the Sabbath. The same expression is found in the section on the man with dropsy (Luke 14:1). These mentioned passages are the only ones in the Gospels where this Greek phrase "lurked around him" can be found. This is not entirely unimportant for the prehistory of Christian anti-Judaism.

thus return the favor. Rather, when you are holding a banquet, invite the poor, the crippled, the lame, the blind. So you will be happy, because they will not be able to repay you. For it will be repaid to you at the resurrection of the righteous." But when one of the fellow guests heard this, he said to him: "Blessed is he who dines in the kingdom of God." But he said to him: ". . ." [Then follows the parable of the great banquet.]

So, according to Luke, Jesus taught this at the meal in the Pharisee's house after he had healed the man with dropsy.[90]

What Jesus wants to convey to the host at the end of his teaching is a beautiful moral lesson. In terms of content, however, it is a variant of the parable of the great banquet that follows immediately afterward. What Jesus told there in the parable now becomes a morally upright piece of advice here! The list is identical in Luke 14:13 and 14:21. The Greek word for "cripple" occurs in the New Testament only in these two passages. On the other hand, this list does not appear in Matthew's version of the parable. There, the landlord simply asks his servants to invite those they find to the wedding. If Matthew is more original, then we will be able to accept "evil and good" as his addition. Matthew seems to have been especially interested in the calling of sinners. Thus the twice-repeated list in Luke is a kind of bracket between the moral advice and the parable that follows. "By repeating this list, Luke makes it clear that he has interpreted the parable as a paraenetic example narrative to 14:12–14: this is how you should do it, like the master of the house in the parable, who in an exemplary manner treated the poor, the crippled, the blind, and the lame who cried at his table."[91] Did Luke find Jesus' words to the host as a variant of the parable in a source and adapt them even further to the parable? Or did he perhaps write them himself? The first possibility is much more likely, but it has not yet been decided whether Luke 14:12–14 comes from Jesus.[92] The fact that one is rewarded for a pious act in the afterlife (Luke 14:14) is a generally Jewish and Christian view. From this, too, we can conclude with probability that Jesus' words of Jesus to the host do not go back to Jesus and that they depend on the parable of the great banquet.

---

90. A cross-connection between the healing of the man with dropsy and the parable of the great banquet is the phrase "to eat" in Luke (Luke 14:1, 15). Literally, it means "eat bread"; this is a Hebrism.

91. Jeremias, *Die Gleichnisse Jesu*, 41.

92. If we knew that the list of guests in the parable (Luke 14:21) came from Luke 14:13 (it is not in Matt 22:9–10), then the direct dependence on Luke 14:12–14 would be proven.

The situation is different with Jesus' words to those invited (Luke 14:7–11). There is an old kernel to the passage there. Luke 14:7 is an introductory passage that places the banquet speeches in the situation of a real banquet and gives the speeches a polemical edge against the Pharisees. As Luke tells us, Jesus noticed that the Pharisees' guests "chose the best places." He therefore rebuked them (Luke 14:8) and advised them not to take "the first place." The same Greek word appears in the anti-pharisaic polemic in Luke 20:46 (Mark 12:39; Matt 23:6). The "first places" in Luke 14:7–8 are therefore certainly a tendentious invention of Luke; the banquet speeches themselves, on the other hand, are by no means a criticism of the Pharisees. This can be easily observed by an unbiased reader based on the content of the speeches themselves. We will also see in a moment that the first saying has grown—so to speak—in Pharisaic soil.[93]

The rabbinic parallels to Luke 14:8–11 are well known.[94] But have they been used objectively? Luke 14:11 goes back to Hillel, who lived before Jesus. Except in Luke 14:11, the sentence still occurs as an independent

---

93. In two Greek manuscripts, one of which is the Codex Bezae, in Latin Itala, and in some Syrian manuscripts, according to Matt 20:28, there is a *Logion* parallel to Luke 14:8–11. Jeremias puts the two texts on p. 21f., claiming that the "two very different Greek versions are due to one and the same Aramaic tradition." Unfortunately, my knowledge of Aramaic is much less than my Greek knowledge. I only know that the Greek of *Logion* (according to Matt 20:28) is a pure vulgar Greek.

94. See Herman Strack and Paul Billerbeck, *Kommentar zum Neuen Testament aus Talmud und Midrasch*, vol. 2 (Nördlingen: C. H. Beck, 1922), 204; Jeremias, *Die Gleichnisse Jesu*, 106, 191. On the two rabbinic sayings, see Bacher, *Die Agada der Tannaiten*, vol. 1, 5f., and the notes there and 413. Regarding the meaning of Hillel's statement, see Flusser, *Hillels Selbstverständnis und Jesus*, FrRu 27 (1975) 172–75, esp. 174. The text quoted is in WaR 1.5, ed. Margulies (Jerusalem, 1953), 16f., where the parallel texts are mentioned in the commentary. Hillel said, "My humiliation is my exaltation, my exaltation is my humiliation." From the wording and the accompanying psalm, we learn what Hillel meant by this: By humiliating myself, I exalt myself, and by exalting myself, I am humiliated. This beautiful existential slogan was then morally vilified. Now, it is no longer man who humbles and exalts himself, but God who humbles and exalts man. In b. Er. 13b, it says, "Whoever humbles himself, the Holy One exalts him, and whoever exalts himself, the Holy One humbles him." In the treatise Derech Eretz 7:36, ed. Higgery, vol. 1:146, we read, "When you humble yourself, the Holy One exalts you." In the Maschtot ze'irot, ed. Higger, 91, says, "Everyone who humbles himself is exalted." This saying of Hillel existed in Jesus' time and appears in the Gospels (Luke 14:1; 18:14; Matt 23:12; cf. Matt 18:4; John 4:10): "Everyone who exalts himself will be humbled, and he who humbles himself will be exalted."

saying in Luke 18:14, Matt 18:4; 23:12, and Jas 4:10. But the decisive text for the whole passage in Luke is the saying of Shimeon ben Azzai (around 110 CE) based on Prov 25:7: "For it is better to be told to you 'Come up here' than to be humiliated before a nobleman." Rabbi Shimeon ben Azzai said, "Move away from your seat two or three seats and then sit down." Descend, so that you can be told: Keep moving up! Don't move up, because you might be told: Get down! It is better to be told "climb up, climb up!" than to be told "descend, descend!" And so, Hillel used to say, "My humiliation is my exaltation, my exaltation is my humiliation. It is indeed said: 'He who exalts himself on the throne, he humbles himself by looking.'" (Ps 113:6).

This would be the right place to repeat the whole passage from Luke 14:8. "Do not take the first place, because you could be told 'Make room!' You would then have to take the lowest place. Rather, . . . go and settle down in the last place, so that they will say to you: friend, keep moving up. . . . For everyone who exalts himself will be humbled, and he who humbles himself will be exalted." We should not have to point out the simple fact that Luke 14:8 and the rabbinic parable are one and the same saying. The variants are by no means greater than between a saying of Jesus recorded in different Gospels. In this proverb, the saying of Hillel is expanded—namely, through the influence of Prov 25:7. Thus a new proverb was created that calls for humility in daily life.[95] Luke 14:8–11 makes it clear that this moral maxim is older than Rabbi Shimeon ben Azzai. This is certain, since Luke wrote his Gospel earlier. It is customary for the rabbinic tradent to pass on what has been learned. In our case, however, although I do not consider it very likely, it may also be that an older saying was mistakenly attributed to Shimeon ben Azzai because Shimeon ben Azzai said something similar in wording but different in meaning. He said, "By your name they will call you, and in the place that is due to you, they will put you, and from yours they will give you."[96] The older saying of exaltation and humiliation, also attested in

---

95. More precisely, in the rabbinic source, there is Hillel's utterance—which is expressly mentioned—according to the utterance of Ben Azzai, whose wording shows no outward signs of being influenced by Hillel's words. But it is quite possible that Hillel's words formed the starting point of the first saying and that they were brought by the inheritors of the tradition together with his own saying as an appendix. It is important that in Luke 14:8–11, the two sayings—that of Ben Azzai and the Hillels—are reflected in the same order.

96. The other saying is attributed to Ben Azzai in b. Yoma. 38a and b. For parallel texts and other attributions, see Bacher, *Die Agada der Tannaiten*, vol. 1, 411f., note 912.

the Gospel, has now been attributed to ben Azzai, because he also speaks—albeit in a different sense—of place that is due. As in the rabbinic parallel, the connection between the proverb of Hillel and the banquet occurs in Luke. From there it is possible, although not provable, that Jesus himself created the connection between the saying of exaltation and humiliation with the rules of the banquet. However, we must not forget that even if we should succeed in freeing a saying in the Gospels from the later Greek adaptations and recognizing its original Hebrew form, it is not yet certain whether the saying originates from Jesus or whether a Jewish saying was attributed to Jesus because it was considered worthy of him. This seems to be especially true for such words in the Gospels that have been heavily edited. We already accepted this for Luke 12:47. However, as in similar cases, it is also theoretically plausible here that Jesus acted like other Jewish teachers: He repeated a traditional saying because he agreed with its content. All these tracks do not lead me, though, to Jesus' authorship of Luke 14:8–11. I suggest that the maxim does not originate from Jesus nor that he adopted it. First, it is too similar to the rabbinic parable; and second (and more importantly), we have already guessed that Jesus' words to the host (Luke 14:12–14) are most likely a secondary formulation. As a result, the originality of the whole banquet speech becomes questionable. Frankly speaking, it seems to me that a morally pious maxim on how one should behave is too uncultured for Jesus! The banquet speeches are described by Luke as a parable. They are not, but people believed Luke and still believe it today. That is why we have examined the guest dinner speeches, and I hope we have even learned some principles in the process.

In Luke 17:7–10, there is the parable of the useless servants:

> "Which of you, who has a servant at the plow or on the field, says to him when he comes home from the field: 'Come here at once and sit down at the table?' Will he not rather say to him: 'Prepare me something to eat, gird yourself and serve me until I have eaten and drunk and afterwards do you like to eat and drink'? Does he need to thank the servant that he has done what he was ordered to do? So it is with you! If you have done everything you were ordered to do, then say 'We are unworthy servants; we have only done our duty.' "

The parable is not connected with either the previous one or the following one. Its subject (17:7–9) is strongly stylized in Greek, and Greek interventions are also noticeable in the interpretation. Jülicher explains the parable as follows:

In contrast to the desire for wages and the conceit that so easily sets in among the pious and righteous, not only among Pharisees but all the time, Jesus inculcates in his disciples that the best can never do more than his duty, that he may therefore make no claims to thanks on the part of God, just as a slave willing to serve raises such claims to his master.[97]

This is the best that can be said about the existing parable. However, if we take a closer look, difficulties arise. The interpretation in verse 10 seems to express a lesson: If we have fulfilled our duty to God, then we have done what we were required to do and must not count it as a special merit. Rabban Johanan ben Zakkai expressed it with the following words: "If you have done many deeds of Torah[98] do not keep it to yourself; that is why you were created."[99] The servant should not therefore demand any thanks from his master for his dutiful performance. Even before the time of Jesus, Antigonos of Socho had warned that the servant should not serve the Master for the sake of reward.[100] It is difficult, however, to understand why the servants who did what they were ordered to do are called "useless."[101] The Greek word can hardly be easily translated back into Hebrew here. In the New Testament, "useless servant" appears only in Matt 25:30. But this parallel does not help with our parable. Perhaps we are useless servants if we imagine that we have done our duty to God, but this is not explicitly stated in the text.

There are two major difficulties in the parable itself. The first difficulty arises when we ask what we can learn from the parable when we read that the servant must not only fulfill his workload of external work but also prepare the meal for the master. Why is the possibility being considered at all that the master can suggest to the servant to go to dinner right after the work in the field? At first, I thought to myself that there was a relic of a version according to which the servant is bad and useless because he thinks he has fulfilled his duty by working on the plow or at the farm and can therefore sit down at the table without further ado. But this is not written in the parable. Rather, it means that the Master requires the servant to fulfill his entire duty. If this is what is meant, however, then it does not seem to me to be expressed very skillfully. In any case, the motif of the demand to fulfill our whole duty is too strongly emphasized within the framework of the parable. After all, the

---

97. See also Jülicher, *Die Gleichnisreden Jesu*, vol. 2, 18.
98. See chapter 6, note 5, below.
99. Av. 2:8.
100. Av. 1:3.
101. See Jülicher, *Die Gleichnisreden Jesu*, 211.

main tendency is a different one. The parable wants to fight against our pride in the fulfillment of what we are obligated to do anyway. This brings us to the second difficulty—namely, verse 9: "Does he [the master] give thanks to the servant for having done what he was commanded to do?" The presupposed answer is no. Perhaps the view that God does not credit the man for doing his duty corresponds to Greek philosophy, but it does not correspond to the Judaism of that time nor to the proclamation of Jesus or Paul. To do our duty to God is to fulfill his will. Of course, they were convinced that this would be rewarded by God. Jesus and rabbinic Judaism emphasized the goodness of God and his mercy toward sinners and warned people against emphasizing their own merits. Jesus and Rabban Johanan ben Zakkai turned against this kind of self-righteousness in the same way. I therefore assume that the original content of verse 9 is inaccurately reproduced in the Gospel. Perhaps Jesus said something like this: "Does the servant take credit to himself that he has done what he was commanded to do?" This would have removed the unevenness between verses 9 and 10. The good Hebrew "so also with you" would then form a direct stylistic and factual continuation. I want to quote a related rabbinic parable here:

> Solomon said before the Holy One: "A king who hires workers, and they do their work well, and he gives them their wages—why is such a king to be praised? When is he worthy of praise? If he has hired bad workers who are not doing their job well and he gives them their wages after all, then it is his great favor." And Solomon also said, "The fathers have done their work and have received a good reward. What kind of favor was it that they were rewarded for their deeds? We are lazy workers—give us a good wage! For it is said 'The Master our God will be with us, as he was with our fathers' [1 Kgs 8:57]."[102]

Even externally, the two parables touch each other. "We are lazy workers," Solomon acknowledges and, according to the parable in Luke, we are also to acknowledge that "we are useless workers." Common to both parables are the main theme of the work ethic and the motif of work well done, which means the fulfillment of our duty toward God. A different paradox is extracted from this motif in both parables. According to Jesus, it is about the right attitude of man before God. If we have done everything that we owe to God, then we should not take it for our own benefit because it was our

102. Ziegler, *Die Koenigsgleichnisse des Midrasch beleuchtet durch die roemische Kaiserzeit*, chapter 6, parable 86; M. Tep., ed. Buber, 217. We usually translate from the better text in YalqM, ed. Buber, 174.

duty to do this and God is entitled to demand it of us. The rabbinic parable, on the other hand, is about the goodness of God: If a king pays workers the appropriate wage for their good work, then there is nothing praiseworthy of the king about it. But if he pays well for bad work, then he grants a great favor to unworthy workers. "We are lazy workers—give us a good wage!" There is no question that Jesus would fully approve of the rabbinic parable, since the same spirit blows in it that moved him in his preaching and parables. It is the spirit of special, often paradoxical sensitivity to the goodness of God and the loving understanding of human inadequacy that characterizes the main stream of rabbinic Judaism, which Jesus passed on to Christianity.

A particularly interesting proof that Jesus adopted rabbinic material, if he agreed with the rabbis' view, is the parable of the house on the rock. The parallels from rabbinic literature have long been known to researchers.[103] The parable is found in both Matthew (7:24–27) and Luke (6:47–49). I quote it here mainly according to the wording of Matthew:

> "Now everyone who hears my words[104] and does them is like a wise man who built a house[105] on a rock. The rain fell, the streams rose, the winds blew and beat that house. But it did not collapse, because it was founded on rocks. But anyone who hears and does not do[106] is to be compared to a foolish man who built a house on sand.[107] The rain came, the streams rose, the winds blew and beat against that house. It collapsed, and its fall was great."

The introductory sentence (Matt 7:24; Luke 6:47) belongs to the parable, which you know is about hearing and doing. If it were missing, then we would only know that the parable speaks of right and wrong action before

---

103. See Strack and Billerbeck, *Kommentar zum Neuen Testament aus Talmud und Midrasch*, vol. 1, 469–70; and Jülicher, *Die Gleichnisreden Jesu*, 267f.

104. Matthew: "These are my words." However, it is better to understand Matt 7:24, 26 as follows: "Anyone who hears these words from me." This construction is good Greek. *BDAG*, 63, cites Acts 1:4: "The promise which ye have heard out of my mouth." Thus, in the course of the history of research, Matt 7:24, 26 has often been misunderstood because of Luke 6:47. If I am right, then Luke read the same thing in Matthew in his Greek text. But he turned it into "my words" by omitting the disturbing word *these*. Also, Luke 21:33 par., where "my words" had already been written in the original, Luke apparently moved to this change. Finally, to align Luke 6:46 with Luke 6:47, Luke no longer speaks in 6:46 (like Matt 7:2) of the doing of the will of the heavenly Father but of the doing "which I say."

105. Matthew: "his house."

106. Matthew: "hear these words of mine and do them not."

107. Matthew: "his house."

God. As in many rabbinic parables as well as in Jesus' parables, the motif of the wise man and the fool appears here.

In the common source of Matthew and Luke, our parable followed a saying of Jesus in which Jesus kept himself from the cult of his person.[108] Matthew gives the first half of the proverb (7:21–23) before this parable, but Luke (6:46) gives only one verse. Jesus blames those followers who, although they worship him personally, do not pay attention to what is the main thing—namely, to do the will of the heavenly Father. The following "rock or sand" parable teaches that it is not enough just to listen—we must also act accordingly. Both sentences in the parable are organically connected with each other by the fact that they contain a right and an opposite wrong action. Outwardly, they sound like each other since they both begin with the word *everyone*. In the common source of Matthew and Luke, the two sections—the section against the cult of personality and our parable—stand at the end of Jesus' great Sermon on the Mount (or in the field). As we see from Matthew and from Luke, the source already mentioned hearing and doing the words of Jesus. This is a fitting conclusion to Jesus' sermon. When Matthew speaks more specifically of "these words of mine," he is referring to the Sermon on the Mount itself. In the source, the expression "my words" probably means the previous sermon. The expression appears there only once—namely, in the introduction of the parable (Matt 7:24 and Luke 6:47). Matthew introduces the phrase "these words of mine" once again in the introduction to the second half of the parable, whereas Luke simply says (in good Hebrew) only of hearing and not doing. The expression "my words" occurs only once more in the first three Gospels: in the concluding verse of another long speech by Jesus—namely, the Synoptic Apocalypse: "Heaven and earth will pass away, but my words will not pass away."[109] Here too, the saying, although not exclusively, refers mainly to Jesus' previous speech

---

108. Cf. in this regard, the articles mentioned in note 68. The continuation of the saying is found in Luke 13:26–30 and Matt 11.

109. The phrase "my words" still occurs in the usual texts of the parallel passages Mark 8:38 and Luke 9:26. But there are textual witnesses with Mark and Luke, in which "words" is missing. It says, "He who is ashamed of me and mine." This makes good sense, and it is easy to understand that "words" has been added secondarily. On the other hand, it is hard to imagine that one would have deleted the word in both Gospels, which would have suddenly created a new, unexpected sense. Another opinion is expressed by Bruce M. Metzger, *A Textual Commentary on the Greek New Testament* (London: United Bible Society, 1971), 99f., on Mark 8:38, who, among other things, did not consider that the word was missing in the

of the Synoptic Apocalypse. As is well known, this saying is a duplicate of Matthew 5:18, where the duration of the law of Moses is compared with the duration of heaven and earth. At the end of the Synoptic Apocalypse, Jesus speaks similarly of his own words. Is this original? Luke 21:33 par. is the conclusion of a speech that, as it is generally rightly assumed, was compiled by someone from the real sayings of Jesus. So, it is very likely that the editor wrote this fitting conclusion of the speech by transferring a real saying of Jesus about the law of Moses to these words of Jesus.

Let's get back to our parable! It opens with, as I have said, the phrase "my words" (Matt 7:24; Luke 6:47). At the same time, it concludes the Sermon on the Mount. Is the phrase "my words" also secondary (i.e., inserted in a way that fits the structure) to signal the conclusion of the Sermon on the Mount? I am inclined to this view, and my previous explanations lead me to this. If I am right, then we have no evidence in the first three Gospels that Jesus himself attached a special charismatic weight to his words as such. After both the Sermon on the Mount and the Synoptic Apocalypse, the phrase "my words" was put into Jesus' mouth by an editor as he wanted to emphasize the importance of Jesus' previous speech. In both cases, Jesus was speaking about the words of the law of Moses. But before we show this for the parable of the house built on a rock, it should be pointed out again that the saying against the cult of the personality of Jesus and our following parable are thematically related to each other. Maybe Jesus had said both on the same occasion. In any case, the two sayings were probably connected with each other in literary terms before the editor changed the words of the law to the words of Jesus to end the Sermon on the Mount with the parable adapted in this way. So, I suspect that the preceding word against the cult of personality came into the Sermon on the Mount together with the parable, because it was already connected earlier with the parable.

If Jesus did not use the phrase "these words of mine" in the parable of the house on the rock, then what did he say? Two possibilities are open, which essentially amount to the same thing. Either he said "the words of the law" or "the words of God." Both expressions are contemporary rabbinic phraseology. An aside look at two episodes in which tensions between Jesus and his family are reported can lead us a little farther here. In the first case, Jesus was told that his mother and brothers were standing outside and wanted to see him. But Jesus said, "My mother and my brothers—these are

---

Lukan parallel in some witnesses. See also Taylor, *The Gospel According to Saint Mark*, 521 and 383.

those who hear and do the word of God" (Luke 8:19–21).[110] In the second episode, a woman is reported to have praised Jesus' mother. Jesus then says, "Yes, but blessed are those who hear and keep the word of God" (Luke 11:27). To hear and do the word of God—or, with another Hebrew word, "keep"—was thus for Jesus the decisive command for people. In this, he agreed with other Jews, and he is an important witness of ancient Jewish thought here. We have already heard about the importance of doing the will of God in the saying against the cult of personality (Matt 7:21; cf. Luke 6:46). According to Jesus and his rabbinic contemporaries, however, we should not only do what is heard; we should also do and teach the commandments of the law. He reproaches the Pharisees for speaking about the law and not doing it (Matt 23:3). This expresses the general point of view of Jesus and contemporary rabbinic Judaism. Paul also adopts this view from his rabbinic past when he writes, "For it is not the hearers of the law who are righteous before God, but the doers of the law who will be justified" (Rom 2:13).

So, when Jesus spoke not of "my words" in Matt 7:24 and parallels but of the words of the law or of the word of God, then he represented the prevailing point of view of rabbinic Judaism at that time. In the second book of Moses (Exod 24:7), we read that Moses took the book of the covenant and read it to the people, and they said, "All that the Master has commanded, let us do and let us hear [it]!" So they put the doing before the hearing.[111] When Israel spoke these words, God called the angel of death and said to him, "Although I have made you ruler over men, you have no authority over these people, for they are my children" (cf. Deut 14:1).[112] So when Israel agreed to do and listen to everything that God had said, a heavenly voice said, "Who has revealed this secret to my children, which the ministering angels use?" For it is written that they "do God's words" and only then "listen to the voice of his word" (Ps 103:20).[113] It is not possible to say for sure whether

---

110. Mark 3:35 and following him Matt 12:50 speak of him who does the will of God.

111. This interpretation of Exod 24:7 can be found, for example, in MHG Shem, ed. M. Margulies, 554, and in MekhSh, 221.

112. WaR 18.3, ed. Margulies, 406; see Bacher, *Die Agada der Tannaiten*, vol. 2, 300. The one responsible for passing on this tradition is Rabbi Eliezer, the son of Rabbi Josse ha-Galili.

113. b. Šabb 88a; see Bacher, *Die Agada der Palästinischen Amoräer*, vol. 2 (Strasbourg: Trübner, 1896), 55. The one who passed it down is Rabbi Eleazar ben Pedath. See also Bacher, *Die Agada der Palästinischen Amoräer*, vol. 2, 165, 197, 394, 406, vol. 3, 139, 391f., 417, 489, 658.

Jesus directly knew and utilized this profound evaluation of this verse when he spoke of hearing and doing in the parable of the house on the rock. It is more important that this understanding of Exod 24:7 in the sense that doing precedes listening (i.e., learning) was an expression of an old Jewish view[114] that Jesus shared and represented outside of his parable sayings. The emphasis of the reality over mere learning was originally—probably in the wake of the appearance of Hillel, who regarded the learning of the Torah as a particularly high value—a reaction against the consequences of a one-sided religious intellectualism. To avert this danger, the best among the Jews declared that learning without doing was futile and fruitless. The deed (*ma'aseh*) means much more in the corresponding sayings than just the fulfillment of the commandments. It is the active realization of the will of the heavenly Father in the world:

> Why does it say "The commandment that I command you to do today" (Deut 11:22)? Because it says (in the same verse): "For if you keep (lit. 'observe') the whole law." One might think that if a person has kept the words of the law, he can sit down and does not have to do them. But it is also written "requests to do." So the purpose of keeping is to do it. If a person has learned the law, then he has fulfilled a commandment. If he has learned it and kept it, then he has fulfilled two commandments. If he has learned and kept and done, then there is nothing greater than this."[115]

It is the same tendency we also find in Jesus' parable of the house on the rock: The main thing is to do it!

Finally, at an important meeting of rabbinic scholars around 120 CE, the following decision was made on the question of whether learning or doing was more important: Learning is more important because it leads to doing.[116] The very nature of the compromise shows how important action was valued in Judaism at that time. Before this decision, there were only sources that considered action more important than learning. Thus Shimeon ben Gamliel, the son of Paul's teacher, whom we also know from the Jewish War of Josephus, says: "All my days I have grown up among the

---

114. On this view, see provisionally Adolf Büchler, *Types of Jewish-Palestinian Piety* (repr., New York, 1968), 81–91.

115. SifDev, ed. Finkelstein, 113. The Vatican manuscript (Assemani 32) reads: line 13 "shimmer," lines 14 and 15 "shimmer." See also Sifra in Lev 26:14.

116. See, inter alia, SifDev, ed. Finkelstein, 84–86. Also, Büchler, *Studies in Sin and Atonement in the Rabbinic Literature of the First Century*, 85n114; and Bacher, *Die Agada der Tannaiten*, vol. 1, 296n3.

wise and have found nothing better for man than silence. It is not the study of doctrine (*midrash*) that is the main thing, but it is the deed, and he who makes many words brings sin."[117] In the generation after the destruction of the temple, Rabbi Eleazar ben Azariah told a double parable on the same subject, which is also similar in motif to this double parable of Jesus:

> "Everyone whose wisdom is more abundant than his deeds, to whom can he be compared? To a tree whose branches are abundant and whose roots are sparse, and the wind comes and uproots it and turns it over. . . . But everyone whose deeds are more abundant than his wisdom, to whom can he be compared? To a tree whose branches are sparse, but whose roots are many and deep. Even if all the winds in the world come and blow on him, they cannot dislodge him from his place."[118]

Let us quote a similar saying of a Galilean contemporary of Jesus, Rabbi Hanina ben Dosa, who said,

> "Anyone to whom the fear of sin is more important than his wisdom, his wisdom will stand. And anyone to whom his wisdom is more important than the fear of sin, his wisdom will not stand." He used to say, "Everyone whose deeds are more abundant than his wisdom, his wisdom will stand. And everyone whose wisdom is more abundant than his deeds, his wisdom will not stand."[119]

Rabbi Hanina ben Dosa was a pious man and a miracle worker. When he died, it was said that the "men of deeds" stopped with him.[120] Hanina ben Dosa was an outstanding representative of this type of man, who were called "the pious men" and "the men of deeds." Without any doubt, Jesus also belonged to this class of people. We probably will not go wrong if we find our anti-intellectualism expressed in the saying "men of deeds." It is even possible that the concept of doing was so broad among these pious men that it included their supernatural deeds (miracles, answers to prayer, and so on). Because they were "men of action," they were accompanied by supernatural forces. Perhaps we suddenly came across a significant characterization of Jesus in the treatment of the parable of the stones. At the same time, we must not forget that the conviction to give preference to doing rather than just learning was common to the charismatics Hanina and Jesus as well as the rabbis.

---

117. Av. 1:17.
118. Av 3:17. See also Bacher, *Die Agada der Tannaiten*, vol. 1, 221.
119. Av 3:9.
120. m. Sot. 9:15.

Later, when the tension between learning and action was no longer fully understood, "deeds" included only "good work," not *opera meritoria* (meritorious works) but acts of love toward one's neighbor. Thus it was possible that the word *good* was interpolated at different times before "the deeds" into such sayings, which express the old tension between wisdom and deeds.[121] This certainly also happened with the rabbinic saying, which is rightly cited in connection with the parable of the house on the rock.[122] Elisha ben Abujah (around 120 CE) said,

> A man who has deeds[123] and has learned much Torah, to whom may he be compared? To a man who first builds with stones and then with bricks. Even if a lot of water comes and stops next to the stones, they do not dissolve them from their place. But a man who has no deeds[124] and has learned the Torah, to whom may he be compared? To a person who builds first with bricks and then with stones. Even if there is only a little water coming, they are about to be overturned.

Apart from minor differences, it is clear that the rabbinic parable and the parable of Jesus are one and the same parable. This becomes even clearer if we accept my assumption that Jesus did not transform a foreign parable for himself in such a way that he gave out the "word of God" or the "words of the law" as his own. I tried to reason that Jesus was speaking of the words of the law and that the change was made by the editor. So, did Jesus simply adopt a rabbinic parable or did Elisha ben Abujah repeat a parable of Jesus? The second possibility needs to be clarified more precisely. It seems to me to be almost certain that the parable was falsely attributed to Rabbi Elisha ben Abujah.[125] If this is correct, then the creator of the parable is unknown and Jesus could well have been that creator!

---

121. This can be found in the saying of Rabbi Eleazar ben Azaria (see note 118 above). In the father's sayings (3:17) the deeds, but in the edited parallel in ARN, chapter 22 of the "good deeds." See Bacher, *Die Agada der Tannaiten*, vol. 1, 221n2.

122. ARN, version A, chap. 24, ed. Schechter, 77. See also Strack and Billerbeck, *Kommentar zum Neuen Testament aus Talmud und Midrasch*, vol. 1, 469f.; Jülicher, *Die Gleichnisreden Jesu*, 267f.; Bacher, *Die Agada der Tannaiten*, vol. 1, 4321, 123; in the text: "good deeds."

123. In the text: "good deeds."

124. In the text: "good deeds."

125. "Elisha, son of Abuja," as Jülicher, *Die Gleichnisreden Jesu*, 267, calls him, should have been known to the learned theologian: it is about the famous rabbi who lost his faith. The fact that the parable was attributed only to Rabbi Elisha

The parable of the house on the rock is told excellently by Matthew. In Luke (6:47–49), it was stylistically and unfavorably edited and the explicit contrast between the wise man and the fool, which we know from the parables of Jesus and from rabbinic parables, has disappeared. The house of the foolish man is not built on sand, as in Matthew, but on land without a foundation. The rabbinic form of the parable speaks of a person who begins construction first with stones and then continues with bricks and vice versa. The type of construction, which is called correct here, was widespread at that time. However, it is very possible that Jesus' version of the rock and the sand is original and the rabbinic variant is secondary.[126] The rabbinic text speaks of a man who has learned the law and either has deeds or does not have them. Jesus is also talking about someone who heard and either did or did not do them. Both expressions correspond to the thinking of that time. We have seen that Jesus also speaks of hearing and doing in other

---

is very likely if you look at ARN, version A, chapter 24, and compare it with the parallel text of version B, chapter 35. After the father's sayings (Av 4:20), Elisha ben Abuja said, "Who learns as a child, to what might he be compared? Ink written on new paper. And who as an old man learns, to what might he be compared? Ink written on erased paper." In verse B of ARN, we read that Elisha invented another parable for the same purpose: "He who has learned as a child is like the lime that is painted on stones and cannot be wiped off by the rain, whereas he who learns as an age is like the lime that is painted on bricks," etc. There is also a parable in version B in which the Torah is compared to a bird that should not escape. Both parables are taken out of their original context in version A. The parable of the lime is now reinterpreted as deeds and learning; see Strack and Billerbeck, *Kommentar zum Neuen Testament aus Talmud und Midrasch*, vol. 1, 69. In version A, three more parables with the same theme are added, of which at the beginning of the chapter, the first parable is ours. This reinterpretation and sequencing could easily happen because our parable is also about stones and bricks. So, in version A of ARN, only those sayings really seem to come from Rabbi Elisha ben Abuja that deal with the privilege of learning at a young age. The reason why one transferred to Elisha ben Abuja parables, which reproach the one who has learned but does not do anything, is easy to understand. Elisha ben Abuja was taught, but his deeds were evil. Eccl 5:5: "Do not give your mouth to sin against your body. . . . Why should God be angry with your voice and destroy the work of your hands?" Cf. Bacher, *Die Agada der Tannaiten*, vol. 1, 431. It should also be borne in mind that at this time, people often built in such a way that they started with stones and continued with bricks. But it may be that on this point, our parable was adapted to the following parable, which also speaks of stones and bricks. So could the parable in ARN, version A, chap. 24, as in the case of Jesus, who once acted from rock and sand?

126. See the end of note 125 above.

ways, whereas the Greek word *manthanein* ("to learn") in the specifically rabbinic pedagogical sense strangely does not appear in the Gospels. The places where *manthanein* occurs (e.g., Mark 13:28 par. Matt 9:13; 11:29) all have the meaning of "to experience, to be taught." Comparing the rabbinic form with the parable of Jesus, we can see not only that the parable of Jesus is better told and more beautiful, but also that we have the feeling that the parable of Jesus is more original. Since it corresponds to the understanding of Judaism that Jesus otherwise represents, we will not be able to deny the parable of Jesus. However, it is not certain that Jesus himself was the creator of the parable for two reasons: first, his parable was also handed down as a rabbinic parable; and second, although it expresses Jesus' point of view, we cannot call the content of the parable "specifically Christian."[127] Why couldn't Jesus have an older parable on his lips that he thought important to share with his listeners? Does this make it less important for Christians? We can learn from the parable of the house on the rock what Jesus meant, for example, in Luke 8:21 (cf. also Luke 11:28) when he spoke of hearing and doing the word of God. This parable of Jesus is no less interesting for the spiritual history of ancient Judaism. It is the oldest datable evidence of a significant concept in Judaism. Here, Jesus also shows himself from his most obvious side: He was a Jew!

The parable of the house on the rock belongs to the kind of parables that can be called the "craftsman's comparisons."[128] In order to vividly bring a person to correct moral behavior, one compares that behavior with properly performed manual work. Such comparisons have been common in Greek philosophical literature since Socrates, who especially distinguished himself in this kind of comparison. Even the rabbis were no strangers to this as we have seen from the parallels to Jesus' parable of the house on the rock. In the Gospels, there are two other "craftsman comparisons" in the double comparison of the tower and the king:

> "For who of you who wants to build a tower does not sit down first and count the cost, whether he has enough funds to finish the project. He is preparing himself so that not, for example, when he has laid the foundation and the

---

127. Jülicher, *Die Gleichnisreden Jesu*, 267.

128. See Olof Gigon, *Kommentar zum ersten Buch von Xenophons Memorabilien* (Basel: Reinhardt, 1953), 62.133C. A fine comparison of craftsmen can be found, for example, in b. Hag. 9b in Hillel's answer to the second question of Bar He He: "Go and learn this in the street of the donkey drivers; ten *parasongs* for one Zuz, eleven *parasongs* for two Zuz!"

execution is not enough, all those watching will begin to mock him and say 'This man began to build but could not complete it!' Or what king, who goes out to make war with another king, will not sit down first and keep counsel, whether he is able to meet with ten thousand men the one who comes up against him with twenty thousand? But if not, then while he is still far away, he sends out an ambassador and asks for peace. So then none of you who has not renounced everything can be my disciple." (Luke 14:28–33)

The double comparison is designed in Greek idiom. We will hardly find traces of Hebrew in the writing style. The Jewish Hellenistic philosopher Philo expresses a similar thought as he speaks of the struggle between vice and virtue:

> She [Virtue], it is said, allows herself to be taken care of, if she is to get in-volved in a scuffle, to test her own strength beforehand in order to succeed if she is strong enough to enter the battle, but otherwise not to venture on the battlefield at all. For it is not shameful that vice is the subject, the essence of which is shame; but it is certainly a disgrace when virtue is the subject, since it is, above all, entitled to beautiful glory, which is why it is accustomed either to triumph or to assert itself unconquered.[129]

Philo speaks of the need for proper assessment before the struggle of virtue with vice. He uses a different comparison: namely, the testing of one's own strength before getting involved in a scuffle.

The stoic philosopher Epictetus[130] advises that we need to think about a matter and check our own abilities if we must decide; otherwise, we will suffer shipwreck. If someone wants to win the Olympic games, he must be aware that he must go through hard training. Before choosing the profession of a philosopher, a person should consider what profession is proper, and he should examine his nature to know what he can do. Caution before deciding to become a philosopher is the main thing, according to Epictetus. The athlete's training is a comparison. Among the Greeks, even according to Philo, the philosopher is often compared to an athlete. Aside for one exception I know,[131] such comparisons are missing in rabbinic literature and in

---

129. Jülicher, *Die Gleichnisreden Jesu*, 206.

130. Epictetus, *Dissert.* 3, chap. 15; see Jülicher, *Die Gleichnisreden Jesu*, 214.

131. The evidence is strengthened in Jalkut ha-Mechiri, *JQR 15* (1924/25), (Jerusalem, 1968), 185, to Hos 7:1–5: "It is I who stretched out their arms to *yasarti*." The author understands the Hebrew *jasarti* as "chastisement," and at the same time, as if written *asarti* ("I have forbidden, I have bound"), and says: "The Holy One

the New Testament. I cite the Greek analogies to the double comparison of the tower and the king not because I consider the double comparison to be non-Jewish because of its Greek style, but because I want to show the kinship between Jewish parables of this kind and their Greek parallels. Later, I will address the fundamental question of whether it is possible that the rabbinic parables are indirect descendants of the philosophical comparisons of the Greeks.

In the double parable of the tower and the king, Jesus "imprints the admonition: think it over carefully."[132] In Luke 14:33, the comparison is followed by an interpretation. However, most commentators assume that this interpretation does not fit the comparison as it is about self-examination, not self-expression. To better understand the situation, we should consider that the entire section (Luke 14:25–35) that deals with the conditions of discipleship was compiled by Luke or a previous editor. Each saying was provided by the editor with the same refrain: "cannot be my disciple" (Luke 14:26b, 27b, 33b). Only the last saying about salt ends with different conclusion: "Whoever has ears to hear, let him hear!" (Luke 14:35b). Before our double comparison, there are two other sayings of Luke (14:25–27): the one about hating one's own family, and the one about carrying the cross. They are taken from the common source of Matthew and Luke and correspond to three sayings in Matthew (10:37–39).[133] The first two are also provided there with a refrain that, however, is different from Luke: "He is not worthy of me."[134] After the double comparison, Luke (14:34) mentions salt, which we

---

said: 'I have said that I will chastise them by prohibitions in this world, so that their arms become strong for the world to come.'" So, the prohibitions are like the straps on the wrestler's fist: they strengthen his arms for the future world.

132. Jeremias, *Die Gleichnisse Jesu*, 195, and chapter 3, note l.

133. Although it seems that in Luke 14:26 two sayings of Jesus, which stand independently in Matt 10:37 and 39, have been drawn together and that the words "yes, his own soul" from the other saying have been inserted there, the matter is not certain. It could be that Luke is the original reading here. Hating one's family and one's own soul in Luke 14:26 may be an allusion to Jer 12:7f.: "I have forsaken my house, I have cast off my inheritance, I have delivered the beloved of my soul into the hand of their enemies. . . . Therefore I hate it [i.e., my inheritance]." Then the verse in Luke 17:32 would be original. Matthew 10:39 and Mark 8:35 par. would then also be imitated in this verse under the influence of the Master's word in Luke 14:26. The whole complex Synoptic situation would still have to be handled. See the following note.

134. The second statement (of the cross) and the third statement (of the soul) from Matthew (10:38) is found in Matt 16:24f., Mark 8:34f., and Luke 9:23f.

find again in Matthew (5:13) and which is heavily edited in Mark. Another thing, according to the Lukan story, Jesus is in the house of a Pharisee for the Sabbath meal (14:1–24), and then (Luke 14:25) the passage in which the double comparison is located is introduced with the words "But a large crowd came with him, and he turned and spoke to them." So, we suddenly learn that Jesus is on a journey.[135] In reality, the verse is an introduction created by Luke or a previous editor to mark the beginning of the section. The question of whether the refrain of Matthew or that of Luke were in their common source is difficult to decide.[136] It is not impossible that Jesus once said, "So none of you who does not renounce everything he has can be my disciple." In fact, Jesus demanded, even if not from all those who wanted to accept the message of the kingdom, yet from those who wanted to follow him, an absolute poverty. However, all these considerations do not lead to the conclusion that Luke 14:33 is a real saying of Jesus. Nor can it be proven that this verse from the beginning relates to the double parable as an interpretive statement. As already mentioned, the interpretation fits quite poorly with the comparison. The verse shares with the double comparison the absence of the Hebrew sound but exhibits the Greek conception. However, Jesus' views were well known to the editor. Since he realized that the double comparison was unclear without an explicit interpretation, he probably attached the sentence he had formulated to the comparison. That is not to say that the double comparison does not come from Jesus either. But where the author got it and what it originally meant, I do not know. If the whole thing were not so Greek, edited and clumsily written, we could perhaps speak with greater courage of an original connection between the comparison and its interpretation. Let us remember that there was a time when it was difficult for a rich man to make the decision to part with his property to follow Jesus (Luke 18:22 par.), so you must think carefully about such a step beforehand. But even this case hardly sheds any light on the murky Lukan double comparison and its interpretation, which do not quite fit together.

Finally, let us deal with the little parable of the two debtors (Luke 7:40–43). Its importance, as far as I see, is not sufficiently emphasized by researchers or by teachers. This parable is embedded in the story of the penitent woman in the house of Simon the Pharisee. This story has a duplicate

---

135. See also Hans Conzelmann, *Die Mitte der Zeit: Studien zur Theologie des Lukas* (Tübingen: Mohr Siebeck, 1954), 60.

136. Klostermann, *Das Matthäusevangelium*, HANT 4 (Tübingen, 1971), 92, considers the Lucan form to be more original.

in Mark 14:3–9 and in Matt 26:6–13, and it does not say that the woman was a sinner. She also did not anoint the feet of Jesus there, but poured the oil on his head. The anointing, which is a part of the story of Jesus' passion there, is interpreted by Jesus as an anointing for his funeral and "where the gospel is proclaimed in all the world, her [the woman's] deed will also be spoken of for her memory." It is often believed that Luke did not write down this parallel story because he had already told our story here, without any relation to the passion. It seems to me that Mark knew something about the story told by Luke and that Mark introduced her to the story of the passion. In doing so, he ignored its central moral tenet and instead interpreted this anointing in the sense of the piety of the cross. He himself later reports (Mark 16:1 and parallels) that the women intended to anoint the dead Jesus. I also trust Mark to have invented the protest of those present and Jesus' rebuke (Mark 14:4–8). Influenced by Mark, Matthew also correctly omitted the first, original story (cf. Luke 7:36–50).[137] John 12:1–9 combines the two variants.[138] At one point, Mark may have preserved the original tradition; he speaks of Simon the Leper and not of Simon the Pharisee (like Luke). Perhaps Luke turned the leper into a Pharisee to clearly distinguish Jesus' love for sinners from the views of his host. Otherwise, the narrative in Luke seems to be the primary form of the story (7:36–50) and the secondary form of the story in Mark (14:39f. and parallels).

Another question is whether Jesus told the parable of the two debtors on this occasion (according to Luke) and how far it was preserved in the original wording. When Simon doubted the prophetic gift of Jesus, because in his opinion Jesus had not recognized the woman as a sinner, Jesus said to him, "Simon, I have something to tell you." Simon said, "Speak, Master!" And then Jesus continued: "A money-lender had two debtors. One owed five hundred denarii, the other fifty. Since they could not pay, he gave it to both of them. Which of the two will love him the most?" Simon answered and said, "I think the one he gave the most to." But he said to him: "You have judged rightly." Then Jesus compared the woman's acts of love with the host's behavior. "That is why I tell you," he said to him at the end, "her sins,

---

137. The story originally ended with Luke 7:47. Verses 48f. are taken from the healing of the man with gout (Luke 5:20f. par.). Verse 50 comes from Luke 8:48 (see par. and Luke 18:42; Mark 10:52).

138. See Raymond E. Brown, "The Gospel According to John," vol. 1, *AYB* (New Haven: Yale University Press, 1966), 449–54. The solution to the relationship between the variants of the story is different there from the one we suggested.

though they are many, are forgiven her; she has shown the most love of all. But to whom little is forgiven, loves little." With this interpretation of the parable, the story ends.[139] The moral proposition is correct, but the parable would be understandable even without it.

There are now two difficulties, though in my opinion, they are not insurmountable. The first is that, according to the framework of the parable, the sinful woman did more acts of love to Jesus than the host. But the parable speaks about the fact that the one who has been forgiven more sins loves God more. The discrepancy between the historical situation and the parable consists, first, in the fact that the doctrine of the parable cannot be smoothly deduced from the situation, and therefore the parable—as is customary with Jesus—does not lead to a properly pure result. But it also consists in the fact that the woman's deeds of love spring from her loving heart and are not the result of her gratitude to God, who forgave her many sins. The woman found out about the forgiveness only after she had accomplished her deeds of love. But perhaps it was so that the parable that Jesus told served, so to speak, as an introduction to the forgiveness of the sins of the woman. The fact that Jesus' subsequent words to the host do not exactly continue the thought of the parable is not particularly serious. Conversations, as well as other events of life, do not always unfold linearly. It is therefore good to keep the discrepancy between the historical framework and the parable of the two debtors in evidence. However, it does not force us to assume that the parable was subsequently inserted into the framework.

The second difficulty lies in the teaching of the parable itself. First, the subject and its motifs are excellent. It is about the paradox that arises when a lender acts in the same way and for the same reason toward the two debtors: he lets the debt go for both of them because neither can pay. On the other hand, one is ten times guiltier than the other. That is why the big difference arises in the gratitude of the two of them. He who is forgiven little loves little. The great sinner, to whom God has forgiven many sins, loves God more than the righteous one. Here we find ourselves clearly in Jesus' real sphere of interest: he did not come to call the righteous, but sinners (Matt 9:13 par.). The difficulty lies in the fact that at first glance it seems that the lesser sinner is being disadvantaged. It also lies in the fact that one does not understand why it should be important here that the sinner loves God more than the righteous one. Otherwise, it is usually the other way around that Jesus and Judaism talk about the overflowing mercy of God for

---

139. See note 137 above.

sinners. Shimon ben Yochai (second century CE) explicitly said that God's love for man is more important than man's love for God. "Israel loves God, but God loves the proselytes." It is written: "Those who love you are like the sun when it rises in its splendor" (Judg 5:31). But who is greater? The one who loves the king, or the one whom the king loves? Of course, the one the king loves! It is said: "And he loves the proselyte" (Deut 10:18).[140] I suppose that Jesus would not have denied that God's love for man is more important than man's love for God. In our case, however, Jesus wanted to establish that the sinner loves God more than the righteous one. Jesus apparently means that the sinner clings to God more than the righteous because of his great love for God. This opinion of Jesus seems, to me, to be sharply defined.

---

140. MekhY to Exod 22:20, ed. Horov., 31, 1; see Bacher, *Die Agada der Tannaiten*, vol. 1, 103.

5

REAL AND SUPPOSED ALLEGORIES

We have examined the framework and interpretations of Jesus' parables and some of his parable images in the Gospels. A first result is urgently needed as the pessimism of modern researchers in this direction is exaggerated! The interpretations of the parables in the Gospels are not as bad as we often assume. Especially with the most important and pronounced parables, they are basically correct. This applies to parables that come from Jesus himself and are sometimes partially edited, as well as to those that perhaps come from the Jewish environment of Jesus and have been editorially inserted into the Gospels.

There are also cases where the editor misunderstood the parable. In these cases, the editor's hand is evident throughout the parable. He also modified the introductions to the parables and the editorial framework. Even in those cases where the introduction and frame are secondary, the editor did not stop before reaching the parable but intervened in it, trying to achieve a new harmony between parable and meaning. Our linguistic investigations have shown that all later editors worked only at the Greek stage of tradition. They had little firsthand knowledge of the essence of Hebrew parables, which included Jesus' parables. Many of them—perhaps all of them—probably did not know that outside of Jesus' parables there were other parables of this kind in the Hebrew tradition of Jesus' time. But even without this knowledge, in most cases, they could easily understand what Jesus meant by his parables. Recording the meaning of the parables was also not so difficult because most of Jesus' parables—like the classical rabbinic parables—generally preached benevolent moral-religious teachings within the framework of the Jewish monotheistic faith.

It should also be noted that Jesus often added an interpretation to his parables, either at the beginning or at the end. He did this mainly whenever the parable would have been difficult to understand without an interpretation. We should therefore fight the temptation to play out the parable against its interpretation at all costs. If we deprive Jesus' parables of their natural protection, then they become free as birds and anyone can insert their own interpretation into the parables without resistance. The modern Christianization of Jesus' parables by today's interpreters is, accordingly, immensely stronger and more profound than the various editorial stages in the Gospels.

One result of our research should be emphasized here: Examination of the changes in the Gospels cannot legitimately start primarily from kerygmatic theological-ideological currents. Rather, it should be literary-critical for the time being. An example of how fruitful such a method can be is the analysis of the Lukan framework of the double parable of the sheep and the penny (Luke 15:1–10). There, we showed that the introduction, by which the double parable became a merciless criticism of the Pharisees and scribes, is a secondary formation of the editor, imitated by the description of another, probably historical incident (Luke 5:29–32). This secondary formation could arise because its author presupposed a constant, hostile rift between Jesus and his Pharisee adversaries. In other words, it is postulated that Jesus' relationship with sinners differs diametrically from the standpoint of Pharisaic-rabbinic Judaism. One should not speak too early of testimonies of a moral revolution when there are rather vulgar distortions behind it. I dare to say this because I know and acknowledge the revolution of Jesus. It was made possible only by Pharisaic-rabbinic presuppositions. Therefore, the parable of God's mercy to the erring was unreservedly acceptable to most "Pharisees and scribes." For the author of the framework, however, it was self-evident that the parable was directed against the Pharisees and scribes, so he had a preconceived opinion. This supposed gap between Jesus and the rest of the Jews is described today, for example, as follows for a broad readership: "In the Jewish law, but breaking its narrowness, Jesus' teaching had to become a 'nuisance' to all directions of Jewish religiosity, especially since the time of the Pharisees and Sadducees."[1] Why must that be? So that Christianity, as an independent religion, could set itself apart from its mother soil of Judaism! Not much has changed in this respect since the pre-Lukan church until today—at most, much for the worse! The ideological prejudice is thus based on the introduction of the double parable. Your author probably did not think much more than his modern descendant, whose words I have just quoted.

The changes in the Greek stage of the Gospels are determined, in particular, by the interaction of two factors: by ideological motifs and by literary "retouching" of the editors who believed this to be right and necessary so

---

1. The Fischer Lexicon, *Geschichte in Gestalten*, vol. 2 (Frankfurt, 1963), 255f.

that the picture would become clearer. The religious motifs and judgments were already understood in the traditional circles from which the editors and the first three evangelists came, and and they are as evident today to simple Christians. But the fact that ideologizations and retouching took place so early is not as strange as it might seem. The central forces of a new religious group usually reach their first standstill after only a few years. The parables in the Gospels were revised at a stage of retardation or standstill. This revision took place more gently than one usually assumes. The editors wanted to retouch the religious-ethical content of parables, rather than proclaim their own ideas or ideologies through the mouth of their Savior. Therefore, one finds in the parables much rarer and much less profoundly settled ecclesiastical-christological motifs than researchers think today. Comparisons with rabbinic parables have also shown that much of what has been explained as Christology or a delay of the parousia has nothing to do with either of these concepts. Even the element of Christian discipline has attacked the very core of the important and pronounced parables less than is often thought. Here, too, the editing is rather external. If we are willing to recognize that Jesus' parables—like rabbinic parables—were originally moral paraeneses culminating in moral demands, then we can understand that not much fundamental change was needed to make their fruitfulness possible, even in new congregations. The editors and the evangelists understood the moral character of the parables without much theology. In this way, the parables were interpreted christologically by the fathers of the church. They are also the ones who allegorized the parables, because they no longer understood them as moral imperatives but mostly as Christ's statements about himself. The allegorization of the parables was a necessary consequence of the christological interpretation of Jesus' parables by the church fathers.

Modern researchers usually assume with Jülicher that Jesus' parables were free of any allegory. But even in the Gospels, they were sometimes extended and edited by allegorical features. The fathers of the church would have then increased this inclination even more. In my opinion, this addresses the issue of allegory in Jesus' parables from the wrong angle. If allegory means that the subjects and motifs of Jesus' parables all represent something else, then his parables are not allegories. However, if allegory means that a narrated event is not merely what occurred but that the narrative is not autonomous and aims at a "moral of the story" and that both the subject and some of its motifs have a precise determinable meaning on another level, then both Jesus' and rabbinic parables are allegories. Before talking about allegory, we should first understand what is meant by this term. It is even more important to clarify the nature of the genre of parables in the Gospels and from the rabbis through literary analyses.

Nevertheless, the question remains whether Jesus' parables were subsequently allegorized in the Gospels. This should be shown mainly in the interpretations. As far as I can see, there is only one true allegorical interpretation in the Gospels—namely, in the explanation of the parable of wheat and the weeds. We have already shown that the allegorical propositions are a secondary addition: "He who sows the good seed is the Son of Man. The field is the world. The good seed, these are the sons of the kingdom. But the weeds are the sons of evil one. The enemy who sows it is the devil. The harvest is the end of the age, and the harvesters are angels." We find a similar phenomenon in the interpretation of the parable in the primitive Christian text the Shepherd of Hermas (end of the first or the first half of the second century CE).[2] There it is said, "The field is this world, the master of the field, the one who created everything. . . . The Son is the Holy Spirit," and so on.[3] The first sentence, "the field is the world," occurs almost literally in the allegorical interpolation of the parable of the weeds (Matt 13:37–40). Reading through the parable and its interpretations in Hermas, one gets the impression that an invasion from the Gospels is unlikely. A similarly pronounced allegorical interpretation can be found in a rabbinic parable of the late type:[4] "The king is God and the city, which is the land of Israel, and the household is David, the king of Israel." As I mentioned earlier, the pronounced allegorical interpretation of the parable of the weeds is certainly a later interpolation of Matthew. The parable of the fourfold field is the only parable of Jesus that is followed by an authentic interpretation

---

2. The last part of the Shepherd of Hermas contains parables that are visions of Hermas. The only parable that is not a vision, but is told by the shepherd to Hermas, is our parable (similitudo 5). At the same time, it is the only parable in this text that is in the style of Jesus' parables and rabbinic parables. On the nature, secondary extensions, and successive different interpretations of the parable, see Martin Dibelius, *The Shepherd of Hermas* (Tübingen: Mohr Siebeck, 1923), 564f. The foundation of the parable is closely related to a rabbinic parable; see SifDev, ed. Finkelstein, 16. One can therefore rightly assume that the author of "Hermas" adopted the parable from rabbinic literature in some way. Unfortunately, this is not the place to treat the parable thoroughly.

3. Shepherd of Hermas 58:2 (Sim. 5.5).

4. M. Tep., ed. S. Buber, 203; Ziegler, *Die Koenigsgleichnisse des Midrasch beleuchtet durch die roemische Kaiserzeit*, chapter 6, parable 15.

with allegorical features; that is, one that comes from Jesus himself (Luke 8:1–15). Stylistically, this interpretation is similar to the two examples just discussed—namely, the Shepherd of Hermas and the rabbinic parable from Midrash Tehillim. The reason for the allegorical anomaly is, as will be seen, that the parable of the fourfold field is not a parable in the full sense. Rather, it consists of four parallel comparisons that are dramatized by an action. The focus is not on the action but on the four comparisons that make up the interpretation. As with the Shepherd of Hermas and the rabbinic parable from the Midrash Tehillim, we can also speak of an exceptional case here. Exceptional cases show that, in their essence, the parables are related to allegorical narratives. Each parable points to a truth that is outside of itself and different from itself.

So, were the parables of Jesus subsequently allegorized in the Gospels? Except for Matthew 13:37b–40, this can hardly be said. Regarding the alleged christological allegorization in the Gospels, Joachim Jeremias says, "Burglar, householder, merchant, king were interpreted as Christ, while originally the Christological self-statement was at most concealed and only in some parables in the background."[5] What Jeremias says about Jesus' references to himself in the parables is basically true. As far as I can see, Jesus spoke of himself only in the parable of the wicked winegrowers (Luke 20:9–19 par.). In addition, in the parable of the stronger and the strongest (Luke 11:21f. par.), he spoke in a veiled way about his messianic dignity. Perhaps the bridegroom in the parable of the ten virgins (Matt 25:1–13) is the coming Son of Man—thus indirectly Jesus himself. But can it be said, for example, that it is an additional allegory if in the Gospels a symbolic figure for God becomes a symbolic figure for Christ? Was the parable previously less "allegorical"? One thing must not be overlooked: Many parable motifs, which modern interpreters claim as christological additions, prove to be motifs are the very essence of Jewish parables when compared with rabbinic parables. The parable of the servant entrusted with supervision (Matt 24:45–51; Luke 12:42–46) can serve as an example. Neither in the Matthean nor in the Lukan final version can I discover a reference to the parousia of Christ.[6] Also, the text "The master of this servant shall come in the day when he does not expect it, and in the hour when he does not know it" does not refer to the final appearing of Christ. We have already discussed the parable of Rabbi Nathan

---

5. Jeremias, *Die Gleichnisse Jesu*, 64; the section on allegorization is on pages 64–88.

6. I am in contrast to Jeremias, *Die Gleichnisse Jesu*, 53f.

about a master who gave his servants silver and gold to trade and who also warned them against mutual robbery. But when the master returned to the servants after a while, he found them outside naked and all their belongings inside, so the king took all their stolen goods away from them. There is then a comparison with the death of the sinner.[7] If this rabbinic parable were to be found in the Gospels, examining it using the usual methods, we would almost certainly run into error. It would be an original Christian paraenesis that exhorts the Christian community "not to be tempted by the absence of parousia."[8] The same would result from a cross-examination: if the New Testament parable of the supervised servant were in rabbinic literature, then it would probably not occur to any Jewish interpreter to infer, based on the unexpected coming of the master, that the main emphasis of the parable is christological-eschatological. It is possible that the author of the common source of Matthew and Luke understood the unexpected coming of the Master as a reference to the parousia of Christ. In the Gospel text as such, however, there are no signs of such a christological interpretation.

In the parable of Rabbi Nathan, it is said that the master gave the servants silver and gold to trade. This idea is also a central motif in Jesus' parable of the entrusted talents (Matt 25:14–30; Luke 19:12–27). As in the rabbinic parable, the master goes far away and then returns. As we have already seen, Luke understood the parable of the entrusted money as fighting against the idea that "now the kingdom of God must immediately appear" (Luke 19:11). He added the idea of the pretender as an additional motif, but it does not seem certain to me whether Luke "saw the Son of Man ascended into heaven and returning to judgment"[9] in the nobleman who takes on royal dignity and demands an account from the servants on his return. Matthew understood the parable as a warning to be vigilant because no one knows when the end time will come. But no christological traits can be found in his version.[10]

---

7. See Jeremias, *Die Gleichnisse Jesu*, chapter l, note 7.

8. See Jeremias, *Die Gleichnisse Jesu*, 55, for a parable of the servant in charge.

9. Jeremias, *Die Gleichnisse Jesu*, 57.

10. See, on the other hand, Jeremias, *Die Gleichnisse Jesu*, 57f. The phrase "enter into the joy of the master" (Matt 25:21–23) is also not certainly christological. Joy is an eschatological gift in Judaism. The phrase found in Matt 25:30, "the darkness without" where there will be "weeping and gnashing of teeth," is secondary. The same is true of Matt 22:13 and very likely for Matt 13:42, 50; 24:51. Matthew 8:12, on the other hand, is original, as the parallel in Luke 13:28 shows where "the darkness outside" is missing.

In the parable of the banquet (Matt 22:1–14; Luke 14:16–24), the Matthean "urge toward the allegorical"[11] itself shows, if one can call an adaptation as such, the purpose of which was to make clear historical allusions—which one would suspect from a parable! According to Matthew, some invitees mistreated the king's messengers and beat them to death. "The king was angry. He sent forth his armies, and slew these murderers, and burned their city" (Matt 22:7). According to Matthew, the meaning of this verse is that Jerusalem was destroyed as punishment for the mistreatment and killing of many of the first generation of Christians by Jews. In the light of this interpretation, the emphasis of the following sentence also becomes clear: "Then he [the king] said to his servants: 'The wedding is ready, but the invited ones were not worthy'" (Matt 22:8). Instead of the unworthy guests, pagans come to the wedding feast. The rejection of the Jews and the transfer of divine election to the Gentiles belong to the ideology of Matthew, who was most likely a Gentile Christian, the oldest witness of Gentile Christian anti-Judaism.[12] Elsewhere, Matthew writes in the same sense that "the sons of the kingdom shall be cast out into darkness" and that others shall come in their place (Matt. 8:11). It is also Matthew who has Jesus say, "The kingdom of God will be taken from you and given to a people who will bear its fruit" (Matt 21:43). The new interpretation was not cleverly incorporated into the parable by Matthew. He thereby distorted its meaning from the theological to the historical. Originally, the parable called for readiness for God; now it was given historical dimensions. The disobedient invitees—a universally human symbol—became an image of the rightly punished and rejected Jewish people. I would not call this an allegorization but a tendentious narrowing of the original, generally valid moral symbolism. Whether the Lukan form of the banquet of the parable alludes to the vocation of the Gentiles instead of the Jews is more than questionable.[13] After Luke 14:21, the host[14] sends messengers to find guests "in the streets and alleys of the city." Perhaps the city was already mentioned in the common source of Mat-

---

11. Cf. Jeremias, *Die Gleichnisse Jesu*, 65. In my opinion, Jeremias goes too far in his identification of "allegorical" elements of the parable.

12. Cf. chapter 4, note 1. See also Flusser, "Some Notes on Easter and the Passover Haggadah," *Immanuel* 7 (1977): 52–60, esp. 53; Ernst L. Abel, "Who Wrote Matthew?" *NTS* 17 (1971): 138–52; and Lloyd Gaston, "The Messiah of Israel as Teacher of the Gentiles," *Interp* 29 (1975): 24–40.

13. Otherwise Jeremias, *Die Gleichnisse Jesu*, 67.

14. Luke—not quite rightly—does not call him "the master of the house." See chapter 2, note 5.

thew and Luke in an indefinite way. Matthew identified it as Jerusalem to indicate Jerusalem's destruction. After Luke 14:24, the host said at the end, "For I tell you, none of those men who were invited will taste my meal." This does not mean the rejection of disobedient Israel. In a rabbinic parable with the same main theme, the host says at the end, "These may eat and drink, but those shall stand, watch, be beaten and mourn."[15] So, we can see how careful we must be in interpreting Jesus' parables.

Was the parable of the wicked farmers (Luke 20:9–19 par.) originally less "allegorical" and then subsequently "allegorized"? This parable occupies a special position among Jesus' parables because his concern is not a moral demand but rather the person of Jesus himself, his mission, and the tragic death threatening him. That is why the symbols, the *dramatis personae* in this parable, have a concrete historical meaning. The number of these symbols (five) is high compared to other parables: the master of the vineyard is God, the vineyard is Israel, the wicked winemakers are the corrupt establishment, the emigrated servants are the prophets, and the son is Jesus. In the parable of the fourfold field (Mark 4:1–9 par.), on the other hand, we find four symbolic objects. The symbolism of this field parable would be incomprehensible without an explicit explanation; it is correspondingly detailed. Those who heard the parable of the wicked winegrowers, on the other hand, knew from the wording what the parable aimed at. An explicit interpretation of the parable would therefore have been superfluous—it would have only disturbed the effect. The listeners who were accustomed to the parable at the time had direct access to the vicarious meaning of the motifs. But whoever today can no longer appreciate this nature of the parables,[16] and must therefore regard the original typology as secondary, transforms the parable from the evil winegrowers through well-intentioned "de-allegorization" into a desolate ruin. If one knows the lighter, rarer laws of parables, then the question becomes "whether the parable as a whole does not emerge so completely from the framework of real life that one must

---

15. Cf. notes 24 and 25 in chapter 2 above. Erich Klostermann, *Das Lukas-evangelium*, HANT 5 (Tübingen, 1975), 153, says that the words "for I tell you" in Luke 14:24 are an indication that the parable is not about the host but about Jesus, the explainer of the parable. This is probable in Luke's case, but not originally. The rabbinic parallel teaches us that Jesus' version was originally about the final words of the host. Perhaps Luke just added the words "I tell you." This is the case, for example, with Jeremias, *Die Gleichnisse Jesu*, 72–75.

16. This is the case, for example, with Jeremias, *Die Gleichnisse Jesu*, 72–75.

nevertheless address it as an allegory."[17] For the parables are not realistic
but pseudo-realistic. Anyone who knows this from being acquainted with
the rabbinic parables will hardly agree with Jeremias here:

> The parable, as Dodd has recognized, realistically describes the revolution-
> ary mood of the Galilean peasants against the large-scale realities of other
> countries and the supposed landowners, as aroused by the zealotism native
> to Galilee. Another supposedly realistic feature in the parable is that the land-
> owner apparently lives abroad. . . . He is perhaps even intended as a foreigner.[18]

The fact that a landlord is absent for a while always occurs in history. In the
parables, as already mentioned, this became a rigid motif. This motif has no
sociological significance but serves the moral imperative of the parable. In
the legitimate search for the *ipsissima verba* of Jesus, therefore, we should
not disregard either the given stylistic rules of the parables or the typological
sense of their motifs. If we take away the typology of the parable from the
evil vintners, then the parable loses its backbone and there remains only "a
threatening word that announces the judgment to the leaders of the people.
. . . You have heaped up rebellion upon rebellion against God! Beware of
rejecting even the last messenger of God."[19] This artificial reconstruction of
the parable sounds like a weak, sublimated echo. Not a word more about the
fact that the vineyard of Israel and the wicked winegrowers are the establishment, that the parable speaks of the sufferings of the prophets sent to Israel,
and not a word of the presentiments about the death of Jesus, the only Son!
Should all this be the result of a subsequent "allegorization"?

Regarding the parable of the fourfold field, we have already pointed out
that an explicit explanation was necessary for understanding its meaning. It
can also be shown that this parable has come to us in a stylistically, greatly
revised form. But is it true that the parable became "allegorical" through
this adaptation? We will also explain through rabbinic parallels that the four
arable groups represent four different types of people. If we were to remove
this typology as supposedly secondary, we would cut and and dismember
the parable. All that would remain would be a poor, morally dour sermon,
as we have heard from Jülicher and Jeremias. Jeremias saw correctly, however, that the expression "the word" in the interpretation of the parable

---

17. Jeremias, *Die Gleichnisse Jesu*, 72.

18. Jeremias *Die Gleichnisse Jesu*, 73f., is influenced by E. Bammel in the legal
considerations he makes. They are not supported by Jewish law.

19. Jeremias, *Die Gleichnisse Jesu*, 74.

"already for linguistic reasons" cannot be traced back to Jesus since it is an imprint of the early church, a "frequently used *terminus technicus* for the gospel; in the mouth of Jesus this absolutely common expression 'ho logos' can only be found in the interpretation of the parable of the sower (in Mark eight times, in Matthew five times, in Luke three times)."[20] Otherwise, as I have already attempted to show above,[21] the expression "my words" in the Synoptic Gospels does not seem to originate from Jesus but from the editor who added it to the end of the Sermon on the Mount and the Synoptic Apocalypse. It was also pointed out that behind the expression "my words" is either "the words of the law" or "the word of God." The latter phrase is still used in two sayings of Jesus in Luke (8:21 and 11:28).[22] They refer to the family of Jesus and sound authentic.[23] The third passage in Luke is the beginning of the interpretation of our parable (Luke 8:11): "The seed is the word of God." In the further interpretation, Luke speaks only of "the word." There is no reason to object to these three Lukan passages. In them, the term "word of God" has nothing Christian in it; the "word of God" means "teaching" in the Jewish sense. In all three cases, Jesus gives Jewish advice: Listen to the word of God. But this is precisely the moral requirement of the parable of the fourfold field. There is therefore no reason to deny Jesus the phrase, "The seed is the word of God."

Even the symbol of the seed, doctrine, is not Christian in our parable but Jewish. It is found in the fourth book of Ezra, a Jewish scripture written around 100 CE.[24] Here, the Jewish seer reminds God of his prophetic words at the time of the exodus from Egypt and the desert migration. God said, "You, Israel, listen to me, Jacob's seed, listen to my words. For behold, I sow my law in you, that it may bear fruit in you, and that you may boast in it forever" (4 Ezra 9:30). In the following sentences, the fruit of the law

---

20. Jeremias, *Die Gleichnisse Jesu*, 75f.

21. Cf. Jeremias, *Die Gleichnisse Jesu*, chapter 4, note 109. The phrase "my words" is also used in the parallel passages Mark 8:38 and Luke 9:26. For some text witnesses, however, "words" is missing.

22. The phrase "the word of God" also occurs in the washing of hands (Mark 7:13; Matt 15:6). However, this section is highly tendentiously edited.

23. In the Synoptic Gospels, Jesus speaks only about "the word" or "the words" in the sense of doctrine: in Matt 19:1, in the secondary word about the eunuchs, "this word." Luke 9:44 ("these words") and Matt 10:14 ("your words") are missing in the parallel.

24. The beginning of the passage (4 Esr 9, 30f.) seems to be a quotation from an older scripture. Other comparisons from the plant world can be found in 4 Esr 8:41–44; 9:17f.

is characterized as imperishable (9:37). The law is taken up by the human heart (9:32–34), as is also stated in the interpretation of the parable of the fourfold field about the seed, which is the word of God. In Judaism, too, the Torah is compared to the world of growth.[25] In a prayer found among the Dead Sea Scrolls, dated by an editor to the middle of the second pre-Christian century, God is asked to "plant your Torah in our hearts."[26] This usage can still be found today in the Jewish table blessing of the Sephardic and Italian rites. The word of God can also be implanted in the heart. Likewise, the blessing, which was apparently originally directed against the Sadducees and is said after the Torah reading, points in the same direction. In it, God is praised "who gave us the Torah of truth and planted eternal life in us."[27] Since the Torah is a tree of life to all who take hold of it (cf. Prov 3:1–8), if it is planted in our hearts, it brings eternal life as a fruit. Around 10 CE, R. Eleazar ben Azariah apparently took up the blessing quoted here. His preaching itself was based on Eccl 12:11[28] where it reads, "The words of the wise are planted." Eleazar ben Azariah said, "As a plant grows and multiplies, so the words of the law grow and multiply."[29] That the word of God is like a seed that can bear fruit in the human heart is therefore not an ecclesiastical allegory. Every Jewish listener at the time of Jesus could understand this image.[30]

It would be futile to examine the further parables of Jesus as to whether their present form was allegorized by the church. Sometimes, they were not quite understood by the Greek editors; but as far as I can see, there is no secondary allegory in the parables of the Synoptic Gospels. I tend to suppose that the bridegroom in the parable of the ten virgins is to be interpreted as the coming Son of Man. I stick to this assumption, although I know that

---

25. Cf. to this and the following Flusser, "Sanktus und Gloria," *Abraham unser Vater* (Leiden: Brill, 1963), 141f.

26. Maurice Baillet, "Un recueil liturgique de Qumran, Grotte 4," *RB* 68, no. 2 (1961): 200.

27. Jesus also thought this way. When someone asked him what he should do to gain eternal life, Jesus asked, "Do you know the commandments?" (Luke 18:18–20 par.).

28. The various versions of this sermon in rabbinic literature are found in Bacher, *Die Agada der Tannaiten*, vol. 1, 224, 4 and 5.

29. Cf. esp. t. Sot. 7:11, ed. Zuckemandel, 307.

30. These images were taken from early Christianity: The word of God grows (Acts 6:7; 12:24; 19:20; Col 1:6, 10) and bears fruit (cf. 7 and 8). Particularly important is Col 1:6; cf. also Isa 55:10f.

the motif of the sudden coming of the master—both in Jesus' and rabbinic parables—otherwise points to God. I also know that the parable of the two dissimilar sons (Matt 21:28–32) would be understandable and effective without the application to John the Baptist, since the subject would not have to be interpreted historically. The actual interpretation of the parable is found in Matt 21:31. The application to the Baptist is not to be regarded here as a secondary allegory. Rather, the Baptist is presented as concrete proof of the validity of the moral teaching of the parable.[31] Jeremias wrote beautifully about the interpretation of the parable of the weeds among the wheat (Matt 13:36–43). But most of the words and phrases he objected to are in sentences we have already recognized as secondary with the help of the interpretation of the parable of the fishing net (Matt 13:49). Although this interpretation has been edited, it is basically original.

To prove his thesis of secondary allegorization in the Synoptic Gospels, Jeremias quotes the apocryphal Gospel of Thomas and asserts that the parables given there have hardly any allegorical features.[32] On the other hand, I very much doubt the importance of the Gospel of Thomas for the study of the words of Jesus, although some parables of the Gospel of Thomas depend on the Synoptic parables; however, they have been adapted only in shortened form. The absence of so-called allegorical features is explained by the gnostic secrecy of the author of the Gospel of Thomas. Every unbiased reader of this apocryphal gospel easily realizes that its parables are difficult—hardly understandable if one does not have a gnostic education. Sometimes it doesn't help much either. The gnostic author also tries to blur as much as possible the traces that lead from his parables to the Synoptic parallels. This also makes it clear that, if possible, he does not want to give an interpretation of a parable. He himself says, "The images are revealed to men, and the light that is in them [that is, in the images] is hidden in the image of the light of the Father. He will be revealed, and his image is hidden by his light."[33]

---

31. Luke 7:29 presents no proof that Matt 21:32 is secondary, but there is proof that Luke knew the parable of the unequal sons but did not pass it along. In my opinion, the same order and conclusion applies in Luke 3:19f. It is not very clever and chronologically prematurely attached to the messianic proclamation of the Baptist. It proves that Luke knew the story of the death and the circumstances of the death of the Baptist but did not mention it.

32. Jeremias, *Die Gleichnisse Jesu*, 86f.

33. In this parable, Jeremias, *Die Gleichnisse Jesu* (28f.), proceeds from the Gospel of Thomas, *Logion* 109. To the form of the Gospel of Thomas, he brings a parallel parable from ShirR to Cant 45:12.

Sometimes the light of Jesus' parables would also be hidden from people if Jesus himself did not interpret the images. Also, because Jesus was not a gnostic, we must not dismiss the Synoptic parable interpretations as secondary. A beautiful example of a necessary interpretation is the double parable of the treasure and the pearl (Matt 13:44–46), with which we will deal here along with its rabbinic parallels.

> "The kingdom of heaven is like a treasure hidden in a field. A man found it and hid it; he went away with joy, sold all that he had, and bought that field. Again, the kingdom of heaven is like a merchant looking for beautiful pearls. Upon finding one pearl of great value, he went and sold all that he had and bought it."

The phrase "he sold all that he had" appears at the end of both parables. It is good Hebrew.[34] At the end of the second parable, it is translated more accurately. That it forms a kind of refrain in both parables of this double parable is beautiful and significant.[35] When we read that the merchant was "looking for beautiful pearls," this expression does not appear to be an afterthought of the evangelist.[36] In any case, the act of searching in the parable is not without significance for its meaning. In the case of the treasure, the search does not occur because of the subject; the man was not digging for treasure and discovered the treasure only by chance. That is why Jesus specifically mentions the man's joyful surprise after he discovered it. In the case of the merchant, on the other hand, who was looking for beautiful pearls, his joy after finding the precious pearl remains unmentioned. It is assumed that he also rejoiced, but his joy was less because the merchant was not as surprised at the man who saw the treasure unexpectedly shining up at him while he was working a field. The manner of recitation of the double parable was therefore dictated by the nature of the two subjects and not by the doctrine the double parable intends to convey. Jülicher correctly expresses the main doctrine of the double parable:

> Thus the parables honor us . . . that nothing, not even father and mother, can be too expensive as a price for the kingdom of heaven; where the acquisition of the kingdom of heaven is endangered by the holding of former possessions,

---

34. Cf. Strack and Billerbeck, *Kommentar zum Neuen Testament aus Talmud und Midrasch*, vol. 1, 674; and Adolf Schlatter, *Der Evangelist Matthäus, seine Sprache, sein Ziel, sine Selbständigkeit* (Stuttgart: Vereinsbuchh, 1959), 447.

35. Cf. Jeremias, *Die Gleichnisse Jesu*, 198, who wants to eliminate this usage in the second instance.

36. On the other hand, see Jeremias, *Die Gleichnisse Jesu*, 198.

it means to let everything go joyfully . . . because if such a price is demanded for it, it is still small compared to what has been bought.[37]

So, all this suggests that "to sell" is not figurative in the two parables but literal. In the same sense, Jesus advises a rich man, "Sell all that you have and distribute it to the poor, and you will have treasure in heaven, and come, follow me" (Luke 18:22).[38] Here, too, Jesus speaks of treasure but in the same sense as in the Sermon on the Mount (Matt 6:19; Luke 12:33f.). Luke was aware of the relationship between the two places. That is why he began the saying about the heavenly treasure with the words "Sell your possessions, give alms" (Luke 12:33). What Jesus said in the Sermon on the Mount is also significant for understanding the double parable (Matt 6:31–34; Luke 12:29–31), and likewise it is about the contrast between possessions and the kingdom of heaven. We should not worry about what we will eat and drink tomorrow because, Jesus says, "Your father knows that you need it. Rather seek his kingdom, and all these things will be added to you." Here, Jesus does not speak of renouncing property for the sake of the kingdom of heaven. However, he combines an "anti-capitalist" view with the search for the kingdom of heaven. He proclaims something similar in our double parable: The merchant who seeks beautiful pearls finds a precious pearl. To acquire it, he sells everything. The pearl symbolizes the kingdom of heaven. Clearly, then, there are relations between the double parable and other sayings of Jesus. The two parallel parables were quite understandable to those who also knew the rest of Jesus' proclamation. They also knew that when anyone finds the kingdom of God, they feel the same joy that seized the man when he unexpectedly found the treasure in the field.

I have asserted without differentiation above that there are no rabbinic parallels to the double parable of the treasure and the pearl (Matt 13:44–46); I now need to clarify that claim. The subject appears in rabbinic literature but with a completely different meaning. There the treasure is Israel, which God has exalted as a special possession out of the world's tribes. In Deut 32:6, Israel is asked by Moses, "Is he [that is, God] not your father, your acquirer?" The rabbis also presented a parable:

Moses said to Israel, "You are dear to him. You are an acquisition, not an inheritance. This is like someone who inherited ten fields from his father. Then

---

37. Jülicher, *Die Gleichnisreden Jesu*, 585.

38. See also Luke 14:33: "So none of you who does not renounce all that he has can be my disciple."

he got up and bought his own field. And he loved it more than all the palaces which his father had given him." And Moses said unto Israel, "Ye are dear unto him; ye are a possession unto him, not an inheritance."[39]

Even more like the subject of the double parable of the treasure and the pearl is a rabbinic parable for Exod 19:5. In the second book of Moses, God says to Israel, "And now, if you obey My voice and keep My covenant, you will be My own possession among all nations, for all the earth is Mine." I have here translated the Hebrew word *segullah* as "own possession." In the Bible, however, according to the ancient Near Eastern court language, it means "the esteemed vassal."[40] In the rabbinic parable, however, *segullah* is understood as valuable personal property. The rabbinic parable of Exod 19:5 reads:

> "Just as a man's own possessions are pleasing to him, so is mine." God is pleased with Israel. "As a man's own possessions are dear to him, so is Israel dear to me." To put it in a parable: This is similar to someone who had inherited many fields. Then he got up and bought a field from his own resources. Now this he loved more than all the others because he had acquired it by his own purchase. So the whole world belongs to him who created it by his word, but only Israel is dear to him. That is why it is said: "You are my own possession from among all nations."[41]

The two rabbinic parables quoted in Deut 32:6 and Exod 19:5 are variations on one and the same parable that speaks of God's love for Israel because Israel is his precious, self-acquired, uninherited possession. Israel is likened to a field prepared by his own hard work, which is loved by the owner more than his other fields that fell to him "only" as an inheritance. Jesus' double parable of the treasure and pearl also speaks of a precious possession to which the purchaser is particularly attached. In the parable of the treasure we hear, as in the rabbinic parable, of the purchase of a field. There is therefore a significant similarity between the subjects, but there are also important differences not to be overlooked. The purchaser in Jesus' double parable is not God, and the acquired precious stone is not Israel, but the kingdom of heaven. As a result, the emphases in the meaning of the parables are set quite differently. The rabbinic parable is indicative, so to speak, and it talks of God's love for his people.

---

39. SifDev, ed. Finkelstein, 349.

40. See Samuel Loewenstamm, *Das Eigentumsvolk in Vorbereitung* (in Hebrew). This investigation is to appear in the booklet for Ben-Haim. The author has thankfully made them available to me in advance.

41. The parable is found in MHGShem, ed. Margulies, 379. It is also in the MekhSh, ed. Epstein and Melamed (Jerusalem, 1959), 139.

The double parable of Jesus, on the other hand, is imperative. Speaking of the incomparable value of the kingdom of heaven, it encourages the hearer to forego everything else to acquire it. Despite these differences, the relationship between the rabbinic parable and the double parable of Jesus is so close that they are latently interchangeable. The rabbis could have used Jesus' double parable to represent God's special love for Israel. Then the treasure and pearl would mean Israel, to which God turns all his love after he has personally purchased it. After this hypothetical exchange, the parable means that the nations of the world are no longer pleasing to God after he acquired Israel. God has sold everything he had to acquire the treasure or pearl. In the rabbinic parallel, however, it is not so harsh with the nations of the world. But as many individual statements in Talmudic literature show, this is quite conceivable in a rabbinic parable. Moreover, the image of the treasure and pearl does not go badly with Israel. Rabbi Levi said,

> Why does the prophet Isaiah speak of a cry in the wilderness [Isa 40:3]? If a man had a pearl in his hand and lost it, where will he look for it, if not in the place where he lost it? Thus the Holy One of Israel lost in the wilderness. "Here in the wilderness they shall be counted, and here they shall die" [Num 14:35]. And there he goes—the voice calls in the desert.[42]

Two other Amoraic parables also fit here. In a parable of Rabbi Shimeon bar Yehuda, Israel is likened to a crown made for the king, adorned with precious stones and pearls.[43] The other parable comes from Rabbi Levi:

> A king had many treasures. But he didn't find it worth the effort to count them. But he also had a small golden container, the contents of which he counted again and again. Asked about it, he said: "Those treasures are not mine; they belong to the state treasury. But this I have acquired for myself as my own property; therefore I count it again and again." Neither did God number the tribes of the world, for they are destined for the fire of hell [Isa 33:12]. But Israel is his own possession [*segullah*]. . . . That is why Israel will always be counted anew [Exod 20:12].[44]

---

42. AgBer 68, ed. Buber, 133.

43. Cf. Ziegler, *Die Koenigsgleichnisse des Midrasch beleuchtet durch die römisch Kaiserzeit*, chapter l, parable 12; Bacher, *Die Agada der Palästinischen Amoräer*, vol. 3, 170.

44. Cf. Ziegler, *Die Koenigsgleichnisse des Midrasch beleuchtet durch die römisch Kaiserzeit*, chapter 9, parable 2; Bacher, *Die Agada der Palästinischen Amoräer*, vol. 2, 408 (from PesR 10,36b). This parable is quoted in reference to Bacher.

This parable is a later "baroque" offshoot of the two variants of the old parable of Israel as God's own possession,[45] except that here we do not read of a field or palace but of a treasure—as in Jesus' parable. By the way, the first variant, in which Israel is first compared to a field and then to a palace, can serve as evidence that the double parable of Jesus and the parable of the rabbis, although variant, come from a common genre.

On the other hand, however, I can hardly imagine that anyone could take offense if Jesus had picked up the old rabbinic parable and referred to the kingdom of heaven instead of creating the double parable of the treasure and the pearl. Jesus could have said, "The kingdom of heaven is like a field that a man has bought. He therefore loved it more than the ten fields that had fallen to him by inheritance. And again, the kingdom of heaven is like a man who had inherited ten palaces.[46] He got up and bought his own palace. And he loved him more than all the palaces he had inherited." If Jesus had told such a double parable, we would miss the "renunciation of all the rest," which is otherwise associated with Jesus' acquisition of the kingdom of heaven. But this experiment can be carried on even further. Surely, Jesus could have easily introduced this motif of renunciation into the hypothetical parable!

What follows from our exchange? First, we can almost certainly say that Jesus's double parable of the treasure[47] and the pearl and the rabbinic parables of Israel as God's own possession have a common main theme. Second, there is the possibility that the main theme was originally invented with reference to Israel and that it entrusted to Jesus the acquisition of the kingdom of heaven. If this assumption is true, then Jesus' revaluation is particularly beautiful and profound. In my opinion, therefore, the following construction is inadmissible: that the "historical" Jesus, like the rabbis, meant Israel when he spoke of the treasure and the pearl; and that the change in the direction of the kingdom of heaven came only from the church, which wanted to eradicate any implication of a positive relationship with Israel as a people of God from the parables of Jesus. This assumption is to be rejected not only because of the depth of the double parable from which we believe that

---

45. Cf. notes 38 and 40 above.

46. Jesus probably would not have spoken of palaces but of houses.

47. According to Matt 13:44, the treasure was hidden in a field. A man, to whom this field did not belong, found it and hid it again provisionally in order to excavate it as belonging to him after the purchase of the field. For the parable, see Strack and Billerbeck, *Kommentar zum Neuen Testament aus Talmud und Midrasch*, vol. 1, 674; Klostermann, *Das Matthäusevangelium*, 124.

we hear Jesus' own voice, but also because the "main business" of the New Testament and classical rabbinic parables is human life. Apparently, for this reason, in the age of Jesus, the theme of Israel was far less important to the genre of parables than it was after the destruction of the temple (70 CE) and the suppression of the Bar Kochba uprising (132–135 CE). It is therefore entirely within the realm of possibility that Jesus converted a parable about Israel into one about the kingdom of heaven without it being perceived as a sensation or even an affront. It cannot be inferred from this change that Jesus was a universalist and that the rabbis were particularists.

From the relationship between the rabbinic parables about Israel as God's own possession and Jesus' double parable of the treasure and the pearl, we can draw a third conclusion: that it is inadmissible to eradicate the interpretation of the parables of Jesus from the Gospels or to ascribe them to the church. If we separate the interpretations in this way from the parables, then the latter become ambiguous and incomprehensible. It is usually not possible to deduce from the parables what they refer to. In this case, the main theme in the rabbinic parables refers to Israel and in the double parable of Jesus to the kingdom of heaven. Both in the rabbinic parables and in the double parable of the treasure and pearl, the interpretation is unquestionably original. Otherwise, the parables would be meaningless.

For this important fact, I would like to provide an additional proof. It is about some sayings of Jesus about the end-time judgment of the world. "When the Son of Man comes in his glory, and all the angels with him, and all the nations are gathered before him, then he will separate them one from another, as the shepherd separates the sheep from the goats. And he will put the sheep on his right hand and the goats on his left" (Matt 25:31–33). On another occasion, I hope to be able to show that the ideas expressed by this picture, which can also be found elsewhere in the New Testament and in the rest of Judaism, originate from the Persian religion. This also helps us understand the dualistic motif of the end-time separation between the pious and the wicked. In Jesus, this eschatological conception plays out in two parables: in the parable of the fishing net (Matt 13:47–50) and in the parable of the weeds among the wheat (Matt 13:24–30, 36–43). The second parable is taken from the plant kingdom, and it connects somehow with the parable of John the Baptist (Matt 3:12; Luke 3:17).[48] The Son of Man

---

48. Another "dualistic" likeness of the plant world attributed to John the Baptist is found in Matt 3:10 (Luke 3:9). There, in the face of fruitless trees, tacitly fruitful trees are assumed.

"has a shovel in his hand, and he will cleanse his threshing floor and bring the wheat into the barn, but the chaff he will burn in unquenchable fire." In Jesus' parable of the weeds and the wheat, the wheat is not juxtaposed with the chaff but with the weeds—or more precisely, the darnel weed.[49] Darnel grows together with the wheat. But at the time of harvest, the landlord will say to the reapers, "First gather the darnel and tie it up in bundles to burn it. But bring the wheat into my barn" (Matt 13:30). The wicked will be cast into the furnace of fire on the day of judgment (cf. Matt 13:42). It is clear that the parable of the Baptist and the wheat and chaff has the same main theme and orientation.

A rabbinic parable from the period around 260 CE, which has been preserved in several variants, aims to depict the salvation of Israel and the rejection of the peoples.[50] I first mention the secondary variant that has been handed down in the name of Rabbi Levi:

The nations are like the stubble [cf. Exod 15:7; Obad 18] that is thrown into the water [cf. Ps 136:15], the thorns that are thrown into the fire [cf. Isa 33:12], the straw and the chaff that are carried away by the wind [cf. Job 21:18]. But Israel is like wheat [cf. Song 7:3], it is the grain of the world.[51]

In a more original form, the parable is narrated in the name of Rabbi Abun:

The straw, the chaff, and the stubble quarreled with one another, and each of them said, "For my sake the field has been sown." Then the grain of wheat said to them, "Wait until the time of the threshing floor comes; then we will know for whose sake the field has been sown." When they came to the threshing floor, the owner came out to thresh the grain. The chaff went into the wind, the straw was thrown to the ground, the stubble burned. But the owner took the bowl and made a heap of grain. And so the peoples of the world struggle.

---

49. Cf. Strack and Billerbeck, *Kommentar zum Neuen Testament aus Talmud und Midrasch*, vol. 1, 667.

50. The parable is found in PesR 10 where R. Levi is given as one who passed down the tradition; in ShirR to Cant 7:3, R. Abun is given as one who passed down the tradition; AgBer 23, ed. Buber, 48 (on prophets); Gen. Rab., 83:4, ed. Theodor/Albeck, 1000f., where further passages are noted; cf. also Bacher, *Die Agada der Palästinischen Amoräer*, vol. 2, 323, where reference is rightly made to Matt 3:12; Bacher, *Die Agada der Palästinischen Amoräer*, vol. 3, 411; Strack and Billerbeck, *Kommentar zum Neuen Testament aus Talmud und Midrasch*, vol. 1, 667.

51. Cf. note 49 above. This variant is cited according to Bacher, *Die Agada der Palästinischen Amoräer*, vol. 2, 323.

Some say, "We are Israel, and for our sake the world was created." The others also claim to be the true Israel in this parable variant.[52] But Israel says, "Wait until God's day comes, which sets the wicked on fire like stubble, and the wind carries them away" [Mal 3:19]. And of Israel it is said, Thou shalt rejoice for ever, and glory with the saints of Israel.[53]

The resemblance between the subject of the rabbinic parable and the parable of John the Baptist (Matt 3:12; Luke 3:17) about the Son of Man threshing the wheat, bringing the grain into the barn, and burning the chaff is obvious. In the rabbinic parable, we also read about the threshing of the grain, the gathering of the wheat and the chaff, and the burning in the fire. The form of the rabbinic parable attributed to Rabbi Abun is more original than that of Rabbi Levi. First, the straw, the chaff, and the stubble argue with one another. Then the wheat comes and advises them to wait. When the time of the threshing floor comes, it turns out that the wheat is the winner. This action is reminiscent of the well-known Aesop fable of the oak and the reed. The oak and the reed quarreled with each other as to which of them was the stronger. Suddenly a storm came. The reed bent according to the wind's direction. The oak, however, resisted and was uprooted.[54] Contrary to this fable, there are more than two antagonists in Rabbi Abun's parable, and the winner appears only at the end of the action. In this respect, however, a rabbinic version is closer to Aesop's basic scheme:

The weeds said to the wheat, "We are better than you, and the rain falls on you and on us, and the sun shines." And the wheat said unto them, "Not that which ye say is true, but that which we say: for the thresher comes and gathers us into the barn, and you are given to the birds for food." Thus the peoples of the world and Israel are mixed together in the world, as it is written: "They mingled with the peoples and learned their works" [Ps 106:35]. The peoples of the world say to Israel, "We are better than you, and the rain falls on us and on you, and the

---

52. See note 49 above. This parable is according to Bacher, *Die Agada der Palästinischen Amoräer*, vol. 3, 411.

53. Bacher, *Die Agada der Palästinischen Amoräer*, vol. 3, 412n1, is right that this parable variant is apparently a reference to conflicting Christian sects. Each of them claims to be the true Israel. The question remains, however, whether this parable—which we only encounter around 260 CE, and which does not speak in all variants of the Israel claim of the peoples—had anything at all to do with Christianity in its older form. The answer to this is rather meaningful.

54. Cf. chapter 3, note 8.

sun shines." And Israel said unto them, "Not that which ye say is true, but that which we say. For the day will come when the righteous will enter Paradise and the wicked will enter Hell [cf. Dan 12:2]."[55]

It is impossible to reconstruct from these variants the original form of the rabbinic parable. After all, the variants point to the rabbinic context in which the Baptist's word and the parable of wheat and weeds are found. In the last variant mentioned, as with Jesus, the weeds and wheat are mentioned. In the first two rabbinic variants and in John the Baptist, on the other hand, there is talk of chaff and wheat. In all rabbinic cases, the subject matter is basically the same as in the two New Testament passages. Could the rabbinic variants here be an additional proof of the relationship between the Baptist's parable and Jesus' parable? This relationship is already evident within the New Testament, although Jesus' parable contains an additional teaching, which goes something like this: "The pious live together with the wicked in this world, but they can rely on the final judgment. Then the wicked will be separated from the righteous and will be judged." The late rabbinic variant tradition in Ag. Ber. 23 expresses the same. There, too, the final court is comforted. But if we return to the more important question, of particular interest to us, of how far the nature of their subject limits the field of view to certain interpretations, then the late rabbinic parable of wheat—together with its parallels in the Gospels—belongs to the kind in which the number of possible solutions is small. This is in sharp contrast to the subject of the parable of the treasure and the pearl. In this case, only the end-time punishment of the evildoers and the salvation of the righteous come into question. This rabbinic parable speaks of the salvation of Israel and the punishment of the nations, whereas the two passages in the Gospels speak of the pious and the wicked. As far as I can see, there is no doubt that the Gospels retained their original meaning and that the rabbinic parable is secondary in its interpretation of Israel and the peoples. In the case of the parable of the treasure and the pearl, we have turned to the reverse possibility—namely, that there the subject originally referred to Israel and that Jesus utilized the same subject to speak of the kingdom of heaven.

We cannot ignore objections and questions here. It is true that the theme of these late rabbinic parables—namely, the example of the Baptist and the example of Jesus over the wheat and the weeds—is the same. But the rabbinic parable was a late parable: it was undoubtedly reshaped and

---

55. Ag. Ber. 23, ed. Buber, 48.

reinterpreted secondarily to refer to Israel and the peoples. Could it even be assumed that the rabbinic parable arose from the two passages of the Gospels? There are after all, researchers who, for understandable reasons, consider using a more or less quiet voice to express the possibility that the Jews learned the art of the parable from Jesus Christ. But anyone who wants to regard the Jews as Jesus' disciples of poetry cannot help but suspect, in our case, that even Jesus himself had a teacher in this art; that is, John the Baptist. His likeness of wheat and chaff, as we have also explained, is closely related to Jesus' likeness of wheat and tares. Despite my strongest concerns, I do not want to rule out the possibility that the late rabbinic parable we have been discussing came into being partly under the influence of the two New Testament passages, or under the influence of the early church's proclamation of these passages. In any case, it should be kept in mind that the two parables in the Gospels express nothing that could not be generally Jewish. Nor do they differ in content from this kind of Jewish parable. So, if the rabbinic parable came from the Gospels or from primitive Christian tradition, then this influence would be possible only because the rabbis did not see a foreign body in these parables but rather flesh from their flesh. If, on the other hand, someone wanted to adopt a common Jewish model for the parable words in the Gospels and for the late rabbinic parables, then they must cope with a long and not quite transparent prehistory of the rabbinic parables. Regardless of this question, the relationship between the example of the Baptist and the example of Jesus already shows that there are probably common roots. From their differences, we can conclude that there were variations on this topic as well, as we know of other topics. The parable is also by nature an oral and fluid genre. The "primeval" theme of all variations was the separation of the wheat from the useless material harvested with it: the gathering of the wheat into the barn and the burning of the worthless material. The purpose here is the salvation of the pious and the torment of the wicked at the Last Judgment.

Three points emerged in this chapter. First, we were able to show once again in the last two examples how the subject of a parable can be more or less ambiguous so that the parable often needs to be explained. Second, we were again able to point to the law of variations on a subject associated with parables. The problem of when and to what extent shifts in the subject point to and condition the meaning of a parable is not easy to solve. The more correct and accurate the solution, however, the better we understand what the parable is trying to say. We will have to return to this problem again. Third, we were concerned with the question of whether the Jewish parables, which include Jesus' parables, are "allegorical." They are not allegories, but they have two levels: that of the subject and that of its teaching. This is why Jesus' parables become wretched ruins when we attempt to "de-allegorize" them. If we consider the interpretation belonging to them as secondary and delete it, then sometimes the disaster has already happened. To live up to the parables, we must know that they are a distinct genre. The next chapter is about following, as much as possible, the origin and prehistory of the genre of Jewish parables.

6

THE ORIGIN AND PREHISTORY
OF JEWISH PARABLES

The essence of the problem of Jesus' parables came to my attention when I became aware of the kinship between a saying of Rabbi Tarfon in the sayings of the fathers (m. Av. 2, 15f.) and the word of Jesus in Matt 9:37f. (Luke 10:2).[1] The rabbinic text in the sayings of the fathers reads:

> Rabbi Tarfon says: "The day is short and the work is great, the workers are sluggish and the wages are rich and the employer urges them on." He also used to say, "It is not up to you to complete the work, and you are not free to be idle. If you have learned much wisdom, your master [literally, the master of your work] is reliable in paying you the reward of your work."[2]

These are not two separate sayings but only one from Rabbi Tarfon, who lived and worked around 100 CE.

According to Matthew and Luke, when Jesus sent his disciples to proclaim the kingdom of God, he said, "The harvest is great, but the laborers are few. So ask the master of the harvest to send workers into his harvest." This

---

1. It was later shown to me that Strack and Billerbeck, *Kommentar zum Neuen Testament aus Talmud und Midrasch*, vol. 1, 527, had already seen the dependency. However, they described the rabbinic saying as "formally similar, but different in content." See also Klostermann, *Das Matthäusevangelium*, 85.

2. The original text here has been reproduced in the mixed version of the Codex Kaufmann (facsimile edition by Georg Beer [Heidelberg, 1929]; published in Jerusalem, 1968). The previous statement of Rabbi Eleazar (ben Arach) also appears in the Codex Kaufmann in its more original form: "Be diligent to learn what you have to answer to an Epicurean [i.e., deist or atheist]. And know before whom you are struggling [cf. Ki 4:8] and who your ally [God] is." This message of encouragement amid the religious distress after the destruction of the temple was adapted in the traditional text to the following saying of Rabbi Tarfon and correspondingly envied. This is why the Codex Kaufmann says at the end "your employer" instead of your "ally." This original type of reading (ally: *bacal beritka*) has been described only in ARN, ed. Schechter, 66, preserved in both versions.

saying is translated exactly from Hebrew. To show the similarity between the word of the Gospel and Rabbi Tarfon's saying, they are juxtaposed:

> "The day is short and the work is great. The harvest is great, and the laborers are sluggish, and the wages are rich; but the laborers are few, and the landlord urges. . . . So ask the Master of the harvest to send workers into his harvest. The Master is faithful in your work, the reward of your work, in paying for his harvest."

Jesus does not speak of wages like Rabbi Tarfon. But as Jesus' parables show, the so-called idea of wages was not foreign to him. Let us first turn to Rabbi Tarfon's saying. The beginning ("The day is short and the work great") forms in the distant sense a variation of the famous, popular saying of the Greek physician Hippocrates (about 460–ca. 370 BCE): "Life is short, art [*techne*] is long."[3] The identity between the Hippocrates saying and the beginning of the Tarfon saying follows from the fact that the Greek word *techna*, which in Hippocrates means "art"—the skill of the physician—corresponds exactly to the rabbinic-Hebrew word *melakhah*. *Melakhah* and *techna* mean "craft" or "work" in addition to "art." Rabbi Tarfon does not speak of short life but says, "The day is short." He did not want his entire dictum to be understood as a proverb but as a parable. In the rabbinic parables and in Jesus' parables, however, a working day is now a symbol of human life. This hardly noticeable but significant change in the Greek saying paved the way for the continuation of the parable. In contrast to the shortness of the day and the enormity of the work to be done, further tensions now arise: Although the wages are plentiful and the work to be done is great, and although the employer insists, the workers are sluggish. But although the employer insists, the person addressed in the familiar form is not only incapable, but also not obliged, to complete the great work imposed. On the other hand, since he is a worker and not an independent man, he must not stand idly by. He can be sure that he will receive his wages from the employer.

In paraphrasing Rabbi Tarfon's parable, we deliberately omitted the mention of learning the Torah ("If you have learned much instruction"). For we suppose that the connection, indeed identification, of the work with the learning of the Torah in the parable is not original. Since the whole saying is kept equal, the mention of the not-equal learning of the Torah

---

3. Cf. August Otto, *Die Sprichwörter und sprichwörtlichen Redensarten der Römer* (Leipzig: Hildersheim, 1965), 375.

acts like a foreign body.[4] Moreover, the sentence lacks any relation to an interpretation. We can therefore omit the sentence about the learning of the Torah altogether. It is only when we make this omission that the saying's inner clarity becomes apparent. I assume that this part of the sentence is not a later interpolation, but that it was already part of Rabbi Tarfon's saying. Maybe he meant, "If you've done a lot of Torah." Such is the formulation of Rabbi Johanan ben Zakkai.[5] Also with the latter, in various traditionally used text editions, the "doing of the Torah" was transformed to the "study of the Torah." It is also obvious that the doing of the Torah fits better into a parable about the work than the learning of the Torah. The Tarfon saying probably goes back to an old way of talking about work. Rabbi Tarfon, or perhaps one of his predecessors, applied this mode of speech to the doing (or learning) of the law. In the original saying, the labor of the workers simply meant the activity of man before God and toward God during his life. Also, in the previously mentioned oldest parable from the first half of the second century BCE, Antigonus from Socho does not speak of the Torah. Rather, he says, "Do not be like servants who serve the Master under the condition of receiving reward. Rather, be like servants who serve the Master without condition to receive reward."[6] So, the Tarfon saying was probably not originally about the Torah. Especially in this case, it is easy to fall under the spell of its special attractiveness and depth.[7] The parable teaches us, among other things, that because of the brevity of his life, the individual cannot complete the work imposed by God on humanity but must not escape this obligation.

We now assume that Jesus knew Tarfon's rabbinic saying in the form he had before the time of Rabbi Tarfon—that is, without mentioning the Torah. Since Rabbi Tarfon lived a few decades after Jesus, he could not

---

4. The last sentence of the traditional version of the parable ("And know that the wages of the righteous are a gift for the future to come") is rightly absent from the Codex Kaufmann.

5. m. Av. 11.8; see chapter 4, note 98. On the phrase "doing the law," see Arthur S. Abramson, *Leshonenu*, 5714, 61–65 (in Hebrew). The usage occurs in the New Testament in John 7:19; Rom 2:14; and Gal 5:3. It is also found in ancient Jewish writings: Sir 19:20; 1 Macc 2:67; 13:48; TestGad 3,2; TestJos 1 l,k; 1 QpHab 7,1 1; 8,1; 12,4f.; CD 17.8. In rabbinic literature, it occurs often and even in the Targum (at Isa 1:27).

6. m. Av. 1.3.

7. This impressive depth remains even in the case where Rabbi Tarfon originally spoke not of learning but of doing the Torah.

have been the one who passed down the saying to Jesus. We can also allow ourselves this presupposition because we are already familiar with the law of variations within the subject of parables. Such a variation most likely took place in the parable itself: the work was no longer understood as a symbol of human activity on earth. It was now interpreted—in a limiting and constricting sense—as the doing (or learning) of the law. This interpretation was incorporated into the parable. With Jesus, however, the parable took a different direction. He is concerned with an urgent mission. Many people are ripe—Jesus thinks—to be won for the message of the kingdom. That is why he does not speak generally of labor but—also limiting and constricting—of the harvest. The disciples he sends out are also called workers, but their task is to harvest. Jesus drastically expressed the same thought to Simon Peter when he called him and said, "From now on you will catch people alive" (Luke 5:10; cf. Mark 1:17; Matt 4:19). Here, people are compared with the harvested grain. According to the custom of his message, Jesus does not say, like Rabbi Tarfon, that the laborers are lazy, but that the number of laborers is too small in proportion to the great harvest. It is therefore necessary to ask the Master of the harvest to send forth workers into his harvest field. The beautiful Hebraism "the Master of the harvest" is to be observed! It corresponds to the phrase "Master of thy work" in the parallel rabbinic parable.

Jesus thus transformed the rabbinic saying for his purposes. He speaks of an urgent task, not of human life. Therefore, the modified saying of Hippocrates would have only a disturbing effect on him. He therefore omits its first half ("The day is short"), which symbolically points to the whole of life. Nor does he mention wages because his image does not align with this. The same applies to the words "It is not up to you to complete the work." Jesus emphasizes that it is important to reap right now. Although there was a sentence about human inadequacy, for Jesus it was no longer relevant. The reference to the urgent landlord was also superfluous for him. On the contrary, one should persuade the Master of the harvest to send more workers into his harvest. The rabbinic saying would fit best into Jesus' parable if he also drew his disciples' attention to the fact that it is not in their will to be idle. However, a parable narrator can freely activate and control the material transmitted to him within certain limits.

But could Jesus, when sending out his disciples, simply have recommended to them the rabbinic saying with no change? Surely, that would have been possible. But if the reader is willing to forget for a while that it is "merely" a rabbinic saying, then if this saying were to be found in the Gospels, he would find nothing non-Jewish about it. Yes, he would probably admire it. But why did Jesus not use the rabbinic saying as it was? Because Jesus wanted to say something toward a different direction that better suited the situation of the disciples. Jesus did not want to encourage the disciples to diligence or to explain their responsibility to God. He mainly wanted to express the urgency of their mission—the harvest is already ripe—with the great willingness of many people to receive the message and the low potential number of missionaries. He therefore varied the subject to better adapt it to the ethical situation. Conversely, could Rabbi Tarfon have used Jesus' form of the saying for his purposes? It wouldn't have been impossible. The Tarfon form, however, corresponds better to Rabbi Tarfon's intentions than Jesus' form.

According to our assumption, Jesus knew the rabbinic parable and edited it for his purpose. His saying is much easier to derive from the Tarfon saying than vice versa. One reason for this is that the rabbinic saying is based on Hippocrates. Jesus could not use this saying for his purposes, so he therefore omitted the first half and adapted the harvest from the work in the second half. The rabbinic saying is more general than Jesus' saying. Both Tarfon's and Jesus' parables are easily understood, and it would be impossible and unnecessary to attach another interpretation to them. As we have seen, most likely someone—Rabbi Tarfon or a predecessor—mentioned the Torah. This is a secondary narrowing of the saying, however, and not an inserted interpretation! Since the listeners at that time were familiar with the equations—working day, human life; work, human work before God; owner, God—they did not need to ask for an interpretation of the parable. In the case of Jesus' parable, our understanding is also further facilitated by the fact that the original situation in which Jesus spoke is also given in the Gospel.

Similar to the fact that we have labeled the words of Rabbi Tarfon and Jesus as parable sayings, we can also do this with the quoted saying of Antigonus from Socho.[8] The words of Rabbi Akiba also belong to this genre:

> Everything is given only as a guarantee, and a fishing net is spread over everything that lives there. The store is open, the owner grants credit. The book is open and the hand is writing. Anyone who wants to borrow can come and borrow. Earners walk around regularly and on a daily basis, claiming debts from people, whether they want it or not. They have something to rely on, and the judgment is a just judgment. And everything is prepared for the feast.[9]

---

8. m. Av. 1.3.
9. m. Av. 3:16.

This parable is based on the comparison between human life and a shop, and the shopkeeper represents God. In addition, three other topics that do not belong to the picture are emphasized and, in the end, it is said that everything is prepared for the feast. Here, the important theme of the meal appears, which plays a major role in Jesus' parables and in the rabbinic parables. The subject of the meal is preceded by that of the judgment. The judgment is to be understood both literally and figuratively in the parable. It is both the judgment against the debtor who owes money to the shopkeeper and the divine judgment over humanity. The third theme here is that of the safety net. This theme arose from an allusion to Eccl 9:12: "Even man does not know his hour. Like the fish that are caught in the evil net, and like the birds that are in the snare, men become entangled in the time of calamity, when it suddenly overtakes them." This Scripture also appears in Luke 21:34f.: "But beware yourselves, lest your hearts be weighed down by intoxication, drunkenness, and worry about food, and that day fall upon you like a net. For it will come in for all who dwell on the earth." We know the suddenness of calamity from Qoheleth, we read from Rabbi Akiba's words that the fishing net is spread out over everything, and we learn the theme of the fishing net from Jesus' parable in Matt 13:47–50.

There is only one parable in the New Testament: the parable we have just discussed. From rabbinic literature, we have come to know two parables: that of Rabbi Tarfon and that of Rabbi Akiba. Also belonging to this genre is the saying of Antigonus from Socho, which is the oldest evidence for the existence of Jewish parables. By their nature, parables are, so to speak, half-developed parables. Typical for them are the paratactically arranged direct statements. It should be noted that these three rabbinic parable sayings go back to a time when there is not much rabbinic material associated with the names of those who passed on the tradition. Most of the rabbinic material from this period is anonymous or associated with a later tradition. The oldest known full parable in which the parable narrator is also named comes from Rabban Johanan ben Zakkai.[10] As is well known, Johanan lived at the time of the destruction of the temple in 70 CE. The parables apparently went out of fashion soon after that. This is probably why so few and such old parable sayings are known to us today.

But can we conclude from all this that the still undeveloped parables constitute the oldest and most original form of the Jewish parables? Nothing is less certain. Our knowledge of the rabbinic literature before the de-

---

10. See chapter 1, note 4.

struction of the temple is very small. Much was lost in connection with the Jewish uprising and the destruction of the temple. One thing, however, is made clear by the Gospels: that fully developed parables existed some time before Jesus. In the course of my explanations, I realized that I could draw their fullness from Jesus. His many parables and the maturity of their form are to be understood only on the assumption that the genus of parables had been formed long before Jesus and that the main themes of the parables, as well as various variations of subjects, already existed.

The nature of the apodeictic, paratactic statements is not limited in the rabbinic literature to the parables. In the writings of the fathers, before the parable of Rabbi Akiba, there is an unparalleled saying: "All things are observed, and authority is given. In goodness the world is judged, and not everything is decided according to the majority of deeds."[11] Rabbi Eleazar Hakkappar once said, "The born are destined to die, the dead to be quickened, the living to be judged."[12] So from the outside, these are a hybrid between full parables and simple sayings consisting of paratactic statements. On the one hand, we could think of the parable sayings as arising from ordinary paratactic sayings. The new thing about them compared to the ordinary sayings would then be their pictorial expression. In a further step, the full parables would have arisen from the parable sayings. On the other hand, we could also make the thesis that the parable sayings are a hybrid between the genre of the apodeictic series of sayings and the real ones. I think the first option is unlikely for many reasons. Regarding the second possibility, it is yet unknown how the parables grew to their full maturity. Perhaps we can make a guess here.

The rabbinic parables are a special literary phenomenon distinct from all other similar genres. They are not even generally Jewish. Outside the rabbinic sources and the Synoptic Gospels, they are sought in vain. It also doesn't take us too far in asking about their ancestors in the Old Testament. The most similar text we can find there is the fictitious legal case that the prophet Nathan presented to King David after his adultery with Bathsheba (2 Sam 12:1–7).

> "Two men lived in the same city. One was rich, the other poor. The rich man had very many flocks and herds. The poor man, on the other hand, had nothing but a single little sheep which he had bought. He raised it, and it grew up

---

11. m. Av. 3:15! "And not everything" is the original reading.
12. m. Av. 4:22.

with him with his children. It ate from his bowl and drank from his cup. It slept on his bosom, and he held it like a child. There once came a guest to the rich man. Because the rich man refrained from taking one of his sheep or cattle to prepare it for the guest who had come to him, he took the poor man's lamb and prepared it for the man who had come to him." And David's anger was kindled against the man, and he said unto Nathan, "As the Master liveth, the man who did this is dead." . . . And Nathan said unto David, "Thou art the man."

This is a fictitious legal case from everyday life and not a parable in the true sense. In it, however, there are many similarities with the subjects of rabbinic parables. A common feature is, for example, the appealing exaggeration in the poor man's loving treatment of the sheep as well as the "non-allegorical" allegory. The rich man is David, the poor man is Uriah, and the lamb is Bathsheba. The visit of the guest who is the cause of the rich man's misdeed, however, does not correspond to any analogy at the level of reality. If necessary, we could only say that the subject has a general validity not intended by Nathan. In Jesus' parables, it also happens that universally valid subjects are applied to concrete persons. The story of Nathan resembles, for example, the parable of the dissimilar sons that refers to John the Baptist (Matt 21:28–32) and the parable of the wicked winegrowers, in which the servants sent out signify the prophets and the son signifies Jesus himself (Matt 21:33–46 par.). But the parable of the winegrowers is an exception among Jesus' parables.[13] The fictitious case in Nathan's narrative might be a parable if the narrative were not interrupted by the words of David's rebellion. The story would have to end much like the parable of the wicked winegrowers: "What will the judge do when the rich man is accused before him? The rich man will die. He will have to replace the poor man's lamb many times over, because he acted in this way without showing mercy." But even after such a change, the story of the sheep would not be a very good parable, because it would not contain a generally valid morality that could easily be discovered.[14] In the rabbinic context or with Jesus, in my opinion, Nathan's narrative could at best have become a cross between an example and a parable. It should be noted that the Nathan narrative is the most comparable Old Testament narrative to rabbinic parables and Jesus' parables. The similarities are due to circumstances in David's life. Therefore,

---

13. The rabbinic parables of the later type (e.g., chapter 2, note 19, above), which are so to speak tailored to the body of biblical persons, are secondary in this respect and thus belong only indirectly in our investigation.

14. An exception, as I said, is the parable of the wicked winegrowers.

the story of the sheep cannot readily be made a precursor to rabbinic and New Testament parables.

The beginning of Rabbi Tarfon's parable quoted above goes back to a saying of the Greek Hippocrates. Can we therefore assume a Greek prehistory of the rabbinic parables, and thus also of Jesus' parables? Further, in connection with the house on the rock, we cited above the Greek craftsmen's comparisons; Socrates was a master of these comparisons. For the double comparison of the tower and the king, we quoted two similar parable pictures from Greek philosophical literature: one from the writings of Philo of Alexandria and the other from Epictetus.[15] We can therefore speak of a possible influence on rabbinic parables from Greek philosophical literature, though this eventual influence did not necessarily occur in the written word. It is also possible that the Jews could have become acquainted with philosophical lectures through conversations with Greek philosophers or with philosophically interested people. In rabbinic literature, one often reads about conversations of rabbis with philosophers or generally with Greek-educated people. These must not have been such celebrities as the Cynical philosopher Menippus of Gadara (first half of the third century BCE) or Antiochus of Ascalon (born between 130 and 120 BCE). One would have to examine Greek philosophical literature, and especially treat Greek philosophical similitudes in the same way we do with rabbinic similitudes, if one wants to go further on the question of the possible effects of Greek literature. Because this immense work cannot be done here, our attempts in this regard are only a prelude. They are based particularly on Epictetus (c. 50–35 CE), whose writings, however, I could not fully work through for our question.

According to the Stoic Cleanthes (304–233 BCE), it is one's intention, not the doing, that is the decisive factor. He illustrates this with the following example:

> I sent two servants to search for Plato and get him out of the academy. One of them searched the whole hall of columns and also went through other places where he hoped to find him. Then he returned home tired and angry. The other servant sat down at the next shop. After he had joined the local workers like a vagabond and loitered and played with them, he found Plato, whom he had not sought. We will praise the servant who, so far as it depended on him, has done all that he had been commanded. But we will punish the lazy one.[16]

---

15. See chapter 4, notes 127–130 above.

16. Cf. Max Pohlenz, *Stoa und Stoiker, Die Gründer, Panaitios, Poseidonios, eingeleitet und übertragen* (Zürich: Artemis, 1950), 128. The text can be found in

This Greek example, too, is told like the mature rabbinic parables in the form of a case that really happened in the past. There is also a story and a moral. The story contains many epic details that are not directly related to its main emphasis. As with many rabbinic parables, the example of Cleanthes is also about servants, who here serve as symbolic figures for man himself. The main theme of a work ethic occurs frequently in Jewish parables. His particular theme is the different actions of two servants—a theme we have mentioned before.[17] The right and wrong actions of servants, sons, invitees, and so on, are particularly important motifs of both the rabbinic parables and Jesus' parables. It is easy to see how similar this example of Cleanthes is to the Jewish parables, if one keeps in mind Jesus' parable of the dissimilar sons (Matt 21:28–32). With Jesus, the same moral problem is illuminated from a completely different angle. There, we learn that saying yes is not enough if this yes is just an empty word. Rather, the son must do the will of the father; even if he at first resisted, he finally fulfilled his task.

In the parable of the dissimilar sons, the father is a symbol of God. This figure of correspondence is missing in Cleanthes's example. In the Greek-philosophical parable images, however, there is also a figure that stands for the deity. When someone asked Epictetus what a man must be like to become a cynic, he replied that one should not accomplish such a great task without God; otherwise, one will be hated by God. "For no one will say to himself in a well-ordered house, 'I will be a steward here.' If he does, the owner will come. And when he sees the man arrogantly ordering things, he will drag him out and beat him. So it is in this great city [that is, the world]. For here too there is a homeowner who orders everything."[18] Epictetus compares the deity, the owner of the world, to a homeowner. In another parable, he compares him to a ship's captain:

When the ship moors on a journey, and you get off to get some fresh water, then when you pick up a snail and a small squid on the way, you have to turn your thoughts on the ship and often turn around, so that if the captain calls you, you leave all these things at his call. Otherwise, you would be thrown into

Seneca, *De Ben.* 6, 10:2; *Stoicorum veterum fragmenta*, ed. Johannes von Arnim, vol. 1 (Stuttgart, 1964), 579.

17. The theme of two unequal persons—either servants or sons—must not always be part of the main theme of the work ethic, as we have seen in chapter 2, note 19, in the rabbinic parable introduced there.

18. Epictetus, *Diatr.* 3.22.2–4; see chapter 2, note 5, above.

the ship and tied up like a sheep. So it is in life: If a wife or a child is given to you instead of a small squid and a snail, there is no objection to it. But when the captain calls, run into the ship and leave all these things and do not turn back! And if you are an old man, do not go far from the ship, lest you ruin the reputation of the captain.[19]

This beautiful picture betrays the Stoic-Cynical worldview of Epictetus. Jesus could have used the same image for another purpose: to make it clear that one must renounce everything—property and connection with one's family—if one chooses to follow him. The call to be ready also belongs to the banquet theme in the Jewish parables. Jesus points either to death—as in Epictetus—or to the end times. In another way, Epictetus uses the picture of a feast: "Now you [that is, God] want that I leave the feast? I go and thank you with all my heart that you have found me worthy to keep the feast with you and to see who you are." The image of the feast is then associated with the thought of death in Epictetus: "When I think about it, when I write this and when I read this—may death come upon me."[20]

Let us now look at a parable of Epictetus from the world of the growth of plants. Some of Jesus' parables come from this world. A man asked Epictetus how to make his brother reconcile with him, and Epictetus replied,

Nothing great suddenly becomes great, not even the grape or the fig. If you tell me now: I want a fig! Then I will answer you: It takes time! Let the tree bloom first, then produce the fruit and then ripen it. If the fruit of a fig tree does not ripen all at once and not in an hour, how will you possess the fruit of a man's disposition in such a short time and so without difficulty? Do not expect such a thing, even if I tell you.[21]

The image is reminiscent of Jesus' growth parables, especially the parable of the self-growing seed:

"The kingdom of God is like a man throwing seed on the land and sleeping and waking up at night and day. And the seed sprouts and bursts open without him knowing it. The earth bears fruit by itself: first grass, then ears, then full grain in the ears. But when the fruit appears, he immediately sends the sickle, for the harvest is here." (Mark 4:26–29)

---

19. Epictetus, *Enchir.* 7.
20. Epictetus, *Diatr.* 3.5, 10f.; cf. also 4, 1.104–106. A beautiful picture of the ripening of ears in the harvest as a symbol of death can be found in 2, 6.11–14.
21. Epictetus, *Diatr.* 1, 15.6–8.

The purpose of this picture in the Gospel is quite different from Epictetus, but the two descriptions of gradual growth are very similar. Perhaps it is no coincidence that this parable occurs only in the Gospel of Mark and that it is composed and thoroughly developed in Greek. It stands in Mark's Gospel before the parable of the mustard seed (Mark 4:30–32), which undoubtedly comes from Jesus. Perhaps it is a replica of this original parable.

Before we hazard our hypothesis based on the Greek examples mentioned, let us now deal with the little parable of the children playing (Luke 7:31–35; Matt 11:16–19). In connection with this parable, Greek materialshould also be mentioned: parable images from Epictetus and a fable of Aesop. In addition, we will also reproduce a parallel rabbinic parable and express the assumption that the small parable may also depend on one or two biblical verses to which Jesus alludes in a deeper sense.

Oddly enough, Jesus' intention, which he wanted to express with this parable of the children playing, is not quite clear in view of the many and varied comparative materials. We almost certainly know the occasion in which he spoke the parable and the historical context in which he wanted to place it. In Matthew and Luke,[22] the parable is a continuation of Jesus' statement about John the Baptist (Matt 11:7–11; Luke 7:24–30). In the case of both evangelists, moreover, the parable is interpreted at the end of the

---

22. Luke 7:29 is certainly a secondary description. It is designed in Greek and shows that Luke, or his source, knew the parable of the unequal sons. There it is said of the tax collectors that they believed John. In our place, they have already been baptized with the baptism of John! John's baptism is also mentioned in the pericope on the question of authority (Luke 20:4 par.). The attentive reader of Luke 7:29f. easily notices that even the pericopes on the question of authority inspired secondary description in Luke. Much more difficult is a question already touched upon above: the beautiful and original saying of Jesus about the breakthrough of the kingdom of heaven (Matt 11:12–15; Luke 16:16) is factually and thematically related to his profound saying about the Baptist in Matt 11:1; Luke 7:24–28. But Luke is lacking in this context. Instead, it is found in edited and shortened form as the first of three sayings (which all are) in Luke 16:16. The three sayings there (Luke 16:16–18) act like the content of an attack against the self-righteous Pharisees based on the preceding words (Luke 16:14). So, did Matthew connect the saying of the breakthrough of the kingdom of heaven (Matt 11:12–15) to the saying about the Baptist because he recognized the saying as materially and thematically related to the saying about the Baptist? Or did Jesus really speak of the breakthrough of the kingdom of heaven on this occasion? Did Luke possibly leave it there because it is also in another place in his version? This latter possibility seems more likely to me.

various reactions of "this generation" about the appearance of Jesus and the Baptist (Matt 11:18f.; Luke 7:33–35). The expression "this generation" here has a critical and debasing tone:[23]

> "To whom do I liken this generation, and to what shall I compare it?[24] They are like children who say to their companions,[25] 'We have piped for you, and you have not danced. We sang lamentations, and you did not mourn.' For there comes[26] John, who neither eats nor drinks. They say, 'He has an evil spirit.'[27] And there comes a man that eats and drinks, and they say, 'Behold a glutton and a drunkard, a friend with tax collectors and sinners.' And wisdom was justified in her works."

The difficulty in accurately grasping Jesus' intention[28] is not that this short parable may have been worked out in the course of tradition or translation into Greek. Rather, the difficulty consists in the fact that the parable already had proverbial features when Jesus spoke it. Proverbial phrases, even if they are figurative, rarely fit exactly what they want to express. The closing sentence, "Wisdom was justified in her works," was probably just a proverb. We can really expect a banalization of the translation here. It was able to emerge because the saying was not properly understood later. As it stands now, the sense of it is unclear, and Luke's variant doesn't help us much: "And wisdom was justified in all her children" (Luke 7:35).[29]

---

23. Here, too, we will try to reconstruct the original text of Matthew and Luke.

24. Jülicher, *Die Gleichnisreden Jesu*, 24, rightly compares the double question in Luke 7:31 with Luke 13:18 (cf. Matt 4:30) and cites Isa 40:18.

25. I think that reading *hetairoi* is better than that reading *heterois*. *Hetairois* is a translation of the Hebrew *haverim*.

26. I translate here twice "here comes" instead of "it came." That way, it is good Hebrew.

27. As we know, the Greek says "the Son of Man." Hugo Grotius has already asserted that "Son of Man" in Hebrew also means "man." In my opinion, it is completely excluded at this point that a messianic title is meant here, and thus the occupation of "the Son of Man" would be justified. On this point, cf. especially Geza Vermes, *Jesus the Jew* (London: Collins, 1972), 182.

28. See Klostermann, *Das Matthäusevangelium*, 101.

29. From a translation back into Hebrew, the following possibility arises: the Hebrew word for the Greek "was justified" is *zadqah*. The Greek *apo* would be *min* in Hebrew. Then the saying would have been: "Wisdom was more correct than her works [or: than her children]." For the Hebrew phrase, see for example, Gen 38:26. But all of this is uncertain.

When Jesus told the parable of the children playing, he probably had Zech 12:10 in mind, a biblical verse that in New Testament times was supposed to refer to the death of Christ:[30]

> And over the house of David and over the inhabitants of Jerusalem I will pour out a spirit of grace and supplication. And they shall look on him whom they have pierced, and mourn for him, as one mourns for the only child. And they will weep bitterly over him, as one weeps over the firstborn.

This is the Hebrew text today. From two New Testament passages, John 19:37 and Rev 1:7, we can conclude that in this verse, already before 100 CE, Jesus was understood as "the pierced one." Even the early church fathers repeated this interpretation.[31] In the rabbinic literature, "the pierced one" from Zech 12:10 is the Messiah the son of Joseph.[32] However, the Hebrew Bible text available to us seems to be corrupted. The Hebrew phrase "they pierced him" is especially suspicious. The Greek translation is "and they will look at me[33] instead of having[34] danced, and they will mourn." Even the Aramaic Targum says "to dance" not "to pierce." The two words have a similar sound in Hebrew: *raqadu* (they danced) and *daqaru* (they pierced). The reading *raqadu* (they danced) is well attested in the witnesses. It is not only in the Septuagint text; the Aramaic Targum also bears witness to it, which is even more remarkable since the Targum rarely gives preference to the variants over the Masoretic text. Through these readings of the Septuagint and the Targum, the Bible text is not without its issues. I would still prefer them. Through them, "the dancing" in the past is opposed to the "mourning" in the present. This is also true of the preacher: "Grief has its time and dancing has its time" (Eccl 3:4).[35]

---

30. See Flusser, "Hystaspes and John of Patmos" (especially notes 120–24). In Jewish medieval apocalyptics, too, Zech 12:10 refers to the Messiah ben Joseph (31); Barnabas letter 7:9; Justinus, Dial.c.Tryph. 7.

31. Barnabas letter 7:9; Justinus, Dial.c.Tryph. 7.

32. Cf. Strack and Billerbeck, *Kommentar zum Neuen Testament aus Talmud und Midrasch*, vol. 2, 292–99; Volz, 229. The oldest temporally fixed rabbinic text after the "pierced one" of Zech 12:10, which refers to the Messiah ben Joseph, dates from the second half of the third century CE.

33. "On me" is also written in the Hebrew Bible.

34. The Greek translator did not have the *Hebrew Qet asher* at his disposal but *tachat asher*.

35. If we choose the reading of the Greek and Aramaic translations, then the Hebrew verbs in Eccl 3:4 and Zech 12:10 correspond.

Jesus makes the children say in our parable: "We have piped for you, and you have not danced, we have sung lamentations, and you have not mourned" (Matt 11:17; Luke 7:32).[36] Did Jesus, in telling the parable of the children playing, also have in mind the words of Kohelet and Zechariah, with the variant read by the Targumist and the Septuagint translator? This needs to be seriously considered! At that time, mourning was not only a movement of emotion, but also a ceremony. The children accuse their playmates that they did not respond to their make-believe lamentations with a make-believe mourning ceremony. It can be assumed that Jesus alluded to Zech 12:10 precisely because the words of Zechariah gave his parable a fourth dimension, so to speak. With the reading "they danced," the word of the prophet could also be understood as a hidden reference to the messengers of God (John and Jesus) and the fickle reaction they received. It corresponds entirely to the way in which Jesus also uses other biblical passages for current references.

The other parallel to Jesus' parable of the children playing is a fable of Aesop.[37] Fables were popular with the rabbis. They developed them and used them often.[38] Jesus also knew the fables of Aesop. I have already mentioned that it was probably no coincidence that Jesus made Aesopian associations three times in connection with Herod Antipas. He therefore regarded the tetrarch and his court as a kind of "animal farm." In Luke 13:32 he calls Herod Antipas a fox. It is possible that Jesus is referring to the cunning nature of Herod. Since we learn nothing from other sources of the craftiness of this man, the word of Jesus would in this case be a real contribution to the characterization of this Jewish would-be-king. But there is also another possibility: In rabbinic literature, "fox" usually refers to a low-minded person of low origin who has great dignity. "The fox is not a lion."[39] This fits perfectly with the originally non-Jewish Herodian dynasty. They were Idumean upstarts and "slaves in the house of the Hasmoneans."[40] When Jesus referred to Antipas as a "fox," he was more likely to associate these latter conceptual complexes with it. When Jesus spoke of the reed that wavered in the wind, he meant courtiers who dwell in the kings' houses and

---

36. The word we have translated as "mourning" is *kopto* in the Greek translation of Zech 12:10; Eccl. 3:4; Matt 1:17. The first two have "mourned," *safod* in Hebrew. Jesus certainly tied in with *safod*. Luke 7:32 turned mourning into weeping.

37. Jülicher, *Die Gleichnisreden Jesu*, 26f., has already referred to it.

38. See chapter 3, notes 2–10, above. In the case of chapter 3, note 23, there is an Aesop fable that bears an external resemblance to the parable of the fishnet.

39. Cf. Jacob Levy, *Wörterbuch über die Targumim und Midraschim*, vol. 4: 589, 657.

40. Thus it is judged of Herod I in bBB 3b.

wear soft clothes (Matt 11:7–9; Luke 7:24–26). He alluded to the court of the Tetrarch and to John the Baptist and related the Aesop fable of the oak tree and the reeds[41] to them. The Baptist is the oak, the courtiers are the reed. The third passage reminiscent of Aesop, but only indirectly (namely, about the Baptist and connected with Herod Antipas) is our parable of the children playing. Jesus told it on the same occasion that he had alluded to the fable of the oak and the reeds. When Jesus makes the children say, "We have piped to you, and you have not danced," these words not only remind us—as we have already said—of Eccl 3:4, but also of another fable of Aesop, which occurs in Herodotus (1:141). According to this fable, a fisherman took a flute and began to whistle. He thought that this would attract the fish to the shore. And when he saw himself deceived in his hope, he took a great net, caught a great multitude of fish, and drew them out. When he saw them fidgeting, he said to the fish, "Stupid creatures! When I piped, you did not dance, but now that I have ceased, you dance."[42] The content of the parable of Jesus is different from that of the Aesop fable: we find the words "When I piped, you did not dance" almost literally in the mouths of the children in Jesus' parable. We already found dancing (without piping) in two passages of the Bible (in Eccl 3:4 and in the variant of Zech 12:10), in contrast to mourning. Piping and dancing, however, can only be found in the Aesop fable. Jesus thus remembered somehow the Aesop fable when he told the parable of the children playing. The already proverbial character of the parable also indicates that Jesus likely slightly modified a literary artifact handed down within Judaism. In this case, the possible influences mentioned could have been effective in Judaism even before Jesus.

In Jesus' parable, the fickle children are the reflection of unreasonable adults. Epictetus also uses this image in a similar sense.

> In every endeavor, one should judge the individual things according to careful consideration. Now they play athletes, then wrestlers again, then they blow a trumpet, then they play a piece about something they have seen and admired. So now you become an athlete, then a wrestler, then a philosopher, then a speaker, and then you are nothing at all with your whole soul: like a monkey, you imitate everything you see. One thing at a time is fun. But you don't enjoy what you're used to.[43]

---

41. See chapter 3, note 9, above.

42. Hausrath, "Corpus fabularum Aesopicarum," 17f.; Stalk 27: 13f. See chapter 3, notes 5 and 10, above.

43. Epictetus 3, 15.5–7.

Let nothing be done without reflection. Elsewhere, Epictetus compares a person who considers the material things to be nothing, but still likes to play with them and deal with them: with children who play with potsherds, they argue about this game, but do not care about the potsherds themselves.[44] Here, too, the children serve as a comparison for human irrationality, a picture that we have also found with Jesus.

The last example from Epictetus has a remarkable parallel in rabbinic literature. The rabbinic parallel deserves special attention, among other things, because it is the only rabbinic parable dealing with unreasonable children, as we also find in Matt 11:16f.; Luke 7:31. Rabbi Shimeon ben Eleazar (second century) said a parable:

> Whom does the matter resemble? It is like children playing with fruit seeds. Whenever in the course of the game a child takes a fruit seed from his playmate, he comes and tears his clothes. But when they have ceased to play, they go and throw away the fruit seeds. Such are the evildoers: they tear away, rob and steal one from another. And when they die, they leave everything they own for others. For it is said, "And to others they leave their wealth."[45]

In content and morals, this parable is reminiscent of that of Rabbi Nathan, who was already quoted above.[46] But the main themes of the two parables are different. Our parable has as its theme the children playing. The parable of Rabbi Nathan, on the other hand, has work ethic, or the master and the servant, as its main theme. Both parables say, among other things, that when you die you must leave all your possessions behind. But the emphasis is different. Although the morality of both parables sounds similar, their subject is adapted to the different emphasis or orientation of the teaching.

The importance of the hour of death as a step from the false to the real is known to the Greeks and rabbis. Both connect with this realization the truth that one must leave here everything that is transitory. The parable of Rabbi Nathan and his covetous servants and that of Rabbi Shimeon ben Eleazar of the children playing with fruit seeds would have sounded familiar to the philosopher of that time. Epictetus also says in his parable picture that, although you may collect snails and small octopuses on the shore, if the captain calls, you must leave everything and hurry into the ship."[47]

---

44. Epictetus 4, 7.5.
45. SemH 3, 5, ed. Higger, 222.
46. See chapter 1, note 7.
47. See chapter 6, note 19.

According to the parable of Rabbi Nathan, people make possessions so excessively important that they fight with their fellow human beings over them. In contrast, the children in the parable of Rabbi Shimeon ben Eleazar are rushing for fruit seeds. But at the end of the game, they leave them and scatter them on the earth. Property is therefore worthless according to the Shimeon ben Eleazar parable. A similar distinction can be found in the parable of Epictetus about the children playing.[48] Like the children in the rabbinic parable, the children in Epictetus know that the toys are worthless. In Epictetus's parable, however, there is an additional nuance: the children involuntarily distinguish between the seriousness of the game and the worthlessness of the seeds. Both the parable of Rabbi Shimeon and the parable of Rabbi Nathan could also be found in Epictetus. On the other hand, Epictetus's playing children would not be a bad subject for a rabbinic parable. Jesus could have said the same thing. But perhaps he would not like to speak of wrongdoers in a parable. Be that as it may, the fickleness of the children playing is in any case a possible parable for the Greeks, for the rabbis, and for Jesus!

This brings us back to the starting point. The Greek-philosophical parable pictures describe cases, situations, and persons from everyday life to depict moral teachings on the level of practical philosophy. The object of moral teaching is man, his problems, and his end. In the Greek parable images, there is sometimes also a symbolic figure for the deity. In our examples, we met this figure as a homeowner and as a ship captain. The moral atmosphere and the problems dealt with are no different from what "classical" older rabbinic parables want to teach us. It is necessary to ask whether and to what extent most of Jesus' parables are quite different. Mature Jewish parables, in relative contrast to Greek parable images, are whole epic stories. They therefore form, like the Aesop fables, a special literary genre. On the Greek side, the parable of Cleanthes[49] is most like the mature Jewish parables. Given all the similarities and dissimilarities, it seems to me well-founded that there was a Greek prehistory of the Jewish parables. A longer inner-Jewish development until the genus reached its end is also to be assumed. The old, "classical" Jewish parable genre, to which the parables of Jesus also belong, forms this end.

Rabbinic parables and their Greek parallel phenomena belong to the layer of thought, which is referred to by the unsuccessful expression "vulgar

---

48. See chapter 6, note 44.
49. See chapter 6, note 16.

ethics." The subjects of the rabbinic parables and the Greek-philosophical parable pictures want to establish a viable morality. They are wisely taken from ordinary daily life. It is generally difficult to trace the influences in the field of "popular ethics." In our case, however, a Greek popular philosophical influence on the origin of rabbinic parables is probable—at least, it is not in doubt. The Jewish parables have a similar moral orientation as the Greek-philosophical parable pictures. The moral realms illuminated by the Greek parable images and the Jewish parables are also similar. The relations between the level of the image and the level of moral doctrine are quite the same in both cases. How far the subject is related or equal among the Greeks and the Jews would result from a thorough examination of the Greek parable images.

We have now touched on the complex and controversial question of Greek influences on rabbinic Judaism, especially Palestinian rabbinic Judaism. Unfortunately, researchers' conclusions sometimes depend too much on their worldview. Jewish Talmud scholars rightly emphasize the special, autonomous character of ancient Palestinian Judaism. Many of them, however, are unwilling to acknowledge more than an outward Greek influence on Rabbinic Judaism. Some Christian scholars, on the other hand, would prefer Christianity not to be committed to a thoroughly Jewish religion. They know that Christianity originated amid Palestinian Judaism and took its first decisive steps there. To detoxify the situation, so to speak, they underline twice and three times that Judaism was not monolithic at the time. At the same time, they overestimate and celebrate the Greek influence on Rabbinic Judaism. One could escape these one-sided accentuations if one were not only better versed in Jewish literature—and indeed in the original languages—but also grasped more clearly how the ancient Greeks taught and wrote prose and poetry. Empathy for both literatures is utterly necessary! One should also increasingly try to develop and use new methods to distinguish, for example, between a Greek influence and analogies within Judaism.

The fact that there was a Hellenistic acculturation in the Middle East after the conquests of Alexander the Great, especially during the reigns of the Ptolemies, Seleucids, and Romans is a well-known fact. It should also be known that the Hellenization has not been far-reaching in many ethnic groups and cultures, and that some Eastern cultures and languages have outlasted the Hellenistic infiltration. Palestinian Judaism, which lay apart from the power centers of Hellenism, also survived Hellenism. It was culturally and religiously so self-confident and powerful that it was able to banish the danger of Hellenistic domination through the Maccabean uprising. Hellenism did not meet with a dying, archaic culture in Judaism. Rather, new forces were at work at that time, mainly in Palestinian Jewry. When later Christianity and Islam emerged from Judaism, these forces worked out into the wider world. On the other hand, because of Greek and Roman domination and Hellenism's civilizational and cultural values, it penetrated, so to speak, into the pores of cultural and national communities that were not decisively subject to it. In particular, the Greek "Paideia," this precious fruit of Greek culture, exerted the greatest influence on all the peoples of that time. The Greek-philosophical parable images originated from the background of the Greek Paideia.

According to Oswald Spengler, the Greek influence on Hebrew culture can be described as "pseudomorphism." The politically empowered culture of Hellenism oppressed Judaism—and other peoples—with great force. It spread to India and southern Asia. This influx of culture was not universally met with hatred or devotion. Although it fertilized Palestinian Judaism, no Greek grafting and no full Greek-Jewish symbiosis arose in Palestine. The Jewish spiritual life did not lose its habitus in its land. The substance and internal structure of Judaism remained. But since the Hellenistic influence was, so to speak, constantly in the air and had to be inhaled somehow, there were changes in access to one's own Jewish heritage. The questions concerning God, man and morality changed. Accordingly, new answers were also attempted. All this happened without rabbinic Judaism being substantially Hellenized. One can roughly cover this process of influencing, on the one hand, and of mobilizing and updating one's own basic abilities, on the other hand, with the term "pseudomorphosis." If I see correctly, the genesis of the rabbinic parable genus is an excellent example of the appropriation of foreign impulses which have initiated an inner growth of a particular literary genre.

If there is to be a harmonious influence on a foreign culture, there must be a willingness to be influenced. In our case, a willingness toward the ethics of Greek popular philosophy, among other things, could be shown. Jews at that time saw an essential relationship between Judaism and Greek thought. Judaism is a moral religion with a philosophical outlook.

Our assumption of a Greek influence on the genus of Jewish parables must sometimes remain hypothetical. The hypothetical character is determined in part by the nature and the lack of exploration of Greek parallels. However, it can be assumed that the Greek influence worked quite early. It had probably already become influential by the pre-Maccabean period, since the resistance against Hellenism before the time of Antiochus IV (175–164 BCE) was not very pronounced among the Jewish "elders and sages." The oldest surviving Jewish parable, that of Antigonus of Socho, dates from shortly before the Maccabean uprising. Even more strongly, an early assessment of Greek influence is supported by literary critical observations. The mature Jewish parables are a developed literary form—so there must be a longer history of inner-Jewish development behind it. Since they were already popular in New Testament times and typical of rabbinic Judaism, takeovers and adaptations must have been commonplace shortly before the Maccabean times at the latest.

7

THE SUBJECT OF PARABLES AND ITS PURPOSE

Since Jülicher, research into Jesus' parables has suffered from, among other things, applying the standards of realistic art theory to them. The parables were conceived as realistic little narratives taken from everyday life. This paved the way for their true understanding. The realistic aesthetics applied by researchers after Jülicher's initial attempt also lacked allegorization. Therefore, it was not recognized that the subject of the parable represents one level and its moral teaching another. In the end, all the explanations of the Jesus' parables found in the Gospels were set aside as secondary.

Modern literary criticism takes a different path. Many contemporary literary researchers—having broken free from the chains of realism—resemble the art researchers of the eighteenth century. In this work, I deliberately connected with eighteenth-century researchers, especially Lessing. I also followed Lessing in that I experimented to examine the possibilities of the genre. In some cases, I even made hypothetical changes. This new approach to literature undoubtedly advises us better than the methods customary since Jülicher, even in the case of parables. The Russian formalists, especially Shklovsky, were good teachers to me. For my investigation, the following sentences are particularly important and characteristic of Shklovsky:

> Inequality requires similarity in order to reproduce its own in order to establish its special system. The fixed forms of art live by and through change. The laws that determine the meanings of the texts in predicted constants will be referred to in the future as "convention." It is those conditions that are known both to the author of the respective signal system and to the receiver. A single altered train of similarities is capable of altering the whole system by its inequality employed in various ways. The inequality of the similar is quite economic, for it makes the system part of a new communication without destroying it.[1]

---

1. Viktor Shklovsky, *Von der Ungleichheit des Ähnlichen in der Kunst* (Munich, 1973), 14. It is worth mentioning some of the works of the philosopher Christian

The literary-critical aspect of my study of the parables could be described in Shklovsky's words as a consideration of the "inequality of the similar" in the parables, or also of the similarity of the dissimilar in them. The achievements of the Russian formalists, as I have already stated several times, are particularly well suited for the exploration of such literary genres, which are often short and at the same time highly stylized and rigid. Rabbinic parables and Jesus' parables undoubtedly belong to these genera.

Parables, Aesop's fables, and European fairy tales are genera with a high degree of stylization. In part, this is because they are popular and passed down orally. In the case of Aesop's fables and rabbinic parables, they take place on two levels: on the visible level of the subject and on the invisible, sometimes not even mentioned, level of moral teaching. This results in a double convention for these two genres: a convention on the nature of the subject, its themes and motifs—the listener is supposed to find something familiar—and, in addition, an unspoken agreement between the narrator

---

Wolff about fables, *Philosophia Practica Universalis* (1738), 2, 302–16, quoted in German translation from Leibfried and Werle, *Texte zur Theorie der Fabel*, 34–42. Wolff makes no distinction—as was customary in his day—between animal fables and parables: "What is invented in the fable shall be known among the people. For the fable is intended to produce the conception of a truth, especially a moral one, in the mind. Therefore, it is necessary that whoever hears them tells an idea of it, or that he can realize what is being told. . . . Thus it is also necessary that what is invented in the fable, if one considers it individually, must be perceived more often beforehand and therefore must also be generally known. And since fables are usually written for the masses, then the fable must be formed from elements that are familiar to the masses. . . . Christ also observes the same in his parables, which fall under the concept of fable. . . . Christ teaches in the parable of the farmer who sows the seed in his field, the efficacy of the divine Word, and in what way it can be hindered in its efficacy, quite vividly. . . . Anyone who wants to create fables must know what is generally known. For what is created in the fable must be known to the broad masses, or what is derived from it must be a generally known thing. It is therefore clear that whoever wishes to create fables must have knowledge of things that are generally known." Not only what Wolff says about the parable of the sower but his whole treatise is excellent. It fits the parables much better than animal fables. Aristotle's literary theory kept eighteenth-century minds from the insight that—in contrast to parables—a certain improbability makes up the charm of the genre "animal fable." What Wolff writes about the literary convention is also important to our discussion and not far from what we have just learned from Shklovsky. But there, Wolff was under the spell of Aristotelian theory; he could not recognize that this convention between the producer and the consumer refers to both the reflected reality and the literary side of fables and parables. The reader or the listener knows what to expect from what is heard or written.

and the listener on the meaning of the subject and its components for the teaching that the listener is supposed to draw from the fable or the parable. The nature of the subject should make the way to "the poodle's core" as easy as possible for the listener.[2] Therefore, the subject and the moral solution are coordinated.

The correspondences between the level of the subject and the level of its moral teaching are stronger and much more precise in the parables than in Aesop's fables. For this reason, the parables are much more "allegorical" than the fables. For the same reason, the rigidity of the convention is more pronounced in the parables. In the fables there are no fixed symbols as in the parables. The fable action is more important to the moral theorem than the subject figures. Most likely, the lion is still intended to represent the king or the powerful of the earth. But what the fox does, for example, shows how cunning people tend to act and warns against them. The fox, the lamb, and the raven as persons, however, should not and cannot be interpreted exactly on their typological equivalents—the typology is too general. It would be banal to say that the fox is a deceitful man and the lamb is pure innocence. One would then miss the main purpose of the fable. Correspondences between the figures of the fable and parallel persons in their moral teaching are not a convention of this genre. In contrast to the genre of rabbinic parables, there is no "cast of characters" whatsoever at the level of the moral teaching of the fables. Such a correspondence between the level of the image and the level of its teaching, on the other hand, is rudimentarily present in Greek philosophical similitudes. We have seen, for example, that in Epictetus God corresponds to the owner of the house and to the captain of the ship,[3] and that in Cleanthes[4] the servants are represented as rightly and wrongly acting men, as is also the case with Jesus and the rabbinic parables. This relationship between Greek philosophical parable pictures and Jewish similitudes may provide further support for our hypothesis that Greek similitudes were a precursor and an approach to the Jewish parables.

So, there was a twofold consensus between the narrator and the listener of each of the parables: on the nature of the subject and on the symbolic content of the subject. The alliance between the narrator and the listener regarding the nature and symbolic content of the subject is the backbone and guide of the parable genre. Without this convention, there would be no rabbinic

---

2. Here, Flusser uses an expression from Goethe's *Faust.* —Trans.

3. Cf. chapter 6, notes 18 and 19.

4. Cf. chapter 6, note 16.

parables and no parables of Jesus. The rabbis said, "Let not the parable be a trifling thing in your eyes, for by a parable man can come to an understanding of the words of the Torah."[5] On the same page of the Talmud, the parables are compared with a handle for carrying, with the thread of Ariadne, with a sickle that makes the way through a cane thicket possible, with handles with which one can move a large box or vessel, and with a rope for drawing cool, good water from a deep well. Aristotle believed the parable should facilitate communication.[6] Jesus' parables also had the purpose of clarification.[7] They belong to the genre of rabbinic parables, which were designed to make it easier for man to understand the teaching. Based on Matt 13:10–15 par., we will also explain that Jesus' words about the purpose of the parables were originally intended to express the same thing. To present the intended teaching pictorially, the subject must be oriented towards the moral principle. That is why Jesus often adds the interpretation of his parable, especially when the subject is ambiguous or even incomprehensible without explanation.

Let us now summarize the convention inherent in the nature of the subject, leaving aside, as far as possible, the question of the influence of moral teaching on the composition of the subject. The structure of the parable subject is more rigid and conventional than the structure of the fable; it is closer to the structure of European fairy tales. As with these fairy tales, the theme, its motifs, and the thematic-motif relationships are often strongly influenced in the parables. They are assumed to be known and welcomed by listeners. In contrast to the rabbinic parables, which include the parables of Jesus, European fairy tales take place on only one level. One can conclude from this that the fixed imprints and the conventional theme of the parables are not solely determined by the correspondences between the level of the subject and the level of the moral. It also follows that the "rule of the game," which permits variations regarding the choice of motifs of parables (or even borrowing from other main motifs) applies not only to rabbinic parables, because the main theme, subject, and motifs point to the level of the moral. Otherwise, it would be incomprehensible that the same rules apply to European fairy tales, which touch only one level. The special charm of fairy tales and parables lies precisely in the variations and enrichments within the framework of the rigid forms and conventions of both genera. What is conventional in the parables and the fixed nature of the subject and its components can also be

---

5. bEr 21b.

6. Cf. Jülicher, *Die Gleichnisreden Jesu*, vol. 1, 71f.

7. Cf. Klostermann, *Das Matthäusevangelium*, 115f.

shown by the fact that the subjects of their main themes and motifs were also retained in later nonclassical or post-classical rabbinic parables, although the level of interpretation of these parables had meanwhile become different. We have already mentioned the fact that in these parables also the subjects no longer served to represent a moral truth figuratively only, but mainly to illustrate biblical verses and acts of biblical figures.

> In the choice of themes, the rabbinic parables differ diametrically from the fairy tales. The fairy tales proclaim the wonderful, the supernatural, the magical. The themes of the parables, on the other hand, stem from everyday practical life. The parable appeals in favor of a new thing to the universally known and recognized of a similar kind. Darkness tolerates this form of speech the least. . . . Illustrare is the tendency of the parable, only the illustre, which is really in luce, can one mind conquer another reluctant mind. What itself is not completely solid can never help to make a neighbor more solid; what itself does not immediately make sense cannot spread light over another. An opaque parable is worse than none at all.[8]

Jülicher thus writes the right things concerning the themes and motifs of the parables. They are usually as simple as possible to give the impression of realism. We have already said that this realism is artificial. In addition, the number of main topics is limited in rabbinic parables and in Jesus' parables. The motifs of the subjects are also conventional. To gain the trust of the listener, the storyteller must tell him something familiar.

Jülicher further says:

> Yes, in the allegory the figurative is to be interpreted, in the parable it is to be interpreted, or more correctly, by its overflowing clarity also its parallel is to make clearer. The figurative character of a parable must therefore not only be taken from the general spheres of perception and experience, but must also be guarded from every ingredient which makes understanding more difficult; for example, it is not advisable to use a metaphor in it. Parables, in which something must first be explained, miss their purpose. Known, clearly secured from any objection, everything must be in the image half of the parable. But if the listener does not simplify to one: this must be so, or: this is so, then the listener is forced, if he shrugs his shoulders, or with one: possible! then the parable-maker wasted time and effort.[9]

---

8. Jülicher, *Die Gleichnisreden Jesu*, vol. 1, 73f.
9. Jülicher, *Die Gleichnisreden Jesu*, vol. 1, 73f.

Jülicher is no longer quite right. If he and his successors were correct that the parables were purely realistic, then a quite realistic case could certainly not emanate a clear moral teaching on the religious-moral level! As far as I can see, even a truly allegorical parable would serve the interpretation better than pure realism. Rather, it must be emphasized repeatedly that the subjects of the parables are not realistic but pseudo-realistic, both for the sake of their interpretability and for their stylized and stereotypical nature. How the subjects of the parables are partly autonomous is also shown by the fact that a subject can be used for very different purposes. I tried to show this about the parable of the treasure and the pearl (Matt 13:44–46).[10] If Jesus had not expressly pointed out to us that this double parable means the kingdom of heaven, it could also be pointed to the election of Israel. The parable of the mustard seed (Luke 13:18f. par.) expresses the growth of the kingdom of heaven very beautifully. But we are only shown the right way to interpret it because Jesus told us this and because the following parable of the leaven (Matt 13:33; Luke 13:20) is also determined by the same interpretation. Without Jesus' reference, could we be so sure that the parable of the mustard seed refers to the kingdom of heaven? Would we find it wholly inappropriate if this parable were related to the growth of the Word of God in the heart of man? We have already seen that the Jews at that time referred the growth of the seed to the development of teaching.[11] We will also be able to see that there is also a parable with the same emphasis in Seneca.[12] Jesus himself also compared the prosperous word of God with the fruitful seed (Mark 4:8, 20 par.). Jesus often interpreted his own parables wisely. The parable interpretations in the gospels cannot be denied to him without serious reasons and transferred to the early church. However, I do not put the emphasis on it here. Rather, I would like to emphasize that Jülicher and his descendants were wrong in their thesis that the images of Jesus' parables were "abundantly clear." In reality, the parables are characterized by a relative independence of their subjects. This is given by the immanent literary formalism in the structure of the subjects and by their limited number. This certain autonomy of the subjects of the parables is dictated by the consensus of the narrator and listener. Because the listener expects a familiar realistic theme and therefore does not want to be surprised, the narrator designs the structure of the subject in a conventional formula. This aspect

---

10. See chapter 5, notes 30–46.
11. See chapter 5, notes 24–30.
12. Seneca, Epist. 8, 38.2.

of the "rigidity" of the parables is not related to the correspondences of the half-image with the moral plane. I will also try to show that the latter also contributes to the conventional structure of the parable genre.

There is also a certain tension between the level of the subject and that of its moral-religious sense in those parables which do not require any explicit interpretation, even if the content of the subject determines the sense of similarity based on the consensus of narrator and listener, and even if the motifs of the subject and its structuring are coordinated with the interpretation. Precisely because the parables—as Jülicher correctly observed—are not allegories, but want to appear realistic, and because the structure of their subjects is strongly stylized, one cannot (and must not) look for a correspondence on the moral level for all the details of the parables. This applies not only to the rabbinic parables and Jesus' parables, but also to the philosophical parable images of the Greeks. In Cleanthes's parable picture of the two servants sent to seek Plato, one searches the whole hall of pillars and must finally return unsuccessful, tired, and angry. The other servant, on the other hand, a lazy one, is lounging around with the town rabble, contrary to his search mission, and accidentally discovers Plato passing by.[13] Through realistic description, the zeal of one servant and the foolish character of the other are clearly accentuated in this parable. This makes the meaning even clearer. But it will not occur to anyone to allegorize these details. The same also applies to Epictetus's parable of the anchoring ship where the sailors leave "to fetch fresh water." If someone picks up "a snail and a small squid" on the way, then he must pay attention to the call of the captain, leave these items he picked up if necessary and hurry back. Otherwise, he will be thrown into the ship and "bound like a sheep."[14] Such images are easily memorized by the listener. If a parable were not pictorial, it would not be a parable. Epictetus compares the small squid and the small snail to a woman and a child. But hardly anyone will have the grotesque idea that the little squid allegorically symbolizes the wife and the snail the children! The number *two* is important for the meaning of the picture, as well as the relative unimportance of the two little animals, on which one can temporarily rely. So, the two cute creatures have a poetic, not an allegorical, significance.

The same is true of rabbinic parables. Take, for example, the rabbinic parable of the children playing around fruit seeds.[15] The children take the

---

13. See chapter 6, note 6.
14. See chapter 6, note 19.
15. See chapter 6, note 45.

fruit seeds very seriously during the game. When a seed is taken from one child, he tears the clothes of the other. When the game is over, however, the seeds are scattered. All this is very clear! The game is human life. The fruit seeds you play with and wave childishly are the fortune you leave behind when you die. So, the fruit seeds in the rabbinic parable have the same function as the little squid and the little snail at Epictetus. The fruit seeds of the rabbis are just as worthless as the animals of the Epictetus. Thus we have learned not only about the epic dynamics of parables, but also about how to adapt a subject to the moral level of a parable!

Let us now examine the rabbinic parable of Eccl 12:7, which I first presented at the beginning of this book,[16] to assess the relationship between the subject and moral teaching. The parable wants to impress on man that he should give back to God the spirit at death as purely as he received it. In the parable, a king gave royal robes to his servants. The wise among them wrapped them up and put them in a chest; the foolish among them went and did their work in them. After a while, the king demanded his clothes back. The wise among them gave them back to him in a clean state, but the foolish among them gave back to him dirty. Then the king rejoiced over the wise, and was angry with the foolish, and said concerning the wise, "My garments are to be brought into the treasury, and they may go home in peace. As for the fools, he spoke. My garments are to be brought to the washer, and they are to be put in prison." I have repeated the most important sentences of this parable here so that the reader can easily convince himself how, in the case of a high-clarity parable, the subject and its motifs are seamlessly adapted to the moral plane so that no explicit explanation is necessary. This assumes the silent agreement between the narrator and the listener that God is signified by the king, and the time from the distribution of the royal robes to their return symbolizes human life from birth to death. The wise and the foolish on the subject plane stand for the just and the sinners on the moral plane. Based on these conventions, the rest becomes clear: The garments distributed to the servants signify the souls which God lends to man at birth and which man must give back to God at death. The pious keep their souls in a pure state; they protect them from dirt in a chest. Sinners, on the other hand, defile their souls with their transgressions—the parable employs the image of workmen doing the dirty work in royal garments to illustrate this. At death, the pure souls of the pious are preserved "in the bundle of life"—according to the parable in the king's

---

16. See chapter 1, note 5.

treasuries. The souls of the wicked who are defiled by sin will be thrown into hell—according to the parable they will be brought to the washer like filthy garments. This will also be clear from the Bible verses quoted at the end of the parable. The bodies of the righteous will "enter in peace; they will rest on their couches" (Isa 57:52), or, according to the parable, they will "go home in peace." On the other hand, there will be "no peace" for the body of sinners (Isa 48:22); according to the parable, they will be imprisoned.

In this parable we have found the following equations, or pairs of equations: The king corresponds to God, the wise servants correspond to the righteous, the foolish servants to the wicked. The royal garment corresponds to the soul, the distribution of the garments to birth, the reclaiming of the garments to death. Filth corresponds to sin and cleanliness to innocence. The treasuries correspond to the bliss of souls. The washer symbolizes the punishment of souls. Returning home means finding rest for the bodies of the righteous. The prison, on the other hand, points to the punishment of the bodies of the wicked. However, although there are so many correspondences between the subject and the moral plane, this parable is by no means a constructed, elaborate allegory. It is nothing more than an excellent parable. The subject has an inner consistency, and the content is interesting. The subject also has a certain autonomy, which means that you cannot interpret all the details completely and easily. This restrained tension and the remarkable unevenness between subject and moral give the parable its freshness. The following details fit here: The foolish servants do their work in the royal robes; this makes the clothes dirty. The work here is an interspersed epic-realistic element. It would be absurd to interpret them symbolically. The same applies to the realistically intended folding of the royal robes and their careful deposit in the treasure chest by the wise servants. In the present parable, therefore, work must not be interpreted as a symbol of human activity in general. No one will say that the parable wants to teach us that the soul should not participate in human activity! Rather, the parable narrator apparently only wanted to say that man should keep the soul away from sin during his life. The treasury in which the clothes are brought is a symbol of the chambers of souls familiar to Judaism. Bringing the dirty clothes to the washer means rejection to the torment of hell—the laundry is not treated mildly by the washer. Only the brutal treatment has its equivalent in the interpretation, but not that the clothes become clean by washing. This cannot be a reference to purgatory, which, by the way, is not entirely foreign to Judaism. Regarding the washer, therefore, there is an imperfect correspondence between the illustration portion and the teaching portion of the parable.

We speak of a perfect parable when the subject and its components are coordinated with the moral plane as successfully as possible. However, in the rabbinic parable we have just discussed, we have found that there is no perfect correspondence between the two levels. I regard such unevenness as a factor belonging to the postulated "perfect parable." A universally balanced, universally harmonious, and universally proportioned correspondence is not desired in the parable. This would interfere with the consistency and probability of the narrative. Furthermore, deviations from absolute correspondences and norms bring about a noticeable poetic spell. We shall yet see, for example, that Jesus' parable of the sower (Luke 8:4–8 par.) violates some "normal" rules of the genre. However, its effect on feeling is not affected by this.

Some motifs and designs of the subject are therefore transparent, others are not. The number of transparent components varies from case to case in the rabbinic parables and in the parables of Jesus. I will also explain that in the parable of the talents (Matt 25:14–30) and in the parallel parable of Luke (Luke 19:11–27) the number of servants and the sum entrusted to them is determined by the subject. For the teaching, only the landlord (or God) and two of the servants who signify a right or wrong action before God are significant. The capital entrusted to the servants signifies what God has given us. The increase of capital by the faithful servant is to teach us that many good deeds can be accomplished if man properly avails himself of the gift of God. Later we will also understand that the punishment of evil expressed in the illustration and the reward of the good servant (Matt 25:28–30; Luke 19:24–26) reflect a Jewish theological view. Further examples can easily be found in the parables of the rabbis and in Jesus' parables, which, on the one hand, show the relative autonomy of the subject and, on the other hand, expose the threads that connect the level of the subject with the level of morality. Furthermore, we have already discussed the tendency to adapt the subject in its motifs as far as possible to the solution of the parable. We have shown, for example, that in Matt 9:37f. and Luke 10:2 Jesus transformed the "great work" that occurs in a common rabbinic saying into the "great harvest." He did this because he spoke not of human life in general, but of the urgency of his message about the kingdom.[17]

The approach of the subject, the theme, and the components of parables to moral teaching and vice versa is determined largely by the consensus between narrator and listener—but not exclusively! The preconditions and

---

17. See chapter 6, notes 2–7.

roots of this understanding lie in the nature of the human soul. It can discover and justify why a particular subject and motif require a particular solution—why they are "transparent" in a particular direction![18] The critical decisions of the soul are not satisfied with the examination of the themes and motifs of the parables. They continue to act on the adaptation of the illustration in the parable even after the crystallization of the genre of parables. In addition to the *a priori* and rational literary convention, intuitive forces of the narrator are also involved in the "moral of the story." Overall, it is not entirely possible to explain intellectually how the mutual relations between the level of the subject and the level of the moral came about in a parable. However, the contributing intuitive component hardly interferes with our understanding of the parable. For this understanding, however, we must learn to understand the essence of the parables as a genre. For the interpretation of Jesus' parables, it is indispensable that we proceed according to the insight that these parables belong to the genre of rabbinic parables.

In parables—as we already know—different motifs and main themes can be used for the same purpose. Whether there is talk of workers or servants, there is not much to it. More importantly, workers or servants are interchangeable in parables because they are dependent on the landlord, and because the landlord has the right to demand a good performance from them. However, a particular motif does not always have to serve a single purpose. In the parable of the wicked winegrowers (Luke 20:9–19 par.) and in some rabbinic parables, the vineyard (because of Isa 5:7) is a symbol for Israel. In contrast, in the parables of the dissimilar sons (Matt 21:28–32) and

---

18. In Bruno Bettelheim's book, *The Uses of Enchantment: The Meaning and Importance of Fairy Tales* (New York: Vintage Books, 1989), he interprets fairy tales according to the rules of classical psychoanalysis. The results sometimes seem distorted to me. However, I must admit that the book betrays a significant person and researcher as an author. Bettelheim's often bizarre conclusions are partly explained by the fact that he is not a literary scholar and barely knows the works of literary researchers. He would have to bear in mind that (European) fairy tales, which he mostly analyzes, form a literary genre that is subject to literary laws. His interpretations are therefore often incorrect. For a similar reason, modern New Testament scholars often misinterpret Jesus' parables. They often do not assume that Jesus' parables are to be considered in connection with the entire literary genre of parables. Despite this limitation, Bettelheim's book is not unimportant. It detects the irrational motifs that play a role in shaping fairy tales. Such intuitive forces undoubtedly also play a role in the design of the parables. They help shape the structure of the subject and choose the individual motifs so that the subject strives for a solution.

of the laborers in the vineyard (Matt 20:1–16), work in the vineyard simply means human achievement before and for God. However, it is also possible that the vineyard in these two Matthean parables is a solution of embarrassment of the Greek translator. It is not excluded that Jesus spoke of an orchard in these two parables. The work in the orchard (Pardes) appears in the rabbinic parables as representative of human achievement. Perhaps the Greek translator found it difficult to find a Greek equivalent for the Hebrew word Pardes. That is why he put the word *vineyard* in, known from other parables. To those who know the rabbinic parables, it seems strange that in the Greek written gospels, the orchard image does not occur.

We have already established that different subjects can also be used for a similar purpose based on two rabbinic parables.[19] The first parable of the banquet, told by Rabban Johanan ben Zakkai, teaches us that one should be ready for the day of the Master. The banquet is an eschatological symbol, both in Judaism and in the sayings of Jesus. In various parables, the image of participation in the "messianic" meal expresses the reward of the righteous. It also points out the punishment of the wicked; they are not only excluded from the meal, but they are also punished differently. At the same time, the parable of Rabban Johanan ben Zakkai also refers to the repentance that should not be postponed until the day of death.[20] The second rabbinic parable, dealing with the king's garments, refers to the hour of death itself. This can already be seen from the introductory verse, Eccl 12:7: "And the Spirit returns to God who gave it." The parable is intended to teach us that at death one should restore the soul to God without blemish. At the end of the parable there is talk of reward and punishment. If one observes the Bible verses quoted at the end of the parable, one recognizes that the parable narrator speaks of the fate of the body and soul after death, and not of the final judgment.

But is the difference in the two parables factually important at all? Is it noticeable at first glance? The second parable speaks of reward and punishment immediately after death, the first of the messianic meal. The first, however, is also focused on the hour of death. The focus of classical rabbinic parables is not the distant future of the end times, but the call to act rightly, not wrongly, in this life. This also applies if they speak of the end-time feast or the eschatological court. Classical rabbinic parables thus serve—even if

---

19. See chapter 1, notes 4 and 5.

20. This is the view of R. Eliezer; to confirm his view, Rabbi Johanan ben Zakkai's parable is inserted in b. Šabb. 153a.

this does not suit many modern theologians—as a primary moral instruction. In Judaism, the hope of future salvation is very strong. This was the case in the time of Jesus and the rabbis. However, the classical rabbinic parables do not reveal much of this end-time tension. The genre did not originate to express the end-time tension. Rather, the parables depict how you and I should live and work rightly and responsibly before God, so that in the end—at death or at the end of time—we can stand before God. Such a pictorial admonition has a grasp of reality! Can the same purpose be presupposed for the parables of Jesus?

Especially since Albert Schweitzer a rediscovery has prevailed in discourse that Jesus and his movement are to be understood in a messianic sense. Previously, the moral-religious meaning of many of Jesus' parables had not been doubted. In addition, it had been emphasized that Jesus' parables contained the church's teaching of Christ. The christological interpretation of the parables was therefore commonplace. So much has changed. Consistent eschatology became modern and underwent many modifications over time. Since one is often Christocentric in a strange way, one tends to understand the parables of Jesus throughout as an existential self-statement of Jesus. Jesus proclaims himself in the parables: "For He whose hidden glory shines forth behind every word and parable, the Savior, has appeared."[21] It seems that Expressionism can feel at home in Christian theology much longer than in the other areas of culture today! This is also related to the fact that the idea of Christian morality tastes bland in the mouths of theologizing Christian researchers. With indignation, they reject Jesus as a sublime moral teacher, as if this moral teacher were an obsolete ghost to be banished. How can one do justice to the moral preaching of Jesus, and how can one grasp the essence of his parables?

The moral-religious content of Jesus' parables becomes clearly definable when one recognizes that they belong to the genre of classical rabbinic parables. Of course, anyone can claim that if two people say the same thing, it does not mean the same thing, and that Jesus therefore adopted the rabbinic parables to change them dialectically. But this could only be true if one could really see that the subjects in Jesus' parables have a different orientation than the same subjects and the same motifs in rabbinic parables. However, such a reversal of the adopted subjects is not detectable in Jesus' parables; that is, if a false ideological view has not already blinded the reader. We have already seen in part that the christological features of

---

21. Jeremias, *Die Gleichnisse Jesu*, 227.

Jesus' parables are secondary and only entered the parables at the Greek stage. This secondary editing process is the expression of the primitive Christian end-time expectation of the parousia. Researchers who indulge in eschatology also admit this. On the one hand they want to remove from the parables what they believe to be secondary expectations of the parousia, but on the other hand, they claim that behind every parable "the hidden glory of the Savior shines forth." But the simple and important truth is that, along with the Sermon on the Mount, the parables are the main vehicle for Jesus' moral message. Jesus made the genre of Jewish parables his own not only for reasons of comprehensibility, but also because *ex natura sua* this genre was able to impress the commandments of moral action on its hearers. Much like classical rabbinic parables, many important parables of Jesus are eschatological only in the sense that the end of human life or the end of time is their point: then it will be shown that the wise will be rewarded and the foolish punished.

I know that I have far from exhausted the manifold theme of Jesus' parables. I have not even mentioned the parables which are completely noneschatological. For the time being, I was only concerned with emphasizing that the subjects and motifs in the parables of Jesus have the same function as in the rabbinic parables. The structures and the interaction of eschatological and noneschatological elements in the parables of Jesus will be dealt with as we examine the individual parables of Jesus. If a comparison between the parables of Jesus and those of the rabbis can critically illuminate the existentially consistent eschatology that prevails today in the interpretation of the parables of Jesus, then the question arises as to whether the monochrome expressionist image of Jesus, which is today drawn by armchair theologians, does justice to the person of Jesus and his message.

8

An Exemplary Parable: The Parable of the Ten Virgins

We have now arrived at a convenient place where we can treat and evaluate in detail Jesus' parable of the ten virgins (Matt 25:1–13). This parable is found only in Matthew, although Luke was also aware of it as I have shown. I also hinted at the context in which the parable stood in the common source of Matthew and Luke, and I pointed out several times that the parable of the ten virgins by no means gives a realistic picture of a village wedding. The two opposing groups of five perform the same actions: one group of girls represents the right action of the wise, and the other the wrong action of fools. It is precisely the high-quality pictorial stylization of how they all appear, or their symmetrical rigidity, that provided an incentive for artists to present this particular parable in their work. The sculptural representation of the parable on either side of the great main door of the Strasbourg Cathedral (around 1280) is rightly famous. In true Gothic style, the artisans used the symmetry from the parable, placing the foolish virgins on the left and the wise ones on the right of the door. Polar dualism is underlined by the fact that there is not only a Christlike groom but also a diabolical seducer. These two figures are followed by three virgins each—for there was no more space on the sides of the door. However, to achieve the original number of virgins, the artisans placed the two remaining figures under a tympanum to the right and left of the door. In addition to their general affiliation to the group of the wise or the foolish, the virgins also show individual traits. These are five variations on the theme of clever virtue and five variations on the theme of the foolish delusion of sin.

The decorative potency of the parable also made it a popular motif of Swedish folk painting. A Swedish folk painting from 1804 was printed on the front of a book. In this painting, the schematic rigidity of the parable offered the folk artist the opportunity to adequately depict the symmetrical ornamentation of the biblical model. In contrast to the virgins in Strasbourg, the ten virgins of the Swedish mural painting have no individuality.

They are stereotypically painted. As a result, the content of the parable does not fully come into its own. On the other hand, however, it becomes clear that the ten virgins are not independent personalities but that they have a decorative function. They are, so to speak, a symbolic manifesto for my understanding of the parables. The decorative folk representation corresponds to the spirit of the parables. Like Swedish folk painting, rabbinic parables and Jesus' parables are all expressions of popular art.

To show the essence and orientation of Jesus' parable as clearly as possible, it is stated here in full:

> "Then the kingdom of heaven will be like ten virgins who took their lamps and went out to meet the bridegroom. Five of them were foolish and five were wise. So the foolish took their lamps and took no oil with them. But the wise took oil in the jugs with their lamps. But when the bridegroom was absent, they all nodded and slept. And in the middle of the night there was a cry: 'Behold the bridegroom! Go out to meet him!' Then all those virgins awoke and prepared their lamps. And the foolish said unto the wise, 'Give us of your oil; for our lamps are gone out.' And the wise answered, 'It would not be enough for us or for you: but go rather to the merchants and buy some yourselves.' And while they went to buy the oil, the bridegroom came, and those who were ready went in with him to the wedding; and the door was shut. Then came the other virgins, and said, 'Master, Master, open unto us.' But he answered and said, 'Verily I say unto you, I know you not.' Watch therefore, because you do not know the day, nor the hour." (Matt 25:1–13)

This beautiful parable is edited only externally and sparingly in Greek. It can therefore serve as an excellent example of the fully developed artistry of Jesus the parable teller. Earlier I mentioned a small but serious intervention by Matthew; he was the one who connected this parable to the kingdom of heaven. On the other hand, I conjectured that the concluding proposition (Matt 25:13) was older than the parable in the Matthean form and arrangement and had been part of the parable from the very beginning. It was apparently shaped by Jesus as an independent moral imperative, which he attached to the parable as his moral teaching.

It is harder to answer another question. Earlier, in two passages of this book, I attempted to reconstruct a saying of Jesus related to the parable of the virgins. In this saying, Jesus resists the cult of his person. He turns against those who call him "Master, Master" but do not do the will of their heavenly Father (Matt 7:21f.; Luke 6:46). Because of the resemblance of this saying to the parable of the ten virgins, Luke 13:25 was shaped in accordance with this parable. In Luke 13:25, the unworthy disciples say to the master of the house, "Master, open to us!" Likewise, the unworthy virgins in Matt 25:11 plead, "Master, Master, open to us!" This repetition of the word *Master* could indeed express the impetuous desire of the virgins standing outside. But in Matt 7:21f. and Luke 6:46, it is more secure as an affirmation of the inappropriate worship of Jesus' person. So, I tend to deduce from the secondary insertion of Luke 13:25 that the words of the parable in Matt 25:11 are themselves influenced by the saying against the cult of personality and that the foolish virgins did not cry out "Master, Master" according to the original wording of the parable, but that they only said, "Master, open to us!" I know that a decision on this issue is not unimportant. After all, the observation of a mutual secondary influence of two of Jesus' sayings regarding the Synoptic Problem and the path to the *ipsissima verba* of Jesus is not without significance.

If we read the parable of the virgins without intermingling it with convoluted thoughts, then we immediately realize what Jesus wanted to draw his listeners' attention to: Be prepared for the call and do not miss the opportunity; otherwise, the opportunity for you may be lost for good. This urgent warning is well known to us from both Jesus' parables and the rabbinic parables. Even in the Essene (or semi-Essene) Damascus Document (CD IV, 9–11), we read an end-time context: "In the completion of time, according to the number of these years, one can no longer join the house of Judah, but everyone must stand on his guard—the wall is built, the statute is far away" (cf. Mic 7:1). Furthermore, in a rabbinic parable of caravansary (a roadside inn), we find the symbolic image of the closed gate: "When I asked you, you did not want to, and now I cannot open it to you."[1]

In both the rabbinic parable and Jesus' parable, the unsuccessful supplicants stand outside the door. In Luke 12:35–38, there is a similar illustration, but it is oriented differently in its subject and in its meaning:

> "Your loins shall be girded and the lights shall burn. And you shall be like men that wait for their master, when he shall depart from the wedding, that they may open to him at once when he comes and knocks. Blessed are these servants whom the Master, when he comes, will find awake."

Here too the lights are burning, but it is the lights of the servants who await the master returning home from a wedding. According to Matthew, how-

---

1. Cf. chapter 1, note 10. In bBQ 80b, it is said, "The door that has been closed will not be opened soon." Quoted in Klostermann, *Das Matthäusevangelium*, 201.

ever, the virgins go out to meet the bridegroom with lamps. In the secondary literature, it is stated that at Arab weddings, the women meet the groom with torches. Does this prove more to the Jews of Jesus' time than what I saw in Delhi, in India, at a wedding? The young groom came riding proudly on his horse, accompanied by a torchlight procession. It means very little today that the torchlight procession receiving the groom is not supported by evidence from rabbinic literature. From rabbinic literature, we at least know that wedding ceremonies took place toward the evening and that it was customary to accompany the bride with torchlight.[2] Elsewhere, it is told how Amram, the father of Moses, after Moses had separated himself from his wife, solemnly took her back at Miriam's request: "He put her in a carrying-chair. Aaron and Miriam each carried wax torches on each side. They went before them." Even if this passage does not quite correspond to the description of the parable, we can rely on the parable reflecting Palestinian wedding customs from the time of Jesus.

In the parable, the foolish virgins beg in vain for the bridegroom to open the closed door for them. In the Lukan parallel (12:35–38), the master, returning from a wedding, knocks and demands that the closed door of his house be opened to him. "Behold, I stand at the door, and knock: he that heareth my voice, and openeth the door, him will I go in, and eat bread with him, and he with me" (Rev 3:20). These two passages are reminiscent of Song 5:2, where the beloved says, "I was asleep and my heart was awake. The voice of my beloved—he knocks: 'Open to me, my sister, my mistress, my dove.'" To this biblical verse, it is said: "God says to Israel, 'My children, open to me an opening of repentance as big as a needle's eye, and I will open to you such an opening through which chariots and carts may enter.'"[3] The rabbinic thought here is certainly not unchristian, and Jesus himself would likely have heard it.

Any analysis, however accurate, of the similarities and differences between Luke 12:35–38 and the parable of the ten virgins does not greatly facilitate the judgment of whether the Lukan passage goes back to Jesus, and if it does, how far back. Surely, the text is stylized in Greek.[4] More important

---

2. Shmuel Safrai, *Compendia Rerum Iudaicarum ad Novum Testamentum*, vol. 2 (Amsterdam, 1976), 758. Safrai quotes PesR 43, 180b, and Friedmann's comment.

3. ShirR to Song 5:2; cf. Bacher, *Die Agada der Palästinischen Amoräer*, vol. 3, 237n1.

4. The structure in Luke 12:35–38 is also influenced by the following parable image of the burglar. Luke 12:38 says, "And he may come in the second and in the third watch." Luke 12:39 speaks of the burglar from the "time" when the

for our investigation is that both the parable of the virgins and the Lukan
parallel speak of waking.[5] I find no reason to deny the demand of waking
up to the "historical" Jesus. I also assume with the same certainty that Jesus
ended the parable by saying, "Watch therefore, because you do not know
the day, nor the hour" (Matt 25:13). But how are falling asleep and waking
up organically related to the subject of the parable? It is obvious that the
story does not end without the falling asleep of all the virgins. The lamps
in the story are "torches [rods wrapped at the top with oil-soaked rags or
flax]."[6] The foolish virgins "were so shortsighted as not to expect a delay in
the wedding feast, and therefore did not think that they would need oil to
refill the torches." The wise virgins, on the other hand, were cautious: they
took vessels with them, "little jugs with narrow necks," filled with oil. The
wait dragged on, and all the virgins nodded off and slept. Meanwhile, the
oil ran out in the burning torches. Falling asleep, however, meant no mis-
fortune for the wise virgins. Although sleep came upon them involuntarily,
when the call came out in the middle of the night, they could refill their
torches with oil. For the foolish virgins, however, falling asleep had serious
consequences. When they woke up, they had no oil supply so their torches
could not burn brightly again. The other girls could not give them any
of their oil, for there might not be enough for everyone. Then the foolish
virgins ran to the merchants to buy oil, but when they returned, it was too
late; the door was already closed.

So, falling asleep and waking up are organic parts of the subject. The
story would not be as good if Jesus had said that only the foolish girls had
fallen asleep while the wise remained awake. The wise virgins could, so to
speak, allow themselves to nod off—it did them no harm. In half of the
image, the parable expresses readiness for the call not by staying awake but
by having enough oil. If Jesus had said that the wise girls stayed awake for
the call, it would be too much of a good thing, if I may say so. Then the balance of the subject would be disturbed and attention would have been di-
verted from the important motif of the oil. In other parables, vigilance can

---

thief comes. Matthew 24:43 speaks in the parallels about the night watches. Luke
has thus transferred the night watch from the following saying about the burglar
into the preceding structure (12:38). In the parable of the burglar (Luke 12:39), he
speaks of the "time" in varying ways. Luke 12:35 is certainly not attributable to
Jesus. The phrase "let your loins be girded" thus should not be attributed to Jesus,
but it is found in 1 Pet 1:13; Eph 6:14.

5. Sleeping and waking are also mentioned in Song 5:2.

6. This and the following quotes are from Jeremias, *Die Gleichnisse Jesu*, 174.

express a person's readiness for the unexpected call of God. In the parable of the virgins, keeping the oil supply ready for the refilling of the torches if needed fulfills the same function. Since the motifs of the oil supply and the waking are interchangeable, Jesus was able to associate the parable with an imperative: "So watch now, because you do not know the day, nor the hour." This conclusion of the parable is therefore original.

Kohelet speaks of oil in a verse repeatedly taken up by the rabbinic parable tellers: "Wear white garments always, and do not let your head lack oil" (Eccl 9:8). We have seen that Rabban Johanan ben Zakkai ties his beautiful parable to this Bible verse.[7] His parable says that one should be adorned "always" so that one may be admitted to the banquet when the cry is heard. In the name of the same rabbi, following the same biblical verse, there is a saying that may have originally been the introduction to the parable:[8] "If Scripture speaks only of white garments, the people have a lot of them. And if only precious oils are mentioned, the rich have a lot of them.[9] In reality, however, the Bible verse speaks of commandments and good deeds."[10] After the parable of Johanan ben Zakkai, another parable follows in the rabbinic text in reference to Eccl 9:8, which is attributed to Bar Kappara (after 200 CE). It is a classic parable in the manner of Jesus' parables:

> The wife of a government messenger (who had to be away from home a lot because of his profession) adorned herself in front of her neighbors. And they said to her: "Your husband is not here; why do you adorn yourself?" She answered, "My husband is a government messenger, and if his time permits, he can come and surprise me. Isn't it better if he finds me adorned and not with a neglected appearance?" So "always wear white garments"—pure from sin— "and do not let your head lack oil"—these are the commandments and good deeds. You should always be prepared for arrival. That's what the rabbi means, and don't think of Christ's parousia![11]

Both in the introduction to the parable of Rabban Johanan ben Zakkai, as well as in the parable of Bar Kappara, the oil in half of the story is

---

7. See chapter 1, note 4.

8. QohR to Eccl 9:8; cf. Bacher, *Die Agada der Tannaiten*, vol. 1, 36nl. The parable itself, which follows there, is brought in the name of Rabbi Yehuda HaNasi. In the manuscript Parma 541 is Rabbi Johanan (ben Zakkai).

9. So, correctly, the reading of the Parma manuscript, 541.

10. The text still mentions the Torah, but it seems to be a gloss. In any case, it is missing in the parable I am about to discuss.

11. Quoted from Bacher, *Die Agada der Tannaiten*, vol. 2, 516f.

understood as "commandments and good deeds." These should never be lacking, so that one does not stand unprepared in the sudden happy event. Did Jesus mean something similar in the parable of the ten virgins with the oil supply? I would say yes to this question because of his other parables. To speak of "commandments and good deeds" would probably be too clumsy and banal a term for Jesus; but in principle, the wise virgins' supply of oil cannot mean anything else.

The parable is about a wedding.[12] In the Apocalypse of John (Rev 19:7, 9), we read of the marriage of the Lamb with his bride. The Lamb is Christ and "the wife or bride of the Messiah is New Jerusalem, according to the mind of the writer of the Apocalypse."[13] On the other hand, when the Synoptic Gospels speak of a wedding, there is never any explicit mention of a bride. Listeners should identify themselves with the participants in the wedding. So, it is in the parable of the virgins. The same is true of the unoriginal verse Matt 22:2. There is talk of a king preparing a wedding for his son. The king represents God and the mention of the son is a blunt motif in the Gospel. However, it will still be shown that in the accepted rabbinic presentation, the son represents the people of Israel. Again, the bride remains unmentioned and those invited to the wedding are to be understood as the hearers of the parable.

More important for understanding the parable of the ten virgins is Jesus' first answer to the question of why his disciples do not fast (Matt 9:15; Mark 2:19f.; Luke 5:34f.). In his second answer, Jesus speaks of cloths and wineskins. As we will see in the next section, this second answer hits the nail on the head. The pericopes would be simpler and smoother if we omitted the first answer about the wedding guests.[14] This does not mean that Jesus did

---

12. The bridegroom concludes by saying to the foolish virgins, "Truly I tell you, I do not know you." The formula attributed to Jesus, "truly I say unto you," is derived from Matthew and given to the bridegroom. The groom is identified with the coming Christ. The words "I do not know you" appear twice in Luke (13:25 and 27; cf. Matt 7:23) in a pericope related to our parable. By the different wording in the parallel in Matt 7:23, it is probable that the twofold "I do not know where you are from" in Luke 13 was marked by our parable, which Luke knew. That seems to me to be the best explanation. Perhaps the foolish girls were only just on their way to the vendors when he arrived; and since their torches were extinguished, the bridegroom could not recognize them in the dark.

13. Wilhelm Bousset, *Die Offenbarung des Johannes* (Göttingen: Vandenhoeck & Ruprecht, 1966), 427. See Christ the bridegroom also in John 3:29; 2 Cor 1:2; Eph 5:32. See also Taylor, *Gospel According to Saint Mark*, 210.

14. Literally, "the sons of the bridegroom"; that is, the bridegroom's guests invited to the wedding. So Strack and Billerbeck, *Kommentar zum Neuen Testament*

not give the answer nor that he did not speak it on this occasion. The only question is whether and how far the saying has come to us in edited form as opposed to the original. The end of Mark 2:19 ("As long as they have the bridegroom with them, they cannot fast") is missing from important manuscripts of Mark as well as in Matthew and Luke. I would certainly not deny these words in Mark.[15] But because they are written in the Markan manner, bring nothing fundamentally new, and are missing in Matthew and Luke, they are more to be attributed to the Markan editors. According to all three Gospels, Jesus says at the end (Matt 9:1–5b; Mark 2:20; Luke 5:35), "But days will come, and then when the bridegroom is taken away from them, they will fast in those days." Various authors regard this verse as a later insertion by the church, because a fast of the disciples after the death of Jesus is mentioned in it.[16] If one wants to reject this sentence, then one should, in my opinion, take another step and assume that the words "while the bridegroom is with them" also come from the pen of the same interpolator who speaks of the time when "the bridegroom will be taken away from them." What remains is the following: Jesus is asked why his disciples do not fast. He replies, "Can the bridegroom fast?" This metaphor would have countered the accusation of not fasting sufficiently and effectively. It was considered a worthy deed to accompany a bride. Even rabbinic scholars interrupt Torah study to render this act of love to a bride along with their disciples. The main duty of the groom's friends and wedding guests is to contribute to the couple's joy during the wedding to the best of their ability. They have even been freed from some religious duties of a more serious nature.[17] We can conclude from this that they were also freed from fasting. Jesus wanted to say, therefore, that a fast of his disciples, who are already participating in the joyful wedding, would be just as absurd as a fast of the bridegroom.[18]

---

aus Talmud und Midrasch, vol. 1, 500, which gives the Hebrew-rabbinic expression there, gives way to the Greek phrase.

15. The words were already in Mark when Matthew used them. The Markan *hoson chronon* in Matt 9:15 corresponds to *ep hoson*.

16. E.g., Jeremias, *Die Gleichnisse Jesu*, 49, notes 3–4.

17. Strack and Billerbeck, *Kommentar zum Neuen Testament aus Talmud und Midrasch*, vol. 1, 504–6, 411.

18. See Jeremias, *Die Gleichnisse Jesu*, 49n3. The term "bride and groom" is literally "the sons of the bridal chamber." Of course, they lose their status as soon as the wedding is over. So, if one is inclined to delete Mark 2:20 and par., then the words "while the bridegroom is with them" are superfluous. But they are necessary in contrast to the time when "the bridegroom shall be taken away from them."

The reconstruction of the saying, which I have just proposed experimentally, makes sense and eliminates various difficulties. But doesn't the result seem more bland and less profound than the proverb as it stands in the Gospels? In it, Jesus expresses his premonition of death, which otherwise oppresses him. Is it a mere allegory when Jesus here compares himself to a bridegroom amid a joyful wedding? Even if we omit everything that we may find concerning, who is the bridegroom of the wedding feast if not Jesus? The main difficulty here is that in the traditional form of the saying, Jesus apparently announces a future fasting of the disciples after his death. Does the joy of the time of salvation cease through the death of Jesus? This difficulty is not entirely resolved when we understand, in the spirit of the Hebrew language, that Jesus said that his disciples "may" (and not "will") fast after his death. You need to have the courage to see these difficulties, but they should not be too lightly eliminated by radical editing.

Even if we take the two (or, according to Mark, three) explicit mentions of the bridegroom from this saying, it would be difficult not to see the bridegroom of the wedding celebration as Jesus, who understands himself at the center of the messianic movement (cf. Matt 12:30; Luke 11:23). This is not to say that Jesus intended to express his messianic claim by equating himself with the bridegroom. The allegory "bridegroom = Messiah" is foreign to the Old Testament. In rabbinic Judaism, in this sense, we find only a fairly late picture.[19] Later on, the bridegroom was considered a symbol of Christ. We have seen that outside of the Synoptic Gospels Christ is not only represented as the bridegroom in the christological sense. In all places (John 3:29; 2 Cor 1:2; Eph 5:32; Rev 19:7, 9), there is also mention of the love of the bridegroom, Christ, for his bride, the church.[20] On the other hand, as already stated, the Synoptic Gospels do not speak of the bride. The wedding is a celebration of joy, not a celebration of love. In Jesus' parables, the wedding is the main theme of the feast. Thus the storyteller is not concerned with the relationship between the groom and the bride but with the problems of the invited guests.

In the parable of the fast (Matt 9:15 par.) and in the parable of the ten virgins (Matt 25:1–13), the bridegroom has the role of host. In Matt 22:2,

---

19. See Jeremias, *Die Gleichnisse Jesu*, 49n2; YalqM to Isa 61:10, ed. Z. Kahana Shapira, 251, and Moritz Zobel, *Gottes Gesalbter, Der Messias und die messianische Zeit in Talmud und Midrasch* (Berlin: Schocken, 1938).

20. For John 3:29, see Rudolf Schnackenburg, *Das Johannesevangelium*, vol. 1 (Freiburg: Basel, 1972), 454: "The evangelist and the Christian listening church will indeed have interpreted the 'bride' as the Messianic church."

the king is the host and his son, the bridegroom, is perhaps a blunt motif.[21] Otherwise, the bridegroom does not appear in the Synoptic Gospels. Thus if the bridegroom performs the same function as the host in the parables of the banquet, then we can easily conclude that the bridegroom represents God in the parable of the ten virgins and the host in the parables of the banquet. In our parable about the ten virgins, the problem raised in the subject is also analogous to the parables of the feast: the virgins should be ready for the wedding, the inviting call of the bell is unexpected, and the foolish virgins, who were not ready, are excluded from the wedding. So, the moral of the story is the same as that of the parables of Jesus and the rabbis. Does the bridegroom of the parable simply correspond to God? I tend to answer no to that question. Although in the Old Testament, the love between God and Israel is likened to the love between a man and a woman, there is neither an early nor a late rabbinic parable in which God is likened to a bridegroom.[22] The reason for this is that a parable in which God acts like a bridegroom would be unpleasantly anthropomorphic. As a Jew, Jesus certainly felt the same, and therefore it is unlikely Jesus would allow himself to use the bridegroom as a symbol of God in one of his parables. We have already seen that in another parable of Jesus the bridegroom does not symbolize God. The second authentic case, in which a bridegroom appears on an equal footing with Jesus, is the saying regarding fasting that we have already considered (Matt 9:15 par.). Even if we remove from the saying every explicit mention of the bridegroom's absence as secondary, the bridegroom is still somehow there—and the bridegroom is certainly not God, but Jesus, in the wedding celebration: he and his disciples around him are the original group until the kingdom of God grows.

---

21. But it is easily possible, as has already been suspected (see Jülicher, *Die Gleichnisreden Jesu*, vol. 2, 419), that Matthew (22:2) inserted the marriage of the king's son into Jesus' parable to express his view that the Jews would be condemned and their city of Jerusalem burned because they rejected Christianity. The Jews had not come to the wedding feast that the king, God, had prepared for his Son Christ. Thus the late and secondary unification of Matt 22:2 would be another testimony to the image that emerged in the early church and quickly became popular there.

22. Rabbinic parables dealing with a wedding are about the wedding of a king's son or a king's daughter. The king is God, the son is Israel, and the bride is the Torah; or the daughter is the Torah and the bridegroom who marries the king's daughter is Israel. The most daring thing that could be said about God and Israel as husband and wife in a parable is that of Rabbi Izhaq; see ShirR to Hl 1, 6; cf. Bacher, *Die Agada der Palästinischen Amoräer*, vol. 2, 291.

Even though I personally think that Jesus understood himself as the Messiah, the wedding joy and fasting are not sufficient support for this opinion. If Jesus presents himself explicitly or implicitly as a bridegroom amid the joyful wedding, then it probably means nothing more than that he is the focal point of a messianic movement, not necessarily the Messiah himself. Let us now examine the parable of the ten virgins in the light of all these interim considerations, although in rabbinic literature, the equation "Bridegroom = Messiah" is found only once in a later version. In the saying about fasting, the bridegroom is hardly God but rather Jesus during his movement. The bridegroom in the parable of the ten virgins fulfills the role of the host, who is otherwise a symbol of God. Because of the rabbinic material, however, it is difficult to imagine that Jesus would describe God as a bridegroom in the parable. So, we cannot fail to recognize in the bridegroom of the parable of the virgins the Coming One—the end-time representative of God. We call him Messiah or the Son of Man. The choice of the figure of a groom is undoubtedly based on the parable: a torchlight procession in honor of the groom. Neither the parable narrator Jesus nor his listeners were disturbed by the fact that the person of the bridegroom in the parable of the ten virgins, as well as in the saying about fasting, was incomplete without his love for the bride. The main emphasis of the parable is about the participants in the wedding feast, not about the love between the groom and the bride.

Although the subject of the parable of the ten virgins is not clearly eschatologically oriented in its essence and in the structure of its motifs, its advice to be well prepared for the sudden call could refer to the hour of death. But if my reasons can be substantiated for believing that the bridegroom in the parable is to be interpreted not as God himself but as the coming Messiah, then the parable must refer to the end times. Only through the motif of the bridegroom does the parable become clearly messianic. But even so, the emphasis of the parable lies not in an eschatological tension but in its recommendation to do good now, for one does not know the time and the hour. Furthermore, just because the parable speaks of the coming Messiah does not yet make it christological. The parable does not provide sufficient evidence that Jesus understood himself as the coming Son of Man. This is also true of his other sayings in which he speaks of the coming Son of Man in the third person. But the other parable in which Jesus speaks of a wedding—namely, his saying about fasting—makes us listen. There the bridegroom is certainly not the coming Son of Man but the present Jesus himself. In our parable, on the other hand, the bridegroom is the coming Son of Man and (far from unambiguously) Jesus himself. As has often been said, the sayings about fasting and the parable of the virgins (in addition to the secondary Matt 22:2) are the only words of Jesus that refer to a bridegroom. Is a syllogism with far-reaching consequences not allowed here? In the saying about fasting, the "present in the feast" or participating in the feast, Jesus is indicated by the bridegroom. In the parable of the virgins, the bridegroom signifies the coming Son of Man.[23] Is it a mistake to see in this a sign from Jesus that enables us to investigate the mysterious depths of his person: Jesus as he who knew himself amid a wedding feast, and as he who is yet to come? In any case, the parable of the virgins is the only sure parable of Jesus in which he speaks of the coming Son of Man.

The parable of the ten virgins is widely treated here because this excellent example can be used to shed light on the complex problem of how the subject matter of the parables depends on doctrine, and how, on the other hand, its subject matter and execution clarify the kind of doctrine the parable seeks to bring to its hearers. Some features of a parable are purely epic and should not be interpreted, as in our parable of the ten virgins. Note, however, that the number *ten* is an even number, for the number of wise and foolish virgins must be the same. It is also a relatively large number. Only two virgins, one wise and one foolish, would not suffice, as a torchlight procession of two girls would seem grotesque. If you were to speak of three girls twice, the number would not only be too small but it could also give rise to misunderstandings. In folk literature, the triad is an "ascending" number, a sort of stepladder. It would therefore also not be aesthetically suitable for symmetrically juxtaposing two equal collective groups. Ten, on the other hand, is an optimal number: two groups of five girls of the same size, acting in the same way, facing each other, like the ten fingers of both hands. If Jesus had spoken of more than ten virgins, then we would be less certain that he was talking about a paradigmatic act. We might have thought he was just talking about a lot of people. The two contrasting groups of five girls—who carry no individuality in themselves, so to speak, but behave in a shadowy manner—are the result of a conscious stylization that removes any realism. Such stylization regarding the subject and the application corresponds to the nature of the parables. The subjects of rabbinic parables and Jesus' parables resemble stylistically rigid, simplified European folk tales. The two contrasting groups of girls in our parable are the pictorial expression of right and wrong action before God.

---

23. In the parable of the wicked vine growers, Jesus is likened to the son of the owner of the estate.

Jesus chose the theme of a wedding for his parable. Furthermore, he did not speak of a host but of a bridegroom because it seemed important to him to point out the coming Son of Man in this case. For the moral of the story, however, reference to the coming Messiah is not decisive. With this choice of theme and these emphases, Jesus wanted to warn his listeners that a man would expose himself to a great danger if he did not prepare for the call. The motif of the invitation, for which one is not prepared, is something we now recognize with Jesus and the rabbis. Today, we can usually see that the fact that the call sounds in the middle of the night has nothing to do with the parousia delay. The late arrival of the bridegroom may, but does not necessarily, mean that the arrival of the Messiah is delayed. The absence of the bridegroom until midnight is perhaps[24] only due to the subject: Because of the late call, the foolish virgins ran out of oil in their torches, and they had no more on hand. The fact that all ten virgins nodded off has little to do with the interpretation. The wise and the foolish girls all fell asleep. For the smart girls, as we have already discussed, this had no negative effect. However, falling asleep is a necessary component of the subject. If the foolish virgins had not fallen asleep, they might have been able to buy a supply of oil during this time, which the wise maidens had done earlier. On the other hand, the supply of oil also has a significance for the moral of the story. We have seen that in a rabbinic parable, oil means commandments and good deeds.[25] Again, with Jesus, the oil corresponds to good deeds. Jesus does not become lesser if he recommends that people do a lot of good so that they are not excluded from future joy in God. He even recommends that we should do better than we consider necessary for securing our future salvation. Therefore, he has the wise virgins bring additional oil in vessels. The fact that the oil runs out after the girls fall asleep should not be interpreted typologically. It belongs only to the subject and allows the continuation of the story, which at this point moves away from the typology and becomes independent. So, when the foolish girls ask their wise colleagues to give them some of their oil, it has nothing to do with the moral of the story. The same applies to the answer of the wise virgins. It corresponds to the fact in

---

24. But it is not entirely impossible that Jesus here also alludes to the Jewish idea that the Messiah will appear in the middle of the Passover night. See the beautiful word from Jerome in Klostermann, *Das Matthäusevangelium*, 201. In my Hystaspes article, I also take up this idea.

25. Bengel, on Matt 25:3, writes that the oil signifies "the holy diligence of man" and rightly compares our parable with 2 Pet 1. I recommend that readers compare the two texts themselves.

the parable that the oil they have will not be enough for everyone. The risk was too great that all ten girls together would run out and everyone's lamps would go out before or during the groom's entrance. For this reason, the foolish girls listen without contradiction to the advice of the wise. However, before they reach the oil dealer, the groom arrives. Confused and without oil, the foolish virgins try to get into the wedding hall. They arrive too late at the door. Since they stand in the dark without light outside, the groom cannot recognize them from the illuminated interior of the house. The door therefore remains locked to them.

The midnight call, the arrival of the bridegroom, the entrance of the wise virgins, the delay of the foolish, and the closed door belong to both the subject and its interpretation. The fact that the groom does not recognize the foolish girls because of the darkness is understandable by the situation of the story itself. But there is a deeper meaning behind this: Whoever has lived in such a way that they are unprepared for the day of the master, the coming Son of Man will not recognize as one of his own. All "transparent" motifs, which have their correspondence in the teaching of the parable, are therefore also an organic part of the subject. Without it, the story would collapse. What would remain would no longer be a real story but only a joke without a punchline or an unepic, flat "narrative" without progressive action. The accuracy of my argument should surely strike everyone as an "aha" moment if they read what remains of this parable as belonging to Jesus—after modern exegetes have blown it up out of neurotic fear of the supposedly primitive pre-Christian allegory. The destructive tearing apart of this parable testifies to the expert inability of these researchers to understand and enjoy this epic of Jesus as literary art. A "super-theology" that is alien to reality can sometimes clog the ears and blind the eyes. To understand Jesus' parables, we must know the nature of Jewish (rabbinic) parables. Jesus' parables belong, as I have often said, to this genre of literature.

The parable of the ten virgins is a good example of an excellently conceived and well-told Jewish parable. In such a case, on the one hand, there are epic motifs that have no correspondence to the moral of the story. On the other hand, the motifs of the subject, which are interpretable in doctrine, are at the same time an organic component of the action and its backbone. The more important the common motifs of the subject and its interpretation are for the action, the better the parable. The obvious motifs of the subject are the hooks on which the teaching of the parable hangs—and hooks should be firmly stuck in the wall! The purely epic motifs of the parable, which do not point to the interpretation, must also be present in the subject of a good parable. Otherwise, there is no correct unfolding of the action. If such epic motifs were missing and all motifs of an alleged parable narrative reflected moral teaching, then this parable narrative would not be a real parable with its own action but a pure allegory with all the disadvantages of that genre. A good parable must not be artificially constructed from the moral of the story.

A bad parable arises when it depends entirely on the morality of history in its motifs, or when such motifs determined by the interpretation are not adapted to the subject in such a way that they can thereby become an extraneous component of the subject. Some later rabbinic parables don't even point to a real moral teaching. Their primary focus is often a biblical verse, a biblical figure, or a historical situation that needs to be made understandable by a conventional subject. Therefore, the action in the subject is often constructed from the point of view of the solution. Furthermore, because some motifs are directly dictated by doctrine, no organic structure arises. The plot of the subject sometimes seems ornate and in certain cases even distorted. Such rabbinic parables are therefore to be regarded as allegories. This impression also arises in such secondary parable images in the Gospels that were written according to the model of Jesus' real parables in Greek, as well as in Jesus' real parables that were revised by a later Greek editor. These Greek-writing Christians had already been denied access to the aesthetic rules of Jewish parables, so they could only understand the parables in a Christian sense. That's why when we read their literary products—properly, this time—we have the unpleasant feeling of an inappropriate allegory.

Such an occurrence hardly happens in rabbinic parables of the older classical type, to which Jesus' parables belong. This does not mean that all rabbinic parables of the classical genre succeeded equally well; not all of Jesus' parables are as exemplary as the parable of the ten virgins. This parable is built on individual motifs. Its story is not an end in itself; it gives the impression of a realistic, exciting story. These positive qualifications are based on the fact that, in our parable, the grave, immanent problems of the parable genre are completely solved: the desired impression that the story has been taken from real life is achieved. At the same time, the subject unquestionably yields the intended moral teaching. In its application, the parable is not ambiguous—though a certain ambiguity does in fact occur in some of Jesus' parables—so that the helpful "moral of the story" is superfluous. The silent consensus between the narrator and listener about the meaning of the subject and its motifs is quite sufficient to understand the parable. There is no need for explicit doctrine. The motifs necessary for the interpretation are so inseparable from the action that they do not protrude, so to speak, from the illustration. The purely epic motifs that are there to create seamless, ever-progressing action are so cleverly arranged that they do not distract the listener from the purpose of the parable.

Here the question arises whether the problems the parable teller must manage artistically exist only for the genre of the parables. Isn't this a problem for all narrative literature? We know the three spheres we have found in the parables: reality, illustration, and its meaning. The task of the epic creator is indeed to harmonize the mutual relationship between these three spheres so harmoniously that a successful work of art can be created. Based on reality, the artist builds a model that is supposed to tell us something about the meaning of reality with the help of the subject. Parables, as well as animal fables, exempla, and allegories, are deliberately about two different realities. The first level is the subject from which the subject and its motifs are taken. The second level is human action, judged from the standpoint of ethics. Parables—including Jesus' parables—thus belong to didactic literature. The artistic program of classical parables is usually "the uncovering of the conflict in the ordinary,"[26] to draw attention to analogous conflicts in the level of morality. In the case of parables, as in the case of related didactic genres, there is an intended use. To lead to it, the two levels were created. The fable teller, the author of exempla, and the parable narrator must work much more intuitively than the allegorist. What a burst of poetic intuition was at work, for example, when Jesus created the parable of the ten virgins!

In less didactically beautiful literature, the meaning of the work is not unambiguous to the same extent as parables. Without any meaning, however, any epic literary work would be meaningless. Even if we sometimes do not want to accept it, we can say the same thing about the entire narrative of beautiful literature as we say about Jesus' parables: The author somehow fictionalizes reality by creatively reflecting it to change the given reality.

---

26. Thus Shklovsky, *Von der Ungleichheit des Ähnlichen in der Kunst*, 28, defines the riddle.

9

THE SYNOPTIC PROBLEM
AND JESUS' PARABLES

It is a truism today to say that the Gospels of Matthew, Mark, and Luke somehow are connected. The scientifically exciting debate begins first with the question of not whether but how they are related. This so-called Synoptic Problem is not only of literary interest. If we try to answer it both in general and in detail, then we argue that the original and the more original should be separated from later editorial ingredients. This opens the prospect of penetrating from today's Gospel texts to Jesus himself and his actual words. This is the main purpose of Synoptic investigations. Knowing who Jesus was, what he thought of himself, what he preached, and what happened to him is not just a historical question. Rather, it should be significant for Christians and all thinking people. The correct answer to the Synoptic Problem also concerns the history of the church since it has much to say to us about the path from the "historical" Jesus to the early church. The fact that the Synoptic investigations also connect to parable research is unquestionable, since Jesus' parables are in the Synoptic Gospels. We need to compare the wording of a parable in the individual Gospels to be able to decide what is original and what was added later. We should take the Synoptic problem even more seriously than we usually do. This would save us a lot of useless speculation. We can see this, for example, in the parable of the burglar (Matt 24:42–44; Luke 12:39–40). A Synoptic comparison of the two texts was sufficient to arrive at a plausible solution regarding which was more original. We have seen that the parallel to Matt 24:42 is missing and that Luke 12:40 is not present in a manuscript family. So, the verse most likely crept into the rest of Luke's manuscripts from Matt 24:44. The remaining saying (Luke 12:39; Matt 24:43) is, in contrast to the enlargement of Matthew and the context in Luke, simple and not contradictory; it casually connects with Matthew's previous words. In this case, then, the mere literary-critical method was sufficient for us to establish that Matthew received the original context and Luke received the original wording of the saying. In addition, it was also advisable to consider the different types of reading of the Gospel manuscripts—which, by the way, should be done constantly and diligently!

If in an individual manuscript or in a group of manuscripts a word, phrase, or sentence is missing that is found in the parallels, then this omission did not necessarily happen through the negligence of a writer. For various discrepancies in text transmission, the process of contamination can also be assumed to be the cause. A piece assumed to be missing was taken from one of the other Gospels or from another manuscript. The decision as to whether it is a subsequent insertion or whether the words originally belonged to the text of the Gospel is to be made based on internal criteria. We should not be blindly guided by the importance of individual manuscripts or a group of manuscripts. The decision about what belonged to the original text and what did not must also not be dictated exclusively by the results of the "family criticism" of the manuscripts. An original reading can even be preserved in a single unimportant manuscript of the New Testament. The New Testament is sacred Scripture. To pass on the required correct wording, the scribes have taken insight into various manuscripts. The individual manuscripts preserved are therefore never entirely "pure." In these circumstances, it is not surprising that an original type of reading has frequently been inherited through unusual channels, irrespective of the ways in which it developed and the progressive division of the texts and their recensions. A secondary mode of reading can be created in three different ways: first, by the successive changes in the handwriting tradition; second, by a contamination of the manuscripts; and third, when a writer alters his text because of a change in his view. In a broader sense, such a correction can be called *lectio facilior*, an easier way of reading.[1] A correction of this kind is made if the writer thinks that the original text, which causes him difficulties in terms of language or content, is corrupted. This is why he "fixes" it. In this sense, this type of correction is not based on the writer's source text. It is the writer's own work or a product of a "logical" translation of the writer. The same "logic" may have run through several writers' minds. The resulting "easier reading" can thus possibly be attributed to several writers. That is why it is possible that in individual cases, the right text can be found quite unexpectedly and, so to speak, by chance in a single manuscript or in a remote group of manuscripts. The right reading style was fortunate; it has simply not been supplanted over the centuries by progressive changes.

---

1. See Vincent Taylor, *The Text of the New Testament* (London: Macmillan & Co., 1961), 4.

Unfortunately, New Testament scholars often did not consider this. They also often do not know that the inner criteria, according to which they decide between different types of reading in the New Testament manuscripts, can work properly only if they possess a knowledge of Judaism. Indeed, to choose the originally correct reading among the different types regarding a New Testament passage, they should know Judaism of the first century CE. Furthermore, they should master Hebrew and Aramaic to such an extent that they can estimate which reading in the Synoptic Gospels is Hebrew (or Aramaic), and how the secondary reading types were adapted to the spirit of the Greek language. Out of ignorance, the *Hebraica Veritas* has often been neglected in the solution of the Synoptic Problem. That is serious. The correct solution of the Synoptic Problem also depends on the structure of the critical apparatus of the Synoptic Gospels and the correct choice of the original reading.

With that, we find ourselves already in the middle of the Synoptic Problem. A false answer to the question of how the first three Gospels are related in literary terms and how their sources were constituted necessarily blocks access to Jesus' words and his teaching. Since Jesus' parables come from Jesus, I must touch briefly on the Synoptic Problem. Only in this way will you understand why I treat the wording of the parables in this way and not in any other way.

The common answer to the Synoptic Question today is this: The first three Gospels are based on two sources. One is the Gospel of Mark. Where the two "secondary witnesses"—namely, Matthew and Luke—have not used it, they follow an additional source: the so-called sayings source, which is a collection of Jesus' sayings. This "two-source theory" is sometimes complicated by smaller hypotheses. Recently, voices have arisen that contradict it and try to replace it with other hypotheses.[2] These new critiques suffer from two evils. First, the literary-critical training of their authors is often inadequate. That is why these authors too rarely have a sense of how a text changes because of editing. Moreover, their Hebrew knowledge is insufficient to decide when the text of the Gospel is closer to Hebrew, when it moves away from Hebrew, and when it is more or less freely conceived in Greek at that time. This knowledge is necessary for a correct Synoptic theory. Jesus did not teach in Greek but in Hebrew. It is only when I can see from my knowledge how and when we progressively moved away from the

---

2. See especially William Reuber Farmer, *The Synoptic Problem: A Critical Analysis* (Dillsboro: Western North Carolina Press, 1976); and Hans-Herben Stoldt, *Geschichte und Kritik der Markushypothesis* (Göttingen: Brunnen, 1977).

assumed Hebrew original form that I may dare to say something authoritative about the relationship of the Gospels to their sources and to formulate a hypothesis about the interdependence of the Synoptics. A new Synoptic theory must not be a mere methodical construction arrived at based on abstract considerations. It should emerge from the interrogation of the individual positions. It is valid if it is used as a working hypothesis in a factual investigation of the Synoptic material and has proven to be successful. In short, it was not invented to block the path to the "historical" Jesus and the events surrounding him. On the contrary, it should help us to learn what actually happened. The Synoptic hypothesis of R. L. Lindsey[3] contains all these positive properties. We can go much further with it than with everything that has been said so far about the Synoptic Problem.

Lindsey, an American Baptist, has lived in Jerusalem for many years, and Hebrew has become his natural language. When he began to translate the Gospel of Mark into Hebrew, he chose this Gospel precisely because he, too, did not doubt that the Gospel of Mark is the most reliable of the three Synoptic Gospels, as it is considered one of the two main sources of Matthew and Luke. During the translation work, however, he was forced to realize that Mark is heavily edited in Greek and that, if there is a Lukan parallel to a Markan passage, the latter is much more Hebraic than the Markan text.

Here I summarize the results of Lindsey's work: The Gospel of Mark is a thorough Greek treatment of the original ancient material but is hardly identical to the ancient account on which it is based. The old account, not the edited one, was available to both Luke and Matthew, who also used the "sayings source." Luke did not know our edited Mark. Rather, it was the other way around. The editor of our Mark used Luke in his work. Matthew, on the other hand, knew the pre-Markan account, but he also drew extensively from our Mark. It follows that if Matthew and Mark offer almost the same wording, then it is our Mark, and not the old record, that is reflected in Matthew. And if Matthew and Luke agree against Mark, then they are credible because then they usually both depend on the old Markan account. Thus through Lindsey's work, the version of Mark that has been handed

---

3. R. L. Lindsey, *A Hebrew Translation of the Gospel of Mark,* Greek-Hebrew Diglot with an English Introduction (Jerusalem: Dugith, 1969). I have just received the book from Joachim Jeremias, *Die Sprache des Lukasevangeliums: Redaktion und Tradition im Nicht-Markusstoff des dritten Evangeliums* (Göttingen: Vandenhoeck & Ruprecht, 1980). The very name shows Jeremias's priority of Mark and his use by Luke. For this reason, his analyses of the non-Markan substance in Luke are also unfavorably influenced by the Mark hypothesis.

down to us was dethroned. The Gospel of Mark is not the oldest and not the most reliable, as it has been significantly restyled in Greek. The influence of the Gospel of Mark on Matthew was therefore unfavorable. Luke, who is pre-Markan, is free from the negative sides of the Markan editorship. Luke is thus lifted by Lindsey, so to speak, to the throne from which he had overthrown Mark. If one is prepared with good reason to follow Lindsey's Synoptic solution, then this, among other factors, results in the following way to approach the original text: If all three Gospels hand down a certain section, then Luke is the most credible. Mark edited the text a lot, and Matthew then mostly further modified Mark. Matthew is especially valuable when he agrees with Luke. In these cases, it often contains the text of the old pre-Markan report better than Luke. The same free choice to choose between Matthew and Luke, of course, exists when Mark is absent.

I have been working with Lindsey for a long time. What interests us now are three questions in particular: How far and where is the text of Luke edited, what changes did Matthew make, and can one know something certain about the original order of the sections in the Synoptic Gospels? A new source-critical hypothesis can be judged only if it is first applied to the texts themselves. It is only correct if it has been proven valuable and leads to factual results. It must be a means to an end.

I will now show by means of some examples the great benefit of Lindsey's Synoptic hypothesis when we analyze Jesus' parables with its help. It will turn out that the new method eliminates many difficulties almost automatically and that we can now better approach the original wording and content of the parables.

I will not use Lindsey's new method only from the first point on. Rather, it has been tacitly presupposed in this investigation from the very beginning. It is, for example, an application of the Lindsey method if I explained above in my analysis of the fasting saying that the second half of Mark 2:19 does not come from Jesus because it is missing in both Matthew and Luke. According to Lindsey, this is hardly original. Rather, it is a decorative extension originating from Mark. A similar but slightly different editorial Markan extension can be found at the beginning of the parable of the evil vintners. Mark introduces this parable as follows: "And he began to speak to them in parables: A man planted a vineyard, put a fence around it, dug a winepress, and built a tower" (Mark 12:1). This is a free reproduction of Isa 5:1f.—even the tower appears there. This rendering is based on the Septuagint tradition, which Jesus certainly did not use or depend on. This makes us pay attention. Matthew depends here (Matt 21:33) on Mark, and

Jesus was referring to Isaiah. As for Isaiah (5:7), the vineyard is "the house of Israel" for Jesus. Was it not enough that Jesus said, "A man planted a vineyard" (Luke 20:9)? It is clear from the continuation that Jesus speaks of the house of Israel. The keyword *vineyard* readily conveyed to Jesus' Jewish audience the association with the famous words of the prophets. Moreover, the parable as such does not get any worse but better if we renounce the ornamental addition from the Greek textual tradition. If we have called Mark 12:1b secondary because these words are missing from Luke, then we did so mainly with the help of Lindsey's new Synoptic hypothesis. However, those under the spell of the usual Markan hypothesis will, in turn, dwell on the beauties of the Markan addition.[4] I, on the other hand, mourn neither additions nor ballast-like explanations. For I am relieved of the difficulty of having to explain why the Markan special material follows the Greek translation of the Bible and does not correspond to Jesus' mother tongue. Just a few more observations: In Luke (20:9) it says, "A man planted a vineyard." Matthew 21:33 says, "A man was a householder who planted a vineyard." This Matthean expression is so Greek that it cannot be literally translated into Hebrew. Perhaps Matthew wanted to imitate the rabbinic expression. That is why he inserts the "master of the house" as usual in parables. Matthew and Luke speak of *a parable* (Matt 21:33; Luke 12:1). Mark, on the other hand, speaks of *parables* (Mark 12:1). According to our Synoptic theory, the agreement between Matthew and Luke is an important fact. The fact that the singular number is original can be demonstrated by an additional investigation. The plural form "parables" occurs only once in Luke (8:10). This deals with the pericope of the purpose of the parables (Luke 8:9f.). The plural is therefore objectively justified at this point, necessary, and therefore original. Jesus spoke "in parables." This fact caused several secondary plural forms in Mark and Matthew. Outside of our position,

---

4. Thus Gerhard Schneider, *Das Evangelium nach Lukas* (Gütersloh: Taschenbücher, 1977), 398f., writes about the Lukan text: "The Markan allusion to Isa 5:1f. is reduced to such an extent that one can hardly recognize the reference to the Isaiah text. Such a reduction, which dispenses with the details in the interpretation of the vineyard, is at the service of greater allegory: one should not dwell on the question of what these details would mean. The fact that the owner entrusts his vineyard to vintners sets the tone." I hope there is little need to challenge this view. For fun, perhaps the reverse could be said: Mark was a disciple of modern New Testament scholars, who wanted to remove the supposed allegory from Jesus' parables. To at least divert the "allegory" and distract readers from it, he inserted the Greek quotation from Isaiah!

Mark 12:1 and 4:2 (Matt 13:2) is Mark's editorial redaction. In Luke, the singular number occurs at the parallel point (Luke 8:4). Mark 4:33f. (Matt 13:34f.) is an editorial summary and is missing from Luke. Mark 4:13 is an editorial specialty of Mark; the plural form "parables" is missing in Matthew and Luke. Matthew 13:53 is Matthean special material that was inserted during the process of editing. The plural form in Matt 21:45 corresponds to the (correct) singular number in Luke 20:19 and Mark 12:12, and "the parables" in Matt 22:1 is missing in Luke 14:16. All these references confirm the exquisite originality of Luke.

Let me quote the parable of the mustard seed in its Markan version (Mark 4:30–32; cf. Matt 13:31f; Luke 13:18) in the translation by Frido-lin Stier, who was able to adapt exceptionally well to Mark's bumpy language style:

> He also said: "To what shall we compare the kingship of God or to what parable should we set it out? It is like a mustard seed: once sown on the earth, though smaller than all the seeds on the earth, but once sown, it rises and becomes larger than all the herbs and drives branches so large that under its shadow the birds of the sky can nest."[5]

(As a brief aside: The Gospel of Mark has been compared to an old folk woodcut, which was to indicate the primordial nature of this Gospel. But are old carvings primitive in the sense of originality? After all, it is known that they too mostly depend on artistic templates or traces of them. Because of their imitative character and indulgent detail, they are labeled in technical language somewhat pejoratively as *gesunkene kunst*.[6] The primitive realism of this art is rarely the result of an impartial gaze but mostly a longing to achieve some kind of memorable completeness. This also applies to the literary level for various popular books such as *Alexander Romance* and *Doctor Faustus*. Pseudo-realistic painting and the craving for blatant effects is typical for this genre of literature. Mark must also be understood in this context. For example, we read in Mark 6:39 that five thousand people were "on green grass," the green grass is only an artistic design and not, as many thought, first-hand information or an implicit calendar date.[7])

---

5. Fridolin Stier, *Die Heilsbotschaft nach Markus (Übersetzung)* (Münich: Kösel, 1965), 146.

6. *Gesunkene kunst* means "degenerate art" or, literally, "sunken art."—Ed.

7. Cf. Klostermann, *Das Markusevangelium*, 63. In Matt 14:19, we speak only of the grass. In Mark 6:35 (and Matt 14:15), it is said that the place was desolate. It

After having taken this little detour, we can now return to the parable of the mustard seed. Luke 13:8 says,

> And he said, "What is the kingdom of God like, and to what can I liken it? It is like a grain of mustard seed that a man took and put in his garden. And it grew and became a tree, and the birds of the sky nestled in its branches."

Luke has preserved the original wording of the parable—perhaps except for the introductory rhetorical question.[8] The parable of the mustard seed is a good example of the accuracy of R. L. Lindsey's Synoptic solution. Through it, we can also better understand the workings of Mark.

Gerhard Schneider writes, "Although the parable of the mustard seed is also found in Mark 4:30–32, only Matthew in Matt 13:31f was influenced by the Markan version, but not Luke. Matthew, for his part, uses the old text, but is also influenced by Mark."[9] The similarities between Matthew and Luke vis-à-vis Mark cannot be overlooked.[10] In our case, it is customary to explain the Synoptic state in such a way that it is assumed there were two different versions of the parable of the mustard seed. One was the Markan,

---

cannot be ruled out that there may also be grass in one place. Historically, however, these are contradictory descriptions. Luke does not share this contradiction. He mentions only the desolate place (9:12), not the grass.

8. Luke 13:18 was edited in Mark 4:30. In Matt 13:31, the rhetorical question is missing, but the dependence on Mark is still visible (Mark 4:30 *thåmen*, Matt 13:31 *paretheken*). Perhaps the rhetorical question was already in the source. But even in this case, one cannot know whether it came from Jesus. The source or Luke could have taken it from the introduction to the parable of the children playing (Luke 7:3; cf. Matt 1:16, where only the first half of the question occurs). In Luke 7:3, the question is certainly original because it is indispensable. It is a little different there than in Luke 13:18. The rhetorical question itself goes back to Isa 40:18: "To whom will ye liken God, and what shall ye set in his image?"

9. Schneider, *Das Evangelium nach Lukas*, 301–3n4; cf. also Josef Schmid, *Das Evangelium nach Lukas*, Regensburger NT, 3; and Taylor, *Gospel According to Saint Mark*, 269.

10. The core of the parable is in Luke and Matthew together: "It is like a grain of mustard seed that a man took . . . and it grew and became like a tree." Only the words "and he put it in his garden" were attenuated by Matthew under the influence of Mark, as well as the introduction to the biblical allusion at the end. In this allusion, however, the shadow does not appear in Matthew or Luke. The original common text of Matthew and Luke was thus interpolated in Matthew by the Markan version. It is also interesting that the parable in Matt 13:31 is still told, as in Luke, in the past tense. In the following verse 32, however, Matthew changes to the present form under the influence of Mark. Cf. Jeremias, *Die Gleichnisse Jesu*, 27.

while the second was in the sayings source shared by Matthew and Luke. The second version is included in today's Gospel of Luke, while Matthew wove both versions into one unit. The solution in this case does not appear to be methodically bad. Otherwise, we find in Matthew an influence on the part of Mark as well as similarities with Luke. However, you do not have to accept that there were two original versions. If you look closely and understand Hebrew and Greek correctly, you will understand the way Mark works. He largely reshaped his fabric. He only had the version we know from Luke in front of him and rewrote the parable. Matthew then combined Luke's template with our Mark.

Also, regarding the final biblical allusion,[11] Matthew largely corresponds to the Lukan template. Both have a free quotation from Dan 4:18. It is not entirely certain whether the Greek translator of the Hebrew source had seen the very similar Greek form of Theodotion. He could hardly have translated any other way. Mark, on the other hand, writes that the birds of the sky could nest under the shadow of the full-grown plant. Mark was able to obtain the image of the shadow from Dan 4:9, Ezek 17:23, or Ezek 31:6. The Markan shade indicates that the plant is unnaturally large. His desire to harmonize probably played a trick on Mark here. Luke 13:19 and Matt 13:32 speak of a tree, but the word *tree* is also found in Dan 4:17. Mark, on the other hand, does not use the word given to Daniel. For him, the contrast between the mustard seed, which at first is "smaller than all the seeds of the earth" and in the end becomes "larger than all the herbs," was important as an artistic contrast. He could hardly speak of a tree, so there is no reason to declare Luke and Matthew as secondary to Mark. And as far as the free use of a phrase from the Bible is concerned, we should know that Jesus and his Jewish listeners were so familiar with the Bible that Jesus could decorate his speech with linguistic details without having to pay attention to objective or even theological conclusions. This biblical reference is just one example among many. So, you are mistaken if you have let the poor mustard plant Jesus spoke about grow into a symbolic world tree! We fail to recognize Jesus' direct access to his Bible when we think that the conclusion of the parable refers beyond Israel to the world of nations that will find its home in the kingdom of God.[12] When you interpret the birds of the sky as the pagans, which is meant as allegory, you do violence to the birds. Moreover, Jesus did not speak of "all" the birds of the sky, as he could have deduced

---

11. See Jeremias, *Die Gleichnisse Jesu*, 27
12. Schneider, *Das Evangelium nach Lukas*, 302n4f.

from Ezek 17:23; 31:6 and Dan 4:9. The birds of the sky nesting in the branches are only there to illustrate the size of the plant.

The mention of the tree in Luke 13:19 and Matt 13:32 means it has a special meaning; the end of the parable is indeed a free quotation from the tree of Dan 4:10–15. Let's look at the difference between Luke and Matthew. In Matt 13:32, we read that the mustard seed "became a tree" —which is a botanical improbability. Luke 13:19 says that the mustard seed "became like a tree."[13] In Hebrew, this means that it grew and eventually became as high as a tree or was tree-like (*we-hajah le-etz*). I have heard—without wanting to engage in botanical subtleties like others—that the mustard perennial can reach a height of four meters (a little over thirteen feet). I see no reason why the fully grown mustard perennial could not be compared to a tree and why birds could not be found in it. The crucial idea here is that from such a small grain, such a tall and multifaceted plant can sprout. The time-word of Luke, which we have rendered with "set," is the Greek translation of the Hebrew *sim*, which best corresponds to the French *mettre*.[14] But is Luke right when he speaks of a garden? Jewish religious practice has nothing against it.[15] It certainly does not mean much that the word *garden* does not otherwise occur among the Synoptics. For if Jesus had told of a field in which mustard seeds had been sown that grew into a small forest of plants, the listeners would have been less astonished at this amazing growth. That is why Jesus speaks of a single grain of mustard seed that a man planted in his garden—and behold, the tiny grain became a tree-like plant. This is much more vivid than a field of mustard plants. The fact that Jesus makes the miracle of growing suitable in a garden that is created for the personal use of the owner is another indication of his high level of storytelling.

Why does the garden not appear in Mark and Matthew? Mark probably did not pay attention to the subtlety of his source text. He read that a mustard seed had been planted in a garden, and he naturally thought of a seed being sown. Therefore, he let the mustard seed be sown into the ground.

---

13. The precision of Flusser's German is difficult to convey here; he means that in Luke, the mustard seed became "tree-like."—Trans.

14. In the Bohemian German of Kafka, it would be said that man has put the seed in his garden. Franz Delitzsch correctly translates *sim* in his Hebrew New Testament, but not so the new Hebrew translation of the New Testament. Franz Delitszch, *Hebrew New Testament* (Tel Aviv, 1976).

15. The rabbinic passages quoted against the garden in Strack and Billerbeck, *Kommentar zum Neuen Testament aus Talmud und Midrasch*, vol. 1, 669, are based on Billerbeck's false halachic understanding.

He put the garden aside, for the farmer sowed "on the earth." In addition to the old model, Matthew also used Mark. From Mark, he took over the first mention of sowing. According to Matt 13:31, the man sowed the mustard seed "in his field." This is more accurately expressed if, as Mark does, one speaks only generally of the earth. Thus the original garden, in which a mustard plant sprang up, became a mustard field.

So far, I have argued only from a literary-critical and not a theological perspective. So, we come to the parable as Jesus said it. Perhaps many will realize that a parable must first be told correctly—in an aesthetic sense. Then it will also be theologically memorable. The Lukan form of the parable of the mustard seed—perhaps except for the introductory rhetorical question—has by far best preserved the original wording of the parable. In this Lukan form, the parable can be easily translated back into Hebrew. Then we become aware of how Hebraically it was thought of and told.[16] In favor of the Lukan form, it should also be noted that Jesus tells the parable in the past tense. In this form, as we have already seen, the perfect parable is told. Mark, on the other hand, chooses the present tense and thus weakens the character of the narrative. Matthew combines Luke with Mark. He begins the parable in the past tense (Matt 13:31) and then bends into the present tense (Matt 13:32).

The theme of the parable is the amazing growth of a plant from a small seed. The small size of the mustard seed is a proverbial image among rabbis. They used to say that something was "small as a mustard seed."[17] Jesus also used this comparison: "If you had faith like a grain of mustard seed, you could say to this mulberry fig tree, 'uproot yourself and cast yourself into the sea,' and it would obey you" (Luke 17:6; Matt 17:20).[18] An inaccurate,

---

16. But it is not certain whether Jesus spoke of the "mustard seed" or only of mustard (*hardal*). However, *hardal* can also mean mustard seed in Hebrew.

17. Evidence from Strack and Billerbeck, *Kommentar zum Neuen Testament aus Talmud und Midrasch*, vol. 1, 669, and J. Levy, *Wörterbuch über die Targumim und Midraschim*, vol. 2 (Darmstadt, 1963), 107.

18. Schneider, *Das Evangelium nach Lukas* (Note: 4), 347f., is correct when he refers to the reference in Matt 17:20 as secondary. Originally, the saying probably included the mulberry or fig tree, which was considered particularly firm and deeply rooted. Strack and Billerbeck, *Kommentar zum Neuen Testament aus Talmud und Midrasch*, vol. 2, 234. Those who have faith can change things against their nature (the tree will continue to grow in the sea). The mountain in Matt 17:20 is taken from Mark 11:22 (par. Matt 21:21). So, here's another example of how Lindsey's Synoptic solution can help us.

popular Greek tradition speaks of mustard seed as the very smallest seed.[19] Mark, writing in Greek, took it over and incorporated it into the parable. It is no longer the growing (the word *growing* is missing from Mark!) that is the focus but rather the stark contrast between the tiniest mustard seed and the huge plant. The mustard seed, under Mark's pen in Greek, became the "smallest of all the plants on earth" and then became the "largest of all herbs" that sprouted "large branches." Matthew took over this contrasting description.

As a result of this shift in emphasis in Mark, the original orientation of the parable of Jesus is obscured. With this parable, Jesus wanted to depict his idea of the expansion of the kingdom of heaven on earth, which begins as small as a grain of mustard seed. But it grows and grows and becomes, so to speak, tree-sized as more and more people are won over to this kingdom and surrounded by it. In my opinion, the meaning of the parable regarding the subject and interpretation is misunderstood if you think you will find an eschatological point in it—although the mustard perennial grows and becomes tree-sized. However, this only marks the greatness of the process, not its goal. The view that end-time salvation will come only when those destined for it are grasped by the kingdom or, in other words, when the expansion of the kingdom is completed could be a scheme of a new sect. It is undoubtedly un-Jewish. Let us not forget that Jesus thought that the day of the Son of Man would come suddenly and unexpectedly; no one knew the time. He also spoke of deep convulsions in human society and the cosmos before the coming of the Son of Man. There is also something important: In Jesus' thought and in rabbinic thought—on which the idea of the kingdom of heaven is based—this idea is not organically linked to the expectation of the Messiah but is an independent idea. "According to their genesis, the Son of Man in the kingdom of God has nothing to do with each other and is not connected with each other in later Jewish eschatology. Their combination was therefore not suitable for Jesus even from the point of view of religious history."[20] Furthermore, the kingdom of God is already here, both for Jesus and according to the rabbinic view: it is being realized now on earth. Thus, based on the subject and other considerations, it can hardly be assumed that "the dominion of God is compared with the end times."[21] The astonishing growth from small beginnings is the decisive factor.

---

19. Evidence from *BDAG*, 1489.

20. Philipp Vielhauer, *Aufsätze zum Neuen Testament* (Münich: Kaiser, 1965), 87.

21. So Jeremias, *Die Gleichnisse Jesu*, 146.

An image like the parable of the mustard seed from the plant world can be found in the Qumran hymn scroll (IQH 6:15f.; 8:4–14).[22] Here, the Essene poet compares the congregation with a tree, "around whose sprouting foliage all the beasts of the forest graze . . . and its branch to all birds. But all the water-trees rise above him." The water-trees represent a wicked environment, and the tree of life itself is hidden. "Unconsidered and unrecognized is his secret seal." God himself hides his secret. The outsider "sees without realizing it. He thinks without believing the source of life." I will also explain that Jesus was opposed to such mystical-separatist esotericism. For the rest, however, the ethereal image for the congregation resembles the parable of the mustard seed. Like Essenism, with Jesus the kingdom of heaven is not only the end-time reign of God, which is already breaking in, but also a divinely willed movement that spreads among people on earth. This kingdom is not only, as in Judaism outside of Essenism,[23] a kingship but also a kingdom—namely, an area that is growing larger and encompassing more and more people. In this context, I do not want to claim that Jesus wanted to found a church, but he did want a movement that would grow.

In the source text, the parable of the mustard seed is followed by the similar parable of leaven. This is the case with Luke (13:20) and Matthew (13:33); this second parable is lacking in Mark. It has been thought that the parable of the mustard seed was originally handed down in two versions: in the saying's source as the first part of a double parable, and in Mark, who passes on only this first parable. Accordingly, the evidence that the parable of the mustard seed in the sayings source was the first part of a double parable is thought to be seen from Luke, who took the double parable from the sayings source, and from Matthew, where the wording of the parable of the mustard seed was also influenced by Mark. Contrary to this common hypothesis, I have tried to show that the Markan version is not to be regarded as independent and that it does not come from another source. Rather, it is the result of a conscious stylistic processing that is typical of Mark. Mark omitted the second parable about leaven because he saw in it a rather useless duplicate. Matthew did the same elsewhere, when Luke (15:1–10) includes the double parable of the lost sheep and the lost penny.

---

22. Cf. Flusser, *Jesus in Selbstzeugnissen und Bilddokumenten*, 87f. It is worth quoting the two passages *in extenso* so that the kinship and disagreement between Jesus and Essenism can appear.

23. Or more precisely, the Essenes did not adopt the concept of the kingdom of heaven.

Matthew (cf. Matt 18:10–14), on the other hand, dispenses with the second parable of the lost penny. He does this for the same reason that Mark omits the second part of the double parable of the mustard seed and the leaven.

Unfortunately, no Synoptic theory can do without a certain casuistry. This also applies to Lindsey's Synoptic solution. According to him, there are not two versions of the double parable of the mustard seed and the leaven. But, we must ask, from what source was it adopted? From the old report, the "Ur-Markus," or from the saying's source? The problem itself is not very important. But if you wish to proceed, then you have no choice but to proceed casuistically. If the double parable was contained in the old report, then there is no difficulty. The old account was available to all three evangelists, including Mark. On the other hand, Mark did not know the source directly. But as Lindsey almost certainly sees correctly, Mark used Luke as a template and the latter drew on the saying's source. Thus, according to Lindsey, the material from the saying's source was transmitted to Mark through the Gospel of Luke. But if the double parable of the mustard seed and leaven was not contained in the old account but in the saying's source, then Mark became familiar with it through reading Luke and omitted the story about leaven as a supposed duplicate. Neither assumptions stands in the way, neither linguistically or stylistically.

In the Gospels, many parables and parable sayings occur in parallels or in contrasting pairs. They usually stand one after the other or form a double parable.[24] Were two parables of Jesus only later coupled together because of their resemblance to double parables, or did Jesus himself compose at least some of them as double parables and then recite them as a unit? In any case, the following pairs should not be separated: the double image of birds and lilies (Matt 6:26–30; Luke 12:22–28), the saying about the cloths and the wineskins (Matt 9:16f.; Mark 2:21f.; Luke 5:36–39), the saying about the mustard seed and the leaven (Matt 13:31–33; Luke 13:18–21; cf. Mark

---

24. Regarding cloths and wineskins (Matt 9:16f.; Mark 2:21f.; Luke 5:36–39); mustard seed and leaven (Matt 13:31–35; Luke 13:18–21; Mark 4:30–32: mustard seed only); treasure and pearl (Matt 13:44–46); sheep and goats (Luke 15:1–10; Matt 18:10–14: sheep only); tower construction and warfare (Luke 14:28–33); double image: birds and lilies (Matt 6:26–30; Luke 12:22–28); salt and light (Matt 5:13–16; at Luke in various places: Luke 14:34f.; 11:38); house on the rock and on the sand (Matt 6:26–30; Luke 12:22–28). Perhaps the parables of the weeds (Matt 13:36–43) and of the fishnet (Matt 13:47–50) belong together; likewise, the parables of the supplicant friend (Luke 11:5f.) and the ungodly judge (Luke 18:1–8). See also the complete list in Jeremias, *Die Gleichnisse Jesu*, 89–91.

4:30–32), the parables of the treasure and the pearl (Matt 13:44–46), the double parable of the sheep and the goats (Luke 15:1–10; cf. Matt 18:10–14), the saying about the tower construction and warfare (Luke 14:28–33), and the contrasting saying about the house on the rock and the house on the sand (Matt 7:24–27; Luke 6:47–49). Further, it should be assumed that Jesus spoke the double parable of salt and light (Matt 5:13–16; Luke 14:34f) on the same occasion. It bears witness to aesthetic deafness when all these inseparable double parables are dismissed as subsequent editorial or redaction work.

It is a peculiarity of Jesus' stories that he loved to share double parables, but he was hardly the inventor of this form. I have found in rabbinic literature only contrasting double parables or opposing parable images that were told by scribes.[25] It is no coincidence that one of the rabbinic double parables parallels Jesus' saying about the house on the rock and the house on the sand (Luke 6:47–49).[26] I have not yet found a rabbinic double parable of which the two parables are parallels, as is typical with Jesus. That probably doesn't mean much. It must be remembered that the interval between Jesus the parable teller and the recording of his parables was incomparably shorter than the interval between the rabbinic parable tellers and the recording of their parables. However, in this relatively short interval between the narrator and the evangelist, we have observed two cases in which the

25. Cf. the double parable of Samuel the Little (dated at the beginning of the second century CE) in Bacher, *Die Agada der Tannaiten*, vol. 1, 371. It is also worth mentioning the double parable of the perfume handler and the tanner: see chapter 3, note 16, above. Concerning the contrasting saying of Eleazar ben Azariah, see chapter 4, note 118. Here, an old rabbinic double comparison should be added, which will occupy us more in the second part. It is about Rabbi Eleazar ben Zadok, who was a respected man during the last decades of the Second Temple: "To whom are the righteous in this world equal? A tree that stands in a pure place in its entirety, but whose foliage leans towards an unclean place. If the foliage is cut down, the tree remains in a pure place. Thus, the Holy One brings suffering brings upon the righteous in this world, that they may one day inherit the world to come." "Your beginning will be small, but your future will be very great" (Job 8:7). "And to whom are the wicked equal in this world? A tree that stands in the whole in an unclean place, and only its foliage inclines to a pure place. If the foliage is cut off, the tree remains in an unclean place. In this way, God gives abundant happiness to the wicked in this world, so that they may inherit the lowest level of hell. It is said: 'Some paths are before man, but his end are paths of death' (Prov 14:12)." bQid 40b, translation according to Bacher, *Die Agada der Tannaiten*, vol. 1, 49, with the help of a fragment from Geniza. Here and often, there is talk of two kinds of trees (cf. Jer 1:2).

26. This double parable is attributed to Elisha ben Abuja. Cf. Bacher, *Die Agada der Tannaiten*, vol. 1, 433; and chapter 4, note 121, above.

second parable of the double parable was omitted as an annoying duplicate. It is easy to imagine that something similar happened to rabbinic parables over the centuries. It may also be that part of an original double parable has been transferred to another place in rabbinic literature.

To return to Jesus: With him, we find that either two parable sayings or two simple, short parables are best suited for a double parable. It is hard to imagine that Jesus would have told two long parables with a rich subject on the same occasion as a double parable. However, I do not think this is entirely impossible. There are rabbinic contrast doublets that are also composed of two short and simple parables.

The double-parable genre of literature can repeat a lesson with the help of two parallel, short parables with different themes; it makes the proclamation memorable and urgent. Jesus uses this method as well. To warn of pending disaster on the day of the Son of Man, he describes two terrible catastrophes of the biblical past: the flood in the days of Noah and the destruction of Sodom in the days of Lot. He continues: "In the same way, it will be on the day when the Son of Man is revealed" (Luke 17:26–35).[27] Furthermore, Jesus sometimes uses a double parable to develop a specific teaching that he communicates in the first parable and then takes the second parable in a different direction with a new aspect. Like a cameraman, Jesus practices the method of gradually sharpening the field of view of his teaching to finally portray it completely before the eyes of the viewers. We should also examine his technique outside of parables, which would facilitate our understanding of his words. It seems to me that a technique of gradually fading and shifting the field of view is typical of Jesus. He may have adopted this method from others, but in any case, he designed them completely. It would be advisable to compare rabbinic paraenesis with Jesus' words to get a clearer picture. The genre of the double parable made it easy for Jesus to slowly shift the focus of his preaching. But those who examine this method in Jesus' argumentation should beware of exaggerations and generalizations, so that they do not seek changes of point of view and direction where they do not exist.

An instructive example of this change of illumination is the double parable of the cloths and wineskins (Matt 9:1, 6f.; Mark 2:2; Luke 5:33–39), to which I shall soon return. The same, however, applies to the double parable of the mustard seed and the leaven, which we are considering right now:

---

27. In Matt 24:37–41, there is no mention of Sodom. See also in Luke 13:1–5 the slain Galileans and the tower in Siloam.

The image of the growth of the kingdom is completed by the second parable. It reads: "The kingdom of heaven is like leaven, which one took and mingled with three measures of flour until it was completely leavened" (Matt 13:33; Luke 13:20).

The parable of leaven is the same in Matthew and Luke.[28] When Jesus spoke of three bushels of flour, he was simply trying to express a large amount, which would have been suggested to him by his Jewish Bible: "A dough of three bushels of flour" is prophesied in Gen 18:6 during the visit of the three men to Abraham. "Flour" in the parable of Jesus means the dough made of flour. This was the common linguistic usage of the time.[29] A woman[30] took the leaven and mixed it into a large amount of dough "until it was completely leavened." Nothing is said about the rising of the dough. That seems to me to be important. Paul probably quotes a Greek proverb when he says twice (1 Cor 5:6; Gal 5:9): "A little leaven leavens the whole dough."[31] In the same figurative sense, we can also find the idea of leaven in rabbinic Judaism. The rabbinic saying about this is an interesting contribution to the understanding of the parable of leaven in the Gospels. Rabbi Hiyyah bar Abba (c. 280 CE), referring to Jer 16:1, said: "If they forsake me (says God), I would be forgiving if they would observe my Torah. For if they forsook me, and observe and study my Torah, and dealt with it, the leaven that was in it would bring them near to me again."[32] Thus the study

---

28. The framework of Luke's words "And again he said" are simple and good Hebrew. The words of Matthew "Another parable he spoke unto them" are scattered. On the other hand, I prefer the introductory words to the parable in Matthew. They are identical with the introduction of the parable of the treasure and pearl (Matt 13:44–46). The Lukan introduction ("To what shall I liken the kingdom of God? It is like a leaven") is apparently aligned with the introduction of the preceding parable of the mustard seed (Luke 13:18f.).

29. See m. Hal. 2.6.

30. The woman who took the leaven also corresponds to the wording of the man who took the mustard seed in the preceding parable. The parallelism of the two parables is thus also indicated stylistically (in Matthew and Luke but not in Mark!).

31. Cf. Franz Mussner, *Der Galaterbrief* (Freiburg: Herder, 1988), 356; Heinrich Schlier, *Der Brief an die Galater* (Göttingen: Vandenhoeck & Ruprecht, 1965), 237; *BDAG*, 672. The saying means that small causes can have far-reaching consequences. This can be understood both positively and negatively. The "leaven of the Pharisees" (Luke 12:1; Mark 8:15; Matt 16:6) has nothing to do with our reasoning; the meaning of the leaven here is negative.

32. yHag 76c; PesK 12 la (Almond Tree, 254); Echa Rabbati, Prooemium 2; cf. Strack and Billerbeck, *Kommentar zum Neuen Testament aus Talmud und Midrasch*,

of Scripture will also bring the one who is far from God back to God. We can only fully enjoy the beautiful rabbinic saying if we grasp its pictorial expression. In Hebrew, "To deal with the dough" means that it is kneaded. If you do this thoroughly, then the whole dough is leavened evenly. If one deals seriously with Scripture, then through the spirit of life hidden in it, its entire content becomes alive and active. Whoever deals with Scripture without thinking of God is brought to God by the leaven contained therein, which leavens the whole of Scripture.[33]

The parable of leaven, the Greek proverb used by Paul, and the rabbinic figure of speech are all based on the observation that a little leaven leavens the whole dough. The rabbinic saying transfers this experience figuratively to the study of Scripture. Jesus uses the image for the increasing intensity and dynamism of the kingdom of God. The tiny mustard seed in the first parable and the small amount of leaven in the second parable represent the small beginning from which the kingdom will grow immensely. But while in the parable of the mustard seed the focus is on the growing itself, the second parable speaks not of the rising of the dough but of the leaven leavening the whole dough. "Similarly," says Jesus, "in the kingdom of heaven: First, when it enters the world, it literally disappears under the mass of the earthly; in the end, there will be nothing left but the kingdom of heaven."[34]

So, this is the crucial difference in the alignment of the two otherwise similar parables. While the first parable describes the growth of the kingdom of heaven, the second parable speaks of the kingdom grasping and "activating" more and more people. But Jesus now says that the leaven will

---

vol. 1, 728; Bacher, *Die Agada der Palästinischen Amoräer*, vol. 2, 197. In yHag, we find the words "and would deal with it."

33. According to bEr 54a–b, the same Rabbi Hiyya bar Abba narrates a not dissimilar saying of his teacher, Rabbi Yohanan: "Why are the words of the Torah compared to a fig tree? Just as you can still find figs on the fig tree, no matter how many times you feel it, so it is with the words of the Torah: No matter how often you immerse yourself in them—you still find a taste in them." Then follows a similar, anonymous saying: "Why are the words of the Torah compared to the breast? With the breast it is so: whenever an infant touches it, he still finds milk in it! So it is with the words of the Torah. No matter how often you immerse yourself in them, you will always find a taste in them." The two parallel rabbinic comparisons quoted here are similar in their double structure to Jesus' double parables. For the words of Rabbi Johanan, see Bacher, *Die Agada der Palästinischen Amoräer*, vol. 1, 237. See also the beautiful double image similar in wording and teaching in SifDev for Deut 32:2, ed. Finkelstein, 336f.

34. Jülicher, *Die Gleichnisreden Jesu*, vol. 2, 598f.

leaven "all" flour. How is this to be interpreted? Leavening of the whole dough is parallel to the transformation of the mustard seed into a tree-sized plant. But the tree-sized plant is not the target in the first parable, while the fully leavened flour is the target of kneading. Does Jesus here express figuratively that, in the end, the kingdom of heaven will reach its goal when he speaks of the fact that in the end all the flour will be leavened? I would at least like to warn against such an interpretation: Jesus did not want to express with the parable of the leaven that the Son of Man will come when the expansion of the kingdom will reach its final stage. I have already mentioned that in the thought of Jesus, in early Judaism, and in rabbinism, the concept of the kingdom of God is independent of the end-time coming of the Son of Man. Jesus said that the Son of Man would come unexpectedly. But did Jesus hope in his heart for this meeting? What does this flour mean? Is it all of humanity, all the people of Israel,[35] or all of those who are being saved? The latter seems most likely to me, if one does not understand it in the sense of predestined election, of which Jesus did not want to know anything. Jesus probably thought that the message of the kingdom would spread and "activate" those people who would then be saved. The imperative in Matt 9:37f. (the saying about the harvest) corresponds to the command of the parable of the leaven. In any case, there are enough words of Jesus that prove that he distinguished between the saved and the damned.

We can already see how many fertile possibilities and riches are hidden in a short parable such as that of leaven. For our investigation, however, it is mainly important that the two parables of the mustard seed and leaven deal with the same subject, but also that the second parable illuminates the growth of the kingdom of heaven from another point of view. The parable

---

35. Just now, a new book is being sent to me by Pinchas Lapide and Ulrich Luz, *The Jew Jesus*. My eyes are on it. For years, the early church was convinced that "the message of the kingdom of God applies only to the Jews." The idea that only Jews are saved contradicts the Old Testament. From Matthew and Luke 11f., it becomes indisputably clear that Jesus, with most of the Jews, believed the righteous among the nations would in the end be redeemed. Another difficult question is whether Jesus and the rabbis, when speaking of the kingdom of God in its specific meaning, considered the peoples included in it. In my book about Jesus (Flusser, *Jesus in Selbstzeugnissen und Bilddokumenten*, 81–89), I tried to show that the rabbinic term "kingdom of heaven" originated from an inner-Jewish, political-ethical problem. If this observation can be confirmed, then the kingdom of God as a term for Jesus has the people of Israel in view, of course without Jesus denying the peoples the salvation from particularistic resentment. The theologians of the peoples may not prematurely dismiss this as an intolerable imposition!

of the leaven therefore deepens the knowledge we gained from the parable of the mustard seed.

Mark omitted the parable about the leaven, "not to be harmed by overcrowding."[36] Furthermore, he inserted the parable of the self-growing seed (Mark 4:26–29) as his special material before the parable of the mustard seed. There seems to be some sort of core in the parable of the self-growing seed that belongs to Jesus. However, it is not entirely Greek though it is conceived according to the taste of Greek parable images. One has already pointed out the parallel in the early Christian letter of the Roman bishop Clement.[37] The parable of Mark says:

> "So it is with the kingdom of God: as when a man throws the seed on the earth and sleeps and wakes up, night and day. And the seed sprouts and grows long, how—he does not know. By itself the earth bears fruit, first stalk, then ear, then in the ear full grain. If the fruit is ready, he will immediately send the sickle, for the harvest is here."

Clement warns Christians against impatience with the following image: "Take a vine. First it puts out the foliage, then a sprout, then a leaf, then a flower, then an unripe grape, then a ripe grape. See how quickly the fruit of the tree comes to maturity!" The Greek philosopher Epictetus also warns against impatience with a stylistically similar image: "Let the tree bloom first, then produce the fruit and then ripen it."[38] This illustrative, step-by-step description of the development of a plant is common to all three Greek comparisons. This is Greek popular taste, however, not Hebrew spirit. This finding is confirmed by the Greek language and Greek style of the parable of the self-growing seed. Mark then includes the parable of the mustard seed, treating it also in the same Greek manner.

In the Gospel of Matthew, the double parable of the mustard seed and leaven (Matt 13:31–33) is followed by the small pericope on the method of the parables (Matt 13:34). It is taken from the continuation in Mark (4:33f.).

---

36. Jülicher, *Die Gleichnisreden Jesu*, vol. 2, 580. It is true that there is a trilogy of seed parables in Mark. But it is not certain that Mark had them in mind them when he inserted the parable of the self-growing seed (Mark 4:26–29) prior to the parable of the mustard seed.

37. *First Clem 23:4 (2 Clem 11:3)*. Cf. Jülicher, *Die Gleichnisreden Jesu*, vol. 2, 540; Taylor, *The Gospel According to Saint Mark*, 267.

38. Epictetus 4, 8.40. Klostermann pointed to this parallel in *Das Markusevangelium*, 44. I also pointed this out above in chapter 6, note 21. Here, I would like to point out the similarity in the presentation.

Then in Matt 13:36–43, the interpretation of the parable of the weeds follows. This interpretation is therefore separate from the parable itself (Matt 13:24–30). Presumably, Matthew thought it sensible to address this interpretation to the general pericope on the method of speaking in parables.[39] This separation of the explanation of the parable from the parable itself imitates what happened in all three Gospels with the parable of the sower. There, too, between the parable and its explanation is the brief, general pericope of the purpose of speaking in parables (Matt 13:10–15 par.). If we consider all this, then it becomes evident that the double parable of the treasure and the pearl in the source of Matthew came immediately after the double parable of the mustard seed and was not connected to the parable of leaven. The double parable of the treasure and the pearl is handed down to us only by Matthew. Further, I have already noted that the double parable of the mustard seed and leaven, as well as that of the treasure and pearl, apart from the problematic parable of the self-growing seed, are the only parables of Jesus that speak unequivocally of the kingdom of heaven. And it was precisely these parables that formed a unity in the source of Matthew. Is this compilation to be understood from the creative endowment of this source, or did Jesus himself on an unknown occasion decide to illuminate the essence of the kingdom of heaven through two pairs of parables?

Thus far I have tried to show that a better Synoptic theory can help us to understand the method of Markan processing so that we can move past Mark to the original text of the parables. I have further explained that this enables us to know more about the original order of the sources of the Gospels. However, I have hardly mentioned the fact that we also can learn more about content-related distortions in the Gospels with the help of Lindsey's Synoptic solution. In many cases, it helps us to understand the original meaning of Jesus' proclamation from the texts we have received without having to include hypotheses that go beyond the text of the Gospels.

I would like to begin with a story about a sentence in the Synoptics that is not in Jesus' parables. When I spoke not long ago about the rabbinic background of the Sermon on the Mount, a New Testament professor ob-

---

39. Matthew assimilates the pericopes on the method of parable (13:34) to the following interpretation of the parable of the weeds: "All these things Jesus spoke in parables to the multitude." And in 13:36, he begins the interpretation of the parable with, "Then Jesus left the crowd and went into the house." He wants to describe the explanation of the parable as being intended only for the disciples. It is also influenced by Mark 7. In the parallel, in the pericopes of handwashing (Matt 15:15), no house is mentioned.

jected: "How can you speak of a rabbinic exegesis of Jesus when we learn from Mark [1:22]—in an editorial sentence—that Jesus taught as one who had authority and not as the scribes?" I answered this theologian with great seriousness: "If Jesus had authority, then he could also argue rabbinically from that authority." It wasn't until later when I was working on this book that I realized how this curious sentence originated with Mark. Without Lindsey's Synoptic theory, I never would have understood the development that led to this sentence.[40]

Now, in the case of this saying about authority from Lindsey's perspective, I would like to enter the path from Luke via Mark to Matthew. For the Synoptic development of the narrative in Luke 4:31–37 and Mark 1:21–28 (cf. Matt 7:28), it is significant that, according to the ancient account, this event took place at the beginning of Jesus' public career[41] when it was first reported that Jesus taught in a synagogue on the Sabbath and Jesus drove the evil spirit out of a man. Luke 4:36 says: "Everyone was terrified. They spoke among themselves, saying, 'What is this that he commands the unclean spirits with authority and power, and they go out?'" Quite literally, the astonished question is actually "What is this thing? What's going on?" Mark understood the question correctly when he wrote, "What is this?" (Mark 1:27). The word we have translated as "thing" is the Greek *logos*. *Logos* usually means "word," but it has already been observed that *logos* can also mean the object or the thing being spoken about.[42] It is also known that the Hebrew equivalent *davar* means "word" and "thing." In the New Testament, too, the Hebrew *davar* is sometimes behind the Greek *logos*[43] in its two meanings. In our day, unfortunately, this knowledge has not been applied to Luke 4:36. But the gifted and sensitive Hugo Grotius[44] knew that

---

40. Earlier, I understood the authority in Mark 1:22 as the ordination of a rabbi, in the sense of the question to Jesus in Luke 20:2 par., by what authority he teaches in the temple. I thought that the crowd was amazed at Mark 1:22 because Jesus taught as if he were an ordained rabbi and yet not like one. David Daube, *The New Testament and Rabbinic Judaism*, 205–23, 206, understood the sentence.

41. In Luke, it is not so. There Jesus' public ministry begins in the synagogue in Nazareth (Luke 4:16–30) because Jesus came from there. But Luke 4:23 speaks of what happened earlier in Capernaum. So, Luke changed the original order.

42. *BDAG*, 944.

43. Peter's answer to Simon Magus in Acts 8:21 is particularly interesting: "You have no share nor lot in this matter [*logoi*]." The passage is literally translated from Hebrew.

44. It is worth quoting in Latin the words of Hugo Grotius, *Annotationes in Novum Testamentum*, vol. 3 (Groningen: Zuidema, 1828), 231: *Posuit hoc Lucas*

those present asked about Jesus' healing miracle: "What is this thing?" The question is literally translated from Hebrew: *Mah ha-davar ha-zeh.*

In the old account, this was probably talking only about Jesus' first miracle of salvation in the synagogue of Capernaum as a continuation of the story that he taught there on the Sabbath (Luke 4:14). His teaching on the Sabbath is mentioned only incidentally. The story had already been translated into Greek when a pre-Lukan editor[45] noticed that in this pericope, a concrete example of Jesus' teaching activity is mentioned for the first time. The editor's discovery inspired his creative imagination. Thus Luke 4:32 emerged as a secondary addition and as a "flashback" of Luke 4:36. Now we read, "And they were astonished at his teaching, because his word was with authority." One could have suspected earlier that Luke 4:32 is an editorial addition, not only because the word *doctrine* (Greek: *didachae*) can hardly be translated back into Hebrew, but also because *didachae* does not appear in the sources of the Gospels.[46] On the other hand, it is easy to see that the Greek text of Luke 4:32 depends on Luke 4:36. This can be shown by the common usages that took on a new meaning in the secondary verse. Luke

---

pro eo quod Marcus dixerat' ti esti touto '; quare verior est interpretatio illa' Quid hoc est rei?' Nam et LXX, cum 'davar' rem significat 'logon' aut 'rema'saepe vertitur.

45. There is no doubt that Luke wrote a Greek text that had been extended by a former editor. Luke 4:32 was written on the premise that Jesus had first appeared as a teacher. That is why the editor thought it appropriate to speak of listeners' amazement about Jesus' teaching. Our Gospel of Luke makes Jesus appear earlier in the synagogue in Nazareth. Therefore, Luke 4:32 is a kind of duplicate to Luke 4:22. The old report was already available to the editor in Greek, for only in this way can it be explained that he used the Greek word *logos*, which means "thing" in Luke 4:36, as "word" in Luke 4:32. But is this "he taught them" in Luke 4:31 (cf. Mark 1:21) original, or perhaps these words also come from the pre-Lukan editor? The earlier Greek-drafted Luke 4:15, which speaks of Jesus' teaching, gives a strong impression of an editorial summary. Luke 4:31 once certainly followed the editorial Luke 4:15. So it seems to me now very probable that Jesus' teaching in the synagogue in Capernaum was inserted by the same pre-Lukan editor. If I understand correctly, then the old account did not speak at all of Jesus' teaching at his first appearance in the synagogue of Capernaum but only of a first healing miracle.

46. The word *didachae* does not appear together anywhere in the Synoptic Gospels except in our pericopes (Luke 4:32; Mark 1:22; Matt 7:28). I assume with Lindsey that Mark here is dependent on Luke, and Matthew on Mark. In addition, the saying as special material occurs twice in the framing sentences of Mark (4:2; 12:38) and once in Matthew (16:12), whereas the word is missing in Mark. Luke (12:1) speaks of the "hypocrisy" of the Pharisees. Matthew 22:33 is an editorial conclusion that repeats what is written in Matt 7:28.

4:36 tells us that "a fear has come upon all" after seeing Jesus' miracle of salvation. According to Luke 4:32, "the hearers of Jesus were astonished at his teaching."[47] Even more interesting are the two other twists. After Luke 4:36, the eyewitnesses of the miracle said to one another, "What is this thing, that he commands the unclean spirits with authority and power?" In the secondary passage, Luke 4:32, the listeners were "astonished" at his teaching "because his word [*logos*] was spoken with authority."

What happened? The editor read in his source that Jesus, while teaching on the Sabbath in the synagogue of Capernaum, had driven the unruly spirit out of a sick person, and that those present had recognized with amazement that this Jesus possessed the authority of God to cast out demons. After this presentation, Jesus first appears as a teacher in the synagogue. The editor thought then that it was insufficient to be content with merely mentioning Jesus' teaching on this occasion. But how and from where should a closer connection be established between doctrine and the power of salvation? There was talk of the multitude who were terrified of the miracle of salvation. The fear of the miracle could therefore be compared to the impression Jesus gave when he first appeared as a teacher in the synagogue. So, the editor thought that from the words of the crowd shaken by Jesus' miracle, one could draw an analogy to their reaction to Jesus as a teacher. He read the astonished question of the crowd only in the Greek translation. He therefore found what he was looking for: the people's astonishment and realization that the miracle-worker Jesus could perform such miracles only because power had been given to him by God. In the editor's opinion, the listeners recognized this and were astonished when they listened to Jesus' teaching, noting that he spoke his word in God's power. The editor mentioned the "word" of Jesus because he found the Greek word *logos* in this passage. Ignoring the original Hebrew meaning of *logos* in Luke 4:36, the editor was able to conclude that Jesus' teaching was distinguished by a special quality: It was done by God's authority. At that time, the listeners would have experienced this in deep shock. By his analogy, the editor thus created an impressive picture of Jesus as a teacher: His word came from God!

According to Luke 4:32, Jesus' teaching is of superhuman quality. Although this quality was not in sharp tension with Judaism at that time, Mark took the first step toward a contradiction. According to him, the hearers at Capernaum "were astonished at his teaching, for he taught them as one

---

47. Mark 1:22 and Matt 7:28 take the expression "they were astonished at his teaching." Mark repeats it in 1:18.

having authority,[48] and not as the scribes" (Mark 1:22). This is a restyling of what was written in Luke 4:32. There, we read that the "word" of Jesus "came with authority." However, Luke 4:32 is an addition adopted from Luke 4:36. As a result of the restyling, the expression "the word" disappeared in Mark. The main word *authority* appears in Mark in a different syntactic context. Mark apparently clarifies Luke by saying that Jesus taught as a bearer of authority. You might think that the text in Mark is an innocent explanation of what Mark read in Luke 4:32. But if we look further, to Mark 1:27, we learn something better. According to Luke 4:36, after Jesus had healed the man, "fear came upon all, and they spoke among themselves, saying, 'What is this thing that he commands the unclean spirits with authority and power, and they go out?'" In Mark 1, on the other hand, we read, "And they were all terrified, so that they spoke with one another and said, 'What is this? A new teaching that is fulfilled with authority?[49] And he commands the unclean spirits, and they obey him.'"

With Mark, therefore, the emphasis shifted from the miracle of healing to the peculiarity of Jesus' teaching. He therefore tends to rewrite Luke's additional words about the Jesus' teaching (Luke 4:32). Furthermore, he says the crowd is amazed not only about the miracle of healing but also a second time about the novelty of Jesus' teaching. In the old account (Luke 4:36), Jesus commands the unclean spirits "with authority." After the addition (Luke 4:32), the word of Jesus "with authority" also takes place by means of a flashback. Mark "harmonizes" these two mentions of authority: one in favor of Jesus' teaching and the other in favor of Jesus' healing. In this sense, he changes Luke 4:36. In Mark 1:27, Jesus' authority no longer manifests itself in the expulsion of unclean spirits but is characterized by the novelty of his teaching.[50] By squeezing this new doctrine into the verse, Mark breaks

---

48. Lindsey made me aware that this expression is also in Luke 19:1–7, but in a slightly different sense. He suspects that the violent expression in Mark 1:22 is linguistically influenced by Luke's text.

49. It is customary to translate this differently because the word *authority* is taken too little seriously here, and because one does not consider that the words "as a result of authority" here should explain why Jesus' teaching is new. The following division does not correspond to the Markan sentence: "A new doctrine! And with authority he commands the spirits." This would correspond to Luke 4:36 but not to Mark, who says in 1:22, "He taught them as one having authority." Cf. Taylor, *The Gospel According to Saint Mark*, 176; Metzger, *Textual Commentary*, 75.

50. Mark 1:27 first interprets Luke 4:36 ("What is this thing?") according to its sense. Immediately afterwards, Mark understands the Greek word *logos* as a word and speaks of a new doctrine. He takes the word *doctrine* from Luke 4:32.

the unity of the original. One sentence now falls into two parts, with the mention of the expulsion of the unclean spirits becoming an appendage.

The progressive changes in the section on Jesus in Capernaum confirm our new Synoptic solution. We are thus able to review and confirm the stylistic and factual changes in the first three Gospels. In many cases, this enables us to advance to the original wording of Jesus' preaching. Above all, we can grasp the essence of Jesus' parables more clearly and interpret them accordingly.

So far, we have gone the way of Luke to Mark. Now let's see what happened to Matthew from the pericope. After literary and philological considerations, I have tried to fathom how the characterization of Jesus' teaching originated in Luke 4:32. It says that his word came with authority. Mark goes one step further and says that Jesus taught "as one having authority and not as the scribes," which then becomes the focal point of the whole pericope with Mark. Predominantly from Jesus' teaching and less from his miracle-working, those present recognized Jesus' authority. Through his stylistic elaboration and apparently the only explanatory addition of the scribes, Mark was able to first point out the heavenly origin of Jesus' teaching, and he could also roughly describe the content of Jesus' proclamation: Jesus taught "as one who possesses authority." His teaching differed qualitatively from rabbinic teaching. Jesus' teaching was "a new teaching with authority." These new achievements of Mark pleased the author of the Gospel of Matthew. He was even so fascinated that he was willing to renounce the whole miracle of Jesus' healing and, following Mark, write: "And it came to pass, when Jesus had finished these words, that the multitude marveled at his teaching, for he taught them as one having authority, and not as their scribes" (Matt 7:28f.). The scribes now have become "their" scribes.[51] And what were the words that Jesus had just finished? The Sermon on the Mount. Anyone who has learned even a little about Judaism knows how much the Sermon on the Mount has its roots in rabbinism and its exegetical method. The Matthean claim that the words of the Sermon on the Mount are quite different from the teaching of the scribes is at least exaggerated.[52] But the

---

51. On this point and on Matthew's tendency to deepen the distance between Jews and Christians, cf. Georg Strecker, *Der Weg der Gerechtigkeit Untersuchung zur Theologie des Matthäus* (Göttingen: Vandenhoeck & Ruprecht, 1966), 30.

52. Starting from Matt 7:28f., where Matthew interprets the nature of the Sermon on the Mount in his sense, an investigation would be worthwhile, as Matthew in the Sermon on the Mount himself manipulated the words of "historical" Jesus by small but significant changes; e.g., in Matt 5:17f. Through his redaction, a

uninitiated New Testament scholar, whom I mentioned above, was confused by this editorial distortion.

When Mark 1:27 is read together with Mark 1:22, it follows that Mark understands the nature of Jesus' proclamation as a "new teaching with authority," which is like the teaching of the scribes. The contrast between the "new" teaching of Jesus and Judaism highlights a poorly preserved papyrus fragment of an apocryphal gospel with the help of a fictitious argument.[53] Jesus is asked by a Jewish adversary, "Why don't you answer? What new doctrine, they say, do you teach, and what new baptism do you proclaim? Answer me!" Hopefully today, it is no longer necessary to prove that Jesus did not want to teach a "new doctrine." Rather, he sought to restore the true, original, divine meaning of Judaism. This knowledge, however, does not free us from the task of finding out what Mark understood by the "new teaching" of Jesus. After answering this question, our path to understanding the double comparison of the cloths and the wineskins will open.

The Markan pericope about Jesus' authority and likewise the Markan double comparison of the cloths and the wineskins state that Jesus is presenting a new teaching regarding Judaism. If we want to clarify the issue here, we must ask about their *Sitz im Leben*; for it is evident that most of Jesus' disciples did not have the impression that his doctrine was something new. There were Jewish Christians who thought that Jesus had not come "to take away from the law of Moses." Rather, he had come "to add to the law of Moses."[54] They,

---

tension arose towards the "law." Strecker, "Die Antithesen der Bergpredigt," *ZNW* 69 (1978): 36–72, however, judges differently about the resulting antitheses. He sees Jesus as the "spokesman of the original antitheses." Then he continues, "His instruction is fundamentally [*sic*] opposed to the tradition of the 'ancients'; it leads in fact to the repeal of individual commandments of the Torah." We should ask ourselves how far such an outlook justifies Jesus and how far it is a modem metamorphosis that continues the centrifugal path of successive secondary editorial offices in the Gospels. In the light of my philological-critical examination of the term "authority" (*exusia*) in the pericope, it is helpful that Strecker, when he asks "for the motivation of Torah cultivation and Torah criticism in the proclamation of Jesus," assumes that "an excellent *exusia* consciousness for Jesus is undoubtedly to be presupposed, without it being possible to call it 'messianic.'"

53. Klostermann, *Das Markusevangelium*, 17f., drew attention to this parallel. It is the apocryphal fragment from Oxyrhynchus No. 1224. It was published by Klostermann himself in *Apokrypha* II, *Evangelien* (Kleine Texte 8), 26. I follow his results.

54. Flusser, "An Early Jewish-Christian Document in the Tiburtine Sibyl," in *Paganisme, Judaïsme, Christianisme: Infleuences et affrontements dans le monde antique: Mélanges offerts à Marcel Simon*, ed. A. Benoit et al. (Paris: E. de Boccard, 1978).

too, were unfamiliar with the idea that Jesus was proclaiming a new doctrine that did not agree with the rest of Judaism. Mark, writing about the new teaching of Jesus, was a Hellenistic Jew. The assumption is not wrong that he knew the Pauline Epistles. As I have tried to show elsewhere, Paul belonged to the second layer of Christianity, to the "kerygma of the Hellenistic churches," whose faith was influenced by Essenism.[55] The Essenes at Qumran saw in their "union" the fulfillment of the promise of Jeremiah (31:30), and they called their covenant the "new covenant." The second, Hellenistic layer of Christianity surpasses this idea. Since then, it has been called the "new covenant" of Christianity.[56] In this layer of Christianity, a contrast arises between the old covenant and the new covenant, which would have been unthinkable among the Essenes. In a still rather mild form, this contrast is expressed in the Letter to the Hebrews (8:13; cf. 2 Cor 3:6, 14). The author of this book comments on the "new covenant" found in the book of Jeremiah in the following way: "By saying, 'a new covenant,' he has declared the first to be obsolete. But what has lasted for ages and ages is near to disappearance." In Galatians, Paul speaks about a sharper contrast between the old covenant on Mount Sinai and the new covenant of Christianity (Gal 4:21–5:).

Paul also speaks of the new existence of the Christian: "Now we have become free from the law, dying to that which held us in bonds, so that we now serve in the newness of the Spirit and not in the oldness of the letter" (Rom 7:6). The Christian dies in Christ, with whom the "old man" is crucified so that we "walk in the new life" (Rom 6:4). The "old man" and this renewal by becoming a Christian are also mentioned in Ephesians (4:21–24; cf. 2:15; Col 3:9f.). As a Pauline summary statement, 2 Cor 5:1–7 can be interpreted as follows: "If, therefore, anyone is in Christ, he is a new creature. The old has passed away, behold, it has become new." However, Paul never thought that the teaching of Jesus was something completely new. He is concerned with the novelty of the existence of the Christian because of the cross.

---

55. Flusser, "The Dead Sea Sect and Pre-Pauline Christianity," ScrHier, vol. 4, *Aspects of the Dead Sea Scrolls* (Jerusalem: Hebrew University, 1958), 215–66.

56. See Flusser, "The Dead Sea Sect and Pre-Pauline Christianity," 236–42. The idea that through Jesus a covenant or a new covenant was made was foreign to Jesus and to the sources of the Gospels. In the original text of the words of Jesus at the Last Supper (Luke 22 according to the Codex Bezae), the covenant is not mentioned. Not so with Mark (14:25), on whom Matthew depends (26:28). Paul speaks in this context (1 Cor 1:25) of the "new covenant." See also Flusser, "The Last Supper and the Essenes," *Judaism* (1973): 23–27.

Christianity and being a Christian in the "kerygma of the Hellenistic communities" means the withering away of the old and the process of becoming new. Usually, a point against the old covenant and against the law becomes visible. But can it be so simply said that Mark's understanding of Jesus' teaching of a new, differently constituted doctrine contrary to the teaching that the scribes delineated is a variation of the polar contrast between the old and the new—corresponding to the kerygma of the Hellenistic-Christian communities? On this question, much can be said in the following treatment of the Markan form of the double comparison of the cloths and the wineskins. Luke, who preserved the original state of the ancient source, knows the qualification of Jesus' teaching as new neither in the pericopes of authority nor in the double comparison of the cloths and the wineskins. Furthermore, when he talks about Paul's visit to Athens in the Acts of the Apostles (17:19–21), the term "new doctrine" has a clearly negative meaning for him. At the Areopagus, Paul is asked, "'Can we know what this new teaching is that is being presented by you? For you bring strange things to our ears. So, we want to know what might be there.' All Athenians and the strangers present there have no other time than to say or hear something new." Luke thus criticizes the Athenians[57] who want to know Paul's new teaching. He does not want the Christian message to be understood as a "new teaching."

Let's go back to Mark. The Markan idea that the doctrine of Jesus is different from the doctrine of the scribes, and that it is a doctrine by virtue of authority, has much in common with the contrast between the old Jewish and the new Christian, as understood by the second "Pauline" stratum of Christianity. However, it cannot be easily deduced from this. Mark's position is still a rather moderate expression of a tense relationship between the new faith and the soil from which it grew. About a hundred years after Mark, Meliton of Sardis expressed this contrast extremely blatantly.[58] A little later, Irenaeus asks, "So what did the Master bring when he came? Recognize that he brought the great novelty by bringing himself who was foretold." What a miracle, then, if Mark transferred this novelty to the teaching of Jesus, and Matthew even says that the Sermon on the Mount was of a different nature from what the scribes taught. If today, some theologians and New Testament scholars apply such conceptions to everything Jesus said, then they block their way to understanding what is characteristic in Jesus' proclamation.

57. Cf. Hans Conzelmann, *Die Apostelgeschichte* (Tübingen: Mohr Siebeck), 97.
58. See his Easter homily. Cf. O. Perler, trans. J. Blank, "Méliton de Sardes, Sur la Pâque," *SC*, 123. Blank uses the quotation from Irenaeus (adv. haer. IV, 34.1), 52.

After this long detour, I would now like to discuss the double parable of the cloths and the wineskins (Matt 9:14–17; Mark 2:18–22; Luke 5:33–39).[59] Since I have already dealt with the parable about the groom, I can omit it here. Unfortunately, Luke already redesigned the double parable and we cannot reconstruct Hebrew wording. Mark stylistically takes the text even further from the Hebrew than the other two Gospels. Matthew knew the old source,[60] but at the same time, he was highly dependent on Mark. Matthew wrote this passage in a simpler form than Mark and Luke; nevertheless, it was usually difficult for him to decide where to reproduce the old source and where to simplify the Markan template. In each case, Luke's double comparison was already available in Greek, and indeed in a realistic imitation. The other two Gospels multiplied embellishments, each independent of the other, and Jesus' original simplicity was lost.

> And they said unto him, "The disciples of John fast,[61] and also the disciples of the Pharisees;[62] but your disciples eat and drink." Then Jesus answered

---

59. I have already said some things about this double parable in Flusser, "Do You Prefer New Wine?," *Immanuel* 9, (1979): 26-31.

60. Matthew and Luke have in common the term *epiballei* (Matt 9:16; Luke 5:36). Mark 2:21 speaks only of *epiblema*; he used this word in reference to Luke 5:36. The pouring out, the last words of Luke 5:37, and *hoi askoi apollyntai* in Matt 9:17 are also shared between the sources. The most important correspondence between Matt and Luke is *bleteon* in Luke 5:38; cf. the second *ballousin* in Matt 9:17. The verbal adjective *bleteon* in Luke is the only adjective in the entire New Testament with the ending *teos*; see Blass, Debrunner, Rehkopf, *Grammatik des neutestamentlichen Griechisch* (Göttingen: Vandenhoeck & Ruprecht, 1976), 52, 65n5. I suppose that Matt 9:1–7 is original and Luke changed "the one who fills" to "one who fills." If Luke writes that new wine should be "put into new wineskins," it may mean that he too may have personally identified the new wine with the new doctrine of Christianity, although he alone received the punchline of the equation. If Mark is dependent on Luke, then he has omitted "to fill" because he considered it superfluous. Some manuscripts omit the words "but new wine into new wineskins" at the end of Mark 2:22. Metzger, *A Textual Commentary on the Greek New Testament*, 79. It seems that the words in Mark are original.

61. In Luke, "They fast often." The word *often* is a reference to the Greek original. The word *fast* in Hebrew means "to fast." Luke says, "And they pray." This addition, which has nothing to do with the content of the pericopes, is explained, first, by Luke's preference for mentioning prayers and, second, probably because according to Luke 11:1 it is said that John the Baptist taught his disciples to pray.

62. The disciples of the Pharisees are lacking in Marcion. Otherwise, they appear in different forms in different places; cf. Klostermann, *Das Lukasevangelium*, 73. Despite all the textual difficulties, I do not want to miss the Pharisees here.

them,[63] "No one cuts a piece of cloth from a new garment,[64] and puts it on an old garment; otherwise, he will cut the new one here, and there the tear will be even worse.[65] And no one puts new wine into old wineskins, or else the new wine will tear the wineskins, and it will flow out and the wineskins will be lost. Rather, they tend to put new wine into new wineskins.[66] And no one who used to drink the old desires the new, for he thinks, 'The old tastes better.'"

If you carelessly read the introductory question in these three Gospels (Matt 9:14; Mark 2:18; Luke 5:33), you get the impression that Mark comes before Luke and that Matthew is dependent on Mark.[67] In all three Gospels,

---

63. Here, I leave out the saying about the bridegroom (Luke 5:34). Luke has the *caesura* after the saying about the bridegroom. That is why he introduces the double comparison with the following words: "He also spoke a parable to them." This sequence formula is typical Lukan stylization; Klostermann, *Das Lukasevangelium*, 73.

64. The Greek word means "garment." It is inferred from this that in Luke the folly of the procedure increases in that the patch is not cut off from a piece of new cloth but from an already finished garment; Klostermann, *Das Lukasevangelium*, 731. In my experience, however, such a distorted move cannot be attributed to Luke's imagination. The solution is much simpler: It is precisely at this point that Luke faithfully adopts the Greek translation of his original. The Hebrew word *beged* was translated as "garment" in this source with the ordinary equivalent. But at that time, it meant not only "dress" but also the fabric from which one makes clothes. This is evident, for example, from bYev 102b. See also M. Jastrow, *A Dictionary of the Targum, the Talmud Babli and Yerusalami, and the Midrashic Literature*, vol. 1 (1950), 137.

65. I have taken from Mark 2:2 (Matt 9:16) the words, "And there the breach is made worse." This is probably the most acceptable way out. In Luke 5:36b, it says, "And there the old cloth will not fit with the new." This is certainly not original, because the Lukan form of the saying about the cloth is not parallel to what is said in Luke and in Matthew in two parts about the old and the new wine. In both parts of the double parable, it has certainly been said in parallel that both the old and the new will perish. Unfortunately, this is not mentioned today in any version of the picture of the cloths. According to Luke 5:36, the new material is cut and the cloth does not fit the old garment; according to Mark 1:21 (and Matt 9:16), on the other hand, only the old garment is torn. What happened to the text of the image of the cloth in the Gospels shows how right Jesus was with the double comparison: The editor or—rather unlikely—Luke himself has attached a new Greek cloth! With Mark, the rift gets worse, and with Matthew, it didn't get better. As far as I could, I tried to fix the condition, so to speak, by means of artificial plugs.

66. On the Lukan *bleteon*, see note 59 above. I read here with Matt 9:37 *ballousin*.

67. Luke 5:33 par. is a nice proof of the correctness of Lindsey's Synoptic solution. The question about the table fellowship (Matt 9; Mark 2:16; Luke 5:30) is

the pericopes about fasting revolve around the passage that deals with the banquet at the house of the tax collector Levi. In Luke (and Matthew), the fasting question is directly linked to the tax collector's meal. Whether this literary sequence corresponds to historical events can no longer be decided. Luke writes, "And they said to him." He is implying that the interlocutors were the same as those whom Jesus had previously exhorted in Luke 5:22. But if we assume that the framework and introductory question in Mark and Matthew depend on the text before us in Luke, then it is difficult to consider the mention of the fasting of the Pharisees as secondary, although this mention is very awkward for Luke.[68] But what about the special fast days of John's disciples? It is to be assumed that they observed such. Of John the Baptist, Jesus himself testified that he "neither eats nor drinks" (Matt. 11:18; Luke 7:33), in contrast to Jesus himself, who "eats and drinks."

---

addressed to the disciples of Jesus in all three Gospels. In Luke 5:30, they are asked, "Why do you eat and drink?" while in Mark and Matthew, they ask why Jesus eats with the tax collectors. In the following fasting question (Matt 9:14; Mark 2:18; Luke 5:33), Jesus himself is addressed, since he had just answered before. He is asked about the behavior of his disciples. The behavior of the disciples of Jesus is thus criticized in the second case in all three Gospels. In the first case, on the other hand, this criticism deals only with the disciples in Luke, whereas in Mark and Matthew the apex is directed against Jesus himself. In both cases, therefore, the disciples were originally criticized regarding the question of fasting, as is still the case in all three Gospels. In the question of the table community, however, only Luke preserves the untimely state. Mark and his followers—Matthew has changed—the whole complex of questions is not without importance for the search for the "historical" Jesus. Who was often criticized by inquiries—Jesus himself or his disciples? According to Luke in the question of the table fellowship, it was the disciples; and according to Mark and Matthew, it was Jesus himself. In the story of the picking of grain on the Sabbath (Mark 2:23 cf. Luke 6:10), it is told only by the disciples, and not by Jesus himself, that on the Sabbath they crushed the grain with their hands. Therefore, the accusation applies only to the disciples. The same is true for the story of handwashing (Mark 7:2 and 5; Matt 5f.). In the story of the clash of Jesus with the Pharisaic high priest in the temple courtyard (Schneemelcher, *New Testament Apocrypha*, vol. 1, 57f.; Jeremias, *Unbekannte Jesusworte,* 60–70), the accusation is directed both against Jesus and his disciples, but the story is apocryphal. Are we dealing here only with stereotypical formulas? Or did Jesus' behavior differ from that of his disciples so that the accused were precisely struck by the criticisms? Or was Jesus blamed for the behavior of his disciples because he also acted like his disciples? The latter is certainly true regarding not fasting.

68. See also note 61 above. If we want to consider the mention of the fast days of the Pharisees in Luke as secondary, then we must assume that this mention from Mark or from Matthew crept into Luke's text.

The same expression is found in Luke 5:33 and applied to Jesus' disciples regarding fasting. Luke learned this from his sources. Could it not be that the mention of the Pharisees is original but that Luke added the disciples of John based on his knowledge of them? This question is not as meaningless as it may seem at first glance.

It is known that Luke was also otherwise interested in John the Baptist and his disciples. In our pericopes (Luke 5:33), he says of John's disciples that they "keep prayers." The mention of the prayers of John's disciples combines the wording of our pericopes with the Lukan introduction to the Lord's Prayer (Luke 11:1). There, it is reported that one of the disciples of Jesus asked him, "Master, teach us to pray as John also taught his disciples." Jesus then taught his disciples the Lord's Prayer. After the discovery of the Dead Sea Scrolls, it became obvious that the Baptist was close to the Essenes. He seems to have belonged to those fringe Essenes who had strong rabbinic tendencies. If Jesus taught his own disciples a competing prayer to the prayers of the Baptist, so to speak, we might surmise that the Lord's Prayer bears some resemblance to the prayers in the Qumran scrolls. This, however, is not the case. The Lord's Prayer is "rabbinic," and its first half is even developed from the rabbinic *kaddish*. If these assumptions and conjectures are correct, then it becomes difficult to bridge the contradiction between the essential root of John's movement and the rabbinic character of the Lord's Prayer.

An analogous problem is hidden in the question about fasting. The fact that the disciples observed special fast days can be regarded as quite certain. Jesus' answers to the question of why his disciples do not fast, in contrast to John's disciples, do not give the impression that he only wants to justify himself to a Jewish sect. But it does seem that here Jesus is criticizing a new religious practice that someone is trying to impose on all Jewry. Sewing a new rag on an old cloak and pouring new wine into old wineskins will not help; it will spoil everything! Although we do not know the special fast days of the disciples of John, we know the new fast days of the Pharisees very well. The Pharisees were then the teachers of most of the Jewish people, and their newly established fast days did not apply only to their group members. Their fasting is explicitly mentioned in our section in all three Gospels. Based on our historical knowledge of the Pharisees' fast days and the textual evidence, we can assume that the proclamation of the Pharisees' fast days in our pericopes is original. If the fast days of John's disciples were not only included in our text based on a historical hypothesis of Luke, then it can be assumed that they also observed such additional fast days that are not prescribed in the Bible. It may also be that they had adopted the new fast days of the Pharisees.

As researchers have correctly recognized, this is not about the fast prescribed by the Bible that everyone had to observe, but about additional fast days, with the greatest likelihood being the twice-a-week fast introduced by the Pharisees: on Monday and Thursday.[69] The Pharisee in Luke 18:12 boasts that he fasts twice a week, and the original Christian Scripture, *Didache* (8:1), also reports about these fast days of the "hypocrite." How many Jews at the time of Jesus kept these fasts, we do not know. In any case, this additional new fasting has not generally prevailed in Judaism. One of the main purposes of Jewish fasting is to make the people repent. The Pharisees—and certainly also John's disciples—wanted to encourage the people to repent again by introducing new fast days. For Jesus, too, repentance was of crucial importance. He maintained that repentance[70] to God was the commandment of the hour. However, he regarded the introduction of new fast days as ineffective and even harmful patchwork. In his opinion, such a partial reform could not achieve a general and profound reflection of the whole people: "If you do not repent, you will all perish in the same way!" (Luke 13:3–5).

After all these considerations and observations, we cannot help but see in Luke 5:39 the point of the double comparison. Mark and Matthew bring no parallel to this point. Because of this lack of parallels, there are manuscripts from which Luke 5:39 is missing. It is easy to explain what happened there according to our Synoptic theory, according to which the development often took place in the direction of Luke via Mark to Matthew. If the punch line is in Luke, then it is probably original. If it has been omitted in Mark for any reason and if in this case Matthew depends on Mark, then the point must also be missing in Matthew.

It is easy to guess why most researchers like the form of the double comparison in Mark and Matthew.[71] Without Luke's point, we can read

---

69. See, for example, Emil Schürer, *Geschichte des jüdischen Volkes im Zeitalter Jesu Christi*, vol. 2. (Leipzig: Hildesheim, 1964), 572f.; Klostermann, *Das Markusevangelium*, 27; Lowy, "The Confutation of Judaism in the Epistle of Barnabas," *JJS*, 5–8; Strack and Billerbeck, *Kommentar zum Neuen Testament aus Talmud und Midrasch*, vol. 2, 241–44; Büchler, *Types of Jewish-Palestinian Piety*, 139; and Büchler, *Studies in Sin and Atonement in the Rabbinic Literature of the First Century*, 442–48.

70. In German and in Hebrew, literally "turning back."

71. I have some English written evaluations of the double comparison in note 58 in the article I mentioned above.

from the double comparison that the "historical" Jesus had set himself apart from fragile Judaism. He himself had proclaimed that the old Jewish message was incompatible with his overwhelmingly new message. "The new I bring is as incompatible with the old as a new patch with an old garment and new wine with brittle wineskins."[72] "One cannot preserve the old cloak of Judaism with new patches, and one cannot preserve the new wine of Christianity in old wineskins."[73] If we read the double comparison in the Markan form as an answer to the fasting question, then we can read from it: "The Cause of Jesus demands a new piety. . . . The Jewish custom is thus declared to be done with. You can't do it."[74] However, it can be assumed that Mark presumably meant that the controversy about fasting concluded with the saying about the bridegroom and that the following double parable was a saying of Jesus independent of the question of fasting. Therefore, the point in Luke 5:39 was incomprehensible to Mark, and he left it out. Furthermore, if we separate the double parable from the question of fasting (and therefore delete Luke's point) then what Jesus says against the unreasonable, bungling innovators becomes fighting words against the fragile Jewish old tradition, which is incompatible with the new Christian religion. If we read the double comparison in a Markan pattern, we can come up with various colorful, denominationally tinged interpretations. "The new wine that Jesus brought needs new wineskins, the new spirit also needs new forms," says a Catholic exegete.[75] And a liberal Protestant New Testament scholar declares with an explicit anti-Catholic jab, "The new thing that Jesus found to be repugnant to everything old was spirit, life, religion."[76]

The differences in the lofty interpretations of modern exegetes[77] are partly because today we think more historically than the fathers of the church. We are therefore forced to consider the fact that Jesus was a Jew and under the law. Marcion had it easier: he was able to justify his dualistic mood with our saying. But Tertullian, in his writing directed against

---

72. Thus Klostermann, *Das Markusevangelium*, 28, describes Mark's concept.

73. So Zahn at Klostermann, 28.

74. So Schneider, *Das Evangelium nach Lukas*, 140. In favor of Schneider, it should be said that he does not consider such a statement to be authentic to Jesus: "This instruction corresponds to the situation towards the end of the first century, in which the synagogue and the Jesus congregation were separated from each other." See also Schurmann, *Das Lukasevangelium*, 298–300.

75. Schurmann, *The Gospel of Luke*, 299.

76. Jülicher, *Die Gleichnisreden Jesu*, vol. 1, 198.

77. Jeremias, *Die Gleichnisse Jesu*, 118.

Marcion, meant that Jesus wanted to show with the double parable "that he separated the novelty of the gospel from the oldness of the law."[78] Irenaeus speaks of the new covenant of freedom and of the new wine being poured into new wineskins—namely, faith in Christ.[79]

Both the patristic exegesis and the modern interpretation of the saying about the cloths and wineskins have a common orientation, which can be roughly described as follows: With this parable, Jesus said that weak, old Judaism is incompatible with his new Christian message. Such interpretations, however, are nothing more than elaborations of the Markan understanding of the double comparison. To get out of this unanimity and to get to the original meaning, I first analyzed Mark's report about Jesus' visit to the synagogue of Capernaum (Mark 1:21–28) in a historical and literary-critical way. It turns out that Mark understood Jesus' teaching as a new teaching. This teaching came into being by divine authority and differed substantially from the teaching of the scribes. It is also possible that the characterization of Jesus' teaching as a "new teaching" in Mark 1:27 was codetermined by the "new wine" in a double comparison. The only question is how far Mark went in distinguishing between Judaism and Jesus' teaching. Apparently, not as far as the church fathers. He probably saw in Jesus' proclamation a new doctrine sanctioned by God, quite different from the doctrine of rabbinism within Judaism. It was marked by the tension between his church and the synagogue. Therefore, reading the double parable in his source, he mistakenly found a confirmation from the mouth of Jesus himself that it was harmful for the young church to pour its young wine into the old wineskins of the synagogue. He therefore concluded that the praise of the old wine in Luke 5:39 is an annoying addition, and that's why he left it out.

Out of fidelity to his source, Luke was the only one who left in the point of the parable (Luke 5:39). But it is not as if Luke did not also think that the new wine signified the proclamation of Jesus.[80] A certain ambiguity, both due to the absence of the point in Mark and Matthew as well as regarding Luke's way of thinking, was transferred to the copyists of the Gospels. Under the influence of Mark and Matthew, some copyists of Luke omitted verse 5:39. Others thought they could fix the verse cosmetically and therefore

---

78. Citations according to Jülicher, *Die Gleichnisreden Jesu*, vol. 2, 198.

79. Irenaeus, *Contra hereseis* 4.33.14; cf. also 4.35.2. For another quotation from Irenaeus in the same direction, see note 57 above.

80. Cf. note 59 above.

wrote: "And no one who drinks old wine wants to drink the new." So it was in the presentation of the gnostic Gospel of Thomas and perhaps also in the Diatessaron of Tatian.[81] This is a pessimistic improvement, which involuntarily exposes how mangled the interpretation of Jesus' saying was by the time Mark had already begun. We must be patient with the finicky drunkard if we want to dissuade him from the bad habit of drinking a good, old wine! Although modern exegetes do not smuggle the word *equal* into the text, they travel the same way to excuse Luke 5:39 from their point of view. This verse is supposed to be "a benevolently humorous concession that one need not be surprised at the tenacious adherence to the habit."[82] And another exegete: "With this rule, Luke makes clear how it is that many lock themselves to the new. The old is (understandably!) more acceptable to them; one can find the negative attitude of the critics of Jesus understandable. The contemporaries of the evangelists should know why many Jews refuse the claim of Jesus in disbelief."[83] Through the new theological "cloths," the whole story becomes colorful. But why, for God's sake, has one (since Mark, so to speak) imbued Christian people in the name of Jesus with an allegorical new wine, when everyone prefers the existing old wine? Is it not strange that though theologians delight themselves in the parable of the new wine, when in the wine cellar, they always order the old wine and drink it with pleasure? Is the novelty of the Christian message compared to rotten Judaism, which apparently does not agree with Christianity, so dear to them that they gladly tolerate a miserable parable from Jesus? Remember, Jesus was a master parable teller and he understood something about wine! He testifies about himself that he is a glutton and a drinker of wine (Matt 11:19; Luke 7:34). So how could he have invented such an unnatural parable, when otherwise he would have avoided such weak, unnatural subjects?

Even if we forget for a while (because of the supposed theological sense) that old wine tastes better than new wine, and we further separate the double image from the fasting question as an independent saying, and even if we finally consider the point of the image in Luke as an addition, we still have not cleared away all the difficulties found in the statements of modern theologians.

---

81. The word meaning *equal* is found in the Arabic translation of the Diatessaron of Tatian (*Diatessaron de Tatian*, ed. A.-S. Marmardji), but not in his Persian translation (*Diatessaron persiano*, ed. Giuseppe Messina, 35).

82. Klostermann, *Das Lukasevangelium*, 74.

83. Schneider, *Das Evangelium nach Lukas*, 141

The pair of parables themselves, however, do not reveal the uselessness of the old for the followers of the new, but the danger of the new for the followers of the old: the old garment and the old wineskins are lost—but here also the young wine.[84]

Another researcher correctly sees the tendency of the double comparison. But to save the young wine and the new cloths for Jesus, he invents a gracious solution:

> Jesus held his hand over the disciples of the Baptist, protecting them from imitating his disciples. Both comparisons show that the old corrupts through the connection with the new and admonishes for the care of the old, for the preservation of the old mantle, which is torn by the still unfinished new stuff, for the preservation of the old cloth, which the young fermenting wine would burst. Thus the parables warn the disciples of John of the hasty, idiosyncratic appropriation of the freedom of the disciples of Jesus. . . . First of all, however, the aim of the parable lies in the fact that the old remains unspoiled.[85]

So let us follow the subtlety of these two researchers and drop the interpretation of the double parable that has been common since Mark! Let us read Jesus' words in their historical context in response to why he is leading his disciples not to keep new additional fasts, and let us apply Lindsey's theory of Luke's priority, and then we shall be well advised. The loss will be that we will not see Jesus as a contrasting figure to the Judaism of his time. But there is also a profit for us; we find ourselves in the promising position of having a fresh perspective about this critical attitude of Jesus in being able to learn from our contemporaries.

To pave the way for understanding Jesus' dual language, some of the rabbinic literature on the symbolic value of wine is useful. The term "new wine" does not appear in the Old Testament. The first time it is found is in the Essene Temple Scroll (19:4; 22:10).[86] Like water, wine is a symbol of Judaic teaching.[87] "In wine you do not get its taste from its beginning, and the older it gets in the jar, the better it gets; and so it is with the words of the Torah: the more they grow old in the body, the better they get."[88] Rabbi Meir used to say, "You shall not pay attention to the jar, but to what is in it. There are some old jars, full of old wines, and some old ones, in which

---

84. Klostermann, *Das Markusevangelium*, 28.

85. Schlatter, *Der Evangelist Matthäus*, 314f.

86. See Y. Yadin, *The Temple Scroll* (Hebrew ed.), I:32; II:61.

87. See the beautiful late parable in Soferim 15:6.

88. SifDev Ekev, ed. Finkelstein, 3.

there is nothing but new wine."[89] In both rabbinic sayings, the old wine is the good wine. Wine is a symbol of the Torah, the doctrine of Judaism. The symbolic meaning of Jesus' saying about the cloths and wine belongs in the broader sense to this complex of rabbinic symbolism.

Now the groundwork has been laid to understand the double comparison and even be able to enjoy it. If we consider the historical situation in which it arose and, moreover, do not neglect the point in Luke, we can then realize that these two subjects strongly express Jesus' teaching. Regarding the charge that Jesus and his disciples refused the newly introduced fasts, he considered it as humorously *reductio ad absurdum*. He was convinced that these fasts could not achieve the purpose of bringing the people back to God. For him, introducing new fast days was just as pointless as cutting a patch out of a new fabric and putting it on an old garment. Doing this will spoil the new fabric and make the tear even worse! In the first parable, both comparison objects are the same type: an old and a new piece of textile. Someone, as the first parable says, wants to patch up a damaged old cloak. He does not notice that the new fabric does not match the torn, softened, and frayed garment and he enlarges the tear instead of fixing it. What should be the advantage of new material aggravates the problem. The new piece of fabric does not help but harms if it is inserted into the old without natural, substance-specific adaptation and harmony. The old cloak is spoiled by the well-intentioned but stupid patchwork with new material. The result is a needlessly cut new fabric and an even bigger tear in the old garment of the rash restorer.

The second comparison of old wineskins and new wine is constructed externally parallel to the first comparison. When new wine is poured into old wineskins, the wineskins break and the wine pours out all over the ground. Both pictorial sayings show that Jesus did not consider the state of Judaism at that time to be ideal. He therefore compares it to an old garment in need of repair and brittle old wineskins. But, just like Jesus, critics of all times judge their own era! Critics of their own time, the Pharisees also wanted to improve Judaism through new fast days.

In addition to all the parallelism of these two images, there is also a particularly striking difference between them. In contrast to the first, the

---

89. mAv 4.20. The name "Meir" appears in many quotations of the saying and in the Codex Kaufmann of the Mishnah. Other manuscripts and ARN (version B, ed. Schechter, 5:75) lack the name, as if the author were the rabbi; i.e., the patriarch Rabbi Yehuda Ha-Nasi.

second comparison describes materials of different types: wine and wine-skins. This material difference is not accidental. What is certain is that the mention of the new wine tearing the skins enables Jesus to introduce a third, contrasting pair of terms in which the contrast between the old and the new is different. In addition to the two pairs of terms—old dress/new cloth, old wineskins/new wine—a third now appears: new and old wine.[90] This new wine has two functions: It contrasts with both the old wineskins and the old wine. This contrast between the new and old wine also stands out to the one who omits the point in Luke 5:39. All exegetes from the patristic period to the present day have based their interpretation on this contrast, even if they had to disregard the point in Luke because of their ideologizing tendency. It seems important to me that in the third, contrasting pair of terms—in contrast to the first two in which the old is worse and the new is better—the old wine is more exquisite than the new. Furthermore, the new wine is not poured in old wineskins to save those old wineskins. In the second picture, the field of view has shifted. I assume that Jesus consciously did this to clarify all aspects of the question and to prevent misunderstandings. This double comparison is thus also a further indication that Jesus sometimes tried to expand and enrich his listeners' field of view by presenting the object like a modern cameraman: by successive illumination taken in a movement.

In the first comparison, the cloth is new and the cloak is old. From this someone could conclude (which is what some have done) that Jesus wanted to say: You need not only a new cloth but a whole new dress. But he could have said that explicitly. He did not do so: first, because he was not a bad parable teller; second, because it was not his intention to replace the teaching of Israel and its law with something new. Jesus did not want to be an abolishing reformer. He did not want to discredit or destroy Judaism. Read the Gospels with a knowledge of Judaism: Jesus did not want to destroy the law but to establish its true meaning. And let us not forget what question Jesus answers with this double comparison—why his disciples do not keep the new fast days. As has already been said, he considers their useless bickering petty, childish, and an inadequate innovation. Moreover, it would be like a square peg in a round hole if Jesus said, "Throw away the old cloak without repair and buy a new one!" That would also be pointless regarding the subject as it would be totally spoiled. Therefore, the importance of the

---

90. The parable of Rabbi Meir just quoted (mAv 4:20) also speaks of old and new wine and tacitly of the old and new jar.

cloth's newness should not be tendentially exaggerated. The Pharisees—and perhaps also John's disciples—wanted to repair the old garment of Judaism by means of a new cloth—that is, new fast days. The image is excellent, and perhaps Jesus even wanted to gently point out, with reservations, the good intentions of these clumsy reformers. But through the second parable, Jesus wanted to avoid a misunderstanding. He certainly did not think that we would understand this parable to be saying that we had to reject everything old and introduce new things on principle. Neither Jesus nor the subject of this double parable even came close to this misunderstanding. Only the evangelist Mark fell for this idea, in connection with his assessment of the situation of his congregation. In my opinion, Jesus wanted the parable of the old wineskins to eliminate another misunderstanding. He wanted to say: "The quality of the new cloth is better than that of the old garment, but don't think that the new fast days are something good in themselves! The new cloth is made of better material than the old garment. But the new wine is inferior, and its newness is certainly no advantage."

The second parable picture in this double comparison, the image of the wine and wineskins, is a representative example of the inevitable dependence of parable narrators on their own creation. On the one hand, they build the subject in such a way that they can communicate as much instruction as possible through these images. On the other hand, limited by the subject, they cannot fully exploit the problematic situation to which they want to respond. To widen the field of view regarding the first parable image, Jesus now speaks of old wineskins and new wine. This second parable is, so to speak, more inward than the first. In it, the contents of the wineskins are mentioned. I have also pointed out that in rabbinism, wine is a symbol for the Torah—for Judaic doctrine. From these two examples, we have also seen that the old wine represents the better teaching. When Jesus spoke of new and old wine, his hearers could not help but think of superior and inferior doctrine. The introduction of new fast days by the Pharisees was an expression of their doctrine or worldview. Jesus therefore did not compliment the Pharisees and their doctrinal attitude when he told the parable of the new wine. Like any serious critic, Jesus thought that present-day Judaism was as ragged as an old garment and as fragile as old wineskins. But he also knew that patchwork—the introduction of new fast days—was no remedy. He was convinced that the situation would only get worse if the old frame was filled with inappropriate or inferior new content.

Although we would like to learn from the double comparison what positive solution Jesus had in mind for the state of Judaism at that time, he was constricted by his own subject. Even the fact that the second parable had to be built parallel to the first limited the freedom of Jesus' parable narrative. In addition, the subject must give the impression that it reflects a reality from everyday life. I believe that I correctly understand Jesus' attitude toward the Judaism of his time when I think that Jesus wanted to strengthen the fragile framework of Judaism to preserve the old, precious content; but then, as a colleague suggested to me, he would have had to say, "New wineskins for old wine."[91] Yet it seems to me that the subject did not allow such a statement from Jesus. Although new wineskins would certainly not harm the old wine, the old wine does not need new wineskins. The wording proposed by my colleague, however, does not fit the real side of the subject. In the reconstruction of the double comparison, I resorted to Matt 9:17, which brings us to the original: "Rather, one is accustomed to put new wine into new wineskins."[92] This is the only practical measure possible if someone wants to store new wine. Otherwise, the new wine would tear the old wineskins, the wine would flow out, and the wineskins would be ruined. The description of how to preserve the new wine is therefore a necessary part of the subject, which should not be interpreted. That Mark seduced interpreters to pour a new wine into the original wineskin is a subject for another chapter.

If we do not disregard the factual content of the double comparison from a preconceived notion, then we become aware that the double image in Mark and in Matthew ends with a shrill dissonance. This is mainly due to the mention of the new, inferior wine. This inevitably awakens the association with old, valuable wine, about which we learn nothing from Mark and Matthew. On the other hand, the conclusion of Luke (5:37) is satisfactory: "And no one who used to drink the old desires the new, because he thinks the old tastes better." The double parable here has reached its end; the conclusion is therefore not meant ironically. It would be ridiculous to

---

91. Shmuel Safrai, who is of the opinion that Jesus' original wording was like this.

92. Cf. note 59 above. Only in Matthew is the sentence indicative and not imperative. At the end of Matt 9:17, it is still written: "then both [i.e., the new wine and the skins] are preserved." This is easy to translate into Hebrew, but I am hesitant to call it original as it is lacking in the other two Gospels. Perhaps Matthew added the sentence to find a fitting conclusion to the parable after omitting the closing sentence with Mark. Because of Mark, however, he did not want to change the previous sentence imperatively. But if the end of Matt 9:17 is original, then it belongs only to the subject and not to interpretation.

imagine that Jesus wanted to "dissuade the drunkard from his bad habit," so to speak. On the other hand, theological exegetes at conferences and in sermons praise the new wine of Christianity—yet still drink the old wine!

Jesus is serious about old wine, at the level of both the subject and the application. Also, people tend to like old wine better; those who refuse to accept the new know what they are doing. In this case, the new is an "improvement" that could only harm. By introducing the concrete, conceptual pairing of "old and new wine," Jesus clearly says that the new institution is worse than the old. This was not clear enough from the illustration of the old cloak and the new cloth.

If we are willing to follow Jesus in the elaboration of his arguments, then we are urged to admire his art and his pedagogical talent. As in the double parable of the mustard seed and leaven, it is also shown here that the genre of the double parable makes it possible for Jesus to expand the listener's view. And again, we have learned how important it is to start from Luke. Without Luke, we would not know the point of the saying. And, hopefully, there is something else we have learned: The tendentious distortion of Jesus' message had already begun in the Synoptic Gospels.[93]

---

93. I also spoke about the later widening of the rift between Judaism and Christianity in patristic literature. The misunderstanding of the double saying had practical consequences in the early church. There was an emotional relationship with the old breeding ground of the church. We already read in the primitive doctrine of the apostles: "But your fast days shall not take place at the same time as those of the hypocrites. They fast on the second and fifth days of the week. But ye shall fast on the fourth day and on the day of preparation. Do not pray as the hypocrites do but pray as the master has commanded in the Gospel"—and then the Lord's Prayer follows (Didache 8:1–3). J. T. Audet, La Didache (Paris: Gabalda, 1957), 367: "L'instruction sur le Éüne ne parait pas le mieux inspirée du œcueil. Pour diriger des chrétiens dans les voies de l'évangile, elle ne trouve rien de plus judicieux à leur proposer que le périlleux sentiment de la "séparation", triste présage de ce que l 'église allait bientôt obtenir, lorsque la mission auprès d'Israel serait remplacée par la littérature adversus Judaeos."

10

Jesus' Parables: A Means of Hardening?

The new Synoptic hypothesis that we discussed in the previous chapter opens the way to the original wording of Jesus' proclamation. We can better understand Jesus, his words become more credible, and the prejudices that had crept into the text of the Gospels disappear as if by themselves. I will now apply this new hypothesis to the passage on the purpose of parables (Matt 13:10–15; Mark 4:10–12; Luke 8:9f.). Our conclusions will have significant consequences regarding the meaning of Jesus' parables.

Today, the section on the purpose of the parables stands between the parable of the sower and its interpretation in all three Synoptics. It also contains the so-called hardening motif in all three Gospels: that is, Jesus speaks openly only to his disciples while to others he speaks in veiled parables so that they do not understand. Now, the hardening motif does not fit at all into the context of Jesus' parables, just as it would not fit into rabbinic parables. Parables are not there to obscure a message but to illuminate. If we do not want, for other reasons, to believe that Jesus brought people down by shadowy means, then we must try to expose his original wording as much as possible with the help of a solid literary-critical method. The fact that this has not been possible until now depends mainly on the fascination with which the Gospel of Mark has been given every temporal priority.

I will now present Jesus' statement, first in the Lukan and then in the Markan wording, and then I will try to reconstruct Jesus' words. According to the usual Luke text, Jesus said, "It is given to you to know the mysteries of the kingdom of God, but to the rest in parables, so that they may see—and yet not see and hear—but not understand" (Luke 8:10). According to Mark, Jesus said, "To you is given the mystery of the kingdom of God, but to them all things are set forth in parables [literally: all things are done in parables], that they may see and yet not see, hear and yet not understand, lest they should repent and be forgiven" (Mark 4:11f.). Instead of Matt 13:11–15, I now bring—although this may be unusual—the reconstruction of Jesus' words:

"To you it is given to know the mysteries of God, but to them it is not given. That is why I speak to them in parables, because they see—and yet do not see—and hear—yet do not hear and do not understand."

Thus, according to our hypothesis, Jesus' original saying is preserved almost literally in Matt 13:11 and 13. Under the influence of Mark (4:12), Matthew literally attached the Greek translation of Isaiah's saying about hardening (6:9f.; cf. Matt 13:14). In Matt 13:11–13, the word of the prophet Isaiah is alluded to, but the whole saying corresponds to what is known of Jesus' parables and the function of the parables in general: that is, they were created to illustrate. There are three main reasons why these words of Jesus have become unpleasant: (1) When the Gospels were written, most people did not know about the nature of Jesus' parables; therefore, individual parables were interpreted as mysterious clues. (2) Like many parables outside the New Testament, Jesus' parables sometimes require additional interpretation. (3) Isaiah's words about hardening took on an ecclesiastical-polemical orientation in primitive Christianity.

You can only preserve the Synoptic versions as Jesus' actual words by means of various, tricky methods. The prerequisite for all these tricky methods is Mark's priority. Joachim Jeremias's attempt is interesting.[1] He translates Jesus' words according to Mark 4:11ff. as follows:

"To you God has given the mystery of the kingdom of God; but to those who are outside, all things are mysterious, so that they may see (as it is written) and not see, hear and yet not understand, unless they repent and God forgive them!"

Then Jeremias continues:

The Logion speaks, that is our result, not at all of the parables of Jesus, but of his preaching in general. To the disciples the mystery of the present *basileia* is revealed, to the outsiders Jesus' words remain obscure because they do not acknowledge his mission and do not repent. Thus is fulfilled in them the dreadful prophecy of Isa 6:9f. Yet there is hope: "If they repent, God will forgive them." The last glimpse is of God's forgiving mercy.

Jeremias translates this verse, "But to those who are outside, everything is mysterious." Mark 4:11 says, "But to those who are outside, all things

_____

1. Jeremias, *Die Gleichnisse Jesu*, 11–14.

are done in parables." According to Lindsey's and my hypothesis, Mark depends on Luke here. According to Luke, it was given to the disciples to know the mysteries of God; "to the rest (they come) only in parables."[2] Mark, therefore, completes the elliptical sentence in Luke and adds the explanatory "they come." What does that word mean? Is it to be understood that the mysterious idea of the kingdom of God should be presented only to those who are not called in a form that makes it impossible for them to understand? The Greek wording of Mark can be understood in a twofold sense: Either "to the outsiders everything happens in parables," or "to the outsiders everything will be related to them in parables." If we take the Markan text as a mere execution of the Lukan line of thought, then Mark also speaks of the fact that outsiders hear parables from Jesus so that they do not understand the mysteries of the kingdom of heaven. Then what Mark means is that Jesus' parables are a teaching method. But if one thinks that Mark wanted to say that everything that happens in parables to the outsiders, then one must also admit that Mark—in contrast to the two other evangelists—does not speak at all of Jesus' parables as a method, but that he wants to say that everything Jesus said is mysterious to the outsiders—in contrast to the disciples. Jeremias's bold interpretation is supported by the fact that Mark—in contrast to the two secondary witnesses—does not speak of "the knowledge of the mysteries." He left out "the knowledge" to be able to say that the disciples were given the mystery of the kingdom of God and that they are in possession of the kingdom. Compared to the disciples, the outsiders grope in the dark and therefore plunge into corruption. It is difficult to decide between the two interpretations that result from the Markan text because Mark is often inconsistent. It is therefore not possible to infer the meaning of the second half of the sentence from the meaning of the first half of the sentence with any certainty. One thing, however, is certain: In all three Gospels, the word *parable* here means "concealment," not "revelation."

The Greek word *parable* in the Greek Old Testament is the translation of the Hebrew word *mashal*, which is ambiguous in the Old Testament. In rabbinic literature, however, it is the designation of a clearly profiled genre: precisely that of rabbinic parables to which also belong Jesus' parables. Jesus and his disciples referred to the parable as *mashal*, and the evangelists followed the wording of the Greek Old Testament. According to the correct

---

2. So, correctly, Heinz Schurmann, 458. See also Schneider, *Das Evangelium nach Lukas*, 184. For Mark 4:11, cf. Klostermann, *Das Markusevangelium*, 41, and *BDAG*, 315.

opinion of the rabbis, however, the parables do not have any meaning to obscure.[3] Aristotle also understands the parable, or the comparison, in the same way.[4] The rabbis, of course, remain aware that a parable is not reality itself, but rather an illumination of reality.

> Once upon a time a disciple sat before Rabbi Schmuel bar Nahmani and said: "Job never existed and was never created but was a parable." And he said unto him, "Because of thee saith the scripture, 'There was a man in the land of Uz, and Job was his name.' But it is also said: 'The poor man had nothing but a single little lamb, which he had bought and raised, etc.' (2 Sam 12:3). This had not happened, but it was only a parable, just as Job was only a parable."

It is instructive that in addition to Job, mention is made of the story that the prophet Nathan told King David. Earlier I argued that this story is the closest we have to rabbinic parables in all of the Old Testament.[5] According to b. San. 92b, the rabbis once considered whether what is told in Ezekiel 37 about the revival of the bones is a poem or whether the prophet really raised these dead. Rabbi Judah said, "This was truly a parable." Then Rabbi Nehemiah said to him, "If it was real, why was it a parable, and if a parable, why was it real? Indeed, it was a parable."[6] Therefore, since the rabbis also knew that parables are not reality itself but only an image of reality, we can also more easily home in on an understanding of Mark, who sharply distinguished between reality and the content of the parables.

Before we turn again to our passage, I would like to briefly mention what the word *parable* means in ancient Christian literature outside of the Synoptic Gospels. Instead of a "parable," the evangelist John speaks in his Gospel of a "proverb" (*paroimia*: John 10:6; 16:25, 29). From John 16:25, we can understand what John imagined Jesus' parables to be. Jesus said, "This

---

3. See also Strack and Billerbeck, *Kommentar zum Neuen Testament aus Talmud und Midrasch*, vol. 1, 653f.

4. See Jülicher, *Die Gleichnisreden Jesu*, vol. 1, 69–72.

5. bBB Isa.

6. The Hebrew text of b. San. 92b can give an impression of the subtlety of the rabbinic discussion. It reads, "Rabbi Yehuda said: '*amat mashal hayah*.' Then Rabbi Nehemiah told him: '*im amat - lammah mashal, we'im mashal—lammah amat? ella, beamat mashal hayah*.'" This Sanhedrin passage is noted as tannaitic (Detanya). On the other hand, a disciple speaks before an Amora in the passage from Bava Batra just quoted. But he also has an older opinion. In other words, this view is also tannaitic. For the rabbinic discussion of the book of Ezekiel, see Louis Ginzberg, *The Legends of the Jews*, 4 vols. (Philadelphia, 1947), 332.

I have spoken to you in parables; the hour is coming when I will no longer speak to you in parables, but will tell you plainly about my Father." At this point, the "parables" are still veiled, mysterious speech for the unenlightened disciples, which "on that day" will give way to an open and free speech about the Father.[7] The word *parable* itself appears outside the Synoptic Gospels in the New Testament only twice: in the Letter to the Hebrews 1:19 and 9:9, which are both difficult. These passages are not at all about parables in the sense of an example from life, but about typological exegesis. The word *parable* denotes a real fact in both passages of the Letter to the Hebrews, pointing to another real fact in the future. The second passage is particularly interesting: "By faith Abraham offered Isaac when he was tempted, and he gave up the only son, he who had received the promise, and to whom it was said, 'In Isaac shall thy seed be called.' But he thought that God was able to raise the dead. Therefore, he also received it as a *parable*" (Heb 11:17–19). The passage becomes easier to understand when one begins with the common assumption in Judaism that Isaac was really sacrificed and then rose from the dead.[8] The rabbinic parallel cited above (b. San. 92b) justifies the opinion of church fathers that in the Letter to the Hebrews the resurrection of Isaac points to the future resurrection of the dead.[9] The section from the Letter to the Hebrews and the debate between the rabbis are about the future resurrection. Rabbi Yehuda's opponent says that the prophet Ezekiel really raised the dead. Rabbi Yehuda, on the other hand, is of the opinion that this narrative is only a parable. And in Hebrews, the real resurrection of Isaac is a parable of the real future resurrection of the dead. The word *parable* is thus used in both texts as a reference to the eschatological resurrection.

Like the related term "wisdom saying" in the Gospel of John, outside of the Synoptics, the word *parable (mashal/parabole)* is never used in the New Testament in the technical sense. In the case of the Synoptics, we must also consider whether a parable is told directly by Jesus or whether a "similar"

---

7. Cf. Rudolf Schnackenburg, *Das Johannesevangelium*, vol. 3 (Freiburg: Basel, 1976), 182n51. See also Schnackenburg, *Das Johannesevangelium*, vol. 2 (Freiburg: Basel, 1977), 358f.

8. See Billerbeck on the passage; Herman Strack and Paul Billerbeck, *Kommentar zum Neuen Testament aus Talmud und Midrasch*, vol. 3 (Nördlingen: C. H. Beck, 1922), 746; and Ginzberg, *The Legends of the Jews*, vol. 1, 282; vol. 4, 251n253 (Heb 1:19); and 254n255. See also Rom 4:17.

9. In addition to b. San. 92b, cf. also WaR for Lev 22:27, Margulies, 627–29. According to Otto Michel, *Der Brief an die Hebräer* (Göttingen: Vandenhoeck & Ruprecht, 1966), 402f., the fathers of the church who understood it this way are Theodoret and Ephraem.

meaning of Jesus' parables is being considered. This indicates what happened in the pericopes that contain the purpose of the parables (Mark 4:10–12 par.)

In the case of the apostolic fathers, the word *parable* often occurs in the Shepherd of Hermas, "which, however, is not independent of the Synoptic tradition. But only once more we find here a real double parable called a parable (Luke 11:18). Otherwise, the parable for Hermas is an enigmatic word, which is soon seen in the face, soon brought to mind in words, but in any case, needs interpretation down to the details."[10] In the apocryphal Epistle of Barnabas, the word *parable* occurs twice (6:10 and 17:2). The meaning of these two passages is not easy to grasp. According to both verses, the parable calls for an understanding of the mysteries of God: "Blessed be our Master, brethren, who has set within us truth and understanding of his mysteries. For the prophet speaks a parable about the Master; who can understand except he who is wise and knowledgeable and loves his Master?" (Barn 6:10). "For if I were to write to you about what has passed or what is to come, you would not understand it, because it is contained in parables" (Barn 17:2).[11] This is similar to what is written in the Ascension of Isaiah (4:20), a primitive Christian apocalyptic play, which also mentions the martyrdom of Peter under Emperor Nero. There the prophet Isaiah says, "And the rest of the vision of the Master, behold, it is written in parables in my words, in that which is written in the book which I have written openly"; that is, in the biblical book of Isaiah.[12]

Three writings from the apostolic and post-apostolic ages can teach us even more about the use of the word *parable* at that time. The book *Kerygma Petrou* is preserved only in a series of quotations from Clement of Alexandria. The first half of the second post-Christian century should be assumed as the drafting period of this writing. The author clearly says in the name of Peter: "But we opened the books of the prophets, which we had, partly in parables, partly in riddles, partly reliably, and in plain speech the words of Jesus."[13] So, the "parables" and "riddles"—as opposed to the "clear words"— are concealed christological references found in the Old Testament.

---

10. *BDAG*, 215.

11. See also Robert A. Kraft, *The Apostolic Fathers*, 3 vols. (Nashville: Thomas Nelson, 1965), 99.133; and Hans Windisch, *Die Apostolischen Väter: Der Barnabasbrief*, vol. 3 (Tübingen: 1920), 335–96; and Eugène Tisserant, *Ascension d'Isaie* (Paris: Letouzey, 1909), 126 (cf. *The Translation of Windisch*, 396).

12. Tisserant, *Ascension d'Isaie*, 126.

13. Wilhelm Schneemelcher in Hennecke-Schneemelcher, *New Testament Apocrypha*, vol. 2 (Tübingen: Mohr Siebeck, 1963), from Clement of Alexandria,

The second text I would like to mention here is the newly discovered Easter homily of Bishop Meliton of Sardis. It was written between 160 and 170 CE and is important for the history of both Judaism of its time and ecclesiastical anti-Judaism. First, Meliton describes the exodus of Israel from Egypt and then explains it typologically in the suffering of Christ and redemption through Christ. Between these two parts, he presents a fundamental consideration of the nature of typology, which thus begins: "Nothing would be, beloved, what has been said and what has happened outside the parable and the (divine) purpose. Everything that happens and is said belongs to the parable: what is said to the parable, what has happened as an example, so that as what is read is shown by the example, so also what has happened is illuminated by the parable."[14] Although Meliton uses the word *parable* first for both categories in this text, here and in the sequel, he consistently distinguishes between parable and model, prefiguration, type. "Parable" refers to what is said in the Old Testament, while "type" refers to the events reported in the Old Testament:

> For thus the salvation and truth of the Master was foretold in the people (Israel), and the doctrine of the gospel was foretold by the law (i.e., the Old Testament). Thus the people (Israel) became the model (type) of an intention and the law becomes the writing of a parable. The Gospel is the interpretation of the law and its fulfillment, and the Church is the place of truth. The example had its value before truth, and the parable was admirable before it was interpreted. That is, the people (Israel) were valuable before the church rose, and the law was admirable before the gospel was illuminated. Just as the example is devalued by giving the image to what is essentially true, and just as the parable is devalued by illuminating the interpretation, so the law was also fulfilled by illuminating the Gospel, and the people (Israel) were devalued by the rising of the church, and the example was dissolved by the appearance of the Master.

We should read the whole work of Meliton in Greek to fully admire the precision of its terminology and its hermeneutical achievements. According to Meliton, what is said in the law, the wording of the Old Testament, is the parable illuminated by the gospel, while the facts reported in the Old Testament are the model, the type of the new present fact: the people of

---

Stromata 4, 15:128. Greek text by Klostermann, *Apokrypha I, Evangelien* (Berlin: Marcus and Weber, 1929), 1:15f.

14. *The Passover Homily of Meliton of Sardis*, chapters 35–43; Meliton of Sardis, *Sur la Pique et fragments*, 78–83 (lines 236–304); and J. Blank, *Meliton of Sardis: From Passover*, 109–111.

Israel is a prefiguration of the church. Regarding the distinction between the meaning of biblical words and the meaning of biblical deeds, Meliton of Sardis anticipates a similar distinction with Thomas of Aquinas.[15] But if he refers to what was said in the Old Testament as a parable, which is illuminated and repealed by the New Testament, then this has very little to do with Jesus' parables and related rabbinic parables.

A few years earlier, Justin Martyr wrote his dialogue with the Jew Tryphon. Justin uses the word *parable* in the same sense as Meliton.[16] Although the Gospels are known to Justin, he never speaks of Jesus' parables. He always uses the word *parable* in connection with the Old Testament, which points to Christ. In the parables of the Old Testament, the Holy Spirit spoke in a veiled way. Justin speaks of "many hidden words and such words as have been spoken in parables or in mysteries or miraculous deeds" (68:6). He says, "Whatever the prophets have said and done, they have revealed through parables and prefigurations, so that most of them may not be easily understood by all; they have hidden the truth in them, so that those who seek to find and learn must strive" (90:2).

So, in the face of this "cloud of witnesses," is it a miracle that a parable is usually understood in ancient Christian literature as a mysterious, veiled signpost pointing to the higher reality? Or that, in contrast to Jesus' parables, we think that a parable is "parable-like"? What does the *chorus mysticus* say at the end of the second part of Goethe's Faust? "Everything that is impermanent is only a parable; the inadequate, here is the event—the indescribable, here it is done." Let us now leap from the Platonizing Goethe to a completely different modern author, Franz Kafka, who has the following paradoxical saying: "Of the parables: Many complain that the words of the wise are again and again only parables, but are useless in daily life, and only this we have. . . . All these parables are really just trying to say that the incomprehensible is incomprehensible, and we knew that."[17]

---

15. St. Thomas Aquinas, *Summa Theologica*, where the quotation from the edition of Petrus Caramellus, vol. 1, p. 9 reads: *Auctor sacrae Scripturae est Deus, in cuius potestate est ut non solum voces ad significantandum accomodet . . . , sed etiam res ipsas.* Thomas depends on Junilius Africanus, who explains his *Instituta regularia divinae legis* (Migne, PL 68, col. 34) in Constantinople around 542. This introduction to Bible study faithfully follows the views of Theodore of Mopsuestia (c. 352–428), the greatest exegete of the Antiochian School. See also A. Funkenstein, "Nahmanides," *Typological Reading of History*, 36f. (Hebrew).

16. Justin Martyr, *Dial.* 36:2, 51:1, 63:2; 68:6, 77:4, 78:10, 90:2, 97:3, 114:2; 115:1; 123:8.

17. Franz Kafka, *Gesammelte Schriften*, 5 vols. (Berlin, 1946), 95.

But classical rabbinic parables and Jesus' parables were invented precisely so that they could be used in everyday life and thus show that the incomprehensibility of God's economy can be comprehensible. So, why should the parable mean anything else? The approach to this change of meaning had already begun in the apostolic age—except in the unedited passages in the Synoptic Gospels, which are translated from Hebrew and date back to Jesus himself and his Jewish circle of disciples. We usually cannot know what the Greek editors and evangelists imagined the word *parable* to mean. Since they were no longer firmly rooted in Jesus' Jewish environment, they probably mistakenly assumed the genre of parable was only typical of Jesus and that he had invented it. Even today, uninformed people still think this way. For the hardening theory in Mark 4:10–12 par., it is crucial that the word *parable* never appears in its original New Testament and rabbinic meaning in the Synoptic Gospels, not even in the New Testament. This also applies to the Christian writings from the post-apostolic era. Incidentally, in the rest of the New Testament and in the following Christian literature, Jesus' parables are never mentioned: in the Gospel of John, Jesus speaks "in proverbs." The proverb is now a veiled, enigmatic word. Most often, parables are spoken of when one means Old Testament passages and prophecies, which were illuminated and fulfilled by the coming of Christ.

So, when the Gospels were written down in Greek, it was hardly known in those Christian circles that there were similar rabbinic parables other than Jesus' parables.[18] At that time, the idea arose that the parable was a veiled riddle. This is one of the reasons why in the three Gospels where the "purpose of parables" pericopes appear (Mark 4:10–12 par.), the parables are considered riddles that obscure the understanding of the outsider. Strictly speaking, this applies only to Matthew and Luke; Mark goes one step further. This can be seen by reading Mark unaffected by the parallel in Matthew and Luke. Even if one does not accept the Lindsey-Flusser Synoptic hypothesis, one can easily become aware of two differences between Mark and the two other Synoptics. According to Mark, the mystery of the kingdom of God is given to the circle of disciples; and according to the other two Gospels, it is given to them to "know" the mysteries. As we have seen, Luke is elliptical and abrupt in the sequel. But what he meant is not difficult to guess: "but to the rest (the mysteries of God are) in parables." Matthew 13:11 is even clearer and more correct than Luke: unlike the circle of disciples, it is not

---

18. This is not an absolute statement. Perhaps Matthew, for example, knew something of rabbinic parables. But more on that later.

given to them to know the mysteries of the kingdom of heaven, and that is why Jesus speaks to them in parables. In Mark, therefore, it is not said that knowledge was given to the circle of disciples. According to him, the mystery of the kingdom of God itself was given to them. Seduced by Luke's abrupt speech, Mark adds a word at the end, apparently explaining it. According to him, Jesus said, "To you has been given the mystery of the kingdom of God, but to those who are outside, all things are set forth in parables."[19] Joachim Jeremias says, "But to those who are outside, everything is mysterious." According to Jeremias, therefore, the purpose of Jesus' parables is not spoken of at all in Mark 4:11f. Rather, Mark wants to say that the disciples possess the mysterious kingdom of God, whereas to the outsiders everything is a parable-like riddle that will bring them down. In fact, Mark exacerbates the contrast between the disciples and the rest of humanity. According to Jeremias, for Mark these are "people who are outside, and so do not participate in the kingdom of God." A strange metamorphosis has taken place: in Mark 4:11f, where the word *parable* occurs—if these interpretations are correct—there is a discrepancy between a "parable" and Jesus' message of love. Does this turn correspond to Mark's worldview? The answer to this question is clear if one accepts our better Synoptic hypothesis. I have already touched on the question of Mark's ideology in two studies. In an article I wrote about the crucifixion report in Mark 19, I concluded that, unlike Luke, Mark lacks the sympathetic Jewish crowd at the crucifixion and that Jesus' enemies—as with Luke—have remained with him. Of Jesus' friends, however, there are only those in Mark who represent the Christian community, so to speak. With Mark, all "non-Christian" Jews are enemies of Jesus. Followers of Jesus are only the Christian women from Galilee and the converted Gentile, the centurion.[20] In another work, I discussed the so-called Synoptic Apocalypse (Mark 13 par.)[21] Among other things, it has been shown that Mark, unlike Luke, eliminates any reference to the destruction of Jerusalem by the Romans and to the end-time salvation of Israel from the prophecy of Jesus. The Synoptic Apocalypse becomes eschatological through and through. More important for us, however, is that in the Markan Synoptic Apocalypse, not

19. In Mark's source text, the Greek, non-Hebrew word order is to be observed, in contrast to the other two Gospels. You can see the author's intervention.

20. Flusser, *Der Gekreuzigte und die Juden*, FrRu 28 (1976), 153–57.

21. Flusser, "Eine Weissagung über die Befreiung Jerusalems im Neuen Testament," *ErIsr*, vol. 10 (Jerusalem, 1971), 226–36 (Hebrew); now in Flusser, *Judentum und die Quellen des Christentums* (Tel Aviv: Sifriyyat Pocalim, 1979), 253–74.

only is every mention of Israel's future eradicated but "the elect"[22] become
the object of prophecy: the master will shorten the days of the end-time
hardships because of the elect whom he has chosen. False prophets will do
signs and wonders "to mislead, if possible, the elect." And in the very end,
the Son of Man will "send the angels and gather the elect from the four winds,
from the end of the earth to the end of heaven."

I do not mean to say that the author of the Gospel of Mark, who was of
Jewish origin,[23] added distinct anti-Jewish traits to his work. Rather, it seems
that, as a follower of the mission of the Gentiles,[24] he wanted to sharply distinguish the Christians (the elect) to whom the kingdom of heaven is given
from those who are outside, to whom everything is presented in parables
and who are rejected, be they Jews or Gentiles.

According to our pericopes in Mark, the outsiders are destined for destruction, so no interpretation helps. Mark unbearably exaggerates the motif
of hardening. In other words, he draws an inhumane consequence that Matthew and Luke did not draw. To the outsiders, "everything is presented in
parables, so that they may see and see—and yet not see—hear and hear—and
yet not understand, so that they may not repent and he forgive them." This
is a paraphrase from Isa 6:9f.: "And he said, Go and say to this people, 'Hear
continually, but do not understand; and see continually, but do not know.
Harden the heart of this people, and make their ears deaf, and blind their
eyes, lest they see with their eyes, and hear with their ears, and understand
their heart, and recover it.'" The Hebrew word *veshav*, which is here translated as "again," the Greek and Aramaic translations probably render this
rightly as "to repent";[25] that is, "lest . . . [the people] should repent and recover." Matthew brings Isa 6:9f. (Matt 13:14) literally from the Greek Bible.

Here, a short philological detour is necessary. Much has been written
about the influence of the Aramaic translation on the paraphrase of the

---

22. Mark 13:20 (Matt 24:22) vs. Luke 21:24; Mark 13:22 (Matt 24:24) is missing from Luke; and Mark 13:27 (Matt 24:3) is missing from Luke. Otherwise, the
chosen ones appear in the Gospels only as special material (in a different sense) in
Matt 22:14 (cf. Rev 17:14) and Luke 18:7. Luke 23:35 speaks of the "Christ of God
the Exalted."

23. He was apparently a Hellenistic Jew. From what we know of historical Mark,
I find it hard to believe that he wrote the Gospel of Mark.

24. "But first the message of salvation must be proclaimed to all peoples" (Mark
13:10, and from there edited in Matt 24:14).

25. So also, Buber-Rosenzweig. "Otherwise, he might see with his eyes, hear
with his ears, discern in his heart, repent, and be healed."

Bible passage in Mark 4:12.[26] But if one assumes that Mark 4:12 depends on Luke 8:10b, then this possible influence is limited only to the end of the Markan verse, which is an addition to Luke. Also, the words are "and they will be forgiven." This is how the last two words of Isa 6:10 are translated in the Targum. In Luke 8:10b, it is written that the mysteries of God come to the rest in parables "that seeing they may not see, and hearing they may not understand." We have already mentioned the Markan form. It is good to expect not only a possible influence of the Aramaic translation on the end of the verse in Mark. In our opinion, the Markan version depends, on the one hand, on Luke and, on the other, on the Greek translation of the Isaiah passage. Look at this in the Greek text of Mark. The first word meaning "with it" is found in Mark as well as in Luke. The whole quotation is pluralized in Mark and Luke in the third person—unlike the second person in the Hebrew and Greek versions of Isaiah. The context of the Gospels requires the third-person plural, because Jesus speaks to his disciples and not to the rest of the people (see also Matt 13:12!). On the other hand, the words "see and yet not see" come from the Greek text of Isaiah as well as "repent." Also in the Markan text, "lest" is taken literally from the Greek Isaiah. There, however, it is written a little earlier: "lest the people see it with their eyes," and so on; and in this, the Hebrew original, the Greek, and the Aramaic translations are agreed.[27] Mark cannot use that word in the origi-

---

26. See Jeremias, *Die Gleichnisse Jesu*, vol. 2, 14.

27. The Aramaic word for "lest" is, like the Greek word, an exact translation from Hebrew. The Aramaic word therefore means "not," hence also "perhaps," where the opinion is presupposed, where something is assumed to be unthinkable or unlikely. See Levy, *Chaldäisches Wörterbuch über die Targumim*, 178. It is therefore not acceptable to assume with Jeremias, 13, that the Aramaic word permits a positive answer and means "whether not perhaps" or "unless so." Mark later uses the Greek term *Min to afisete na symveí* and then Jeremias translates the Greek word derived from the Septuagint back into Aramaic in the sense he assumed: "The 'mepote' Mark 4:12 is therefore an equivalent of a *targumic dilemai* which must be reproduced here with 'unless.'" After his unclean and linguistically questionable manipulation, Jeremias arrives at the returned translation: "But to those who are outside, everything is enigmatic, so that they [as it is written] see and yet do not see, hear and yet do not understand, unless they repent and God forgives them." I understand what Jeremias has done to these dubious shifts. First, he assumes the priority of Mark and therefore considers the Markan form to be a rendition of the *ipsissima verba* of Jesus. Second, he cannot accept that Jesus was so inhuman. That is why he is forced to understand Mark: thus the terrible prophecy of Isa 6:9f. is fulfilled in them (the outsiders). Yet there is hope: "If they repent, God will forgive

nal place. He has already taken "with it" from Luke. That's why he uses the Greek particles later. Mark writes, "that they may see and see—and yet not see—hear and hear—and yet not understand, lest they should repent and be forgiven."[28] As will be seen, this arduous investigation was necessary so that we could free ourselves from Mark 10:12 when we later examine the connection between Matt 13:13 and Luke 8:10b.

Thus the motif of hardening occurs in our section in all three Gospels. In Mark, however, it comes to the fore with special vehemence. While Matthew and Luke make a reflection on parables the subject of Jesus' parables, Mark deals with the contrast between those who possess the mystery of the kingdom of God and those who do not: to those who are outside, everything[29] is presented in parables. The troubled gaze of the outsiders, who are outside the kingdom of heaven, leads them to not see and hear, "lest they should repent and be forgiven." One could argue that this extreme consequence is found already in Isa 6:9f., but that is not true. There, it is written that the prophet Isaiah is to harden the heart of the people, "that they may not see and hear, and that their heart may understand and recover," but the time in which the people are not to repent is limited until the coming and unfortunately necessary healing catastrophe. This is not the case with Mark.[30]

If we read Isa 6:9 by tearing it out of its context, then the words can serve as a threat against Israel. This threat then justifies the church's turning away from unbelieving Jewry. Indeed, even in early Christian times, the intra-Jewish admonition became a pronounced expression of a tense relationship

---

them." The last glimpse is of God's forgiving mercy. Such a Jesus is not wholly comfortable even to me.

28. In the Hebrew and Greek texts of Isaiah, instead of the Markan phrase "lest," it is simply "and."

29. Even the superlative "all" is logically lacking in Matthew and Luke!

30. But Mark is not entirely consistent. After Jesus pronounced condemnation on the outsiders, he returned to the parable of the sower and explained to his disciples when asked about the parables: "You do not understand this parable, and how do you understand all the parables?" (Mark 4:13). Mark did not notice that his Jesus had just said that his disciples possessed the mystery of the kingdom of God. Cleverly, this dramatization is inappropriate. However, there is no irreconcilable contradiction. Jesus does not say, as with Matthew and Luke, that it is given to the disciples to "know" the mysteries of God. The Markan Jesus can therefore grant his disciples a little incomprehension of the parables—but whether Mark thought so is not certain. About the incomprehension of the disciples in Mark, see also Mark 8:14–21. Later, we will discuss the secondary plural "parables" in Mark 4:10 and 13, which is also not very clever and was caused by Mark 4:2.

with Judaism.[31] The word of the prophet is given its new meaning in a significant place in the Acts of the Apostles (Acts 28:25–28). Standing at the end of Acts, it constitutes, so to speak, the ultimate consequence of the work that seeks to describe the path from the Judaism of the early congregation to the Christianity of the Gentiles. Paul is at the end of his journey in Rome. He invites to himself the leaders of the Jewish community in Rome and introduces himself to them as a faithful Jew. One day, as he explains faith in Christ in detail and tries to convince them of the law of Moses and of the prophets from Jesus, some are persuaded by his word, but the rest remain unbelievers. Having disagreed among themselves, they set out after Paul said, "The Holy Spirit spoke aptly to your fathers through the prophet Isaiah." Paul then closes his address to the guests by saying, "So be it known to you that this salvation was sent to the Gentiles, and they will hear." I believe that a researcher does not see the intention of Luke wrongly when he says that even though a part of the Jews had converted, Luke no longer reckons with the success of the Christian mission among "the Jews." Rather, the time has now come for the Gentile Christian church, which has assumed the inheritance of Israel.[32] So, the function of the Old Testament word about hardening is clear.

But what about the biblical passage concerning hardening in John 12:37–43?

> Although he had done such great miracles for them, they did not believe in him. That's why they couldn't believe it, because . . . Isaiah said, 'He has blinded their eyes and hardened their hearts, lest they see with their eyes and understand with their hearts and repent and I would heal them.' Nevertheless, even from the authorities many believed in him; but because of the Pharisees they did not openly confess it, lest they be excluded from the synagogue.[33]

These are the words of the Synoptics and not of the Johannine Jesus.

---

31. To Isa 6:9f. in the New Testament, cf. Krister Stendahl, *The School of St. Matthew: And Its Use of the Old Testament* (Uppsala: 1954), 129–32. Isaiah is also referred to in Justin Martyr (*Dial.* 12.3; 33.1; 69.4). The passages are collected in Conzelmann, *Die Apostelgeschichte*, 149f.

32. Conzelmann, *Die Apostelgeschichte*, 149. What Luke says here in the Acts of the Apostles is not in such sharp contrast to the Romans, as Conzelmann thinks. Who says that Luke meant that the "hardening" of the Jews was final? What is written in Acts 28:25–28 does not fit so badly with what we can read in Rom 1:1: "Because of their transgression salvation has come to the Gentiles."

33. Concerning the wording of the quotation from Isaiah to John, see Schnackenburg, *Das Johannesevangelium*, vol. 2, 517–19.

These two references are more similar than it seems at first glance. In John 12:37–43 and Acts 28:25–28, the biblical text about hardening refers to unbelieving Judaism. In both cases, there are also Jews who have become believers in Christ. According to the Acts of the Apostles, some are persuaded by Paul's Jewish listeners, while others remain unbelievers. According to John, even many of the authorities believe in Jesus. As we have seen, John subsequently tends to weaken the faith of individual Jews. But even so, the resemblance remains. If I am not mistaken, this can only mean that historical reality has not allowed the word about hardening to be applied against the whole of Judaism, because the early church was Jewish and because after the event of the cross, other Jews also joined Christianity. The word about hardening therefore explains biblically the unbelief of that part of Judaism that remains outside. Is this understanding of the prophetic word about hardening connected with its function in the pericopes of the "purpose of parables" speech in the Synoptic Gospels (Mark 4:10–12 and par.)? According to Luke, and even more so with Mark, the words of the prophet Isaiah serve to prove that only the disciples can understand the nature of God, whereas the others, those outside, are condemned to spiritual blindness. This is not stated in Matthew (13:1–13). But he also adds, probably under Mark's influence, the word about hardening from the prophet (Matt 13:14). Isaiah 6:9f. is therefore also used in our pericopes in the early church sense. It serves to exclude believers and those who understand from the unbelieving, and therefore spiritually blind, environment. So, what happened? In his saying, Jesus alluded to the words of the prophet to show that those who do not belong to the circle of disciples need educational guidance through illustrative parables because otherwise they would not understand his preaching. But since he used the prophetic word stylistically for this purpose, the word of Isaiah aroused other associations among the evangelists—associations Jesus did not intend. Isaiah 6:9f. is a hardening word, which was used in apostolic times to biblically justify the unbelief of the non-Christian environment. Once again, the usual thing happens: the editor or evangelist intervenes half unconsciously when he misunderstands a traditional word or phrase and then, almost unintentionally, carries his own ideas into the Logion. It then happens that he changes the word or the phrase without worrying that the whole Logion has become meaningless. The editors and the evangelists usually wake up only for a moment and almost always at the wrong moment.[34]

---

34. Flusser, "Die konsequente Philologie und die Worte Jesu," *Almanach auf das Jahr des Herrn* (Hamburg, 1963), 25f.

Mark pushes the futility of the hardening of the unbelieving environment to the extreme. But here, as elsewhere, he is involved in stark disagreements. Through Jesus, he proclaims that the mystery of the kingdom of God is given to Jesus' disciples. And immediately in the next sentence, he has Jesus accuse his disciples of incomprehension (Mark 4:13).[35] Literally, this is a continuation of the thread that begins with the editorial introduction to the parable of the sower (Mark 4:10), continues with the heavily edited introduction to our pericopes (Mark 4:10), and ends with the heavily edited introduction to the interpretation of the parable (Mark 4:13). In all three places, Matthew is more or less influenced by Mark. Mark 4:1f. advances on the typical Markan stilts: "Again he began to teach by the lake. A great multitude gathered around him, and he got into a boat and sat down in the lake, while all the people were on the land by the lake. And he taught them many things in parables. In his speech he spoke to them." We have already demonstrated that the word *doctrine* (*didachae*) did not belong to the original part of the evangelical report.[36] We have also tried to show that the plural form of "parables" is secondary everywhere except in our statement about the nature of the parables (Matt 13:13; Luke 8:10; Mark 4:1) where the plural is the only meaning. On the other hand, the plural form in the editorially redacted introduction to this saying is secondary. This introduction (Mark 4:10) is one of the highlights of Mark's almost unbearable stylistic manner: "When he was alone, those around him with the twelve asked him about the parables." In Greek, the style is even worse, and therefore Matthew (13:10) was forced to simplify the sentence. The original text of the introduction is preserved in Luke 8:9: "And his disciples asked him,[37] 'What is this parable?' "—and the answer is found in Luke 8:11a. Luke 8:9 thus connects seamlessly to Luke 8:11a. This will be decisive for the assumption that Jesus' statement about the nature of the parables (Matt 13:1, 13) was taken out of another context and inserted between the parable of the sower and its interpretation.

So, the sentence in Luke 8:11a is original. In Mark 4:13, it says, "You do not understand this parable, how will you understand the parables?" There is talk of the parables at all only because Mark continues the train of thought of Mark 4:2 and 4:10. But there is also a new motif: the incomprehension of Jesus' disciples, to whom the mystery of the kingdom of God is

---

35. See also note 28 above.
36. See chapter 9, note 45, above.
37. According to some witnesses, perhaps the word *his* should be omitted.

given! The statement about understanding the parables can be interpreted only as a reproach.[38] There is a parallel remark in Mark 7:17f. (cf. Matt 15:15). There, the saying that "what enters into man and does not defile him" is called a parable. And when the disciples ask Jesus about the meaning of this "parable," he answers, "So you too do not understand? Do you not perceive that whatever enters a man from without cannot defile him?" The disciples show a similar lack of understanding in Mark in another paradoxical saying, which, however, was not described by Mark as a parable: "Beware of the leaven of the Pharisees." You can also read this saying in Luke. With Mark (8:14–21), it is embedded in the continuation of the narrative of Jesus' second distribution of bread (Mark 8:1–10; Mark 8:15). The whole second distribution of bread is not present in Luke, and Matthew depends on Mark. The extent to which this feeding of the four thousand is a work of Mark is difficult to say. In any case, the conversation about leaven (Mark 8:16–21) seems to be Mark's invention.[39] I leave it to the reader to read the whole thing. "And he recognized it and said to them, 'What are you discussing, that you have no bread? Do you not yet know and understand? You have eyes, and you do not see, and you have ears, and you do not hear, and you have no memory"[40] (Mark 8:17). The word about the eyes and ears in Mark 8:18 (lacking in Matthew) is the language of the Greek Bible in Jer 5:21 (cf. Ezekiel; it also recalls Isa 6:9f., which we have just seen used in Mark 4:12 against the non-Christian outside world!). At the end of the discourse on leaven (Mark 8:21), Jesus said, "Do you not yet understand?" After the second feeding miracle, the disciples seem more distant from understanding

---

38. William Wrede, *Das Messiasgeheimnis in den Evangelien* (Göttingen: Vandenhoeck & Ruprecht, 1969), 103. He brings to Mark those passages according to which the disciples in the course of history show themselves to be incapable of understanding Jesus (101–7). Not all passages have the same value, and Wrede is so strongly convinced of Mark's priority that he does not touch on the Synoptic Problem. Although his interpretation of the question seems to me to be unimportant, the book is important, wise, and noteworthy.

39. Lindsey thinks that the whole of the second miracle of bread was invented by Mark to support the saying about leaven through some kind of act. Bread distribution is suitable because leaven is necessary for the bread. I tend to accept Lindsey's conjecture because I believe I know the way Mark works. The Pharisees' demand for a sign (Mark 8:1–13; cf. Matt 16:1–4) was placed here by Mark between the distribution of bread and the discourse of the leaven of the Pharisees, because those who demand a sign from Jesus are the Pharisees. This is, therefore, a literarily good transition from the distribution of bread to the leaven of the Pharisees.

40. See Taylor, *The Gospel According to Saint Mark*, 367.

Jesus than ever, for they grossly misinterpret his word about the leaven of the Pharisees and have not drawn any teaching from the food.[41]

Very curious is the remark in Mark 6:52 that refers to the first distribution of bread. Matthew leaves it out, apparently because he couldn't swallow it. After the first distribution of bread, the story of walking on the lake follows only in Mark (6:45–52) and Matthew (14:22–33); it is missing from Luke. When everyone saw Jesus walking on the water, they were dismayed. "Immediately he spoke to them and said to them, 'Take courage, it is I; do not be afraid.' And he went up to them into the boat, and the wind was calm, and they were utterly astonished. For they had no understanding of

---

41. Wrede, *Das Messiasgeheimnis in den Evangelien*, 14. The motif of the incomprehension of the disciples and the early Christian view that the parables were there to be veiled could understandably be adopted in the gnostic milieu, as a Coptic text from the library of Nag Hammadi shows (see *The Nag Hammadi Library in English*, 32). I offer the section in English from the Christian gnostic script: The Apocryphon of James. "At first, I spoke to you in parables and you did not understand; now I speak to you openly, and you [still] do not perceive. Yet it was you who served me as a parable in parables, and as that which is open in the [words] which are open. For after the [end] you have compelled me to stay with you another eighteen days for the sake of the parables. It was enough for some [to listen] to the teaching and understand 'The Shepherds' and 'The Seed' and 'The Building' and 'The Lamps of the Virgins' and 'The Workmen' and 'The Didrachmae' and 'The Woman.'" You can see that this new text is not insignificant for our questions. Today, it is possible to collect these parable pictures and the parables from gnostic (and Manichaean) literature: those related to the parables of Jesus and those that were reinvented. It will be shown that this kind of religious literature is about a specific development, the roots of which can be found in the primitive, un-Jewish understanding of the parable as an expression of a mysterious doctrine. Noteworthy, for example, is the variant of the mystery of the lost sheep (Matt 18:10–14; Luke 15:3–7), which is found in the gnostic gospel Veritatis 32 (*The Nag Hammadi Library in English*, 44; and in German in Robert Haardt, *Die Gnosis: Wesen und Zeugnisse* [Salzburg: Otto Müller, 1967], 183). The gnostic writer combines this parable with another word of Jesus in Matthew (12:11), where it is said that a sheep fell into a pit on the Sabbath, and the Sabbath is symbolically interpreted. It is not certain that the author of the gnostic scripture did this because Matthew connected the Sabbath saying (Matt 12:11) with the parable, speaking in the Sabbath saying of a single sheep (or lamb), which does not belong to the matter but only obscures the Sabbath saying. The parable of the lost sheep is also found in the gnostic Gospel of Thomas (107). Those certainly unimportant variants of Jesus' parables, such as the Gospel of Thomas, have often been overly stressed by researchers. But we should write about this in particular.

the loaves, but their hearts were hardened."[42] The associative connection with the previous distribution of bread was not very successful. One can only say that disciples' shock due to the miracle on the lake is somehow psychologically related to the previous incomprehension of the distribution of bread. In all three Gospels, we will look in vain for any incomprehension of the miracle of bread on the disciples' part. The simplest explanation for the realization of Mark 6:52 is that Mark was no longer thinking about the first distribution of bread when he wrote down these words, but that he already had the second distribution of bread in mind—or, more precisely, the conversation about leaven that follows. Also, in the second distribution of bread, the "stubbornness" of the disciples does not refer to the miracle itself but to the saying about the leaven of the Pharisees (Mark 8:17f.). Mark's work is certainly not perfect.

So why is it that in Mark's account the disciples of Jesus are so unintelligent that they understand the words and deeds of their master so poorly, especially when it comes to figurative speech? This fact, or motif, was certainly not in the original report. As far as I can see, this intellectual "hardening" of the disciples does not occur in Luke. Therefore, this motif seems to be an invention of Mark. But what gave him the impetus for such a view? The involuntary author of this was probably Luke or, more precisely, a pre-Markan redactor writing in Greek. This person did not speak of a general ignorance of the disciples, but only of their inability to comprehend the suffering of the Son of Man and his resurrection. After the second prophecy of suffering, we read in Luke (9:45; cf. Mark 9:32; Matt 17:23 lacks the expression "not understanding"): "But they did not understand this word, and it

---

42. Also, the disciples' fright is mostly the result of an editorial intervention in Mark. Not even Matthew is involved. Once again, the Markan shock was apparently awakened by a paradoxical teaching of the master—and this is important for our investigation. Jesus said it was hard for a rich man to enter the kingdom of heaven. "But the disciples were troubled because of his words" (Mark 10:24). And after Jesus had spoken his word concerning the camel, the disciples were "utterly troubled" (Mark 10:26). Here Matthew (19:25) follows Mark, but he leaves out the word *utterly*. At the transfiguration, Peter did not know what to say, "for they were terrified" (Mark 9:6b). Here, too, Mark remains alone with his remark. It is his work, in order to show the fright of all the disciples present, that he leaves the singular (Peter) and speaks in the majority. Even with his addition to Jesus' agony at Gethsemane (Mark 14:40b), Mark remains alone when he says, "And they did not know what to answer him." On the other hand, the mention of the disciples' fear in the first storm on the lake is common to Mark (4:4) and Luke (8:25), but it is missing in Matthew (8:27).

was veiled from them, lest they should understand it; yet they were afraid to inquire of him concerning this word." Then there is the third proclamation of suffering, this time only with Luke (18:34): "And they understood nothing of this, and this word was hidden from them, and they did not understand what was said." According to Luke, therefore, in Jesus' lifetime, the meaning of the cross is veiled from his disciples. They can't understand Jesus when he talks about it. Mark transfers this incomprehension to other areas: with him, the disciples do not have the ability to understand Jesus' deeds and words.

But is Luke's influence the only reason Mark sees Jesus' disciples as unintelligent, or is this view also related to Mark's own understanding of Jesus? We have already seen that according to Mark (1:22 and 27), Jesus' proclamation was a new teaching that was fundamentally different from the teaching of the scribes. After one of Jesus' healing miracles, which did not contradict the Jewish religious practice of that time, "the Pharisees immediately went out with the Herodians to make a decision against him to kill him."[43] Soon after, according to Mark, the hostile atmosphere thickens around Jesus:

> And he came home, and again, a crowd came together, so they couldn't even eat. And when his own heard it, they departed to take possession of him; for they said that he was mad. And the scribes who came down from Jerusalem said, "He has Beelzebub," and, "By the prince of demons he casts out demons."

In the end, on the cross, Jesus dies all alone, humiliated and abandoned. Few of them were nearby. His cry on the cross shows that he feels abandoned even by his heavenly Father.[44] Even in the "little apocalypse," the Markan apocalyptic Jesus is not concerned with his people but only with the elect (Mark 13).[45] We have also already seen, according to Mark, that only his own possess the mystery of the kingdom while to those outside, everything happens in parables. The latter will be denied conversion to God

---

43. See also Flusser, *Jesus in Selbstzeugnissen und Bilddokumenten*, 48f. Again, the pre-Lukan editor has taken the first step. After the criticism of Pharisaism, he adds the following: "And when he had departed from there, the Pharisees and the scribes began to fiercely oppose him and to besiege him with questions" (Luke 11:53). First, this sentence is conceived in a rather distorted folk Greek and, second, it fits badly with the Lukan conception.

44. See my article in note 19 above.

45. See my article in note 20 above.

and will not be forgiven (Mark 4:11f.). The Markan superhuman miracle-rabbi Jesus is not even understood by his own disciples. Sometimes, Mark literally falls out of his own concept and isn't consistent. Matthew sometimes behaves uncertainly toward Mark, which is partly because Matthew also had better sources. Sometimes, the Markan character sketch of Jesus is too crass for him. Primarily, however, wherever Mark precedes him, Matthew is under his spell. Luke, on the other hand, could not be seduced by the magic of Mark's one-sidedness because, according to our hypothesis, he did not know Mark. The adherents of Mark's importance can argue that Luke has softened it. But for many reasons, it is impossible to say. In Luke, Jesus' disciples understand his teaching and his parables. Their question about the meaning of the parable of the sower is justified because this parable, in its essence, requires an explanation. In this point, Luke faithfully reflects the historical episode because he records the original account literally (Luke 8:9, 11). What is written in Luke 9:10, as we shall see, is the work of the pre-Lukan editor.

The image of Jesus designed by Mark is certainly not identical with the gnostic Christ, but it has some similarities with him. For Mark, Jesus works in an environment foreign to him, even hostile, in which only the elect understand him. Besides, not even Jesus' disciples are able to fully understand him. It is no coincidence that the Johannine Jesus is painted with some brushstrokes reminiscent of Mark's craftmanship. It will suffice to illustrate this with a few words from the famous prologue of John's Gospel: "The world did not recognize him, he came into his own, but his own did not receive him. But to all who received him he gave the power to become children of God, to those who believe in his name" (John 1:1–12). Today, it is generally assumed that John's prologue is based on a song or hymn that the evangelist used for the beginning of his Gospel.[46] "His own, who did not accept the Logos when he came into his own" were perhaps identical in the original hymn with "the world that did not recognize him."[47] But

---

46. See Schnackenburg, *Das Johannesevangelium*, vol. 1, 200ff. and additional bibliography, 530f.; Jack T. Sanders, "The New Testament Christological Hymns," *SNTS 15* (Cambridge, 1971), 29–57.

47. The next parallel to the supposed content of the hymn, which underlies the prologue in John and in John 1:10, is found in the Ethiopic Enoch, ch. 42 (see also 94.5 there). I have not found this parallel recorded in any scientific debate. Only R. H. Charles, *The Book of Enoch* (Oxford: Clarendon Press, 1912), 82, says that Enoch 42 reminds him to a certain extent of the Johannine prologue. And here is the saying, according to chapter 42 of the book of Enoch: "Wisdom found no place

according to John, the unbelieving Jews are Jesus' own who did not receive him. They are contrary to those "who believe in his name." So, the Johannine view is like Mark's. In addition, Jesus stands with Mark and John not only in opposition to the world but also in incomprehension on the part of his disciples, even if he speaks in parables. We have already seen that John shares the primitive Christian view that the parables are a veiling, pictorial way of speaking and that he calls Jesus' parables "wisdom sayings" (John 10:6; 16:25, 29). After the disciples realize that Jesus is now speaking openly and not in idioms, they declare,

> "Therefore we believe that you came from God." Jesus said to them, "Do you believe now? Behold, the hour is coming, and it has already come, that you will be scattered, each for himself, and leave me alone. But I am not alone, because my Father is with me." (John 16:29–32)

If Jesus now questions the faith of his disciples and establishes this doubt with the prediction of their impending flight, the present hour remains in the same perspective of their incomprehension and weakness.[48] Even Jesus' loneliness at the end is reminiscent of the image Mark had drawn.

If it is permissible to apply to John—and, with less justification, to Mark—the gnostic threefold division of mankind, then the elect are the pneumatics, the disciples are psychics, and the rest of humanity belongs to the lowest level of carnal humans. This also applies to the incomprehension of Jesus' enigmatic parables. Concerning the general character of the unbelieving Jews and their delusion, I would like to quote a saying of the Johannine Jesus: "Why do you not understand my language? Because you are unable to hear my word! You have the devil as your father. And because I tell you the truth, ye believe me not. He who is of God hears the words of God; therefore, you do not hear, because you are not of God" (John 8:42–47). This is also accompanied by the reaction that follows the Johannine illustrative discourse of the shepherd and his sheep (John 10:1–5). The evangelist observes, "This is what Jesus said to them, but they did not know

---

where she could dwell; there she was given a dwelling place in heaven. Wisdom went out to dwell with the children of men, but she found no dwelling place; then wisdom returned to her place, and took her seat with the angels. And the iniquities came out of their chambers, which she had not sought, and dwelt with them, as the rain in the wilderness, and as the dew in the thirsty ground." This is strongly reminiscent of Hesiod, *Works*, 197–201, and Ovid, *Metamorphoses*, 1.1490.

48. Schnackenburg, *Das Johannesevangelium*, vol. 3, 186.

what the words he said to them meant" (John 10:6). A modern exegete makes the following comment:

> In our passage, the "riddle speech" intensifies the function that Jesus' revelatory word has at all because of the strangeness and incomprehension of the non-believers (cf. 8:43–47). Because the hearers are blinded (9:39), they cannot comprehend the illustrative speech and prove to be those who do not belong to Jesus' sheep and know his voice. The proximity to Mark 4:11f par. is unmistakable.[49]

So, it is a matter of our hardening motif, and this connection excuses the long road we have taken so far. I cannot rule out the possibility that John is also influenced by Mark in his opinion of Jesus' parables and their effect. The centrifugal path from Jesus as he lived and taught on earth to the Johannine Jesus and to the gnostic Christ is, it seems to me, not without danger!

The rabbis and Jesus rejected every secret doctrine. In Deut 13:7, the rabbis commented as follows:

> "In secret," from this we say that they say their words only in secret. It is written: "In the twilight, at the end of the day, at the time of night and darkness" (Prov 7:9). But the words of instruction are said only in public. It is written: "Wisdom calls in the streets, in the open squares she raises her voice, on the walls she preaches" (Prov 1:20).[50]

This beautiful rabbinic word is not only anti-gnostic but also anti-Essene. We know from the Dead Sea Scrolls and from Flavius Josephus that the Essenes also kept their doctrine secret from their environment. According to Josephus (Bell II:141f.), a new member of the Essene community was obliged to swear a terrible oath, in which it was stated, among other things, that the Essenes should not "hide anything from the followers of the sect, nor betray anything from them to others, should one also use violence until death" and that they "must strictly guard the books of the sect as well as the names of the angels." The Dead Sea Scrolls provide further evidence that the Essenes kept their teachings hidden from the outside world. A rebellion arose against an Essene poet in the sect, as is customary.[51] When the men of his clan became stubborn and grumbled, the poet said, "About the secret

---

49. Schnackenburg, *Das Johannesevangelium*, vol. 2, 538.
50. SifDev to Deut 13:7, ed. Finkelstein, 151.
51. This division can be read in 1QH 5:22–36 and 6:19–22.

that You have hidden in me, the children of evil are slandering." According to the poet, although these circles sought to betray the sect's secret teachings to the unbelieving environment, God provided. The abusive traitors had not grasped the true meaning of the secret doctrine: "Because of their guilt you have hidden the source of insight and the true secret," so that those people who sold only their false ideas, and not the true doctrine of the sect, to the outsiders (IQH 5:23–28). In another hymn, the poet compares the sect to a sacred planting.[52] The sacred seed is hidden, "unnoticed and unrecognized is its secret seal. You, God, have shielded his fruit by the mystery of the reins of power and of the holy spirits. And the torment of the fire shook, so that no one could reach the fountain of life. For he sees without knowing and thinks without believing in the source of life." As later with the gnostics, so also with the Essenes: their doctrine is a secret doctrine. It should be kept secret. It must not be betrayed to the unbelieving world because it is supposed to be, by its very nature, a mystery—an esoteric, mysteriously profound, and immediate revelation of God, which unbelievers cannot understand. When the evangelists turned Jesus' words regarding the nature of the parables into a saying about hardening under the influence of the Isaiah passage, they certainly did not think of stamping the message of Christianity into an arcane discipline. But apparently, they liked to understand Jesus' words, especially his parables, as mysterious in a different sense: as a deep revelation of God through Christ, incomprehensible to the outside world.

The evangelists, to the extent just described, use the word of Isaiah and their preconceived opinions to transform themselves into an unhistorical image of Jesus in our place. Not even Mark—who, compared with the other two Synoptic Gospels, increases the vehemence of the saying about hardening—was able to constantly turn his back on reality. Following his series of parables, he sums up the workings of the parable-teller Jesus quite reasonably: "And in many such parables he spoke the word to them as they could understand it. Without a parable, however, he did not speak to them; but when they were alone, he explained everything to his disciples" (Mark 4:33f.). Matthew (13:34) uses Mark's summary while Luke does not. What

---

52. 1QH 8. Not by chance does the parable recall Jesus' parable about the mustard seed. See Flusser, *Jesus in Selbstzeugnissen und Bilddokumenten*, 87f. The important difference is that Jesus does not speak of the mysterious growth of the mustard plant and Jesus' tall plant is not hidden like the symbolic trees in the sectarian song.

Mark says here is better than his earlier saying about hardening (Mark 4:11f.). There, Jesus intends that outsiders should not understand his parables. Here, it is reported that Jesus speaks to the people in parables because doing so helps the understand what he is saying. Mark is partly right, but the section is not very clever. In sharp contrast to the saying about hardening, Mark knows that Jesus uses parables to facilitate the understanding of simple people; but on the other hand, it is absurd to claim that Jesus spoke to the people only in parables. Did not the "historical" Jesus also teach the people in a different way? And if the parables are adapted to the understanding of simple people, then why does Mark claim that Jesus explained everything just to the disciples and not to the multitude? Were the parables universally comprehensible, yet interpretations were withheld from the multitude? We have already seen that there are self-evident parables that do not need a more precise interpretation, while other parables are ambiguous without an interpretation. In those parables, every listener is faced with this ambiguity—both the disciples and the less initiated people. Thus Mark is once again inconsistent. On the one hand, he knows that the parable is an aid for the simple; but on the other hand, he is under the spell of the systemic constraint he has created. He is obliged to both the saying about hardening he knows from Luke 8:10 and his own warped image of Jesus, according to which the superhuman miracle-worker stands frighteningly alone with his chosen ones. Therefore, in Mark 4:33f., Jesus feeds the multitude only with parables, while he explains these parables only to his disciples.[53] Regarding any distortion, however, it is correctly said here that these parables are not a means of hardening but an aid to better understanding.

---

53. We find the same mental construction in Mark a little earlier in the pericope about the purpose of parables. Again, Jesus explained the parable of the sower to his disciples as a private matter, "when he was alone" (Mark 4:10). These words are not found in Luke or Matthew. The latter (Matt 13:10) is indeed influenced by Mark, but it also knows and uses the old, unspoiled source. The word *disciples* is common to both Matt 13:10 and Luke 8:9 (but not Mark 4:10). So, it seems that Matthew did not find the Markan "when he was alone" in his good source. That's why he left out the words, even though he had read them in Mark. The same view that Jesus explained the parables only to his disciples is also found in the pericopes of the handwashing, again in Mark. In this Gospel, it is emphasized that Jesus told the parable of the clean and unclean to the multitude: "And again . . . he called the multitude and said to them, 'Listen to me all and take hold of it'" (Mark 7:14). This also carries with it Matthew (15:10) a little shortened. Mark says, "And when he was come home from the multitude, his disciples asked him about the parable" (Mark 7:17). Here also, the explanation is granted privately. What happened to

In addition to the words about the purpose of parables (Luke 8:9ff.), which are found today in the Synoptic Gospels in the parable of the sower and its interpretation, all three conclude their series of parables with a special treatise on the nature of parables. First, Luke includes the parable of the sower and concludes with the saying about the right use of the parables (Luke 8:16–18). Next, Mark uses this passage (4:21–25), which is beautiful proof of Mark's dependence on Luke! Mark then continues the series of parables and concludes it with the section on the method of parables (Mark 4:33f.). Finally, Matthew uses this passage (Matt 13:34), which proves Matthew's dependence on Mark. Matthew then continues the parables and ends with a little parable saying, which I intend to deal with later (Matt 13:51).[54] Actually, one might be surprised that this and similar cases have not been considered over the course of the many Synoptic investigations. Otherwise, we would have been able to find the right Synoptic solution sooner.[55]

We now turn to the sayings concerning the proper use of the parables (Luke 8:16–18; Mark 4:21–25). As we can easily verify, all of these have their parallels elsewhere. I assume that our section has been put together by a pre-Lukan editor as Matthew does not include the whole passage. Appar-

---

Matthew? As in Matt 13:10, here the separation of Jesus from the multitude is lacking. The question of the disciples is thus introduced in Matt 15:12: "Then the disciples came and said to him." But these are the same words the pericopes of the purpose of the parables introduced in the same Matthew passage (13:10)! They're probably from there. Matthew repeats it consciously more often. Also, Matt 15:13a ("but he answered and said") is identical with Matt 13:11a. What else Matthew has put together does not concern us here. Only one thing should be noted: the term *phrazein* appears in the New Testament only in Matt 15:15.

54. That the saying about parables according to Matthew serves to conclude the parable is evident from its introduction: "'Have you understood all this?' They said to him, 'Yes'" (Matt 13:51).

55. I have another observation to make: We can follow the same direction from Luke to Mark and from Mark to Matthew when we compare Luke 20:40, Mark 12:34b, and Matt 22:46b. The final sentence comes from Luke (20:40): "For they dared not ask him any questions." The sentence is varied in the other two Gospels. With Luke, the sentence closes the Pharisee's question, and Mark includes the following question about the Great Commandment (Mark 12:34b). The pericopes of the Great Commandment are elsewhere in Luke (Luke 10:25–28). In Luke 20:40, the questioning is finished. The following pericope of the Son of David is a *logion* in Luke (20:41–44) and Mark, which Matthew (22:41–46) converted into a dialogue. Therefore, in Matthew, the questioning ends only after this pericope and Matthew puts the mentioned sentence at the end of only this section (Matt 22:46b). Again, it seems to me that Lindsey's theory has been confirmed!

ently, however, he knew the passage in the Markan form (Mark 4:21–25): "For he that has, to him shall be given, and he shall have abundance: but he that has not, to him shall be taken away even that which he has." This fits into the section like a square peg in a round hole. Matthew, however, inserted these words because they speak of giving and taking. Furthermore, the previous original verse says, "To you it is given to know the mysteries of the kingdom of heaven, but to them it is not given" (Matt 13:1). So, Matthew thought he had done something sensible when he rescued this from the string of sayings in Mark 4:21–25. This Matthean opinion, however, can hardly be applauded from a literary-critical point of view. From Luke 8:18, we can see what function the pre-Lukan author intended for the saying. After affixing two words of Jesus directed against the secrecy of doctrine (Luke 8:16f.; cf. Mark 4:21f.), he continues: "Now pay attention to what you hear! For whoever has, to him will be given; and whoever does not have, to him will be taken away what he thinks he has" (Luke 8:18; cf. Mark 4:23–25; Matt 13:12). So, the Lukan editor referred the saying of giving and taking to the success or failure of the right or wrong reception of this teaching. However, this giving and taking has its natural place elsewhere—namely, in the parable of the talents (Matt 25:14–30); or, as Luke calls it, in the parable of the minas (Luke 19:11–27). There (Matt 25:29; Luke 19:26), the saying forms the conclusion and the point of the parable: the unworthy servant is deprived of what he has, and it is given to the good servant.

I could not help following a Synoptic odyssey of a saying of Jesus. An attentive reader who has the Gospels in hand can learn much about the origin of the Synoptic Gospels. It goes without saying that the end phases of the saying did not remain unaffected by their long journey: Mark 4:25 descends from Luke 8:18; and Matt 13:12 is influenced, on the one hand, by Mark 4:25 and, on the other hand, by Matt 25:29.[56]

---

56. The words "and he shall abound" are found in both Matt 13:12 and 25:29. They are missing in all other forms of the saying. Otherwise, Matt 13:12 is similar to the statement in Mark 4:25 and not in Matt 25:29. Where, then, are the words "and they shall abound" originally, in Matt 13:12 or 25:29? I think the second option is more likely. As I said, Matt 13:12 is taken from the discourse in Mark 4:21–25. In Mark 4:24, it is written before our saying: "By what measure you measure will be measured to you. And this will be given to you." From there, apparently, Matt 13:12 took the occasion to say, "and he will have abundance." The whole series of sayings in Luke 8:16–18 follows the parable of the sower. The pre-Lukan editor did this because the preceding parable speaks of the word of God and how to hear it. By the following series of sayings, he wants to show that one should not proclaim the word of God in secret and that one should pay attention to how one hears.

The first two sayings of the section on the right use of the parables (Luke 8:16f.; Mark 4:21f.) stand in sharp contrast to the previous hardening motif. Also, we derive from them a decisive rejection of any esoteric secrecy. The pre-Lukan editor took both of Jesus' sayings from elsewhere: the first saying (Luke 8:16; cf. Mark 4:21) is found in Luke 1:33 and Matt 5:15, and the second (Luke 8:17; cf. Mark 4:22) in Luke 12:2 and Matt 10:26. Both verses originate in the source of the saying since they are only in this pericope, which is to be attributed to the pre-Lukan editor. Although Mark documents this, they are otherwise missing from Mark.[57]

It may be difficult to reconstruct the original wording of Luke 8:16f., which is a pericope from the pre-Lukan editor, but both sayings deserve to be looked at in their source before being edited in Luke 8:16f. In Matt 5:13–16, the first saying is part of the second half of the double saying about salt and light: "You are the light of the world: a city that lies on the mountain cannot be hidden. Nor do they light a lamp, and put it under a bowl, but on a candlestick, and it shines to all in the house. Let your light so shine before men, that they may see your good works, and glorify your Father who is in heaven."[58] The double saying about salt and light seems to be well preserved in Matthew and illuminates the profession of the disciples. The disciples form, to a certain extent, the spice and preservative of the world and they serve as light. Just as a city sitting on the mountain cannot be hidden, so also a lamp is placed on the lampstand so that it can illuminate everything. The last sentence (Matt 5:16) shifts the original meaning by referring not to the work of the disciples but to their conduct or good works when speaking of "the light." Therefore, the verse in Matthew seems to be a secondary addition. The saying of the light originally ended as a punch line with the invitation: "So shine your light in front of the people!" Jesus did not want his disciples to be hidden from the world.

The second saying in the pericopes about the use of parables (Luke 8:17; Mark 4:22) is the same in the sayings source (Matt 10:26; Luke 12:2). The

---

57. Whoever is willing not to cling to the priority of Mark will find from this situation further proof of the correctness of Lindsey's theory. He becomes aware that Mark 4:21–25 depends on Luke 8:16–18. Luke 8:16 speaks of a bed, whereas Mark 4:21 asks, "Does the lamp come to be placed under a bowl or under a bed?" Mark 4:21 combines the bed in Luke 8:1–6 with a bowl (Matt 5:15; Luke 11:33). From this, it is likely that Mark knew both Luke and the bowl in the source of the saying (by Luke 11:33). Taylor, *The Gospel According to Saint Mark*, 263f., necessarily had to get into trouble in this context.

58. In my remarks, I follow Klostermann, *Das Matthäusevangelium*, 39.

pre-Lukan editor modified it stylistically. He also pulled it out of a broader context, as he did with the previous sentence. In the source of the saying, it forms only part of an entire passage: the call to fearless confession (Matt 10:26–33; Luke 12:2–9). The first two sayings of this series (Matt 10:26f.; Luke 12:2f.), of which our saying is the first, are closely related. It says,

> "So do not be afraid of them.[59] For there is nothing hidden that will not be re-vealed, and nothing hidden that will not be known. Therefore, everything you have said in the dark will be heard in broad daylight. And what you whispered in your ears in the chambers will be sounded on the roofs."[60]

Being secret for fear of the consequences will not help the disciples, because they cannot hide their words from others. Experience teaches that what is whispered in an inner room will eventually be heard when all the birds on the roofs chirp to each other. So, it makes no sense if the disciples, who are supposed to be the light of the world, conceal their master's teaching because of their fear of persecution. Because concealment is meaningless, the disciples should not seek it. It was a different yet similar idea for the Essenes who held to secret doctrine: "No thing that was hidden from Israel and found by someone who searches, he hides from them [the Essenes] for

---

59. I took this beginning from Matt 12:26a. It is missing in Luke 12:2, but it was in the original text; for this "do not fear" does not open the following counsel of Jesus only to Matthew (10:28) but also to Luke (12:4). Luke omitted the words because he wanted to closely follow the call to fearless confession with the warning against the leaven of the Pharisees. This made the whole passage (Luke 12:2–12), which speaks of outspoken confession and persecution, a continuation of the dis-course against the Pharisees (Luke 11:37–12:1)! On the other hand, the context in Matthew is much more convincing and probably original: the call to fearless confession there follows the dark word about the future persecution of the disciples (Matt 10:17–23; 24f. does not belong here).

60. Except for the beginning, I am following Luke 12:2f. here. Matt 10:27 says, "What I say to you in the dark, say in the light, and what you hear in the ear, preach on the housetops." Such a reinterpretation certainly does not hit the heart of the matter. Luke—and Jesus—wants to say that nothing will help you if you do not speak openly out of fear; it will nevertheless, even against your will, become public. This is a paradoxical general wisdom typical of Jesus. According to Matthew, on the other hand, Jesus speaks of a future revelation of received mysteries through the secret teaching of Jesus. The veiled, what Jesus whispered in the dark to the disciples, the disciples are to reveal later in the light, to make it fully known, to openly proclaim. I cannot take part in such a skillful alteration of Jesus' words. I therefore give preference to the original reading in Luke that sounds closer to Jesus.

fear of apostate spirit."[61] An Essene was not allowed to hide anything new from his fellow sect members. He was not allowed to give in to his fear that he would be accused of heresy or that his innovation would lead others to heresy. The rejection of fear in teaching a doctrine to others is common to the Essenes and Jesus. However, unlike the Essenes, who were strictly forbidden from communicating specific sectarian teachings to outsiders, Jesus obliged his disciples to communicate true doctrine to the whole world. How then can we suppose that Jesus fully preached his sermons to his own disciples while sharing with others only mysterious parables?

Jesus' anti-esoteric attitude observed in the parables also applies to other topics in his message. It is highly questionable whether Jesus ever used the phrase "mystery of the kingdom of God" (Mark 4:11), since this expression is almost more in line with Qumran Essene thinking. In a hymn scroll, the Essene poet compares his congregation to a tree that is hidden, "unnoticed and unrecognized by his secret seal" (1QH 8:1; cf. 1QH 6:150). Jesus, on the other hand, says nothing like this in his parable of the mustard seed (Luke 13:18f. par.), which is a picture of the growth of the kingdom of heaven. On the contrary, it is known that Jesus sent his disciples to proclaim the kingdom of heaven to all. It is also known that Jesus did not have to explain the concept of the kingdom of God to his listeners; they knew what it meant. Jesus wanted his disciples to speak openly. The assumption is quite absurd that for Jesus the kingdom was shrouded in mystery.

It is different with Jesus' self-image of his person, his divine sonship, and his messianic status. Jesus never spoke openly about this, and the Greek editors of the Synoptic Gospels and the Gospel of John raised this authentic inner tension to a "messianic secret." Furthermore, there are many modern New Testament scholars who deny that Jesus had any sense of kingship or messianic consciousness. Although the nature of New Testament statements does not make such doubts seem entirely unreasonable to scientists, modern "post-Easter" Christology has lost much of its legitimacy since the Dead Sea Scrolls were published. From them, we can see that in ancient Judaism around the time of Jesus, there were religious leaders—such as the Essene teacher of righteousness and the poet of the Essene hymns—who were convinced they had immediate and unique access to the mysteries of God and a key position in the divine economy. Their supporters believed them. It is said of the Essene teacher of righteousness (1 QpHab 7:4) that

---

61. 1QS 8:12. My explanation is based on Jonathan Licht, *The Rule Scroll* (Jerusalem: The Bialik Institute, 1965), 110.

God "made known to him all the secrets of the words of his servants the prophets." The Essene hymn poet says, among other things, about himself:

> You set me as a sign to the elect of justice and as an interpreter of knowledge in wonderful mysteries, to test the men of truth and to test those who love instruction. . . . [I am the man] in whose mouth you have put and whom you have taught understanding. You have put it in his heart to open a fountain of knowledge for all who understand.

These and similar passages in the Essene Hymnbook are significant because they expose a new aspect in Jewish apocalypticism. Until the discovery of the scrolls, apocalyptic pseudepigraphy only knew of a lofty self-image of biblical figures. But the Qumran scripture now shows us that there were Jews at that time who themselves spoke and wrote about their inspired self-conception and their direct access to the mysteries of God. Why should not Jesus of Nazareth have been one of them, though with special, much more human qualities? A man who never completely surrendered his claim to sovereignty but also never completely concealed it, whose proclamation was never esoteric since he offered it to all as the only right way? To this proclamation also belonged his parables, the purpose of which—as with the rabbis—was to bring moral teaching to humanity with utmost urgency.

11

JESUS' CRY OF JUBILATION AND THE BLESSED EYEWITNESSES

In our context, we must also consider Jesus' cry of jubilation (Matt 11:25–27; Luke 10:21).[1] It only became understandable after the publication of the Essene Hymnbook (1QH). Today, it would not be difficult to see Jesus' cry of jubilation as authentic. With it, Jesus intended something unusual. He made use of the ecstatic form of Essene hymns and the inspired missionary consciousness of their poet to find adequate expression for his intimate connection with the heavenly Father. The reason why Jesus' claim of sovereignty was preserved in the Synoptic Gospels was because of its poetic form and a hymn that entails memorizing. Jesus said:

> "I thank Thee, Father, Master of heaven and earth, that Thou hast hid these things from the wise and prudent, and hast revealed them to the simple. Yes, Father, for so was the will before You. Everything is given to me by my Father, and no one knows the Son except the Father, and no one knows the Father except the Son, and to whom the Son wishes to reveal himself."[2]

---

1. See, among others, Schneider, *Das Evangelium nach Lukas*, 242–45 and bibliography; and Erik Sjöberg, *Der verborgene Menschensohn in den Evangelien* (Lund: C. W. K. Gleerup, 1955), 184–90, 230–33. Primarily, the first passage in Sjöberg should be mandatory reading! This is also true of the unfortunately little-noticed Eduard Meyer, *Ursprung und Anfänge des Christentums*, vol. 1 (Berlin, 1921), 280–91. Meyer rightly criticizes Eduard Norden, *Agnostos Theos: Untersuchungen zur Formengeschichte Religioser Rede* (Darmstadt, 1956), 277–308. Norden thinks the *Logion* was not of Jesus and seeks its origin in the mystical-theosophical milieu of Asia. This view is related to the atmosphere that prevails in the circle around Reitzenstein. I fear that this Reitzensteinian ideological orientation will soon become a dream of the future again for various researchers, to which not only the world situation but also the new gnostic finds and fatigue with Christianity will contribute. But most likely, the representatives of this new wave will no longer be as thorough and learned as Norden was.

2. It is tempting to claim the following word in Matt 1:28–30 as the hymn of Jesus, because it seems to be a direct statement about Jesus and is in the same hym-

In their personal prayers, even then, Jews turned to God with the following introductory formula: "Let the will be before you . . ."[3] Here, Jesus thanks his heavenly Father that it was his will to keep this hidden from the wise and discerning and to reveal it to the simple. The phrase "wise and understanding" belongs to the Old Testament. The Greek word we translate as "simple" is in Hebrew *peta'im*. It is found chiefly in biblical wisdom literature and denotes the ignorant or foolish who have not learned the wisdom of godliness.[4] But even in biblical wisdom literature, the word does not always have a negative connotation. In Essene literature, *peta'im* has a positive, specific meaning. However, the contrast between the wise or intelligent and those who are simple is indicative of Jesus' meaning. From a different point of view, we see the contrast as well in his Beatitudes and proclamations of woe. From there, for example, we can also understand Jesus' ambivalent relationship with the Pharisees and his affection for the poor and disenfranchised. We must, however, pay close attention: the juxtaposition of the wise and intelligent, from whom this is hidden, and the simple, to whom this has been revealed, indeed expresses Jesus' anti-intellectualism. But this is not identical with the difference between those to whom it is given to understand the mysteries of God and those to whom one must speak in parables because otherwise they would not understand. In Matt 13:11–13,

---

nal style. However, these two verses are missing in Luke, so they were not known to him. As will be seen, they may not have belonged to the hymn for serious Synoptic reasons. Only Matt 11:28–30 mentions the hymns of wisdom in the book of Ben Sira (ch. 24 and the closing chapter, which is not from Ben Sira and is also in the psalmist's scroll of Qumran, where it is attributed to King David). See J. A. Sanders, *The Psalms Scroll of Qumran Cave 11* (Oxford: Clarendon Press, 1965), 70–85. See also Sjöberg, *Der verborgene Menschensohn in den Evangelie*, 232. Matthew 10:27 is more original than Luke 10:22. Matthew exemplifies the Father's knowledge of the Son and the Son of the Father through a universal truth that applies to every father and son, while Luke 10:22 writes, "No one knows who the Son is except the Father and who the Father is except the Son." This is no longer spoken of generally, but now specifically of the Father-God and Son-Christ. What is interesting is that Luke was led to this all too blatant christological interpretation by the Greek unemphasized *tis*. The Greek text of Luke's source of sayings is therefore identical to Matthew's.

3. Cf. Strack and Billerbeck, *Kommentar zum Neuen Testament aus Talmud und Midrasch*, vol. 1, 607, 785; and Joseph Heinemann, *Prayer in the Period of the Tanna'im and the Amora'im: Its Nature and Its Patterns* (Jerusalem: 1967), 113. See also Matt 1:26; 18:14. Heinemann's book is also available in English: *Prayer in the Talmud: Forms and Patterns*, Studia Judaica 9 (Berlin, 1977).

4. Cf. Sjöberg, *Der verborgene Menschensohn in den Evangelien*, 185f.

the wise and prudent are left out. The wisdom of the world—to speak on Paul's terms—prevents them from grasping the message, even if they are spoken to in parables in a popular and figurative way. As we shall see later, it is almost certain that Jesus' cry of jubilation is the reason for perpetuating his saying about the parables. In this case, too, Jesus applied his art of gradually shifting perspective in his proclamation.

When Jesus says "No one knows the Father except the Son," this itself sounds so sublime that many are inclined to deny that the entire hymn belongs to Jesus. Earlier in ancient Egypt, Pharaoh Akhenaten said to the sun god, Aton, "There is no one else who knows you, except your son [Akhenaten], the only-begotten of Ra."[5] However, parallelization is not entirely possible with Jesus as Jesus is truly speaking of his unique relationship with his heavenly Father. But by using an example from parent-child relations, Jesus reveals to his hearers what God ultimately wants in this hour of the Son's mission. Even among humans, "no one knows the son except the father, and no one knows the father except the son, and to whom the son wants to reveal it." Jesus thus transfers the human father-son relationship to his relationship with his heavenly Father and to God's innermost will.[6] In order to understand correctly what Jesus is doing here, we must know that the Hebrew word that means "to reveal" has not only a religious but also an everyday meaning. It signifies both divine revelation and normal communication of a previously unknown fact from person to person. We can only fully grasp the depth of Jesus' cry of jubilation if we free ourselves from its Greek form and focus on the Hebrew. God reveals to the simple what is hidden to the wise and learned, and so Jesus reveals the hidden will of his heavenly Father to those to whom he wants to communicate it, because the same applies among humans. No one knows a son and his intentions better than his father, and the son is the one who knows his father best. The son can also, if he wants, best inform others about his father and his intentions. The Hebrew word for "reveal" has the same double meaning in the blessing (Matt 16:17) that bursts forth from Jesus after Peter alone recognizes and pronounces Jesus' messianic status: "Blessed are you,[7] Simon Bar Jonah,[8]

---

5. Cf. *ANET*, 317; Erik Hornung. *Der Eine und die Vielen. Ägyptische Gottesvorstellungen* (Darmstadt: Wissenschaftliche, 1971), 244f.

6. cf. Gustaf Dalman, *Die Worte Jesu* (Leipzig: Kessinger, 1898), 231–33.

7. The expression "Blessed art thou" also means "Praise thee."

8. "Bar" is Aramaic for "son" and occurs in Hebrew sentences with name references. Peter's father was called Yohanan: see John 1:42 (where Jonah appears in individual manuscripts) and John 21:15–17. For the Jew, "Yonah" is a short form

for flesh and blood has not revealed this to you, but my Father in heaven." "Flesh and blood" is quite common in Judaism as an expression for humans in contrast to the deity, and also occurs in the New Testament otherwise. Jesus, therefore, praises Peter because no human has communicated to him that Jesus is the Messiah, for everyone else considered him to be the prophet of the end times (Matt 16:14). Jesus' messianic position could only have been revealed to Peter through God. It is obvious that not only the double meaning of the word *reveal* but also Jesus' messianic sonship are common to his cry of joy in Matt 11:25–27 and Matt 16:17.

Not only is the free rhythm of Jesus' jubilation common to Essene hymns but also his opening phrase, "I thank you." This is how most of the hymns in the Qumran hymnbook (1QH) begin. Jesus used the form of an Essene hymn when he shouted for joy. Like the Essene hymnist, he was convinced he had direct access to the mysteries of God and that he could pass on this experience and knowledge to others.[9] Jesus differs from the Essene hymnist, however, in knowledge of his sonship, which he organically inserts into his hymn.

Do we have to admit that Jesus also represented a certain esotericism? Yes and no. He gives thanks that God has revealed to the simple what is hidden from the wise and discerning, and that God communicates it to those to whom he wishes to reveal it. For the time being, this target audience is his disciples, to whom the mysteries of God are given. Perhaps one can also put it this way:

---

of Johanan. This short form also occurs in rabbinic literature; cf. Levy, *Wörterbuch über die Targumim und Midraschim*, vol. 2 (Darmstadt, 1963), 226; cf. also the form "Yahnah" for the magician Jannes (Yohanan) in CD 5, 18; this magician is also called "Yonah" in bMen 85a.

9. To this end, Sjöberg, *Der verborgene Menschensohn in den Evangelien*, 188, rightly quotes Ethen 48:6f. and 62:7 about the Son of Man: "And this is why he [the Son of Man] was chosen and hidden from him before the world was created and forever. And the wisdom of the Master of Spirits has revealed him to the saints and to the righteous. For from the beginning the Son of Man was hidden, and the Most High preserved him in the presence of his power and revealed him to the elect." There is no mention of the Son of Man as the transmitter of revelation. See, however, Sjöberg, *Der verborgene Menschensohn in den Evangelien*, 44f., and Ethiopic Enoch 51:3, 46:3; 61. According to the apocryphal "Songs of David" (which I discovered and will publish in a Hebrew article for the time being, and which probably come from Qumran), at the end of days, the king and prophet David will address all the kings and peoples; all the rulers of the earth will gather "to see the power of your right hand and to understand the mystery of your holy words."

This is the deepest knowledge of the hidden nature of God. Jesus' relationship to apocalypticism does not consist in simply adopting apocalyptic conceptions. Apocalypticism has created the milieu that was the necessary prerequisite of his activity; but in the formation of his own intuition and message, he has not only used the apocalyptic ideas but at the same time transformed them.[10]

But surely, Jesus was not concerned with the proclamation of any conception of the hidden form (*toar*) of God. Such an interpretation diminishes the strangeness of Jesus' exultation. But our difficulty also lies elsewhere—namely, that Jesus' cry of rejoicing somehow contains a kind of social esotericism of its message. This has a lot to do with the nature of his parables. The fact that many things remain hidden from the "wise and intelligent"—not only God's ultimate kairological will, which is comprehensible to the simple—has occurred since Socrates and will continue until the end of time. It is especially true when these wise and intelligent people practice their scholarship professionally. For this reason alone, it is obvious that the simple are not limited to the disciples. The Hebrew word for "simple" (*peta'im*) that Jesus uses here also has a special meaning in the theology of the Essenes.[11] The hymnist says about himself, "And I will become a trap for the wicked, but a cure for all who repent of sin, for the simple to gain prudence (according to Prov 4:1; 8:5) and for a firm mind for all who are troubled in heart" (1QH 2:8).[12] The "simple" is therefore an honorable self-description of the Essenes, like the humble and spiritually poor.[13] In addition, commentaries of the sect speak of the "simple men of Judah, the doers of the law" (1 QpHab 12:4) and of the "simple men of Ephraim" (4QpNah 3:5). It is about "laymen" who are not full members of the two hostile communities: on the one hand, the Essene *yahad*, which is typologically identified with Judah; and on the other hand, the Pharisaic cooperative, which is

---

10. Sjöberg, *Der verborgene Menschensohn in den Evangelien*, 189. Sjöberg speaks of the "hidden nature of God." This is not very fortunate because Jesus was certainly not such an apocalyptic. As we shall assume later, what was hidden from the wise and discerning was the meaning of the apostles' healings and their message of the kingdom.

11. Sjöberg, *Der verborgene Menschensohn in den Evangelien*, 186.

12. See the fragment of the Essene hymnal (14:5): "To instruct the simple in the breadth of Thy power." On the honorary titles of the sect that leads our text and on the other self-descriptions, see Jacob Licht, *The Thanksgiving Scroll* (Jerusalem: Bialik Institute, 1957), 47f.

13. See Flusser, "Blessed are the Poor in Spirit," *IEJ* (1960): 1–13.

typologically called "Ephraim."[14] But at the end of time, the Essenes hope, the evil deeds of the Pharisees will be revealed to all Israel, "and many will recognize their sin and hate it and find it repulsive. . . . And when the glory of Judah the Essenes shall be revealed, the simple of Ephraim [the Pharisee community] shall flee from the midst of their community, and forsake those who do them, and join Israel" (4 QpNah 3:3–5). According to the Essene view, therefore, there is a legitimate hope for the "simple" who have been seduced by the Pharisaic heretics. Jesus was certainly not that much against the Pharisees.[15] I quoted the passage from the Nahum-Pesher because we can see from these texts that "the simple" in the opinion of the Essenes was not only an honorable self-description. Rather, this expression also meant the simple people who can be redeemed and who will recognize the truth. If the Essenes had already thought this way, then how much more are we to assume that Jesus, who left many narrow-hearted and narrow-minded people far behind him, wanted to denote his discipleship with those who are simple to whom this was revealed. Jesus certainly did not mean organized simplicity, but simplicity as a quality.

In his cry of jubilation, therefore, the real difficulty consists in a single phrase—namely, that only he knows the Father "to whom the Son wills to reveal it." This is the case with Matthew (11:27) and Luke (10:22). That may sound good and "Christian," but is it authentic to Jesus? For an Essene, such a phrase would sound quite natural. For example, the hymnist compares himself to a gardener who irrigates trees:

> By my hand you have opened its fountain with its streams. When I wave my hand to chop their trenches (the irrigation channels for the trees), they strike their roots in the pebbles. . . . But if I draw back my hand, it will be like juniper in the wilderness and its rootstock will be like weeds in salty steppe. (1QH 8:21–26)

If the Essene teacher and preacher wants to impart divine knowledge to someone, it depends on his will whether or not this happens. Can you imagine such a thought with Jesus? Although his jubilation call is conceptual and imitates an Essene hymn, did Essenism have an influence without Jesus wanting to say the same thing as an Essene proclaimer? However, we should bear in mind that Jesus' words about the son who speaks to others

---

14. See Flusser, "Pharisäer, Sadduzäer und Essener im Pesher Nahum," *Essays in Jewish History and Philology* (1970), 149f. The essay will soon be published in German in *Qumran: Wege der Forschung*, vol. 14.

15. See Flusser, *Jesus in Selbstzeugnissen und Bilddokumenten*, 50–55.

about the nature of his father should be understood as an example from everyday human life. Both his sayings about the parables and the blessed eyewitnesses (Matt 13:16f.; Luke 10:23f.) certainly exclude the possibility that Jesus wanted to teach an exclusive doctrine. We will also see that Jesus' joyful cry, his comment about the parables, and his statement about the blessed eyewitnesses form a literary unity.

First, some observations about the blessed eyewitnesses. Jesus says to Peter, "Blessed are the eyes that see what you see, and the ears that hear what you hear! Verily I say unto you, that many prophets and righteous men desired to see what ye see, and have not seen, and to hear what ye hear, and have not heard" (Matt 13:16f.; Luke 10:23). In this form, this statement is a reconstruction from both Matthew and Luke.[16] Matthew 13:16 says, "But your eyes are blessed, that they may see; and your ears, that they may hear." For literary reasons, Matthew has Jesus turn to the disciples because this follows the passage on the purpose of parables (Matt 13:10–15). This concludes in his account with Isa 6:9f., where he speaks about the hardening of people in the third person. That is why Jesus changes his personal address to Peter and now turn to the disciples. Luke is the original: not only did Jesus praise the disciples but also all who see and hear. This is similar in the pseudepigraphic Psalms of Solomon: "Blessed are they that shall live in those days, to see the benefits of the Master, which he shall do unto the generation to come" (Pss. Sol. 18:7; 17:50).[17]

Did Jesus speak to Matthew (13:17) of the righteous or to Luke (10:24) of kings? At first glance, the righteous fit better. What would kings have to do with hope for the future? But perhaps this is precisely why we might suspect that the kings in Luke 10:24 can be traced back to a mistranslation or a spelling error in the original Hebrew. For this reason, Matthew would have transformed the not very meaningful "kings" into "righteous ones." Perhaps Jesus spoke of angels (*male 'akhim*) who then became kings (*melakhim*).[18] This seems to be the solution. Jesus spoke of prophets and angels who desired to see and know, but they did not see the future salvation and did not hear. First Peter 1:10–12 says,

---

16. I suppose that the affirmation found in Matthew, "amen, I say to you," is original. Luke probably overlooked the mention of the ears. However, the ears belong here, as can be seen from the following mention of hearing, which is given to both evangelists.

17. This is an allusion to Ps 31:20: "How great is your goodness, which you have delivered to those who fear you."

18. I thank my student and friend Michael Mach for this suggestion.

The prophets who prophesied about the grace that was upon you sought and inquired about this salvation. They inquired as to what would be the time of the Spirit of Christ dwelling in them, who testified beforehand of the sufferings awaiting Christ and of the glory that would follow. Then it was revealed to them . . . what has now been preached to you by those who preached the gospel to you. . . . Things that angels desire to see.

It is to be assumed that these words from Peter's epistle are an expansive elaboration of an older saying. Contrary to Jesus' word about the blessed eyewitnesses, here the prophets foretold the future salvation. The angels, however, desire to see into these future mysteries, but they are not permitted to do so. Even the Greek word for "desire" is common to both 1 Pet 1:12 and Matt 13:7. The assumption is therefore not so erroneous that Jesus also spoke of prophets and angels, who were forbidden to see and hear what they so desired—namely, the present salvation. Then, unlike the angels, the prophets in the Epistle from Peter would have been seen by the ignoran5t. The author of Peter's letter shared the Christian conviction that the prophets are witnesses to Christ.[19] With 1 Pet 1:10–12, and even more so with the word of Jesus from the blessed eyewitnesses, the quotation from an unknown scripture in 1 Cor 2:9 is closely related:[20]

As it is written:

> "What no eye has seen,
>   and no ear has heard,
>   and what no human heart has conceived,
>   the things God has prepared for those who love him."

---

19. Regarding the kinship between Matt 13:16f. and 1 Pet 1:10–12, Bengel, *Gnomon Novi Testamenti* (Stuttgart: Steinkopf, 1891), has already dwelt on this: see 972f. However, it may be that Luke 10:24 is influenced by Isa 52:15.

20. See Alfred Resch, *Agrapha, Aussercanonische Schriftfragmente* (Darmstadt: Wissenschaftliche, 1967), 25–29, 110f. On p. 28, Resch draws attention to the relationship between 1 Cor and Luke 10:23 (Matt 13:16). He also shows (110) that both in Const. ap. 7.32, as well as in Clem. Al. Protr. 94:4, the agraphon ends with the words "And they shall rejoice in the kingdom of God." Also, in the second letter of Clement 1:7, the kingdom of God is mentioned in this context: "If we do righteousness before God, we will enter into his kingdom and receive the promises, which no ear has heard and no eye has seen, and of which no man has had a clue." I'm not sure if the conclusion originally belonged to the agraphon and Paul left it out. See also the important Jewish material quoted by Strack and Billerbeck, *Kommentar zum Neuen Testament aus Talmud und Midrasch*, vol. 3, 327–29. For the phrase "of which no man's heart knew," see Isa 3:16; 7:31; 19:5; 32:35; 44:21; 2 Kgs 12:5; Ezek 38:10; and especially Isa 65:17.

The lost scripture from which this was taken could have been a Jewish work. The basic passage is from Isa 64:4:

> Since time immemorial no one has heard,
> No ear has perceived,
> No eye has seen any God besides you,
> Who acts on behalf of those who wait for him.

Although Jesus never mentions this verse in the Gospels in the way it was understood in Judaism, it is central to Jesus' understanding of the breaking in of salvation into the world. This verse is often associated in rabbinic literature with another Bible passage, Ps 31:20:

> How abundant are the good things
> that you have stored up for those who fear you,
> that you bestow in the sight of all,
> On those who take refuge in you.[21]

The good that God keeps stored up for those who wait for him will be given to them in the future. But no eye has ever seen, and no ear has ever heard, except God, what he has prepared for those who wait for him. One day, the salvation that is hidden from all eyes and ears and known only to God will be revealed. The oldest surviving testimony to this view is found in Deut 3:26 when God said to Moses, "Enough is enough for you." In Tannaitic times, the following Midrashic commentary was given:

> God said to Moses: Much has been stored up for you; much is kept for you. "How great is your goodness, which you have delivered to those who fear you" (Ps 31:20). Furthermore, it is said: "And from ancient times it has not been heard, nor perceived by the ear, no eye has seen, O God, except for you, who works for him who waits for you" (Isa. 64:4).[22]

---

21. Cf. Lib. Ant. 26:13. Pseudo-Philon, *Les Antiquités Bibliques*, ed. D. J. Harrington, vol. 1, 210–12; vol. 2, 58; M. Philonenko, *Quod oculus non vidit*, 1 Cor 2:9, 5: "*Quod oculus non vidit nec auris audivit, et in cor hominis non ascendit.*" The mentioned apocryphal script is Jewish and was written before the destruction of the temple; there are no Christian interpolations. As can easily be seen, this is not a direct quote from Isa 64:3. Here, the first two verses are quoted from a Jewish nonbiblical quotation, the three verses of which are in 1 Cor 2:9. This seems to me to prove the Jewish origin of the quotation in 1 Cor 2:9, 21. See also note 17 above.

22. SifBam 135, ed. H. S. Horowitz (Jerusalem, 1956), 181.

Rabbi Levi said, "Come and see how great is the good that God has saved the righteous for the future. It says: 'How great is your goodness, which you have delivered to those who fear you, which you show to those who trust in you, in the sight of the children of men'" (Ps 31:20).[23] At this point, Rabbi Yohanan follows with a statement that is also handed down elsewhere in rabbinic literature: "What God has preserved for the righteous for the future, the eye cannot see and the ear cannot hear. No ear has heard, and no eye has seen, O God, except you, who doeth so for him who waiteth for you" (Isa 64:4). Not only has this interpretation of Rabbi Yohanan of Ps 31:20 and Isa 64:3 been handed down several times but this as well: "All the prophets have prophesied to us until the days of the Messiah, but as for the world to come, it is said: 'No eye has seen, O God, except you, who is acting thus for him who waits for you'" (Isa 64:4).[24] These two statements of Rabbi Johanan complement each other: The prophets prophesied only until the time of the Messiah, but no eye has seen the inbreaking of salvation and no ear has heard, not even the prophets! Concerning the apocryphal quotation in 1 Cor 2:9, it is rightly said that there is no reason to suppose that this interpretation of Isa 64:4 was not yet common in the days of the apostle Paul.[25] But does this interpretation apply to Jesus himself?

An Essene author said, "God told Habakkuk to write down what will happen to the last generation, but he did not tell him the end of time." To the teacher of righteousness, on the other hand, according to the same author, God "made known all the secrets of the words of his servants the prophets" (1QpHab 7:1–5). While this is not exactly what the rabbis and Jesus meant, the common view is that the prophets prophesied to the last generation, but the completion of the time was not made known to them.

According to the early rabbinic view, Moses did not know the details of the future salvation. According to a Tannaitic midrash,

> The Israelites said to Moses, "Our teacher Moses, tell us what good things God will give us in the future." And he said unto them, "I know not what to say unto you. Look to what has been prepared for you. To that belongs a parable: A man gave his son to an educator. He walked around with him and showed him

---

23. SifDev 13:25, ed. S. Buber, 73.

24. References at Strack and Billerbeck, *Kommentar zum Neuen Testament aus Talmud und Midrasch*, vol. 3, 327–29; and Bacher, *Die Agada der Palästinischen Amoräer*, vol. 1, 336.

25. Strack and Billerbeck, *Kommentar zum Neuen Testament aus Talmud und Midrasch*, vol. 2, 329.

everything. And he said unto him, 'All these trees are thine, all these branches are thine, all these olive trees are thine.' When he was tired of showing, he said to him, 'Look, what has been prepared for you!'" Moses also said to Israel, "I do not know what to say to you. Look to what has been prepared for you." "How great is the good that God has saved for those who fear him" (Ps 31:20).[26]

Moses' ignorance is put into perspective by this parable. It is not absolute ignorance but still one limited to the Israelites. On the other hand, it is not said in the parable that Moses knew about future salvation.

That the apocryphal quotation in 1 Cor 2:9 and 1 Pet 1:10–12 belongs in this context seems to me to be self-evident. From the First Letter of Peter, we learn that the prophets sought to learn about the coming grace and that angels desired to see into this mystery. Jesus said that many prophets—and perhaps also the angels—"desire to see what you see, and have not seen, and to hear what you hear, and have not heard." "Blessed are the eyes that see, and the ears that hear," since salvation is now present (cf. Matt 13:16f.; Luke 10:23f.). How can we not think of the rabbinic interpretation of the word of the prophet: "And from ancient times no one has heard, nor ear perceived, no eye has seen, O God, except you, who act thus for him who waits for him" (Isa 64:4). The prophets, the rabbis said, prophesied only until the time of the Messiah, but they did not see salvation in the future.

Didn't Jesus say the same thing elsewhere? John the Baptist had sent two of his disciples to Jesus to ask him, "Are you the one who is coming, or shall we wait for another?" Jesus said to them, "Tell him what you hear and what you see. Blessed is he who is not wrong about me!" And then Jesus began to speak to the crowd about John and how John is more than a prophet:

> "Truly I say unto you, among them that are born of women, none is equal to John: but the least in the kingdom of heaven is greater than he. From John until now, the kingdom of heaven is breaking through, and the in-breakers are tearing it down. For all the prophets prophesied[27] until John, and if you will receive it, he is Elijah, who is to come." (Matt 11:2–15; Luke 7:8–23)

---

26. SifDev 352, ed. Finkelstein, 429. On Jacob's forgetting of the eschatological secrets before his death, see L. Louis Ginzberg, *The Legends of the Jews*, vol. 2 (Philadelphia, 1947), 140; and vol. 5, 336f. The end times are also hidden for other reasons, people, and angels, but I have touched only on the aspect that concerns us now.

27. Here in the source (Matt 11:13; Luke 16:16), "and the law" is inserted. "The Law and the Prophets" means "the Old Testament" both in the Gospels and accord-

Here, too, there is talk of hearing and seeing—of hearing and seeing the mighty deeds of Jesus: "If I cast out demons with God's finger, the kingdom of God has already come upon you" (Luke 11:20). And here, too, we read that the prophets prophesied only until John and that after John, the kingdom of heaven will break through. So, we are grounded on Jewish thought, which Jesus creatively transformed from his experience.

Did Jesus praise the eyes that now see and the ears that now hear only because they have been given what was forbidden to the prophets, or did he only want to praise those who also correctly grasp the meaning of what they see and hear? For although the salvation that the prophets—and among them the last and greatest, John the Baptist—had desired in vain is now present, and although the kingdom of God is now breaking through, it must only now grow like a mustard seed from small beginnings and include more and more people. It must be proclaimed by royal messengers. The harvest is great, but the laborers are few (Matt 9:37; Luke 10:2). That is why not only the saying of the blessed eyewitnesses (Matt 13:16f.) is in place here but also the saying about the parables (Matt 13:11–13 par.). In Jesus' parable, there is also the distinction between those who are given to understand the mysteries of God and those to whom one must speak in parables in order that they may understand them. That is why Jesus' cry of jubilation (Matt 11:25–27; Luke 10:21–22) speaks of the wise and intelligent and the simple, as well as of the Father and of the Son who reveals the essence of the Father to others.

After these detours, we can now return to the saying of the purpose of the parable. I explained above that Mark 4:10 is secondary to Luke 8:9 and that Matt 13:10 depends on Mark. But it turns out that here Matthew used the original report in addition to Mark. Matthew has "the disciples" in common with Luke, which are missing in Mark 4:10. The question of the disciples was, "What is the parable?" (Luke 8:9b). In Luke 8:11a, "The parable is" follows this question seamlessly. Both the question and the answer resemble good Hebrew. The disciples rightly asked about the meaning of the parable of the sower, and Jesus also rightly gave them his interpretation. The parable needs an explanation to be properly understood. The pre-Lukan

---

ing to Jewish parlance. That is how this inserted comment should be understood. At this point, however, the law does not belong to the matter. The fact that it was inserted later can also be seen from this because it is only in second place (after the prophets). I am also not happy with the words "so far" in Matt 11:12. Without them, the saying would sound better. Perhaps the inserted words originated because of the "until the days of John the Baptist." I write "to John" according to Luke 16:16. See Flusser, *Jesus in Selbstzeugnissen und Bilddokumenten*, 35–40.

editor took the opportunity to have Jesus say a word in principle about the purpose of his parables because the disciples had asked for the meaning of the parable. The editor tore the words out of their original context and edited them in the sense of the hardening motif. Matthew (13:13) did the same with reference to Isa 6:9f. The fact that Jesus himself alluded to the hardening motif seems to me to arise from the Matthean context. However, the pre-Lukan editor did not want to accept that Jesus only touched on Isa 6:9f. in an untheological, nonprincipled sense—in a playful way, as it were. The stylistically adorned allusion to Bible passages was also common in Judaism. For the most part, rabbis were not concerned with the original weight of a biblical saying. They were not historical-critical Bible writers. But because the words from Isaiah (6:9f.) became particularly important in primitive Christianity because of the alleged anti-Christian hardening of the Jews and because the word *parable* was then interpreted as a mysterious way of speaking, the pre-Lukan editor interpreted the words of Isaiah in an almost principled sense.

The Lukan blunt motif is reinforced by Mark (4:10–12). There is no evidence that Mark knew any other source besides Luke 8:9f. Luke is therefore not original here, yet more original than Mark. This fact is important for our pericopes. In this way, we can decide which was the original reading of Luke. This correct reading will clarify the content of Jesus' words. In most of the manuscripts, we read in Luke 8:10, "It is given to you to know the mysteries of the kingdom of God." But the word *kingdom* is missing in some manuscripts. It is also missing in the quotation from the church father Eusebius, who had the excellent library of Caesarea at his disposal so his reading style is therefore important.[28] It is easy to understand why other manuscripts have inserted "the kingdom." Such is the case with Mark 4:11. Each copyist was tempted to believe that these words from the original had been carelessly left out. It is a miracle that we possess any witnesses at all who did not allow themselves to be confused by the wrong reading! The expression "of the kingdom" slipped into most of Luke's manuscripts by a contamination from Mark. Matthew, for his part, is influenced by Mark when he writes, "You have been given to know the mysteries of the kingdom of heaven." In fact, Matthew often preserves the reading "kingdom of heaven." He is so accustomed to this turn of phrase that here he adapts the kingdom of God in Mark 4:11 to an expression belonging to Jesus. Again,

---

28. Another example of the weight of the manner of reading of Eusebius is given in Flusser, "The Conclusion of Matthew," *ASTI* 5 (1967): 110–20.

Matthew is committed to Mark on the one hand and to the original account on the other. Mark 4:11 says, "To you is given the mystery of the kingdom of God." Compared to Matthew and Luke, therefore, he omits "recognize" and changes the good Hebrew plural "secrets" into the singular "mystery," which is possible in Hebrew but more difficult. It sounds easier in Greek. The omission of "recognize" is intended by Mark. Behind Jesus' words, Mark suspected that Jesus wanted to announce to his chosen disciples that the kingdom had been given to them. That's why he added the word *kingdom*. The knowledge of any secrets was insignificant to him.[29]

Mark thought, then, that Jesus had given the mysteries of the kingdom to his elect, but we read of this mystery of the kingdom of God only here, and such an idea is even contrary to Jesus' philosophy, but we have already talked about this. Jesus publicly proclaims the kingdom and offers it to all through his messengers; his kingdom is certainly not shrouded in mystery.[30] But if, according to the better text of Luke, we read of the mysteries of God that are made known to Jesus' disciples, then the word of Jesus becomes meaningful. The term "mysteries of God" (*raze 'el*) is typical of the Essene world of ideas.[31] This is not difficult to understand because Jesus' utterance, of which his comment about the essence of the parables is only the middle link, partly breathes an Essene spirit.

In addition to the "mysteries of God," the Essenes also speak of his "wonderful mysteries." The Essene teacher has the duty to "guide the members

---

29. That such a conception existed in primitive Christianity is shown by the secondary Lukan verse in Luke 12:32, which is lacking in the parallel with Matthew: "Do not be afraid, little flock! For it pleased your Father to give you the kingdom." However, as the continuation shows, this is not about the present kingdom but about future salvation; cf. also Luke 22:29.

30. A friend, sadly deceased, intended to write a book about the parables of Jesus. He proceeded from our pericope in its Markan version and wished to show that Jesus' parables have little to do with rabbinic parables for they speak in a veiled sense of the mystery of the kingdom of God connected with the mystery of the figure of Jesus. It was a pity that this friend was not allowed to write the book! It would certainly have been successful and would have provoked a debate that is bitterly needed. Erasmus once wrote that a man will not be condemned by God if he has made a mistake, but God does not like mistakes. I think Erasmus is right. But it also seems to me that there is hardly any error—especially in the Holy Scriptures—which would not necessarily produce new errors, even if the original error arose out of carelessness. This is even more true if the error arose from a prejudice. That is why the *Erasmian bonae jitterae* are so necessary today!

31. See 1QpHab 7:8; 1QS 3:23; 1QM 3:7; 16:11, 16; and see Yadin's last comment. Cf. also Ethiopic Enoch 63:3.

of the union into knowledge and also to teach insight into the true, wonderful mysteries" (IQS 9:18). The Essene hymnwriter praises God: "You set me as a sign for the elect of righteousness and as an interpreter of knowledge in wonderful mysteries" (IQH 2:13). Jesus certainly did not mean it so haughtily and so esoterically when he said to his disciples, "It is given to you to know the secrets of God," although apparently the Essene way of thinking discolored something. Much depends on our understanding of the words "you have been given."[32] Jesus apparently does not speak here of an esoteric determination of God's grace, which gives the true gnosis to the disciples. He wants to say to the disciples that through his life and in his words and deeds, the mysteries of God have become tangible,[33] while he must speak to the others in parables so that they may understand. To the disciples, he revealed the nature of his heavenly Father. Only so far can he be compared to an Essene teacher and revelator.

We have already seen that Jesus' original saying about the nature of the parables in Matt 13:11 and 13 is well preserved. The framework in Matt 13:10 is a secondary formation influenced by Mark 4:10, and Matt 13:12 does not belong to the topic.[34] In the saying itself (Matt 13:11), under the influence of Mark 4:11, the kingdom of heaven is mentioned; otherwise, Jesus' words remained intact with Matthew.[35] How can we explain this unusual fact of such a small influence of Mark on Matthew?[36] The correct explanation for this is that there is a source of sayings that both Matthew and Luke knew and used. Either Mark knew the piece only from the Lukan adaptation or he took it from the Lukan context. Matthew is influenced by Mark only in one point. The pre-Lukan editor took Jesus' saying about the purpose of the parable out of its original context and put it between the parable of the sower and its interpretation because the disciples at that time

---

32. Perhaps Jesus here alludes to Deut 29:3: "But the Master has not given you heart to know, and eyes to see, and ears to hear, until this day." The relationship with our pericopes is obvious.

33. See Heinz Schürmann, *Das Lukasevangelium*, vol. 1 (Freiburg, 1969), 461.

34. See chapter 10, note 55, above.

35. Perhaps we should not read in Matt 13:11 "To them it is not given" but "To the rest it is not given"; see Luke 8:10.

36. Schürmann, *Das Lukasevangelium*, 461, writes. "The surprising differences common to Luke and Matthew are hardly all accidental, but can hardly be explained with certainty in their conclusion. . . . One might be tempted to assume that Luke and Matthew read a common source." See also the bibliographic information there.

asked their master for the meaning of the parable. The editor thought this would be the right opportunity to have Jesus teach his disciples about the purpose of parables.

Can we still determine today the original place of Jesus' saying on the nature of parables in the sayings source? The answer must be positive and should also be able to explain to us why the saying in Matthew is hardly influenced by Mark. Matthew has constrained the saying under Mark's influence between the parable and his interpretation. Although he hardly changed the wording of the source of the saying, he was so impressed by the motif of Mark's hardening that at the end (Matt 13:14ff.) he added the Isaiah saying (Isa 6:9ff) in the form in which it occurs in the Greek Bible because he apparently noticed that the motif of hardening was missing in the sayings source.[37] Thus, although Matthew accepted the Markan order, he copied—with a slight deviation—the sayings source (Matt 13:1–13). According to the Greek quotation from Isaiah, he again follows it (Matt 13:1–6f.). So, the saying about the blessed eyewitnesses in the sayings source is the continuation of Jesus' words about the nature of the parables.

Can we still know what came before the saying about the purpose of the parables in the sayings source? To do this, we need to turn to Luke. There (Luke 10:23f.), the saying about the blessed eyewitnesses follows Jesus' joyful cry (Luke 10:21). We have just seen from Matthew that Jesus' word concerning the nature of the parables in the sayings source was in place prior to the word concerning the blessed eyewitnesses. From this follows the following connection in the source of the saying: the cry of jubilation (Matt 11:25–27; Luke 10:21),[38] the purpose of the parables (Matt 13:11 and 13 par.), and the blessed eyewitnesses (Matt 13:16f.; Luke 10:23). Luke does not put the second part of the triptychs in its original place. Rather, he tears it out of its natural context and places it between the parable of the sower and its interpretation. Matthew, however, knew from his source the correct sequence.

Was this tedious source-critical investigation worthwhile? Have we learned anything from this about the nature of the parables of Jesus? I am sure that we now not only know more about the parables but that we have

---

37. Concerning the word of Isaiah in Matt 13:14, see Stendahl, *The School of St. Matthew*, 130f. Stendahl tries to explain the purely Greek form of the quotation from Isaiah by adopting a post-Matthaean interpolation.

38. This connection would disrupt the call of salvation (Matt 11:28–30). The call of salvation was an independent saying, which is missing in Luke 21. See also note 2 above.

also gained a great deal of knowledge about Jesus' proclamation and his self-conception. This is not trivial. I also think that with a little goodwill, we can see that the whole saying is made of one piece and not composed of three different components by the sayings source. Jesus spoke the words on a single occasion, and when we listen to the saying, we notice the fourth dimension, which is inherent in many of Jesus' sayings. But let us listen to the word of Jesus himself:

> "I thank Thee, Father, Master of heaven and earth, that Thou hast hid these things from the wise and prudent, and hast revealed them to the simple. Yes, Father, for so was the will before You. Everything is given to me by my Father, and no one knows the Son except the Father, and no one knows the Father except the Son, and to whom the Son wishes to reveal himself.

> "To you it is given to know the mysteries of God, but to them it is not given. That is why I speak to them in parables, because they see—and yet do not see and hear—and still do not understand. Blessed are the eyes that see what you see and the ears that hear what you hear. Truly I say to you: Many prophets and righteous ones [or angels] longed to see what you see and have not seen it and to hear what you hear and have not heard it."

Although I wrote the whole saying in brief lines, I don't want to give the impression that the whole thing was pure poetry. The hymnal exultation, which is an imitation of the Essene hymns, is certainly a poem. The rest is also poetic, yet we should not forget that not only is the Hebrew prose of the Old Testament rhythmic, but it is rabbinic prose as well. Often there are series of parallel sentences in it, so that it is sometimes hardly possible to distinguish between poetic prose and pure poetry. Since Jesus began his statement about the revelation of God in the present with a poetic hymn, it is natural that the continuation is also strongly rhythmic and poetic. And another thing: Because of the poetic form, it will hopefully be difficult for doubters to deny the sublime word about the revelation of God through Jesus.

Can we at least try to guess on what occasion Jesus said this word of rejoicing? Matthew follows the cry of jubilation and the woe over the Galilean cities (Matt 11:20–24), and it is not much different with Luke, where between the cry of woe (Luke 10:13–16) and the cry of jubilation, there is only the passage about the return of the seventy (Luke 10:17–20). The cry of woe about the cities and the shout of joy were thus not far apart from each other in the sayings source. But this opportunity for the saying about revelation does not seem to me to be very appropriate. The saying better fits the moment when the apostles returned from the journey with joy and Jesus said to them, "I saw Satan fall like lightning from heaven" (Luke 10:18). If Jesus said the great word after the return of his messengers, then it can be explained what he meant by what is hidden from the wise and learned and revealed to the simple: namely, the meaning of the healings of the apostles and their proclamation of the kingdom. This also corresponds to the further content of the saying. But that remains a guess.

Musically speaking, the whole saying is magnificently composed and characterized by variations on some motifs in different formations and keys. Jesus works particularly artfully with the disciple motif. First, he works out a contrast between the wise and the intelligent contrapuntally. But the simple are certainly broader to grasp than the disciples of Jesus. We are already closer to the pure disciple motif when we hear of those to whom the Son wants to reveal the essence of his Father, and only immediately afterward does the disciple motif sound in its pure form when Jesus says, "You are given to know the mysteries of God." The influence of the Essene apocalypticism, by which the cry of rejoicing was formed, also extends to the concise term "the mysteries of God." From apocalyptic Essenism is also to be understood the second leitmotif: the revealing and the hiding, the knowing and the not knowing, the seeing and the not seeing, the hearing and the not hearing, the recognizing and the not understanding. This second main motif varies during the saying, and Jesus gradually passes—which we saw already in his words about the parables—from the essential sphere into the thought world of rabbinism. To the disciples of Jesus are revealed the mysteries of God. But those to whom this knowledge is not given are certainly not the same as those from whom God hides his knowledge, for Jesus speaks to them in parables, because otherwise they would not understand. Their failure to see and to hear is not a result of a hiddenness willed by God, but it is the simple people to whom Jesus did not impart the mysteries of God. Although they are somehow simple, they have nothing to do with the privileged simple to whom God has revealed his essence.

However, both groups—the disciples and the unspecified simple—understood that salvation is already present and that the prophets endeavored in vain to see and hear it. The word of revelation—the triptych—begins with Jesus' shout of joy and thanksgiving to the Heavenly Father and ends triumphantly with Jesus' praise for those who hear and see the kingdom of God that they have longed for from the beginning and that is now revealed. To move from the musical sphere to the visual sphere: here, too—I already noted this above—we see how masterfully Jesus continuously shifts his camera to give a panoramic view. Even before the eye of the dissecting and reconstructing researcher, a partial view arises first of its own accord followed by a multidimensional image of meaning.

I already explained that Jesus' saying about the essence of the parables is neither related to the parable of the sower nor is it an answer to disciples' question. Rather, it is an organic part of Jesus' saying about revelation. Jesus explains to his disciples why he speaks in parables to those who have not been given the understanding of the mysteries of God. If he did not, then they would not understand his teaching. The word is therefore not to be characterized as a saying about hardening but that Jesus wanted to communicate his pedagogical method with them. Like the rabbis, he deliberately used parables as a vivid guide to make it easier for the simple person. We understand Jesus' parables correctly only if we regard them as belonging to the genre of rabbinic parables. From Jesus' word about the purpose of the parables, we learn that Jesus told parables for the same reasons as the rabbis.

12

THE EPIC STYLE OF JESUS' PARABLES

We have come a long way with many surprises. Our path led us from different lookout points to the essence of the parables of Jesus and the rabbis. Jesus' parables are a testimony, a representation of the literary genre of rabbinic parables. Hence the assumption arises, as if by itself, that Jesus' epic presentation of his parables in the Gospels must have been similar to that of the rabbis. In this final chapter, we will now verify this assumption, as this can assist us in our efforts to advance to the original wording of Jesus' parables. In this context, it is advisable to conduct genre research in the right way: that is, to also compare the genre of parables within the field of epic style with similar minor literary minor of world literature. Unfortunately, I can only do preliminary work here, because so far there are hardly any satisfactory works on the stylistics of ancient rabbinic literature. Even a superficial observer will soon realize that there was a conscious poetics behind ancient rabbinic oral literature according to which they communicated in a fixed oral and then written transmission. From this point of view, rabbinic literature belongs to genres like original oral folk literature. Since parables—like comedies, exempla, fables, anecdotes, and folk tales—are not reports of actual events but fictitious inventions, literary design is more pronounced in them than in factual reports. On the other hand, rabbinic parables—as also Jesus' parables—belong to the externally unadorned rabbinic prose, which of course did not lack a master builder's grace. Rabbinic parables—and rabbinic animal fables—stand out from other rabbinic prose by the fact that they were deliberately conceived as artworks of fiction. An examination of those artistic laws of rabbinic parables that are common to other rabbinic forms, and of those that distinguish them from other rabbinic genera, would also benefit Jesus' parables. But such an investigation is still pending.

According to modern New Testament research, however, the question of the original style of Jesus' parables would have to be considered hopeless. For it is almost universally thought that Jesus' words have been thoroughly altered through the kerygma of the Christian community, which also applies to his parables. On the other hand, I am of the firm opinion, together with researcher friends of mine, that it is possible to penetrate quite far into the original wording of Jesus' proclamation: that is, when we apply the usual literary-critical method to the text of the Synoptic Gospels, and when we are also able and willing to be guided by knowledge from within the Jewish field. We admit that Jesus' words, including his parables, were first edited by Greek editors and then by the evangelists. But we also think that with the help of a better Synoptic theory, it can often be possible for us to distinguish the core from the shell. The result of such an approach is then actually always confirmed by our knowledge of the Hebrew language of the time of Jesus and of Judaism at that time. The parables of Jesus belong—as I already emphasized—to the genre of rabbinic parables. Therefore, valid statements can be made not only about the essence but also about the poetics of Jesus' parables only if we have dealt with the essence and the literary form of rabbinic parables.

The question we are now dealing with belongs to the field of aesthetics. Aesthetics, however, is not just a descriptive science; value judgments are also inherent within it. Otherwise, it cannot do its job. In my opinion, we cannot understand art if we try to explain it from a misunderstood addiction to sterile objectivity prior to asking the question of whether and to what extent a work of art achieves the tendency immanent within it toward a possibly perfect aesthetic realization. In other words, the question of how far a work of art succeeds is not only legitimate but also necessary if we want to talk about art. Unfortunately, it seems to me that today many modern researchers only want to be literary proponents but not judges of art. They are often shameful aestheticians at best and do not want to use the standards according to which we can decide what is aesthetically better and what is worse. Their ancient colleagues did not think so, nor did the art critics of the eighteenth century. Hopefully, my view does not lead anyone astray that today we often are beginning to overcome this realistic and positivistic paralysis. The works of Shklovsky and Lüthi, which helped me at the beginning of this book in assessing Jesus' parables, seem to provide me with proof of this. Their methods, as well as the results of Lessing's investigations, can also help us to reflect on the characteristics of the presentation of parables and similar folk forms, such as European fairy tales, comedies, animal fables, and anecdotes. The question of the optimal style of parables is also not only justified regarding Jesus' parables, but it is also urgent. The man Jesus was an excellent storyteller. That is why his parables had such a lasting effect on his listeners. His listeners appreciated them and handed them down to us.

The narrative style of the parables is poetic but outwardly unadorned. As a contrast to this, I will first look at a random example of modern art prose:

> A man ran through in front of us without looking around. His bright blue tracksuit glowed under the covered trees. He ran clumsily, but regularly, as on a rail, through the midst of the thicket. . . . After a few steps we were faced with a wet sawdust trail. Then the blue figure emerged beyond the clearing and pushed his elbows back and forth. The clearing was a sports facility, in the middle of the forest, a regular spot of well-kept green, around which ran a red track with white stripes. . . . The staff who moved here were young and colorful, light blue, ochre yellow, red in all shades, most often red: wine red, scarlet, purple, blood red.[1]

I certainly do not want to deny this play of colors its certain appeal, especially for readers who are used to such a diet, but such descriptions are lacking in both rabbinic parables and Jesus' parables. We are not told anything about the physical nature of the heroes in them, unless it is important for the action. There are also no descriptions of nature and no local flavor. Size and color are mentioned only if they are functional for the parable. The man in the parable, for example, looks for beautiful pearls and finds a precious pearl at the end. We must know this to understand why he sells everything to acquire this pearl (Matt 13:45).[2] In various parables, some are called wise and others are called foolish: for example, in Jesus' parable of the ten virgins (Matt 25:11–13). The parable is excellently told, and it is also very memorable and inspires the listener's imagination. We think we can hear the nocturnal call and see the torchlight procession, although in the parable there are no descriptions whatsoever. This is because Jesus knows how to tell the story in such an exciting way that his listeners are carried away. They listen to the successful story and at the same time become aware of the

---

1. "Another Wish," narrated by Adolf Muschg, 13. Continued in *Neuer Zürcher Zeitung*, no. 192 (August 1979). The story will be published by Suhrkamp-Verlag. The author was born on May 13, 1934, in Zollikon near Zurich.

2. Again, in this regard, Mark is secondary to Luke. In the parable of the cloth, Mark 2:21 (cf. Matt 9:16) speaks of a piece of uncoated cloth. Surely, he was thinking something about it. Luke says only that the garment was new (Luke 5:36). The contrast of old/new is there with Luke, as in the following picture of the wineskins. This contrast is a component of the subject in the parable picture. Did Mark have a penchant for the handiwork of a tailor? In his description of the transfiguration, only he (Mark 9:3) says that the garments of Jesus became quite dazzling "as no bleach on earth can make them so white."

teaching that Jesus wants to teach through this parable. If necessary, Jesus helps them with an additional hint or explanation.

Other ancient Hebrew accounts that lie beneath the Gospels were also poor in such descriptions since they were not necessary for the action. This applies both to the words of Jesus himself and to the events reported. The old accounts were less ornamental in this respect than the Synoptic Gospels we are discussing. Experience has taught me that in Luke, we find the least dramatic and unnecessarily embellishing elements. These few aesthetically disturbing factors are perhaps all the work of the pre-Lukan editor. Mark multiplies and increases such dramatizations and exaggerations, which Matthew sometimes takes from him. But sometimes they are too colorful for Matthew, and he leaves them out.[3] The relatively unadorned prose in which the Hebrew sources of the Gospels were written is certainly closely related to the unadorned, compact prose of rabbinic literature of that time.[4]

---

3. So that I may be understood, I will provide some examples. In the story of the healing of the withered hand, we read: "And looking at them all around, he said to him . . ." (Luke 6:10). This verse is a work of the pre-Lukan editor. The words are missing from Matthew, who is committed to an excellent source. Mark, on the other hand, depends on Luke at this point, but he increases the dramatization unbearably: "And looking at them all around with anger, saddened by the obstinacy of their hearts, he said to the people. . ." (Mark 3:5). Another example: What could we want to read out of the "green grass" in Mark 6:39! This is based on an eyewitness. You can even determine the exact time of the year in which the miracle happened! Furthermore, it is very likely that Jesus embraced the children and blessed them by laying his hands on them (Mark 10:16; cf. Matt 19:15). But it is missing in Luke and was added by Mark in Greek. It is also interesting that we read only about the capture of Jesus at Luke 22:47 and how at that time Judas approached Jesus to kiss him—so the kiss of Judas did not have to be explicitly mentioned. From an inappropriate *horror vacui*, Mark 14:45 (cf. Matt 26:49) writes, "And when he came, he immediately approached him and said: 'Rabbi!' and kissed him." Incidentally, Mark 14:44 (Matt 26:48) is also an explanatory addition designed by Mark in Greek.

4. Rabbinic parables are a part of rabbinic prose, which is a result of Jewish oral teaching and instruction. Compare the concentrated simplicity of rabbinic prose with the treatment that J. G. Herder gave to the "Jewish poems and fables" from rabbinic literature! In two volumes of the *Teutscher Merkur*, which came out in the year of Lessing's death (1781), twenty-two of these "poems from the Oriental saga" were first printed. A third collection appeared in 1887. This collection was printed in 1936 in the library of the Schocken Verlag (Berlin) under the title *Blätter der Vorzeit: Dichtungen aus der morgenländischen Sage (Jüdische Dichtungen und Fabeln)*. It would be worth comparing all the originals with Herder's edits. I bring here only a small characteristic example of Herder's new style—namely, the beginning of the story "Lust und Liebe" (Schocken, 12f.): "In the beginning

Whether this fact is related to the fact that by its very nature, oral literature is often more straightforward than written art prose, or whether the relative unadornment of both rabbinic prose and Hebrew sources of the Gospels can also be explained by the fact that in both cases these are factual accounts, would have to be examined in more detail. But while we note this, Jesus' parables were very likely no poorer in descriptive embellishments than what is otherwise reported about his deeds and words. This also applies to the style of rabbinic parables in comparison with other rabbinic genera. On the other hand, we can easily see that the exempla of Jesus, such as the story of poor Lazarus or of the Pharisee and the tax collector, are richer in dramatic embellishments than the parables because here stories are told. However, we must not forget that while parables are poor in embellishments, at the same time their manner of presentation was designed out of a conscious will to create art.

In the approximate description of the historical framework in which the style of Jewish parables developed, we have come across the purely aesthetic problem of the causal connection between the way the parables are presented and the optimal style of related literary genres. The question is not as simple as it seems at first glance. We can raise two objections against the art critics, such as Lessing and Lüthi. First, the question is justified as to whether there can even be an optimal style for a literary genre. Second, the question was raised as to whether the outwardly simple style of certain oral genres did not sometimes arise from the fact that their later written texts no longer actually reproduced the full oral wording but, so to speak, merely

---

everything was desolate and empty, a cold abyss of the sea; the elements of things were wildly confused. Then the breath of life blew from the mouth of the Eternal and broke chains of ice and stirred the warming mother wings gently like a resounding dove. In the dark depths everything was stirring now, pushing for birth. Then appeared the firstborn, the delightful light. The hollow light united with the mother-love which hovered over the waters; they swung up to the sky and wove the golden blue; they drove down to the depths and filled them with larvae; they carried up the earth, an altar of God, sprinkling them with ever-young flowers; they animated the smallest dust." Herder approached not only biblical legends with his poetics but also rabbinic parables. The latter, however, resisted Herder's unfolding more successfully than the just quoted biblical genealogical text. Two "Schillerized" (for readers unfamiliar with German literature, this would be like saying "Shakespearized") rabbinic parables are printed in the Schocken volume: The day before death (81f.) and in this book in chapter 1, note 4. The wages of the future world (Schocken, 83f.); see Ziegler, *Die Koenigsgleichnisse des Midrasch beleuchtet durch die roemische Kaiserzeit*, chapter 7, parable 15.

a simplified statement of content. Such a simplification, it is said, can happen with a narrator from whose mouth we recognize a fairy tale or similar
genre, if this narrator did not memorize the wording of the story. This is
certainly true to a certain extent for European folktales. In the Germany of
the Brothers Grimm, people did not memorize fairy tales with their actual
wording, as is still customary among other peoples and regions today. Many
years ago, I helped write Aramaic fairy tales from the oral culture of Kurd-
ish Jews. These storytellers didn't just know the content of these epic fairy
tales; they also knew the actual wording by heart. If we did not understand
something, then they repeated the sentences almost verbatim at our request.
The simple style of European fairy tales can therefore be partly explained by
the fact that those who passed them along did not memorize them word for
word. One researcher even found that some Russian fairy tales learned from
the oral culture of the people contain descriptions that can be explained as
decayed cultural artifacts from what was originally a courtly style. If this
researcher wants to cite this as proof that other European fairy tales lost
their ornamentation due to the loss of narrative culture in Western Europe,
then he has, in my opinion, spoken about himself without wishing to do so.
For if the descriptions of the Russian fairy tales are a diminished cultural
artifact, then they may also be a secondary adaptation to the style of higher
social classes.

I have heard another explanation of why European fairy tales are told
in a simple style: narrators were indirectly influenced by the pragmatic,
journalistic nature of Italian novels. Such theses and theories may have
something true in them, but they do not hit the core of the problem. In the
case of comedies, parables, fables, exempla, and European fairy tales, their
simple, relatively unadorned form corresponds to the content and purpose
of the genre. It is true that Asian fairy tales, unlike European fairy tales, are
sometimes much more decorated. But not always. We also do not compare
Western fairy tales with Eastern fairy tales. (The latter, by the way, are a
variant, at least from a literary-critical point of view.) Nor do we want to
examine the question of how the European folk tale came into being when
it reached its end and its formative literary laws were fully formed. Likewise,
the question of the possible influence of elements from other literary genres
can remain aside. As the possible parents and ancestors of the European
fairy tale, the aesthetics of the genre should be of little concern. This is part
of the historical research of folklore. In aesthetic research, literary-historical
circumstances must be considered, but they must not become dominant.
Even if, for example, it is not ruled out that the simple, stereotypical epic

rigidity and relative lack of ornamentation of European folk tales arose only secondarily, who could and should judge the strict legality if the rigorously epic is so excellently exposed as a form of decay? Doesn't a pebble have a perfect shape even if it was created by abrasion?

Perhaps, then, the unadorned nature of the European folktale is a result of its development, influenced by Westerners' inability to memorize and pass on an oral text verbally. This does not apply to rabbinic parables. Their unadorned narrative is primary. We must not forget that, unlike modern Europeans, the culture of ancient rabbinism has always been an oral tradition in form. The Jews, then, must have been masters of memorization if they were to receive and transmit doctrine. They also memorized the wording of the parables with the help of a pronounced mnemonic technique. This laid a solid foundation for a fairly faithful later written tradition. Like the rest of oral rabbinic doctrine, the style of parables had to be such that they could be kept in their wording. In addition to the internal nature of the genre, this circumstance also resulted in the simple style of the parables. Jesus' disciples were ancient Jews to whom it was self-evident that they must endeavor to pass along the words of the master as he spoke them. They were also convinced that their salvation related to the words of the master. The amount of time between the day Jesus spoke the words and when they were written in Hebrew is much shorter than the time between a rabbinic utterance and writing. How, then, can we explain that the parables and other words of Jesus are preserved in the Gospels in such varied forms and that they often betray Greek—not Hebrew—diction? The question contains the answer: These sometimes significant changes were mainly caused by the radical change of the milieu. I say with exaggeration that Jesus' words express the *faith of Jesus*, while the main purpose of the Gospels is to proclaim *faith in Jesus*. My inexact statement here tends to make the change of atmosphere clear. In addition, it must not be forgotten that the translators, the editors, and finally the evangelists spoke Greek and that, because of their situation in a different kind of civilization, they were not skilled in the art of standing as faithful servants in the stream of an oral tradition. Because they were far removed from the "rabbinic" milieu of Jesus and his disciples, they hardly knew any other Jewish parables besides Jesus' parables. It is even questionable whether most of them knew of the existence of other Jewish parables apart from Jesus' parables and were not aware of the stylistic laws of a parable. From all this, it becomes clear why Jesus' parables have often come to us in such a highly edited form. To advance to the original discourses of the parable narrator Jesus, we should not only work synoptically but we should also always bear in mind rabbinic parables. These have preserved the original wording and the peculiarity of the genre very well, even though they were written down quite late. In their case, no change of milieu took place and the stream of tradition was not interrupted. The rabbinic collectors who secured the Jewish parables in writing knew the peculiarities of rabbinic parables because they had many before them and because they lived within the rabbinic environment in which parables were still told—just as in the past. Therefore, even the "editorial" changes they introduced correspond to the spirit of the rabbinic parable genre. It is therefore a stroke of luck that we also know rabbinic parables in addition to Jesus' parables. For our present purpose, it is significant that the simple style of rabbinic parables is not a consequence of development but has always been ingrained in them—perhaps in contrast to fairy tales.

Max Lüthi writes:

> Mass and moderation determine the construction of the European folk tale— also the one kind of economy, a housekeeping bypass in the sense of a power- fully goal-conscious formation. . . . Growing pleasure in making comparisons, poetic metaphors, so-called poetic decorations in general are far from the narrator of folk tales. This partly arises from a lack of talent; it nevertheless benefits the narrative; it is, within its framework, stylish.[5]

European folk tales have in common with the already mentioned oral folk genres the simplicity of narrative style. As with other genres, the simple form is not a coincidence but is, so to speak, adapted to its inner shape. Something else seems to have played a role in European folk tales: their rigid-looking structure seems to have crystallized through a process. In any case, they often look like a surrealistic lunar landscape to which the simple style fits excellently.[6] Unlike fairy tales, parables simulate reality and logic.

---

5. Lüthi, *The European Folktale*, 126 cf., on the other hand: *Es war einmal* (Göttingen: Vandenhoeck & Ruprecht, 1968), 33–35. Among other things, what Lüthi says in *Es war einmal*, 34, is important for our purpose: "When the Brothers Grimm report on the long, crooked nose or red eyes of a witch, it is usually their own ingredient. The real folktale says only: an ugly witch, or an old one."

6. It should also be kept in mind that the style of European folktales may somehow also be related to the way in which epic prose was written in medieval Europe. In this case, the already mentioned Italian novels of the Renaissance, in their simple style, would be only a variation within general usage. We would have to ask ourselves again how far medieval written prose literature is influenced on its part by oral narrative. This complex of questions should be investigated more

Regarding their juxtaposition of fixed and interchangeable motifs, however, they are in turn like European folk tales. In contrast to fairy tales, though, parables are not independent but point to a moral doctrine outside of them. The externally unadorned narrative style is also necessary for the structure of the parables to remain transparent.

Even Aesop's fables did not arise without relation to their morality. Yes, their raison d'être is determined by their morality. As a result, their optimal style is also short and sweet. Lessing writes about it: [7]

> How should the fable be recited? Is here Aesopus, or is Phaedrus, or is La Fontaine the true pattern? It is not clear whether Aesop wrote his own fables and put them together in a book.[8] But this is so well known that, even if he did, not a single one of them has come to us with his own words. . . . Judging by these fables we have received, his presentation was of the utmost precision; he placed no value on descriptions; he got straight to the point and hurried to the end with every word; he knew no "happy medium" between the necessary and the useless. This precision and brevity—in which he was such a great master—the ancients found so appropriate to the nature of the fable that they

closely. I am satisfied here with the reference to the French narrative *Aucassin et Nicolette*, ed. Jean Dufoumet (Paris: Garnier-Flammarion, 1973), from the beginning of the thirteenth century. This magical story is told alternately in songs and in prose. To my mind, the prose of this narrative is reminiscent of the style of European folktales. Here is just a small, purely accidental example of a description from the beginning of section 12: "Aucassin was taken to prison, as you have already heard, and Nicolette was elsewhere in the room. It was in summer, in the month of May, where the days are warm, long and clear, and the nights quiet and quiet. Nicolette lay on her bed one night, saw the moon shine clearly through a window, and heard the nightingale singing in her garden. She remembered her friend Aucassin, whom she loved so much."

7. Lessing, *Werke*, vol. 5 (Munich: Carl Hanser, 1979), 406–10.

8. The style of Aesop fables is very interesting, though not in the sense of Lessing's view; August Hausrath in "Corpus fabularum Aesopicarum," vii–viii, speaks of the *floridum atque loquax genus dicendi, quod magis convenit narrntiunculis illis popularibus, quae de hominum vita temporibus mythicis consociata referunt.* About the myths of fables, it is not worthwhile to lose a word here. As examples of his assertion, Hausrath brings fables 1, 9, 35, and 37. These fables are excellently told—in the manner of the best rabbinic parables! However, their presentation is certainly not "flowery." Any external ornamentation or useless description is missing. All property words found there are strictly functional. They are part of the action and do not elaborate. Shortly, I will discuss the "chatty" style of these fables, which is also characteristic of a good parable.

made a general rule out of it. Theon among others penetrates expressly to that.[9] If I am to become aware of a moral truth through the fable, I must be able to look over the fable at once; and in order to be able to look over it at once, it must be as short as possible. But all ornaments are opposed to this brevity; for without it, it could be even shorter: consequently all extra elements, insofar as they are empty extensions, are at variance with the intention of the fable.[10]

These words of Lessing are not only relevant for Aesop's fables but also for parables. However, some cautious questions that set the stage for differentiation must be asked. What about the short and unadorned presentation of the parable genre and the fable genre? Is the simple style and relative brevity of fables and parables advisable only because they are supposed to be clear so that one can successfully become aware of a moral truth? I have already emphasized that the deliberately unadorned style is characteristic of fables, parables, and other genres of oral folk literature. Fables and parables—sometimes also exempla—also have this in common: they point to a moral doctrine, although not (as Lessing thinks) to a single moral proposition. But since in fables, and even more in parables, many important

---

9. Lessing, according to De Lamoite (409): "The narrative of the fable should be even more planned; it should be compressed as much as possible without all ornaments and figures, satisfied with the only clarity."

10. In 1791, Christoph Gottfried Bardili wrote instructive insights about the style of the fable under Lessing's influence: "Therefore the fable poet may tell everything so short and simple; for he has no need, like the philosopher, always to use psychological reasons to determine action; he has no need, like the speaker, to seek out external motifs; he must not decorate in the same degree as other poets, for his truth already gets all the light from the story itself, in which he imparts to the same reality, the case already brings everything essential with it by its nature. . . . Due to the characteristic nature of the case, which the fable poet, as such, chooses, the mode of treatment of the same is already prescribed to him: shortness and simplicity, avoidance of all ornamentation, simplicity of action." Leibfried and Werle, *Texte zur Theorie der Fabel*, 65. Excellent words, which also apply to parables! Johann Gottfried Herder, *Blätter der Vorzeit*, 66–76, also assumes Lessing. But he brings in views typical to him; for example, "The most beautiful and actual fables are thus torn leaves from the book of creation; their characters are alive—perpetual eternal types. . . . [The fable] was to them a textbook of nature, which only a weak person or madman dared to contradict. . . . Simple is the grace of nature; high naivety is the grace of fables. . . . The nature fable imitates it [nature]; its highest and most enduring charm is silent greatness, silent grace, especially in the fables of fate." Herder applies Wincklemann's classicist concept of beauty to the fable! From Herder, a path leads to Jülicher, *Die Gleichnisreden Jesu*, vol. 1, 294.

parts of their subject matter have a correspondence in moral application and are indispensably bound to an external region. Because of this bond, the ornamentation of fables and parables, which would uselessly loosen this bond, is taken away. Lessing is right when he says that the fable and the parable must be short so that they can be looked over quickly. Only in this way can they point to moral wisdom without being twisted. On one point, however, I cannot agree with Lessing: the fable poet and the parable narrator do not hurry to the end with every word. If so, then the fable and the parable would not be an effective work of art but a factual account. We already know that the fable and the parable have quite a problematic relationship with reality. So, with these genres there is no flowery style in place. However, a certain chatty tone gives fables and parables a higher artistic value. Their subjects, which are only half the picture, want to artfully tell a story. What Bardili says about the fable—that it is a "sensitization of a truth by individualizing it, and thereby giving it as much universality as possible through individualization"—also applies to the parable.[11] So, if the narrator were too hasty to get to the moral as quickly as possible, the fable or parable would lose its effectiveness.

Before we take a closer look at this point, let us dwell briefly on another question. It is debatable whether we are at all inclined to speak of an optimal style. I foresee the authoritative fear of the literary historian and folklorist of the danger of speaking not only of what is present but also of what is to be. Can we do justice to the material if we avoid value judgments? Aesthetic values are inherent in the creation of artists and other people. They vary from creator to creator, from one literary genre to another; they are different according to the historical conditions and the environment. But they always, consciously or unconsciously, guide the creator in his work. So being a bit of an art critic, as was customary in the eighteenth century, cannot hurt today. An art critic knows that a literary genre strives for a form best adapted to it and a narrative style that expresses the structure of the literary work of art in the most effective way. A critic has the right to decide what is better literature and what is worse. Also, for the examination of narrative folk literature, it is not inappropriate for us to be art critics. The parable belongs to narrative folk literature, and an assessment of the aesthetics of parables serves this understanding. There are excellent and less excellent parables, better and less well-told parables—both with the rabbis and with Jesus!

---

11. Bardili, *Texte zur Theorie der Fabel*, 65. It is a pity that it is precisely he who denies this quality to parables.

The optimal mode of presentation of certain genres to which parables also belong is therefore an outwardly unadorned style. This is what Lessing means regarding Aesopian fables and Lüthi regarding European folktales. But how can it be judged if writers and poets seize on a simple, oral, popular art genre, cast it into a written art form or an art poem, and then work it according to the sense of style that suits them? Although simple prose is best suited for fables and parables, this does not mean that the variety of La Fontaine's fables and his imitators would not exist fully. The art fable in verses is a poetic variation of the fable told orally, and it is precisely the tension between purely epic content and poetic ornamental form that makes up the special charm of these little jewels. This also applies to the colorful and humorous retelling of the fairy tales of a Basile, a Perrault, and the brave Musaus![12] We must admit that in these adaptations of animal fables and European fairy tales, there are different laws of art than in the original genre that the sometimes willed discrepancy between content and a new art form can result in the epic framework that causes the plot to suffer; and that it can happen that some details of the original subject become almost unrecognizable. Overall, however, the new art form is aesthetically justified and satisfying; it gives the reader many pleasures. We must also bear in mind that it was hardly possible for an educated reader before Lessing and the Brothers Grimm to enjoy a fable or folktale in its unadorned, popular forms without prejudice or internal reluctance. Art-critical norms prevailing at that time had a blocking effect.[13] So, you can wrap a written European fairy tale or a

---

12. On Basile and Perrault see, for example, Max Lüthi, *The Fairy Tale as Art Form and Portrait of Man*, 74f. Basile's fairy tales were published in 1633 and edited by Perrault in 1697. The text of the Basile: Giambatista Basile, *Lo cunto de li cunti* (Gius: Laterza, 1976). Regarding metaphor, see Italo Calvino's introduction to Giambatista Basile, *Il Pentamerone, traduzione e introduzione di Benedetto Croce*, vol. 1 (Gius: Laterza, 1974), v–xix. The best edition of Musaus is J. K. A. Musaus, *Volksmärchen der Deutschen* (Jena: Eugen Diedrichs, 1912).

13. In this context, it is worth mentioning one of Martin Buber's early books, *Die Geschichten Des Rabbi Nachman: Ihm Nacherzaehlt* (1906). The book is a retelling of mystical fairy tales told by the Hasidic Tsaddik Rabbi Nachman of Braslav (1771–1810) and recorded by his disciple. Rabbi Nachman then read the transcript himself. Although the records are not impeccable, they preserve the unadorned manner of the presentation of European fairy tales with all the merits of this style. The imitation of Buber, on the other hand, is late Romantic in style and adorned with short descriptions, thereby weakening the epic power of the original. It is worth comparing the original from this aspect with the repetition that Buber offers.

fable in a magnificent, colorful robe. I am convinced, however, that such an undertaking would fail in a rabbinic parable or a parable of Jesus.[14]

Now, I would like to say a great deal about how far individual genres can tolerate external ornamentation. This will help us to better understand Jesus' parables. European folktales are sparse in their descriptions, but these must not be missing because they are somehow part of the essence of the genre. Fairy tales want to have a visual and an acoustic effect.[15] Their world is one-dimensional and is described abstractly. Their linear or two-dimensional objects remain metallically rigid and unchanged. Rarely does the fairy tale mention feelings or characteristics for its own sake or to create atmosphere; it mentions them when they influence the action. And it doesn't like to call them by name either; characteristics and feelings are expressed in actions. The fairy tale shows us flat figures, not people with a living inner world. It tells us little of mental distress or conflict, and it distributes different possibilities of action into different forms. The right behavior shows itself in the hero, the failure in his companions. The rich distinction between people is dissolved in the fairy tale. The different behavioral possibilities—which are sharply separated from each other—are shared between several figures. It is not an inner excitement but an outer excitement that drives the fairy-tale figure forward. If the exterior is described in a fairy tale, then there is a unity to the type of description: a city made entirely of iron, a large house, a large dragon, the young king, a bloody struggle, and so on. This concise description outlines and isolates items with a firm contour. The fairy tale prefers clear, unmixed color: golden, silver, red, white, black, next to it a little blue. Only a few things and shapes are given a color designation. As a result, they stand out from the others, which are designated as colorless. The European fairy tale is important for the parables of the rabbis and Jesus, as well as for the characterization of literary genres that are cultivated and handed down by people. Lüthi saw this clearly. In contrast to other genres, the fairy tale does not move along without some limited description. How many embellishments the other genres endure in their popular form is difficult to imagine. In my opinion, the animal fable is closest to the European fairy tale in this respect, and then exempla and comedies follow. The most unadorned are anecdotes and parables.

---

14. Nor did Herder dare to pour rabbinic parables into his poetic prose. See also note 4 above.

15. For depictions in European folktales, see Lüthi, *The European Folktale: Form and Nature*, 8–36.

I have made some observations about the names of persons in different genres. If in a historical example, a comedy, or an anecdote, for example, Napoleon, Caesar, Rothschild, Fugger, or a master thief is mentioned, then only the family name and not the first name is mentioned. Characteristic individual traits (a powerful man, a wealthy man, a donor, etc.) are typically associated with family names. If names in these genres are not strictly necessary, then they are avoided. For example, if an illustration emerged from a true story, then individuals become anonymous. The name is veiled because the story has become archetypal. Personal names that sometimes appear in European folktales (the funny Ferdinand or the faithful John, etc.) are typifications. A similar phenomenon also occurs in exempla.[16] Once, in an exemplum in the Gospels, one person is given a name: in the exemplum of the rich man and poor Lazarus (Luke 16:19–31). Lazarus is a common name of a priest (Eleazar); however, the rich man remains anonymous. Unnamed also are the acting persons of the exemplum of the prodigal son (Luke 15:11–32). When the Dutch playwright Gulielmus Gnapheus (1493–1568) wrote a Protestant Latin school drama about it in 1528,[17] he provided them with names: the father is called Pelargus and the prodigal son is Acolastus. Apart from the name "Lazarus," therefore, all persons in Jesus' exempla are nameless. The acting persons of all parables are also nameless, not only in Jesus' parables but also in all rabbinic parables. A parable cannot bear the names of persons. The figures of the parables are referred to merely by their social position and their profession or their family affiliation. Only the relationships of people with one another and with the world are important. Therefore, even a randomly summoned personal name, such as Lazarus in this case, would cause intolerable damage to the efficacy of a parable.

As already mentioned, the fairy tale cannot do without a limited description of people and circumstances. Likewise, external descriptions also

---

16. There is only one example of Hebel's exemplum "Der Schneider in Pensa" from *Rheinländischer Hausfreund*, in Johann Peter Hebel, *Werke*, vol. 1 (Frankfurt: Insel Verlag, 1968), 298. At the beginning of the story, the good tailor is nameless. Only in the course of history is his name called as follows: When the German prisoners call him to their homeland, "then it passed through the whole tailor like a warm dissolving thaw. 'And I am from Bretten,' said the glorious mind, Franz Anton Egetmeier of Bretten, as Joseph said in Egypt to the sons of Israel." The tailor mentions only his homeland; the author adds the name. The mention of Joseph in Egypt is instructive: the biblical Joseph remained incognito as long as possible!

17. Gulielmus Gnapheus, *Acolastus*, ed. P. Minderaa (Zwolle: Tjeenk Willink, 1956).

occur in other related genres in sparse form. They are not inappropriate for style, but most of the time, we can get by without them. They are just an addition or illustration; however, they do not belong to the actual structure of these genres. Only in parables and probably in anecdotes are descriptions of the environment and the external appearance of a figure sparingly used. They are used sparingly because they disturb the story. Therefore, they are lacking in rabbinic parables and in Jesus' parables. In parables, there is also no mention of descriptive color if it does not play a role in the subject matter. In his parables, Jesus never uses this kind of descriptive color. If there is any color in exempla, fables, or comedies, it is the clear, unmixed colors of the European fairy tale, such as when a black raven and a white dove appear in an animal fable. In Hebel's famous exemplum, *Kannitverstan*,[18] one color is mentioned once—in the description of the funeral procession:

> Four horses, disguised in black, pulled a funeral chariot, also covered in black, slowly and sadly, as if they knew that they were leading a dead man into his rest. A long train of friends and acquaintances of the deceased followed, couple after couple, wrapped in black coats and silent. In the distance rang a lonely bell.

The mention three times of the black mourning color is important for the action. The other descriptions in the story give a strong, fresh impression, although the objects are not as clearly delineated. Thus the house of the supposed Mr. Kannitverstan is "an expensive building, the six fireplaces on the roof, the beautiful cornices and the high windows, larger than at the father's house." The house is beautiful, with the windows full of tulips and star flowers, and so we could proceed with further descriptions from this story.

For further clarification, I will mention a comedy from Georg Wickram, *Das Rollwagenbüchlein*,[19] with the subtitle "Where does it come from that one says: Hey, you poor devil, and back again: This is just the devil's thanks." The little book came out in the year 1555, and its content is not intended for modern delicate ears, but I like it:

> It was a good simple man who came into a church where the image of Christ was painted; to him he lit a little light or a candle of wax and prayed before him. And as he wandered about to look at the churches, when he had never been in them before, so he finds the devil painted in a dark corner in the most hideous

---

18. Hebel, *Werke*, vol. 1, 51–53. *Kannitverstan* means "I can't understand you!"—Ed.

19. Georg Wickram, *Das Rollwagenbüchlein* (Stuttgart: Reclam, 1968), 61f. We modernized the spelling.

way, that he immediately was frightened of him, and so he thoughtlessly said: "O you poor devil, how did you stand so poorly! I want to light a light for you too!" This good man dreams long afterward, as the devil meets him in a forest, and says: "Good morning, you first lit a light for me; therefore, it is reasonable that I should also repay you and pay you an honor. Therefore, come with me, and I will show you a place where a great treasure is buried. You shall dig it up and enjoy it because of me." And he brought him with him with these words to a hollow tree and said, "Go home, and fetch pricks, shovels, and picks, that you may dig it up." The good man rolls in his sleep, as he says: "Yes, but I will not be able to find this tree again." The devil said, "[expletive][20] you'll find him again." The man follows the devil and thinks he's defecating by the tree. And when he woke up, he had defecated in the bed and lay in the filth, whereupon his wife cursed him badly, because she had to wash the bed again. Thus said this poor man: "This is the devil's thanks!" And he told his wife what had happened to him; she only mocked him more for it.

I include this rough comedy because it seems to me to be a model of the unadorned tale but is at the same time a chatty narrative style that is peculiar to comedy, exempla, and parables. Georg Wickram was not tempted by the picturesque scenery of history to paint in any more detail. No color is mentioned and nothing is pictured. The image of Christ is only said to have been painted in the most beautiful way, and the image of the devil was painted in a dark corner in the most hideous way. The narrator speaks generally of a forest and not of a deep forest. That the tree under which the treasure is supposedly buried is hollow seems to be included because treasures are often hidden in hollow trees, although this is not in keeping with the devil's demand that the man dig up the treasure. The narrator brings together two different narrative motifs. Therefore, the story is not a mere account but a work of art. It is told in a lively way; the narrator does not hurry, he has time.

Comedies are so closely related to exempla that there are boundary cases in which a story can be counted as both comedy and exempla. In contrast to an entertaining story or a comedy, an exemplum is there to teach a moral. In contrast to a parable, however, there are not two levels in an exemplum. The subject of a parable and some of its motifs have equivalents in the moral level, while the exemplum is simply a doctrinal moral story. There are borderline cases here too. Jesus' story of the good Samaritan (Luke 10:29–37), the foolish rich man (Luke 12:13–21), the rich man and

---

20. The expression in Wickram's text is *scheiss darzu*, which means "I'll defecate on it." The whole comedy is written in a strong, folksy German dialect.

poor Lazarus (Luke 16:19–31), and the Pharisee and tax collector (Luke 18:9–14) are all exempla. The latter exemplum approaches the genre of the parable because of its inclusion of a hero and an anti-hero. The exemplum of the prodigal son (Luke 15:11–32) also possesses a hero (the prodigal son) and an anti-hero (the elder son), as well as a gracious father who makes the decision. We could therefore also say that it is a parable—namely, of the types of two dissimilar sons (or servants).

Comedies are also related to exempla in that their narrative is richer in epic motifs than most parables. This also affects their presentation style, which we can see in Jesus' exempla.[21] (By the way, it should be noted that there is no mention of color in not only the Synoptic parables but also the Lukan exempla.) By their very nature, Jesus' exempla paint a picture more often than his parables. A helpful example of this is his story of the good Samaritan (Luke 10:33–34):

---

21. The characteristic differences between parables and exempla also affected art history. As far as I can see, only one parable became a popular theme for the performing arts: the parable of the virgins. The decorative symmetry of this parable was stimulating for artists. Far more than his parables, Jesus' exempla attracted painters. The exempla can be represented artistically because they are complete stories with a moral. That is why these stories were painted and poetically redesigned: the good Samaritan, the rich man and poor Lazarus, and the prodigal son. We read an instructive description in the children's book by Johanna Spyri, *Heidis Lehr und Wanderjahre* (Münich, 1978) at the end of chapter 10, 134. There are three pictures about the prodigal son, which are supposedly in an imaginary picture book (we find the example itself and its effect in the last chapter of *Heidis Lehr und Wanderjahre*, 186–88): "Heidi always liked to look at the green heath and the shepherd in the middle of the flock, as he leaned so pleasantly on his long staff, because there he was still with the beautiful flock of the father and only followed the funny sheep and goats, because he was pleased. But then came the picture where he ran away from his father's house and was in a foreign country and had to look after the pigs and had become quite thin, because he still had to eat alfalfa. And in the picture the sun no longer shone so golden, when the land was gray and foggy. But then another picture came to the story: then the old father came out of the house with outstretched arms and ran to meet the returning repentant son to receive him, who came quite fearfully and emaciated in his torn coat." Here we can observe well what happens when an exemplum changes the medium twice. First, it is depicted by Spyri in a series of three imaginary images portrayed with colors, shapes, and areas. Then these pictures are interpreted in writing, and now we talk about feelings and moods. The shepherd leans "pleasantly" on his long staff; it "pleased" him to be with the "merry sheep and goats." The third picture of the "repentant" son is portrayed as quite "fearful and emaciated." The atmosphere thus changes twice, depending on the nature of the medium.

"But a Samaritan who was on his way came near him, saw him and felt sorry for him; he came and bandaged his wounds, poured oil and wine on them, lifted him up on his own animal, brought him to an inn and cared for him. And the next day he took out two denarii,[22] gave them to the innkeeper and said, 'Take care of him! And whatever more you spend, I will pay you when I come back.'"

Such a broad, loving description has more place in an exemplum than in a parable. A particularly impressive example of a broad epic account of events and situations is the exemplum of the prodigal son (Luke 5:11–32), a masterpiece of narrative folk prose. You should read the whole story. The wretched son "went and clung to one of the citizens of that country, who sent him to herd the pigs in his fields. And he longed to fill his belly with pods that the pigs were eating, and no one gave them to him." And when the son was on his way home, "his father saw him and felt compassion, ran, fell on his neck and kissed him." And the father said to his servants, "Quickly take out the best robe and put it on him, and put a ring on his hand and shoes on his feet, and fetch the fattened calf, slaughter it, and let us rejoice." And so, the story continues—with music and dance—to the end. We find the same broad type of description in the example of the rich man and poor Lazarus (Luke 16:19–31). I hope I have been able to show the gradual difference between the stricter narrative of Jesus' parables and the broader epic of his exempla.

I have mentioned this gradual difference because sometimes accompanying details are also mentioned in parables, though the subject could get along by itself without them. I am not talking here about indispensable motifs, without which the action would be fragmentary. In parables, of course, there are details conditioned by the nature of the subject that do not correspond to the moral level of the parable. The developed parable wants to tell a story that has happened. It doesn't want to build an allegory. But besides that, in parables—though not or broadly—accompanying events are mentioned, which are supposed to enliven the parable. Very often, the boundary between what is necessary for the subject and what invigorates the parable is difficult to draw. This applies to Jesus' parables, rabbinic parables, and Greek parables. From this aspect, let us return to the parable of the Stoic Cleanthes:[23]

"I sent two servants to look for Plato and to get him out of the academy. One of them searched the whole hall of columns and also went through other places

---

22. This is a large sum.
23. See chapter 6, note 16, above.

where he hoped to find him. Then he returned home tired and angry. The other servant sat down at the next shop. After he had joined the local workers like a vagabond and loitered and played with them, he found the passing Plato, whom he had not sought."

Here, the description literally slows down the action, the content of which is the search. Also, in Epictetus's parable of the ship passengers,[24] the snails and small squid have their counterpart in the moral teaching, but they are also there to illustrate the wandering of the passengers on the shore in a manner that slows down the action. The same is true of the details in other parables of Epictetus, which we have already discussed.

Let us now turn again to rabbinic parables. I will discuss here only the last two of the rabbinic parables already quoted, and that quite briefly.[25] The subject of the first, that of Rabbi Meir, I share once more:

A king prepared a meal and invited guests to it. He did not set a time when they should leave the meal. The wise among them got up at nine o'clock and entered their houses and climbed their beds while it was still light. Others got up at sunset, and the shops were still open and the lights were on, and they entered their houses and climbed their beds by the lamplight. Others got up at two and three o'clock in the night. Some shops were still open and others were already closed, some lights were on and some were extinguished. They entered their homes and climbed their beds in darkness. The rest who remained at supper were drunk with wine, and wounded one another, and killed one another.

An excellently told parable by an excellent parable narrator! Through the treatment of the individual groups of returning guests, the parable becomes vivid and stimulates the imagination of the listener, although no pictures are painted in the process. The rabbinic parable of the caravan is also lively. The head of the station invites the guests to stay inside because outside the wild animals and robbers can be dangerous. The many conversations in it are typical for both exempla and parables—including Jesus' exempla and parables. As we shall soon see, it is precisely the words of the characters that offer the appropriate opportunity to introduce realistic details that enrich the subject to bring the small story to life. Outside of the conversations, parables of this type are much poorer than exempla. In the parable of the caravan, the head of the station ironically takes up the words of the caravan driver.

---

24. See chapter 6, note 19, above.
25. See chapter l, notes 8 and 10, above.

Now, there is something to be said about how Jesus mentions incidental circumstances in his parables. For example, how excellently he tells the parable of the ten virgins (Matt 25:1–13)! All the details are rooted in the subject, perhaps with one exception (the mention of the call in the middle of the night), but even there the decision is difficult. Particularly rich in details of individual circumstances is the parable of the laborers in the vineyard (Matt 20:1–16). In his rich structure and description of different groups, Jesus' parable is related to the parable of Rabbi Meir just quoted. Likewise, this parable is also enlivened by the many conversations within it. On the other hand, the double parable does not speak of the lost sheep or penny (Luke 15:3–10; Matt 18:12–14). Only after the man has found his lost sheep and taken it on his shoulders and carried it home does he call his friends and neighbors and say to them: "Rejoice with me that I have found my lost sheep." The woman who searches for the lost drachma lights a lamp and sweeps the house, searching diligently until she finds it. Her words to her friends and neighbors correspond to the words of the man who had found his sheep. Together, they form a kind of refrain of the double parable.

In parables, descriptive details are often found in the words of characters. So it is in the parable of the supplicant friend (Luke 11:5–8). The man is asked by his friend at midnight to lend him three loaves of bread, "for a friend of mine came to me on the journey, and I have nothing to set out for him." The man replies, "Don't bother me. The door is already locked and my children are in bed with me; I cannot get up and give you anything," but in the end the friend gets what he asked for. The parable of the Great Supper (Matt 22:1–14; Luke 14:15–24) is also rich in movement and conversation. The host says, "Behold, I have prepared my supper; my oxen and fattened cattle are ready; come to the wedding." But one of the guests says, "I have bought a field and must go out and see it; I beg you to excuse me." And another says, "I have bought five yokes of oxen, and I am going to test them; I beg you to excuse me." And another says, "I have taken a wife, and therefore I cannot come." The words of the host are detailed and justified in Matthew (22:4), whereas according to Luke (14:17), the host is content with the invitation: "Come, for it is now prepared!" In contrast, Matthew (22:5) lacks the answers of the various invited guests. There it stands short and concise: "They did not pay attention to it, but went away, one to his field, the other to his business."[26] This reminds us of the only descriptive

---

26. Matthew 22:6 is a tendentious addition.

sentence of a similar parable of Rabban Johanan ben Zakkai:[27] "The foolish among them (the invited ones) went to their work and said to themselves: Is there a meal without preparation?" However, the Lukan speeches of the stubborn invited ones should be given preference. The words of those in the parables are indeed among the dramatizing elements and main means of slowing down the action. This "chatty" way of speaking is an important advantage for the most successful parables.

The conversations found in parable-speech, counter-speech, and self-talk form a constitutive element of parables. In this respect, too, parables are related to fables. The conversations have two functions that are both polar and complementary to each other. Conversations, on the one hand, promote epic and dramatic tension. They form an urgent element toward catharsis or toward the moment at which the parable (and the fable) reaches its end. On the other hand—and this is the dominant function—the conversations in both genres slow down the speed of the course of the story. In the parables of Jesus and the rabbis, conversations are a suitable point of detention for citing such details that would carry a certain dissonance elsewhere in the parable, which is unadorned. It is important to note that all the details, even if they are sometimes outside the dialogue, are factual in nature; they therefore determine reality and do not paint it. All statements in Jewish parables and in Jesus' parables are epic, never lyrical.

In the parable of the fig tree (Luke 13:6–9), the main content of a living dialogue is determined:

> "One had a fig tree standing in his vineyard. He came to look for the fruit and found none. And he said to the husbandman, 'Behold, three years have passed since I came, and have sought fruit on this fig tree, and have found none. Pull it out, why should it weaken the ground?' But he answered him, 'Master, please let it alone this year until I have dug around it and put fertilizer around it. Perhaps it will bear fruit in the future—if not, you may have it cut out.'"

Both the owner's words and the employee's response contain realistic agricultural data. We even learn that the fig tree has not borne fruit for three years. This is the only indication that we could miss in the parable—but so, the parable is better. Just as rich and lively is the dialogue in the parallel rabbinic parable I mentioned above.[28] (It would be good if you would read this rabbinic parable again in the present context.) Both parables end

---

27. See chapter 1, note 4, above.
28. See chapter 4, note 54, above.

with the request for provisional protection of the plants. In Jesus' parable, this ending is also due to the fact that he is calling for repentance, which could prevent the future catastrophe of the destruction of Jerusalem and the temple by the Romans. From the parallel rabbinic parable, however, it becomes clear that the very nature of the subject demands such an ending. Jesus' parable ends with the conversation in which it remains undecided whether the listeners have taken the call to repentance to heart. Not so in the rabbinic parable. It is part of the certainty of faith that the spared vineyard will prove itself. The vineyard is Israel, which God wanted to destroy because of the construction of the golden calf. However, Israel was spared through Moses' intercession, which proved to be right. But the parable does not say that the vineyard produced good wine.

Like Jesus' parable, the rabbinic parable ends in conversation. Jesus' parable ends with intercession for the fig tree because its future is still uncertain but also because the subject has essentially reached its end. Another proof of the decisive influence of the subject on the form of such parables is seen in the parable of the weeds mixed with the wheat (Matt 13:24–30). Again, it is about growth and fruit; and here, too, the significance of the parable lies in the conversation between the owner and his servants. The end of the conversation is also the end of the parable: the owner decides, of all things, that the weeds should be spared for the time being. In contrast to the rabbinic parable of the vineyard just mentioned, and to Jesus' parable of the fig tree, it is clear what will happen with the weeds in the end. In all three cases, therefore, the parables end with a conversation although their content and purpose are different. Because of the structure of the subject, continuing the story after the conversation would be distracting. We can therefore establish a new rule here: Such parables, the focus of which is a conversation, reach their conclusion with the end of the conversation—after which nothing follows. This applies to Jesus' parables about the fig tree (Luke 13:6–9), the weeds (Matt 13:24–30), the great banquet (Luke 14:15–24), the ungodly judge (Luke 18:1–5), the laborers in the vineyard (Matt 20:1–14), the minas (Luke 19:11–27), the talents (Matt 25:14–30), and the ten virgins (Matt 25:1–13).[29] The same rule also applies to Jewish parables in rabbinic literature. In four of the six examples of rabbinic parables that I presented in the first chapter,[30] conversation is their backbone. They all end

---

29. This category also includes the parable of the unequal sons (Matt 21:28–32). The parable of the supplicant friend (Luke 11:5–8) has an addendum.

30. See chapter 1, notes 4, 5, 6, and 10.

with the words of one of the acting figures. So, where a parable is carried by a conversation, it finds its end with the last words of that conversation. This rule concerning the genre of parables could certainly be further clarified by further investigation. One would still have to find out whether and in what contexts there are exceptions to this rule and how these possible exceptions are made.[31]

Even parables, the focus of which is not a conversation, sometimes end with a direct comment. In these cases, someone who represents God is usually the one who speaks. Not only in the dialogical but also in the more epic parables, a statement can serve as an appropriate conclusion that points to the moral teaching of the parable. A later rabbinic parable, which belongs to the early types of parables,[32] can serve as an example for us. This parable seeks to inculcate the honor of father and mother:

> "The Master God made coats of skin for the man and his wife and put them on them." . . . To what can this be compared? With a king of flesh and blood. He had a servant. The servant ran away from him. He wandered through all countries. Then he fell (again) into the king's hand. He let him be brought in. And when they had brought him before the king, the king took him by the hand, and brought him into his house, and showed him silver, and gold, and precious stones, and pearls, and all that was his in the house. Then he led him out into the open and showed him the gardens and orchards and everything he owned. Then he showed him his sons, the older and the younger. Then he showed him his servants, the older and the younger. After he had shown all things, he said to him, "Have you seen that I do not need you? But come and do the work together with my sons and servants, whether they are older or younger. So you will honor me and have respect for me, as the people here honor me and have respect for me." Thus the holy God has equated his honor

---

31. Another remark: Shklovsky, *Von der Ungleichheit des Ähnlichen in der Kunst*, 128, writes, "In the Gospel the fairy-tale parables are repeated in various places. You end up with a question. They are puzzles with a new solution, because the basis of the solution—morality—has diminished." That the question at the end of a parable is to be understood from the relationship of parables to riddles is correctly observed. But we cannot speak of a new morality in the parables in the Gospels because such questions also occur at the end of rabbinic parables, if the subject so requires; for example, at the end of a parable of Rabbi Shimeon ben Yochai (see chapter 4, note 139, above): "But who is greater than he who loves the king, or he whom the king loves? Of course, the one the king loves!" We should not be guided by preconceived opinions in literary investigations.

32. Tanna debe Eliyahu, *Eliahu Rabba and Seder Eliahu Zuta*, ed. M. Friedmann (Jerusalem: Bamberger & Wahrmann, 1960), ch. 25, 136.

with the honor of father and mother. For it is written, "A son honors his father, and a servant honors his master." If I am a father, where is my honor? If I am Master, where is the respect for me, says the Master of hosts" (Mal 1:6).

The moral of this classically beautiful parable therefore encompasses more than just the commandment to honor one's father and mother. It also applies to the active honor of man toward God, who loves him unselfishly and forgives him. This parable is remarkable not only because it closes with the words of the king, but also because it shows how a good parable is filled with vivid details to make the action visible to the listener without having to insert sympathetic pity or an elaborate celebration. Jesus the Jewish parable-teller possessed the same art inherited by the Jews throughout the centuries. The paratactic mention of small details, which sometimes also occurs in his parables, is therefore generally his own work and not an extension by the translators, editors, or evangelists.

To illustrate the matter, I again quote his double parable of the house on the rock and on the sand (Matt 7:24–27; Luke 6:47–49):

> "Everyone who hears my words and does them is like a wise man who built his house on rocks. The rain fell, the rivers came, the winds blew and hit that house. But it did not collapse, for it was founded on rocks. But everyone who hears and does not do is like a foolish man who built a house on sand. The rain fell, the rivers came, the winds blew and beat on that house. It collapsed, and its fall was great."

One reason that Jesus loved to tell double parables was because their parallel construction captures, underlines, and enhances the parallelism of the elements in the included single parables. Unlike Jesus' other double parables, this double parable is built in contrast. This is also often the case with rabbinic parables, that they show the difference between right and wrong action. The epic naming of the rain, the streams, and the wind occurs in both halves of the parable in parallel, identical sentences, with the difference that they "fell on" the house on the rock while they "struck" the house on the sand. The stronger verb in the second case is correct, because the house built on the sand collapsed. So, it is very likely that Jesus used two different verbs to bring a substantiated increase into the two parallel propositions. It is also stylistically not coincidental that the parable speaks of three elements that threaten the house. The triad is popular in fairy tales[33]

---

33. See Shklovsky, *Von der Ungleichheit des Ähnlichen in der Kunst*, 121f.

and in parables. This belongs to the abstract nature in both genres and expresses a gradual increase. Jesus does this in this parable by naming the rain, the streams of water, and the wind. These two parallel short sentences are found in Matthew (7:25, 27) but not in Luke, who does not include them out of ignorance of the aesthetic laws of parables.[34]

We have already talked about the triad in parables. For example, when three servants appear in the parable of the minas or talents (Matt 25:14–30; Luke 19:11–27). In the parable of the workers in the vineyard (Matt 20:1–16), three groups of workers are explicitly mentioned (vv. 2, 3, 6), even though we hear only of the protest of the first group against the wages of the third group of latecomers. Here, therefore, the contrasting duality is combined with the popular threesome. But even this schematic is not yet complete. After the owner of the vineyard hired the second group, he went out at "about the sixth and about the ninth hour" and hired another two groups of workers (v. 5). In addition to the threesome and the duality, there is therefore a third schematic outline in the parable of the workers in the vineyard. The first group is hired "in the morning," the second group "at the third hour," the third group at the sixth hour, the fourth group at the ninth hour, and finally the fifth group at the eleventh hour. The parable thus speaks of five groups of workers sent to the vineyard at intervals of three hours—that is, one group at the beginning of each day's watch! Thus a full working day is evenly structured and completely covered. We can certainly not call this scheme realistic. In this volume, I have already pointed out several times that parables are not realistic but rather pseudo-realistic. Of the five groups of workers, only three are dealt with in more detail because of the importance of the threesome. The five working groups are highlighted because they memorably mark the progress of the working day. The three groups do not serve to increase the content; they only point to the temporal progressive course of the action. The main motif is the conflict between the first group and the last group. Although there can be no question of a three-tiered gradation in the subject, there is a stylistic increase in our parable: to the first group, the employer says nothing; the owner saw the second group "standing idly in the market and said to them: 'Go you also into the vineyard, and whatever is right I will give you.' " The third group (which is actually the fifth) is not only addressed by the owner, but it also develops into a conversation. The owner found them standing there and

---

34. For the worst rabbinic parallel to the double parable of the house, see chapter 4, notes 121–26, above.

said to them, "What are you doing here all day?" They said to him, "No one hired us." He said to them, "You also go into the vineyard." It is therefore a question of a successful stylistic gradation, whereby the conversation with the third group becomes credible because the workers must explain to the owner why they are standing idle all day.[35] We cannot admire enough Jesus' art and how he stylistically adapts his epic to the abstract laws of the subject.

The importance of the triad is therefore indisputable not only for fairy tales but also for parables. "There are usually three levels. A violation of the triple number, its exceeding, will be punished as it is at the same time."[36] In two of Jesus' parables, the threefold number is preserved, but the fourth element, which serves for clarification, is greatly corrupted; the triple number is obviously deliberately exceeded. In Matthew's version of the parable of the great banquet (Matt 22:1–14), the master sends his servants out to the guests three times. Both Matthew (22:5–6) and the Lukan version speak of three groups of invitees who react negatively to the invitation in different ways. By means of the additional fourth element, the triad is cancelled in both versions and comes to a rupture: After the landlord becomes angry over the refusal of the three groups he had invited, he invites a fourth group (Matt 22:8–10; Luke 14:21, 24).[37] The original invited guests proved unworthy of the invitation, and now random passers-by are brought from the streets to the feast. The behavior of the evil vinedressers is directed differently (Matt 21:33–41; Mark 12:1–9; Luke 20:9–16). In Luke and Mark, three servants are sent in succession to the evil vinedressers; in Matt 21:31, the triad is only

---

35. The idle standing of the workers until the eleventh hour results from the subject. The reasoning of the workers, that no one has hitherto hired them, is credible and fits nicely into the narrative. Jeremias, *Die Gleichnisse Jesu*, 330 has missed the point when he says, "Even if the last hired ones themselves are to blame for sitting idly chattering in the market in the late afternoon (in the time of the pressing grape harvest!), even if their excuse, no one has hired them, is nothing but a lazy excuse . . . , which is to cover their genuinely oriental indifference—they feel sorry for the vineyard owner." This is an overly realistic distortion of the parable—not to mention the arrogance of the European toward lazy, lying Asians, which can arise if the literary laws of parables are not observed. If Jesus had understood the answer as a lazy excuse, he would not have concealed it. But he could not have thought so, for by such an assumption, he would have ruined the parable and removed the balance between the three groups.

36. Shklovsky, *Von der Ungleichheit des Ähnlichen in der Kunst*, 121.

37. The fifth group of guests in Luke (14:22) cannot belong to the matter because of the rules of parables. That it comes from elsewhere, we hope to show in the following volume.

indicated. The fate of the three servants is told in such a way that it is worse from one to the other. So, in the parable of the wicked vineyard workers there is a gradation.[38] The first servant is beaten and sent home empty-handed; the second is beaten, insulted, and sent away empty-handed; the third servant, on the other hand, is wounded and driven out by the tenants. The three servants here are representative of the prophets who were persecuted and killed by the Jewish leadership. Jesus knew that the Jews knew about the violent death of the prophets, and he also talked about it himself. According to the original wording of the parable in Luke, none of the three servants is killed. Why did Jesus avoid speaking about the slaughter of the servants? If he had done otherwise, he would have spoiled the parable. To create a strong contrast between the three characters and the fourth, contrasting extra character, Jesus the masterly parable teller is compelled to spare the violent death for the son. Now, no more servants are sent out.

> "Then the owner of the vineyard said, 'What shall I do? I will send my beloved son. I want to send my only[39] son, maybe they'll shy away from him.' And when the peasants saw him, they reasoned among themselves, saying, 'This is the heir; let us kill him, that the inheritance may be ours.'[40] And they brought him out of the vineyard[41] and killed him."

---

38. The correct increase in the treatment of the three servants by the tenants is preserved in Luke (20:10–12). Mark (12:2–5) ruined it. With him, the third servant is already killed and many others are sent: "some they beat, some they killed." In Matt 2:33–46, the matter becomes even worse. He takes over most of the servants from the expanded addition in Mark 12:5b and writes, "And the builders took his servants, and they struck one, they stoned one, they killed one. Again, he sent other servants, more numerous than the first, and they did the same to them." Matthew therefore knows that the servants sent on behalf of the owner are the persecuted and killed prophets, and that is why he speaks (according to Matt 23:37 and Luke 13:34) of killing and stoning.

39. This is the Hebrew meaning of the Greek word. The "only son" here is not just a contrasting increase!

40. All this is an allusion to Joseph and his brothers (Gen 37:18–20).

41. The Greek word here means "to lead out," not to throw out, push out, or the like. See *BDAG*, 471. In the New Testament, the Hebrew verb is thus translated. Matthew 21:39 agrees with Luke 20:1–5 against Mark. According to our Synoptic theory, this is proof that the original text reads like this: The wicked vinedressers commit a "perfect crime." They lead the son outside the vineyard, and only then do they kill him, hoping they won't be discovered; but it doesn't help them. Mark (12:8) understands the Greek verb in the usual sense as "throwing out." That is why he thinks he must correct his submission and writes, "They seized him, killed him and threw him [i.e., his body] out."

Here, therefore, the threesome is exceeded, and the fourth "superfluous" character is by no means a simple increase, but rather a disturbing message of calamity. Exceeding the three characters therefore triggers a sharp dissonance here.

Let us return to the double parable of the house on rock and on sand. Here, a triad also appears—namely, in the two parallel sentences in which it is said that the house is endangered by rain, streams of water, and wind. This proposition is repeated twice, in both halves of the double parable. Therefore, in this double parable, the triad appears, so to speak, macroscopically—that is to say, in the events—and microscopically—that is to say, as a stylistic means. In the already mentioned example *Kannitverstan*,[42] both in the subject and stylistically, the number three appears also in the great narrator Johann Peter Hebel, whose importance for understanding parables as a genre should not, in my opinion, be underestimated. This example is about the "inconstancy of all earthly things." A German craftsman "came to truth and knowledge in Amsterdam through error." A large and beautiful house "appealed to him," and when he had asked a Dutchman about the owner of this house, he received the answer, "*Kannitverstan*," which in Dutch means "I cannot understand you," and he thought this was the name of the owner. A second time, he received the same Dutch answer when he asked about the owner of a large merchant ship. And when he saw a great funeral procession, he asked who the dead man was and for the third time, he received the answer, "*Kannitverstan*." The triad appears in this exemplum of Hebel not only in reference to the great house, the rich ship, and the narrow grave, but it also appears on a small scale in the description of the funeral procession: "Four black-covered horses pulled a likewise black-covered hearse. . . . A long train of friends . . . followed, couple after couple, wrapped in black coats." The triad is thus also emphasized by the same color: black covered and black coated.

What applies to the triad also applies to doubling: it occurs in the parables both macroscopically and microscopically. Macroscopically, it appears as a contrast between the right and wrong actors. Microscopically, it works as the smallest number for a paratactic series. Therefore, there are not only contrasting double parables but also parallel double parables, which emphasize and bring forward the central idea through the doubling. We have

---

42. Hebel, *Werke*, vol. 1, 51–53. This example is discussed in the introduction, xxviii–xxx. Among other things, there is an important sentence that also applies to successful parables: "Fine threads are spun, and what seemed to be just a flourish next becomes the function bearer in a well-considered architecture through the differentiated repetition."

seen that already. Particularly touching is the refrain in the exemplum of the prodigal son (Luke 15:11–32). When the son returned, the father said to his servants, "Let us eat and be merry, for this son of mine was dead and has come to life again; he was lost and has been found" (Luke 15:24). The father repeats this sentence in response to the older son and with him the exemplum is concluded (Luke 15:32). In his words to the servants, the phrase is an expression of pure joy. In his words to the older son, he receives the sting of a mild reminder. The double mention of this sentence testifies to fine poetry. The same applies to the self-talk of the repentant son (Luke 15:18): "I will go to my father in fear and say to him, 'Father, I have sinned against heaven and before you; I am not worthy to be called your son.'" In Luke 15:21, the son then repeats this sentence to his father. Although he originally wanted to ask him additionally to be hired as one of his day laborers (according to Luke 15:19), he did not get the chance because he was so overwhelmed by his feelings and capable only of expressing remorse. Or did Jesus, out of stylistic intuition, find the practical request disturbing and therefore omit it? In the rabbinic parable of the caravan,[43] the station manager alludes ironically to the words of the caravan leader.

Neither Jesus the parable teller nor the rabbinic parable tellers endeavored to reach the end of the parable as quickly as possible. It is part of the style of their parables that they reluctantly approach the ending. This stylistic means of slowing down can be epic or dramatic, but not lyrically, broadly expansive and embellishing. A "chatty" style is possible and repetitions are popular, but everything needs to have a function in well-constructed architecture. To refresh these findings, we could reread the parable of the ten virgins (Matt 25:1–13). How excellent is this parable! But I don't want to repeat myself, so we will look at the parable of the wicked servant (Matt 18:23–35) to illustrate the same point. The moral teaching of that parable is: "So shall my heavenly Father do unto you, if you do not, every one of you, forgive your brother from your heart." Also, on another occasion Jesus said, "For if you forgive the sins of people, your heavenly Father will also forgive you; but if you do not forgive the people, your Father will not forgive you the sins"[44] (Matt 6:14f.; Luke 11:25f.). This is a general Jewish teaching. For our parable, it is important what Ben Sira (27:30–28:7) said around 185 BCE:[45]

---

43. See chapter 1, note 10, above.

44. See Klostermann, *Das Matthäusevangelium*, 59, which also refers to Ben Sira, among other things.

45. I have already mentioned these words in *Jesus in Selbstzeugnissen und Bilddokumenten*, 65–67.

Jealousy and fury, even they are abominable,
and the wicked man holds them fast.
He who lights these in himself receives vengeance from God,
and all his sins are held against him.
Let go of what you have in your heart, and then pray,[46]
and all your sins will be forgiven you.
One man keeps the wrath of another,
and from God he asks for healing?
With a man like him he has no mercy,
and he asks for mercy for his own sins?
He who is flesh keeps the fury,
who will forgive him his sins!
Think of the end and refrain from enmity,
from hell and death and persist in the law!
Remember the commandment, and do not grieve your neighbor,
the covenant of God, and overlook the transgression.

This is the new Jewish sensitivity of the Second Temple period, which interprets the rule "measure for measure" in such a humane way. To illustrate this theology of morality, Jesus tells the parable of the wicked servants. Containing two parallel acts, the parable is told vividly and dramatically. At the end of the second act, the situation of the end of the first act returns. The servant to whom his master had given ten thousand talents falls at his feet and says, "Have patience with me, and I will pay you everything." The king forgives him his trespass. But then this servant "found one of his fellow servants who owed him a hundred denarii. And he seized him, and strangled him, and said, 'Pay what you owe.' So, his fellow servant fell down and said to him, 'Have patience with me, and I will pay you.'" The parallelism between the situation in the first and second acts is thus emphasized by an identical request. But the servant has no mercy on his fellow servant; therefore, his master forces him to pay his debt through torture.

I have not quoted or even interpreted the whole parable here. I have highlighted only such points that seem to me to be particularly important for our current investigation. Perhaps it should be pointed out that we also learn that the fellow servants were witnesses to the wickedness of the merciless servant.[47] They were grieved at this and reported to their master all that

---

46. This corresponds to Luke 11:25.

47. Joachim Jeremias thinks of this parable as a final judgment parable: "God has granted you—through the gospel, through the promise of forgiveness—a remission of grace that exceeds all comprehension"—therefore apparently the high

had happened. The mention of this fact is very well built into the subject; it is better than if Jesus had simply said, "The Master knew of the iniquity." Thus the parable offers continuous action. The role of the fellow servants in the second half of the picture should not be interpreted; they merely form an active choir in the action that is not only present but also participates in the action. (This was also the case in Greek tragedy.) In the first act of the parable, the king orders the servant to be sold, as well as his wife and children and all his possessions. At the end of the parable, the master hands over the ruthless servant to the torturers until he paid all the debt. From this difference, nothing can be learned about the nature of the moral proposition: the motif is simply varied.

The story of the wicked servant shows how Jesus knew how to increase the tension of listeners through detailed narrative. Although listeners were familiar with the rules of the genre and knew where certain motifs were going, Jesus' parables as well as rabbinic parables are still thought of as exciting stories as they did not know the exact course or solution of the story. Familiarity with these types of stories is intended to trigger agreement among listeners, both in relation to the outcome of the action and the solution at the moral level. Parables are not only short stories, but they also have something of a riddle in them. In contrast to the riddle, however, there must be only one solution to the parable. A parable of Rabbi Akiba is illustrative here.[48] It deals with the same main theme as the parable of the wicked servant—namely, connection with a debtor:

> There were people who were in debt to a king. He set a time limit for them to pay the debt to him. But they did not think to honor the king and to give him a present. However, there was one of them who paid homage to the king on a daily basis. He used to ask about his welfare and bring him gifts, for he said to himself, "It is good to be kind to the doctor before you need him."[49] When the term had expired, the king sent [his servants] to collect the debts. So the debt collectors came to the man who had honored the king. Then he said to them, "You are coming to collect from me? I can pay my debt, lead me to the king!" And they went with him. The king had been waiting for his coming. When he

---

sum of 10,000 talents—"Jesus, as usual, takes up the Jewish doctrine of the two measures, but completely transforms it; it is no coincidence that there are no Jewish parallels to our parable," and so on. I cannot follow such statements.

48. *Midrash Zuta to Song of Songs*, ed. Buber, 19; ed. Solomon Schechter, 563–81. See also Bacher, *Die Agada der Tannaiten*, vol. 1, 331f.

49. A free quote from Ben Sira 38:1.

saw him, he reached out his hand, greeted him first, and said to him, "Come in." The others, who also owed to the king, stood by and saw him sitting by the king's side. They said to themselves, "What does the king gain from doing him such honor? He also owes the king—and not only that he will not be seized, but he will receive such an award!" Then the king said to them, "This was because he had honored the king, brought him gifts, and had always hastened to greet him. And you? You did not honor him and did not greet him." And those who should have seized the man when they saw him sitting in his place of honor were glad that they had not done so. They said, "If we had seized him, because he is so loved and honored by the king, we would have died. And what brought such honor to the man? The gifts he gave to the king." And the debtors began to slap themselves in the face and said, "Why didn't we do the same?" And what is the gift according to which the Holy One is pleased? Mercy.

May I praise this parable? I think it is excellent! I do not want to point out here that the subject, as in various parables of Jesus, is unscrupulous in what the characters say as in the parables of the pleading friend (Luke 11:5–8) and the ungodly judge (Luke 18:1–8). Although the teaching of this parable, or these parables, aims at human improvement, I am concerned here only with Rabbi Akiba's rich structuring and the way in which it is told. Precisely because the parable is not straightforward, because there is lively action in it, because the cast of characters not only acts but also speaks, it is exciting. As soon as the wise debtor appears and gives gifts to the king, we know that in the end the debt will be forgiven. The good ending belongs to the pragmatic "morality" of the subject. So, the listeners are waiting for a happy ending, even if they are not told who the king is in the parable. On the other hand, the parable forces them to participate eagerly in the action, even if they can foresee the happy ending from the beginning. This is achieved through the successful interlocking of epic and dramatic motifs. We observe similar factors in the parable of the ten virgins (Matt 25:1–13) and especially in the parable of the wicked servant (Matt 18:23–35).

In the parable of the wicked servant, there is a king, a ruthless servant and his sacrifice, as well as fellow servants. In the parallel rabbinic parable, we hear of a king, a wise debtor, other debtors, and collectors. In both parables, all persons actively intervene in the action. For the moral doctrine in Jesus' parable, the fellow servants would not need to be mentioned. Even in the rabbinic parable, a mere mention of the collectors would suffice. The conversation between fellow debtors who feel disadvantaged and the king, for his part, is reminiscent of the reproof of the owner of the vineyard, which Jesus addresses in the parable of the workers in the vineyard to the apparently disadvantaged workers (Matt 20:1–15). And how abundant is the epic supplement that fills the parable of Rabbi Akiba! Fine threads are spun! What seems to be only incidental, seen through the course of the action, has a function in well-planned architecture. The above applies not only to our rabbinic parable but also to the whole genre, and therefore also to Jesus' parables. Although a parable is an illustration of a moral, the subject must be free enough to be told in an exciting way. The suspense is achieved by an interesting plot, rich texture, and a successful narrative.

In connection with the narrative art of parables, we must once again ask ourselves to what extent the original wording has come to us in rabbinic parables and in Jesus' parables. In the case of rabbinic parables, we would have to compare the different versions that are in the collections of rabbinic literature. This, of course, applies not only to rabbinic parables but also to rabbinic literature in general. The situation with rabbinic parables is not as difficult as it seems at first glance. As already mentioned, rabbinic sayings were first verbally memorized and handed down. As a result, they often achieved a fidelity and reliability that is much greater than with the mistakes of written literature.[50] We know that over the centuries, new parables were invented in Palestine. They understood the rules of parables and applied them basically all the time. This is another reason why the presentation of traditional parables did not change significantly over time. If someone sometimes modified an old parable, they did this in the spirit of the genre. As for Jesus' parables, we are faced with a real but by no means insurmountable problem. Unlike rabbinic literature, Jesus' words and deeds were fixed in writing not long after his death by Jews skilled in the art of memorization. Then the old Hebrew reports, as experience in dealing with the texts available today has taught me, were literally translated into Greek. These ancient accounts form the basis of the Synoptic Gospels, but the editors and evangelists were Hellenistic Jews and non-Jews. They belonged to a different culture than Jesus and his disciples, and Christianity was structured differently. From their different situation, their faith, and their preconceived opinions or lack of knowledge of Hebrew reality, they worked differently on the Greek translations of the original reports. There is something else about Jesus' parables: These Greek-thinking, Greek-speaking, and Greek-writing Jews and non-Jews perhaps knew no other Jewish parables apart from Jesus' parables as presented to them. They were unfamiliar with the artistic rules

---

50. Interesting in this context are the conjectures of Caesar (*De bello Gallico* 4.14.4) about why the Gallic Druids maintained an oral tradition of their teachings.

of rabbinic parables and were far from the stream of the rabbinic parable tradition. As a result, it could happen that in their editorial work, even out of ignorance of the stylistic peculiarity of the genre, they misrepresented or blurred the structure of the parables and their original method of presentation, as I already said above.[51] However, it testifies to the sense of responsibility of these editors that there are parables of Jesus that have been fairly faithfully preserved in their content and in their original manner of speaking.

It is surprising that the wording of such parables, which are found only in Matthew[52] or Luke,[53] is generally well received and has not been subjected to a thorough Greek restyling. In the Lukan special material, however, the Greek hand can be felt much more strongly. In Luke, there are also parable-like Greek formations, which we have ignored here.[54] With the parables

---

51. "Narrated things are not continuously related to each other. Passages of scenic detail are replaced by passages through which the narrator rushes, although it urges us to catch an enlightening word from him. Assigned different levels and different ranks are matched with fidelity to tradition. Uneven, rugged things are therefore obvious, as soon as one avoids helping by bridging." Friedrich Neumann wrote this about the Nibelungenlied in *Das Nibelungenlied in seiner Zeit* (Göttingen: Vandenhoeck & Ruprecht, 1967), 176. The reasons for the similarity of the situation with the Synoptic Gospels are somewhat different. But in both cases, it is about works that are not personal creations of an independent and autonomously shaping author, but rather writings that work from the traditions. It can also be said about the Synoptic Gospels that the secret of their unusual effect lies in the fact that they are not "finished" (181). And just as there are three Synoptic Gospels, so the Nibelungenlied is preserved in three complete manuscripts (A, B, C) from the thirteenth century, these manuscripts representing three versions of the song. In the thorough manner of editing, manuscript C is reminiscent of the Gospel of Mark.

52. Matthew 13:24–30, 36–43: Weeds among the wheat (slightly edited; interpretation secondarily extended); Matt 13:47–50: fishing net (stylistically worked); Matt 13:44–46: treasure and pearl; Matt 18:23–35: the unforgiving servant; Matt 20:1–16: workers in the vineyard; Matt 21:28–32: unequal sons; Matt 25:1–13: ten virgins. Matt 22:11–13: guest without robe is strongly styled by the same hand that objectively intervened in the preceding parable of the great supper (Matt 22:1–10).

53. Luke 7:41–43: The two debtors (edited in Greek, but otherwise well preserved); Luke 10:30–37: merciful Samaritan; Luke 11:5–8: praying friend (edited in Greek); Luke 12:13–21: foolish rich man; fruitless fig tree; Luke 14:28–33: tower construction and warfare; Luke 15:11–32: lost son; Luke 16:1–9: unjust steward; Luke 16:19–31: rich man and poor Lazarus; Luke 18:1–8: godless judge; Luke 18:9–14: Pharisees and tax collectors.

54. Luke 13:24–30; 14:7–11; nor do we deal here with those parables that are problematic in content and form, occurring in one, two, or three Gospels: Mark 13:33–37; Luke 19:12f.; 12:41: Matt 25:14; 24:43f.; Luke 21:29–31; Matt 24:32f. The

preserved in Matthew and Luke but missing in Mark, the situation is not so simple. If these parables are almost identical in both Gospels, then their wording is quite well preserved.[55] It happens, however, that one evangelist changed more and the other less.[56] In the three parables that are common to all Synoptic Gospels, the influence of Mark on Matthew, as expected, also has an unfavorable effect in the wording of the parables.[57] Thus our stylistic analysis independently leads to the same result as the Synoptic theory, and they both confirm each other. It has been shown that the knowledge of the aesthetic style rules of the parables can be very useful—indeed necessary—for us in the reconstruction of the original wording.

The style rules of Jesus' parables resulted from the aesthetic evaluation of his parables and from the comparison of these parables with one another. In addition, I have constantly consulted the Jewish parables of rabbinic literature. Not only in their subject matter, subjects, motifs, and dialectical connection between subjects and moral teaching do Jesus' parables belong to rabbinic parables, but also in the common, aesthetically effective manner of speaking. We have seen that the style of rabbinic parables was propagated for centuries substantially unchanged. We could also observe

---

last verse is not a parable but a parable image; we omit parable images here. The parable of the self-growing seed is found only in Mark (4:26–29). As I have already explained, the parable comes from Mark himself: he conceived it in Greek.

55. Matthew 12:43–45; Luke 11:24–26: unclean spirit; Luke 7:31–35: children playing; Matt 24:45–51; Luke 12:42–46: the faithful and wise servant and his adversary.

56. The parable of the building of the house (Matt 7:24 –27; Luke 6:47–49) is better preserved in Matthew than in Luke. The parables of the lost sheep and the lost drachma (Matt 18:12–14) are not badly preserved. But in both Gospels, there are important differences. The drachma is missing in Matthew. The two parables of the money entrusted (Matt 25:14–30: Luke 19:12–27) and of the great supper (Matt 25:14–30; Luke 19:12–27; 14:16–24) give up special problems. Both their wording and content are different in both Gospels. The first parable introduces the subject to Luke's political elements, and the second to Matthew's political motifs. The parable of the great supper is better preserved in Luke.

57. The parable of the evil farmers (Mark 12:1f.; Matt 21:33–44) is well preserved in Luke; it is gradually corrupted by Mark and then by Matthew. As for the parable of the mustard seed and the leaven, it should be noted, first, that the parable of the leaven is missing in Mark, and second, that the good Hebrew wording in Matthew was infected by Mark. In the parable of the fourfold field (Matt 13:1–9; 18–23; Mark 4:1–9, 13–20; Luke 8:4–8, 11–15), Mark exerts an original blurring influence on Matthew; but in this case, the parable was already heavily worked out in Luke.

that Jesus' parables, although written down in Hebrew and literally translated into Greek after a short period of time, were subjected to more or
less strong Greek processing. In both cases—in rabbinic parables and Jesus'
parables—the way to their original wording is generally open. Because of
the circumstances mentioned, however, this is not safe and is sometimes
even blocked in Jesus' individual parables. Apart from these particular difficulties, we cannot avoid the question of whether in the oral transmission of some embellishments in the rabbinic parables and Jesus' parables,
some epic and dramatic "flourishes" were lost. That possibility exists. When
parables passed from mouth to mouth, they could have lost some of their
richness: something could be said more simply for convenience. But the
wording of some parables has been well preserved in the Gospels. From
these parables, we can understand why Jesus was famous as a parable teller
and why he loved to tell them. His parables were generally excellent. They
were interesting, lively, and exciting, carried by epic and dramatic accents,
and rich in epic side motifs. Although destined for the people and therefore
generally Jewish and situational in moral teaching, in many of them, we
can feel the deep nature of Jesus' proclamation, its fourth dimension, and
its ironic side-tone.

With Jesus, let us consider only the general human level! It reveals itself particularly impressively in Jesus the parable teller. Let us forget for
a while—pious readers may forgive me this—the shocking thing in the
message, in the person, in the life, and in the death of Jesus! With these
reservations, we may perhaps say that we can learn a great deal about the
nature of his parables and about Jesus as a parable narrator from the short
stories of Johann Peter Hebel. Hebel is somehow complementary to Jesus
in his richness of motifs, suspenseful narrative, irony and the ambiguity of
the morality of the subject, and crystal-clear, pure—as Walter Benjamin
says—"prose goldsmithing."[58] Benjamin also says that for Hebel "everything
factual was already theory, especially since the anecdotal, the criminal, the
possessive, the local as such was already moral theorem." Hebel, who "knew
how to pull all the stops from the lowest levels to the bestowal of generosity,
was not the man to overlook the demonic in bourgeois working life." Is it
so absurd to quote these words in a book about the Jesus the parable teller?

Hebel also wrote a book about biblical stories, which was published
in its entirety in 1824. Working on the book was sometimes difficult for
this man who was marked by the Enlightenment. Therefore, the text is not

---

58. Hebel, *Werke*, vol. 2, 510–13.

always as poetic as in his diary stories, and Hebel is often too committed to the text of the Luther Bible. He also edited Jesus' parables in his book, including the parable of the fourfold field,[59] which he tells mostly according to Matthew. Hebel's interpretation shows, however, that he correctly understood Jesus' intention. This is evident from his own epilogue:

> What does a child want to take away from this parable and its interpretation? Is not the school like such a field? Doesn't Jesus touch the tender hearts with so many beautiful sayings and sow the word? What about his heart? Save me, my God, from carelessness, from thoughtlessness, from evil desires! Receive in me a fine and good heart! May my life be fruitful in good intentions and deeds!

That is, in its clever restricted language, really the meaning of the parable.

Likewise, this book of mine works best if you take it with an open heart. It was written so that Jesus' parables might be understood today as they were meant to be. I wanted my readers to free themselves in their hearts from the restraining rigidity of prejudice, for only in this way can they be open to the words of Jesus. For this is hidden from the wise and prudent. Unfortunately, I was forced to do a great deal of scholarly work so that, to the best of my ability, I could turn my readers into Jewish listeners to whom Jesus spoke in parables. They understood his parables because they knew exactly what parables were and what to expect from a parable. This knowledge has been lost to modern man. That is why I had to make clear to my readers the nature of the rabbinic parables to which Jesus' parables belong. I have no objection to the fact that pure research has gained something as a result.

---

59. Hebel, *Biblical Arch.*, 114.

Select Bibliography

The following abbreviations are based generally on the abbreviations list volume of the *Theological Real Encyclopedia*, compiled by Siegfried Schwertner (Berlin 1976). Unless otherwise noted, the Mishnah and Talmud quotations were taken from traditional editions.

Abel, E. L. "Who Wrote Matthew?" *NTS* 17 (1971): 138–52.

Aboth de Rabbi Nathan. Edited by S. Schechter. 1887. Reprint, New York, 1945.

Aggadath, Beresith. Edited by S. Buber. Krakau, 1903.

Ancient Near Eastern Texts. Edited by J. P. Pritchard. Princeton: Princeton University Press, 1950.

Apocrypha Testamenti Novi: Neutestamentliche Apokryphen. In *deutscher Übersetzung*. Edited by Edgar Hennecke and Wilhelm Schneemelcher. Evangelien. 1. Tübingen 1959; 2. Apostolisches, Apokalypsen und Verwandtes. Tübingen, 1964.

Artedimus von Jaldis. *Das Traumbuch übers v. Karl Brackerz*. Zürich, 1979.

Audet, J. T. *La Didache*. Paris, 1957.

Bacher, W. *Die Agada der Tannaiten*, 2 vols. Strassburg, 1890–1903.

———. *Die Agada der Palästinischen Amoräer*, 3 vols. Strasbourg, 1892–1899.

Baillet, M. "Un recueil liturgique de Qumran," Grotte 4. *RB* 68 (1961): 195–250.

Basile, G. "Lo Cunto de li Cunti." Laterza, 1976.

———. *Il Pentamerone, Prefazione di Italo Calvino*. Laterza, 1974.

Baur, W. *Griechisch-deutsches Wörterbuch zu den Schriften des NT*. Berlin, 1958.

Bengel, J. A. *Gnomon Novi Testamenti*. Stuttgart, 1891.

Bettelheim, B. *The Uses of Enchantment: The Meaning and Importance of Fairy Tales*. New York: Penguin Books, 1978.

Blank, J. *Meliton von Sardes, vom Passa, Sophia*. Vol. 3. Freiburg im Breisgau, 1963.

Blass, Fr. A. Debrunner, and Fr. Rehkopf. *Grammatik des neutestamentlichen Griechisch*. Göttingen, 1976.

Bonner, C. *The Last Chapters of Enoch in Greek*. London, 1937.

Bousett, W. *Die Offenbarung Johannis*. Reprint, Göttingen, 1966.

Brown, R. E. *The Gospel According to John*. Anchor Bible. Vol. 1. New York, 1964.

Büchler, A. *Types of Jewish-Palestinian Piety*. Reprint, New York, 1968.

———. *Studies in Sin and Atonement*. Reprint, New York, 1967.

Bultmann, R. *Die Tradition Geschichte der synoptischen*. Göttingen, 1957.

Conzelmann, H. *Die Mitte der Zeit*. Tübingen, 1954.

———. *Die Apostelgeschichte*. Tübingen, 1963.

Corpus fabularum Aesopicarum. Edited by C. Halm. Leipzig, 1875.

Corpus fabularum Aesopicarum. Edited by A. Hausrath. Leipzig, 1970.

Dalman, G. *Die Worte Jesu*. Leipzig, 1898.

Daube, David. *The New Testament and Rabbinic Judaism*. London, 1956.

Delitzsche, Fr. *Hebrew New Testament* (in Hebrew). Tel Aviv, 1963.

Diatessaron de Tatien. Edited by A. S. Marmardji. Beirut, 1935.

Diatessaron persiano. Edited by Giuseppe Messina. Rome, 1951.

Dibelius, M. *Der Hirt des Hermas*. Tübingen, 1954.

Die Schrift, zu verdeutschen unternommen von Martin Buber gemeinsam mit Franz Rosenzweig. 15 vols. Berlin, 1926–1939.

Dodd, C. H. "The Fall of Jerusalem." *JRS* 37 (1947): 47–54.

———. *The Parables of the Kingdom*. London, 1969.

Dufournet, John, ed. *Aucassin et Nicolette*. Paris, 1973.

Eichner, S. *Die Prosafabel Lessings in seiner Theorie und Dichtung, Bonner Arbeiten zur deutschen Literatur*. Vol. 25. 1974.

Epicletus. *The Discourses: The Manual and Fragments*. 2 vols. London, 1966–1967.

Farmer, W. R. *The Synoptic Problem*. New York, 1964.

Feliks, J. *Animal World of the Bible*. Jerusalem, 1967.

Fischer Lexicon. *Geschichte in Gestalten*. Vol. 2. Frankfurt, 1963.

Flusser, David. "Blessed are the Poor in Spirit." *IEJ* (1960): 1–13.

———. "The Conclusion of Matthew." *ASTI* 5 (1967): 110–20.

———. *The Dead Sea Sect and Pre-Pauline Christianity*. Scripta Hierosolymitana, 215–66. Vol. 4. *Aspects of the Dead Sea Scrolls*. Jerusalem, 1958.

———. "Der Gekreuzigte und die Juden." *FrRu* 28 (1976): 153–57.

———. "Die konsequente Philologie und die Worte Jesu." *Almanach auf das Jahr des Herrn*. Hamburg, 1963.

———. "Do You Prefer New Wine?" *Immanuel* no. 9 (1979): 26–31.

———. "An Early Jewish-Christian Document in the Tiburtine Sybil." *Paganisme, Judaisme, Christianisme, Hommage à M. Simon.* Edited by M. Philonenko. Paris (1978): 173–78.

———. *Eine Weissagung über die Befreiung Jerusalems im Neuen Testament* (in Hebrew). Eretz Israel. Vol. 10. Jerusalem, 1971.

———. "Hillels Selbstverständnis und Jesus." *FrRu* 27 (1975): 172–75.

———. "Hystaspes and John of Patmos." In *Irano-Judaica. Studies Relating to Jewish Contacts with Persian Culture throughout the Ages.* Edited by Sh. Shaked. Jerusalem, 1982.

———. "Jerusalem in der Literatur des Zweiten Tempels." *FS Rubin Mass* (in Hebrew). Jerusalem (1975): 290–93.

———. *Jesus in Selbstzeugnissen und Bilddokumenten.* Hamburg, 1968.

———. *Judentum und die Quellen des Christentums* (in Hebrew). Tel Aviv, 1979.

———. "The Last Supper and the Essenes." *Immanuel* no. 2 (1973): 23–37.

———. "A New Sensitivity in Judaism and the Christian Message." *HThR* 61 (1968): 111–18.

———. "Pharisäer, Sadduzäer und Essener im Pescher Nahum" (in Hebrew). *Essays in Jewish History and Philology.* Hakibbutz Hameuchad (1970): 149f.

———. "Sanktus und Gloria, in: Abraham unser Vater, FS Otto Michel." *Leiden* (1963): 129–52.

———. "Some Notes on Easter and the Passover Haggadah." *Immanuel* no. 7 (1977): 56–60.

———. "Two Anti-Jewish Montages in Matthew." *Immanuel.* Jerusalem (1975): 39–43.

Funkenstein, A. "Nahmanides' Typological Reading of History" (in Hebrew). *Zion* 45. Jerusalem (1980): 36f.

Gaston, L. "The Messiah of Israel as Teacher of the Gentiles." *Interp.* 29 (1975): 24–40.

Gignon, O. *Kommentar zum ersten Buch von Xenophons Memorabilien.* Basel, 1953.

Ginzberg, L. *The Legends of the Jews.* Vol. 4. Philadelphia, 1947.

Grotius, Hugo. *Annotationes in Novum Testamentum.* Groningen, 1828.

Gulielmus Gnapheus. *Acolastus.* Edited by P. Minderaa. Zwolle, 1956.

Hebel, Johann Peter. *Biblische Erzählungen.* Munich, 1958.

———. *Werke.* 2 vols. Edited by V. E. Meckel. Introduction by R. Minder. Frankfurt, 1968.

Herder, Johann Gottfried. *Blätter der Vorzeit*. Berlin, 1936.

Hesiod. *Werke: Hesiodi Opera et dies, Scutum*. Edited by Fr. Solmsen. Oxford, 1970.

Hornung, Erik. *Der Eine und die Vielen, Ägyptische Gottesvorstellungen*. Darmstadt, 1971.

Jastrow, M. *A Dictionary of Talmud Babli: Yerushalmi, Midrashic Literature and Targumim*. New York, 1950.

Jeremias, Joachim. *Unbekannte Jesusworte*. Gütersloh, 1963.

————. *Die Gleichnisse Jesu*. Göttingen, 1970.

Jülicher, A. *Die Gleichnisreden Jesu*. 2 vols. Darmstadt, 1963.

Kafka, Franz. *Gesammelte Schriften*. Vol. 5. Berlin, 1946.

Klemm, H. G. "Die Gleichnisauslegung Adolf Jülichers im Bannkreise der Fabeltheorie Lessings." *ZNW* 59 (1969): 270–82.

Klostermann, E. *Apokrypha I* (KIT 3). Berlin, 1933.

————. *Apokrypha II, Evangelein* (Kleine Texte 8). Berlin, 1929.

————. *Das Lukasevangelium* (HANT 5). Tübingen, 1975.

————. *Das Markusevangelium* (HANT 1). Tübingen, 1971.

————. *Das Matthäusevangelium* (HANT 4). Tübingen, 1971

Kraft, Robert A. *The Apostolic Fathers*. Vol. 3. New York, 1965.

Lapide, Pinchas, and Ulrich Luz. *Der Jude Jesus*. Einsiedeln, 1979.

Leibfried, E., and J. M. Werle. *Texte zur Theorie der Fabel*. Sammlung Metzler. Vol. 169. Stuttgart, 1978.

Lessing, Gotthold Ephraim. *Werke*. Vol. 8. Munich, 1970–1979.

Levy, J. *Chaldäisches Wörterbuch über die Targumim*. 2 vols. Leipzig, 1867.

————. *Wörterbuch über die Targumim und Midraschim*. 4 vols. Reprint, Darmstadt, 1963.

Licht, J. *The Thanksgiving Scroll* (in Hebrew). Jerusalem, 1957.

————. *The Rule Scroll* (in Hebrew). Jerusalem, 1965.

Lindsey, R. L. "A Modified Two Document Theory of the Synoptic Dependence and Interdependence." *NT* 6 (1963): 239–64.

————. *A Hebrew Translation of the Gospel of Mark*. Greek-Hebrew Diglot with an English Introduction. Jerusalem, 1973.

Lowy, S. "The Confutation of Judaism in the Epistle of Barnabas." *JJS* 11 (1960): 5–8.

Lüthi, M. *Das europäische Volksmärchen*. Munich, 1978.

————. *Das Volksmärchen als Dichtung*. Düsseldorf, 1975.

Maier, J. *Die Texte vom Toten Meer*. I Übersetzung, II Anmerkungen. Munich, 1960.

————. *Die Tempelrolle vom Toten Meer.* UTB. Munich, 1978.

Masechtot Zeirot. Edited by Michael Higger. Jerusalem, 1970.

Mechilta d'Rabbi Ismael. Edited by H. S. Horovitz and I. A. Rabin. Jerusalem, 1960.

Mechilta d'Rabbi Schimeon b. Jochai. Edited by J. N. Epstein and E. Z. Melamed. Jerusalem, 1959.

Meliton von Sardes. *Sur la Pâque et fragments. Sources Chrétiennes* no. 123. Edited by O. Perler. Paris, 1966.

Metzger, B. M. *A Textual Commentary in the Greek New Testament.* London, 1971.

Meyer, Ed. *Ursprung und Anfänge des Christentums.* 3 vols. Berlin, 1921–1923.

Michel, O. *Der Brief an die Hebräer.* Göttingen, 1966.

Midrasch Bereschit Rabba. Edited by J. Theodor and Ch. Albeck. Jerusalem, 1965.

Midrasch Haggadol on the Pentateuch: Exodus. Edited by M. Margulies. Jerusalem, 1956.

Midrasch Tehillim (Schocher Tob). Edited by S. Buber. Wilna, 1889.

Mischna-Handschrift des Codex Kaufmann. Edited by G. Beer. Heidelberg, 1929.

Musäus, J. K. A. *Volksmärchen der Deutschen.* 1977.

Mussner, Franz. *Der Galaterbrief.* Freiburg im Breisgau, 1974.

The Nag Hammadi Library in English. Leiden, 1977.

Neue hebr. *Übersetzung des Neuen Testaments.* United Bible Societies. Jerusalem, 1976.

Neumann, Friedrich. *Das Nibelungenlied in seiner Zeit.* Göttingen, 1967.

Norden, E. *Agnostos Theos.* (1913). Reprint, Darmstadt, 1956.

Otto, A. *Die Sprichwörter und die sprichwörtlichen Redensarten der Römer.* Reprint, Hildesheim, 1965.

Perrault, Ch. *Contes de ma mère l'Oye.* Edited by G. Rouger. Paris, 1967.

Pesikta de Rav Kahana. Edited by S. Buber. Lyck, 1868.

Pesikta de Rav Kahana. Edited by B. Mandelbaum. New York, 1962.

Philonenko, M. "Quod oculus non vidit." *ThZ* 15 (1959): 51f.

Philonis Alexandrini opera quae supersunt. Edited by L. Cohn, P. Wendland and S. Reiter. 7 vols. Berlin, 1896–1930.

Pohlenz, M. *Stoa and Stoiker, Die Gründer.* Zürich, 1950.

Pseudo-Philon. *Les Antiquités Bibliques.* Edited by D. J. Harrington. 2 vols. Paris, 1976.

Resch, A. *Agrapha*. Darmstadt, 1967.

Sancti Iustini Philosophi et Martyris cum Tryphone Iudaeo Dialogus. Edited by C. Th. Otto. Jena, 1877.

Sanders, J. A. *The New Testament Christological Hymns*. Cambridge, 1971.

———. *The Psalms Scroll of Qumran*. Oxford, 1965.

Schapira, Z. Kahana. *YalqM zu Jes 61*, 10. Reprint, Jerusalem, 1964.

Schechter, S. *Aspects of Rabbinic Theology*. New York, 1961. Edited and translated by A. Kaempfe. Munich, 1973.

Schlatter, A. *Der Evangelist Matthäus*. Stuttgart, 1959.

Schlier, Heinrich. *Der Brief an die Galater*. Göttingen, 1965.

Schlowskij, V. *Theorie der Prosa*. In Russian, Moscow, 1925. In German, Munich, 1966.

———. *Der Weg der Gerechtigkeit*. Göttingen, 1966.

Schmid, Josef. *Das Evangelium nach Lukas*. Regensburger NT 3. Regensburg, 1960.

Schnakenburg, Rudolf. *Das Johannesevangelium*. 3 vols. Freiburg im Breisgau, 1972–1976.

Schneider, Gerhard. *Das Evangelium nach Lukas*. Gütersloh, 1977.

Schürer, E. *Geschichte des jüdischen Volkes sim Zeitalter Jesu Christi*. 3 vols. Leipzig 1901–1909. Reprint, Hildesheim, 1964.

Schürmann, Heinz. *Das Lukasevangelium*. Part 1. Freiburg im Breisgau, 1969.

Schwarzbaum, Haim. "The Mishle Shuᶜalim (Fox Tables) of Rabbi Brechiah ha-Nakdam: A Study in Comparative Folklore and Fable Lore." *Institute for Jewish and Arabic Folklore Research*. Kiron, 1979.

Siegert, Folker. *Drei hellenistisch-jüdische Predigten*. Tübingen, 1980.

Sifre ad Deuteronomium. Edited by L. Finkelstein. Reprint, New York, 1969.

Sifre d'be Rab Fasciculus primus: Sifre ad Numeros adjecto Sifre Zuta. Edited by H. S. Horovitz. Jerusalem, 1956.

Sjöberg, Erik. *Der verborgene Menschensohn in den Evangelien*. Lund, 1955.

Spyri, Johanna. *Heidis Lehr- und Wanderjahre*. Munich, 1978.

Stendahl, Kr. *The School of St. Matthew*. Uppsala, 1954.

Stier, Fridolin. *Die Heilsbotschaft nach Markus*. Munich, 1965.

Stoicorum veterum fragmenta. Edited by J. von Arnim. 4 vols. Reprint, Stuttgart, 1964.

Strack, H., and P. Billerbeck. *Kommentar zum Neuen Testament aus Talmud und Midrasch*. 4 volumes. Munich, 1922–1928.

Strecker, G. *Das Judenchristentum in den Pseudoklementinen*. Berlin, 1958.

———. *Von der Ungleichheit des Ähnlichen in der Kunst*. Munich, 1973.

Tanna d'be Eliahu, Eliahu Rabba, and Seder Eliahu Zuta. 1904. Edited by M. Friedmann. Jerusalem, 1960.

Taylor, V. *The Gospel According to St. Mark.* London, 1957.

———. *The Text of the New Testament.* London, 1961.

Thoma, Clemens. Preface by David Flusser, 6–32. *Christliche Theologie des Judentums.* Aschaffenburg, 1978.

Tisserant, E. *Ascension d'Isaïe.* Paris, 1909.

Tosephta. Edited by M. S. Zuckermandel. Reprint, Jerusalem, 1970.

Treatise Semaḥot and Treatise Semaḥot of R. Hiyya and Sefer Ḥibbuṭ ha-Keber. Edited by Michael Higger. Jerusalem, 1970.

Vermes, G. *Jesus the Jew.* London, 1973.

Vielhauer, Ph. *Aufsätze zum Neuen Testament.* Munich, 1965.

Weiser, A. *Die Knechtsgleichnisse der synoptischen Evangelien.* Munich, 1971.

Wickram, Georg. *Das Rollwagenbuchlein.* Stuttgart, 1968.

Wrede, William. *Das Messiasgeheimnis in den Evangelien.* Gottingen, 1963.

Yadin, Yigael. *The Temple Scroll* (in Hebrew). 3 vols. Jerusalem, 1977.

———. *Milḥemet bne 'ôr bibne ḥôšekh.* Jerusalem, 1955.

———. *The Scroll of the War of the Sons of Light against the Sons of Darkness.* Oxford: Oxford University Press, 1962.

Yalqut ha-Michiri. Edited by S. Buber. Reprint, Jerusalem, 1964.

Ziegler, Ignaz. *Die Königsgleichnisse des Midrasch, Beleuchtet durch die römische Kaiserzeit.* Breslau, 1903.

Zobel, Moritz. *Gottes Gesalbter, Der Messias und die messianische Zeit in Talmud und Midrasch.* Berlin, 1938.